WHERE DID IT ALL GO RIGHT?

WHERE DID IT ALL GO RIGHT?

A. Alvarez

RICHARD COHEN BOOKS • London

To Torquil and Anne Norman

First published in hardback in Great Britain in 1999
by Richard Cohen Books,
an imprint of Metro Publishing Limited, 19 Gerrard Street, London W1V 7LA

British Library Cataloguing in Publication Data. A CIP record of this book
is available on request from the British Library.

ISBN 1 86066 173 4

10 9 8 7 6 5 4 3 2 1

Typeset in Palatino by MATS, Southend-on-Sea, Essex

Printed in Britain by CPD Group, Wales

CONTENTS

Charcoal portrait of Al Alvarez
by Charles Blackman

PREFACE

'I got the wrong script, the wrong director, the wrong cast.
Where did it go right?'

Zero Mostel in *The Producers*

For two years, beginning in 1958, I was the drama critic for the *New Statesman*. God knows why. My qualifications for the job were the same as Max Beerbohm's – I knew almost nothing about the theatre and didn't much like it – but, unlike Beerbohm, I had no talent for the work. It was a dreadful time. My first marriage was on its last legs, I was chronically depressed and my state of mind wasn't improved by having to trek into the West End at least four times a week and sit through plays with titles like *The Amorous Prawn*. There were occasional, miraculous consolations – Olivier's Coriolanus, Paul Robeson's Othello – but the best of them all was a production of *Ulysses in Nighttown*, starring Zero Mostel as Bloom. When I wrote a rave review of the play, a mutual friend gave me Zero's telephone number and said, 'Call him up. He's a lovely guy and he doesn't know a soul in London. I think you'll like each other.'

Zero was as unlike the pinched life I was then leading as it was possible to conceive. He was a huge presence in every sense. 'Success didn't go to my head,' he once said. 'It went to my waistline.' He had a great wobbling overripe body but he moved like a cat; his eyes rolled and swivelled like pinballs; his face seemed to be made of some high-tech material that he could manipulate into any shape he wanted; he sang; he danced; he bellowed like a bull and cooed like a dove; he imitated wallpaper; he turned himself into a coffee percolator. Once, in a pub off Jermyn Street, he stuck his hand in Joan Littlewood's face and said, 'Blow me up'; so she blew on his thumb and he became a balloon, floating around the bar, seemingly untethered from gravity. He was funnier off-stage than on, as though his mission in life were to make everyone laugh. His wife Kate was tough and glamorous – she had been one of the high-kicking Rockettes when they met – and she kept him in line with side-of-the-mouth, New Yorker wisecracks. They sometimes gave each other a hard time – he was demanding, she was asthmatic – but that didn't seem to matter. They were affectionate and easy-going, they made each other laugh, they enjoyed whatever it was that made them different and were devoted to the good times they had together.

Zero and I were close friends for two decades. When I first met him, he seemed to represent everything that was lacking in my life. He was a galleon in full sail, laden with pleasure, I was a castaway, clinging to the wreckage. Being exposed to all that appetite and energy and hilarity made me realize that there was a world elsewhere. By the time of his sudden death, in 1977, I had learned from his example and my own life had become – in a lower key – as rewarding and enjoyable as his. That is the story in this book: gloom and doom turning into pleasure.

I have written about some of the things that have happened to me in other books, in particular two episodes that were important to me: a description of working my passage on an ancient steam drifter and a night out on a rock face when it seemed likely that my companion and I would freeze to death. Since both the books in which those stories first appeared are no longer in print, I have repeated them here. Two other crucial episodes are only briefly mentioned: my first marriage, which I described at length in *Life After Marriage*, and the suicide attempt that ended it, which is recorded in *The Savage God*.

I owe special thanks to Richard Cohen and Barbara Neil, who read the manuscript with scrupulous care and made innumerable subtle suggestions for improving it. My wife Anne, as always, has read and reread it from the start, kept me going and, in every way, made both the book and its happy ending possible.

PART ONE

1

PROVENANCE

———◆—————

In 1938 my elder sister Anne came home from finishing school in Switzerland, very upset by what was happening just across the border in Germany. One afternoon she persuaded my father to tune in to a short-wave broadcast of one of Hitler's Nuremberg rallies. The only short-wave radio was in my father's gramophone, a state-of-the-art, polished-walnut monster as big as a modern washing machine, but with a loudspeaker behind a fretwork grille instead of a plastic window. Only my father, who loved music and played records late into the night, was allowed to touch it.

My parents knew nothing about world politics but they were proud of their daughter's newly acquired sophistication, so my sister Sally and I were summoned down from the nursery to listen in – not for our political education but to admire Anne's skills as a linguist. We sat in front of the big radiogram, listening to the Führer's crackly voice rising and falling through the static, while Anne stood beside it and translated, like a teacher in front of a class. I was only eight years old, but even I registered that the news was grim.

Every so often Hitler's ravings were punctuated by a great roar from the crowd: '*Sieg Heil! Sieg Heil! Sieg Heil!*'

Finally my mother spoke: 'I don't like it much myself, but it's delicious the way Minnie does it,' she said.

'Minnie?' said my father.

'Minnie the cook. Who else?' my mother answered loftily. 'She parboils it, then finishes it off with minced onion and butter.'

'What in God's name are you talking about?' my father asked.

'Seakale,' said my mother. 'Of course, it's not in season at the moment.'

Apart from her genius for translating everything into food, Katie Alvarez was an innocent, scatty woman, too bogged down in her own misery to have much interest in the world outside. But this was in 1938, the year Neville Chamberlain sold the Czechs down the river at Munich and the Germans marched into Austria, and what baffles me is that this conversation didn't take place in some hick town in the great American heartland where no one had heard of Europe; it took place in the London borough of Hampstead, and Hampstead was full of German refugees.

Like my mother, I was born in Bloomsbury, but my parents had moved a couple of miles north to Hampstead when I was a few months old, not just because it is one of the prettiest of the inner suburbs, with the Heath on one side and Primrose Hill on the other, but also because it was full of their kind of Jews – comfortably off and thoroughly Anglicized. Three or four years later Hampstead was flooded with German Jews fleeing from Hitler. Many of them were professional people – professors, lawyers, doctors, psychoanalysts, including Sigmund Freud himself – and because my parents were good-hearted, they felt sorry for their dignified, confused new neighbours who had been uprooted from their nice lives and forced to start again in a country they didn't know or much like. But feeling sorry for them didn't mean they welcomed this alien intrusion into their own delicately balanced lives. And it certainly didn't mean they recognized that what had happened to the refugees might also happen to them.

My mother did not read newspapers – she didn't read anything – but my father slogged through the *Daily Telegraph* every day, so he must have known about the Nazis. Yet what he read didn't properly seem to concern his life. It was something happening off there in Germany, hundreds of miles away, and it never crossed his mind that we, too, would be in deep trouble if war broke out and the Germans invaded Britain. War, however, was not a problem he took seriously. Neville Chamberlain had waved his brolly and promised 'Peace in our time' and my father was not a man to argue with a Conservative Prime Minister. Meanwhile he and my mother had other things on their minds; instead of worrying about what the Nazis might do to them and their family they worried about the damage all those German accents were doing to the image of the English Jews.

It seems unimaginable now to have been so blithely cut off from political reality when the Holocaust was about to begin. But then everything about the first decade of my life seems unimaginable now, starting with the style of life my parents maintained: a nanny, a cook, two parlour-maids in stiff cotton dresses, frilly white aprons and mob caps, a chauffeur for my father and an under-nurse to take care of my sister Sally when she was laid up for a year. These days only the seriously rich live that way unless someone else – the Government, the company – is footing the bill, but 60 years ago, when wages were low, the trappings of wealth came cheap. Even so, my parents were strictly middle-class and, more importantly, they were permanently strapped for cash. Katie thought about food, Bertie thought about music, but shortage of money was the one subject they had in common. It was what they talked about, fought about and grieved for.

It all seems unimaginable now, wrong from the start, confused, confusing, a mixture of strange fears and stranger snobberies. So where did it all go right? The more I think about my past, the less I understand it. Or rather, I have no trouble with the facts of my life because, give or take a few details, what happened to me is more or less like what happened to any other conventionally educated middle-class Englishman who came of age in the boring 1950s. According to Freud, 'All cases are unique and similar', and what makes my childhood unique for me was the brief interlude of the London Blitz when conventions went out the window and life was anything but boring. My past isn't a problem. It's my origins that bother me – what art dealers would call my 'provenance'.

I have a photograph of my maternal great-great-grandfather, the man who set my mother's family on the road to fortune by peddling 'general goods' – anything and everything that was ready-made, useful and hard to get – door to door in the west country. His customers were mostly farmers' wives and by the look of him he would have seemed to them a familiar kind of a man: stocky and curly-haired, with a truculent mouth and combative stare. The photograph – a daguerreotype – must have been taken later in his life, when he was already going up in the world. His hairline is receding on his wide forehead and his clothes are quite elegant – a velvet collar on his jacket, lapels on his waistcoat, a heavy watch-chain and signet ring. But his suit is rumpled and carelessly worn, as though he didn't much care about his appearance. Apart from his height – all my mother's family were short and the chair the photographer sat him on seems disproportionately large – the farmers' wives would have taken to him without trouble because he himself looks just like a farmer. What he emphatically does not look is Jewish. Yet his name was Abraham Levy and, in Hardy country during the first half of the nineteenth century, that must have sounded as alien as Abdul the Bulbul Emir or Ivan Skavinski Skavar.

Despite his name, Abraham Levy was a native Englishman. According to the records, he was born in Middlesex in 1800 – in those days, Middlesex included the East End of London – and by 1800 the Levys had probably been in England for at least a generation. The Alvarezes, despite their name, may have arrived even earlier. After the Jews were expelled from Spain in 1492 – or from Portugal four years later – the family most likely drifted north and settled in Amsterdam, then crossed to England some time after the Resettlement, in 1657, when Cromwell readmitted the Jews. There were Alvarezes in London from then on and, according to a family tradition, all the Jewish Alvarezes in Britain are related. Most of those who get a mention in the early documents were merchants or bankers or jewellers – too wealthy to belong to my lot – but in Spain and Portugal Alvarez is a name as common as Smith is in England, and before the national census began, in 1801, no one bothered to document the poor. So there may have been other London Jews called Alvarez scrabbling along at the bottom of the heap.

Apart from my immediate family, the only Alvarez I ever met – I was very young at the time – was my grandfather's brother Harry, a diminutive old man with an inflamed face and a spiky manner. I got the impression that he and my grandfather didn't much like each other and that this was normal in their branch of the family. They were blood relations, but it was bad blood and none of them cared for each other. The first ancestor I have been able to trace is Aaron Alvarez, my great-great-great-grandfather, who was born in 1773, though the records don't say where. The records, however, say a great deal by implication, and I have a stack of birth certificates, marriage certificates and death certificates which set out, in meticulous copperplate, the occupations and addresses of my remote forebears. Aaron Alvarez's death certificate describes him as a 'general dealer', his son Abraham was a 'pen-cutter'. Both of them married illiterate wives who had to make their marks on the marriage certificates, and all of them, wives as well as husbands, lived where each wave of immigrants settles when it washes ashore in London: in the warrens of little streets that made up the East End boroughs of Whitechapel and Stepney, places with names like Fleur de Lys Court, Three Tun Alley, Gravel Lane, Mulberry Court – most of them now vanished. The Jews from the Iberian peninsula came first; the Ashkenazis from central and northern Europe – the Levys, for example – followed soon after; then, late in the nineteenth century, a flood of Jews from Eastern Europe arrived, fleeing the pogroms and conscription in the Tsar's army. These days, the area belongs to refugees from the old Empire – Indians, Pakistanis and Bangladeshis. The great slow-moving river of London churns the races together and turns them into something else. That something else includes British citizenship, the right to vote and a British passport, but unlike the American melting-pot, which takes one generation to produce a freshly minted authentic American, in England the sense of being foreign is never quite washed away.

Hannah Arendt once wrote, 'While the self-deception of assimilated Jews consisted in the mistaken belief that they were just as German as the Germans, as French as the French, the self-deception of the intellectual Jews consisted in thinking that they had no "fatherland", for their fatherland was actually Europe.' Because of the Second World War, Europe did not figure in my life until relatively late; although I specialized in languages at school, I was 18 before I crossed the Channel. So maybe all I am saying is that the self-deception I call my provenance is a city, not a nation. I am a Londoner, heart and soul, but not quite an Englishman.

Or maybe it is more complicated than that. Neither the Alvarezes nor the Levys were altogether assimilated – most of them went to synagogue on Saturdays and few of them married Gentiles – but long before I was born both families were irredeemably English in their habits, their style, their expectations and manners, as well as their voices. No Jewish accents in our crowd, no pushiness, no unseemly outbursts in public. Not even many dietary peculiarities. In my parents' house we ate cold fried fish on Friday nights and my mother sometimes lit candles; but we children also ate bacon for breakfast, like most of our friends at school.

My father and mother were not religious people and, in their timorous way, they were well on the road to assimilation, though they would never have admitted it to their own parents. Since whenever it was they arrived in England, the Alvarezes had worshipped and married at Bevis Marks, the ancient Sephardic synagogue in the heart of the City of London. Bevis Marks is England's oldest and most beautiful synagogue, unchanged since it was built, in 1701, and still lit by candles, though it is hard to find now because it is surrounded on all sides by skyscrapers, like a jewel at the bottom of a well. My grandfather Alfred eventually relaxed his principles enough to join a Reform synagogue, where he went most Saturdays and, in double-quick time, became a warden. Yet, unusually for a Jew at that time, he was also a Justice of the Peace, a member of a gentlemen's club in Pall Mall, and he played golf at a high-toned club in Surrey.

In other words, like all members of the Anglo-Jewish Establishment, my family was more English than the English, and that confused me when I was a child. Once or twice a year my parents press-ganged my sisters and me into going with them to synagogue, and every time I came away bewildered. I simply couldn't work out what was going on. On one hand, the gabbled prayers in a language I didn't understand, printed in a back-to-front prayer book in a script I couldn't read; on the other hand, the crowds of English gents in Savile Row suits and bowler hats, looking as if they had just stepped out of a painting by Magritte. What was it about? Where did I fit in? Where did it fit in with *Hymns Ancient and Modern* and the *Book of Common Prayer* we used every day of the week at school (and twice on Sundays, when I went off to boarding school)? I knew great tracts of both those books by heart, but I also knew that they, too, didn't have much to do with me. So far as they and what they stood for were concerned, I was like a foreigner who will never quite understand the local customs, no matter how long he lives in his adopted country or how fluent he is in the local language. Having a Spanish name reinforced my eerie conviction that I didn't belong – neither at the synagogue in Upper Berkeley Street nor at the Church of England morning prayers and Sunday chapel at school. What kind of Jew is called Alvarez? It would have been less confusing if my name had been Levy, if my complexion had been less pale, if my hair, when I was a child, had been dark instead of blond.

The Alvarezes were already rising in the world by the time my grandfather Alfred was born. His father, my great-grandfather Barnet Alvarez, one of the sons of Abraham the pen-cutter, was born in 1849, in Gravel Lane, Houndsditch. When he died, in 1912, he was living at a posh hotel in Brighton and most of his seven children had prospered. Apart from my grandfather, I never knew any of them – it was not a close family – but my mother told me that one of the sons, the youngest, made a fortune in the motor trade, then retired to the south of France and married a French Catholic with a title. (She also said that one of the sons committed suicide and the only daughter was 'a ne'er-do-well' whose name was never mentioned.) Two other sons were also in the motor trade and two were clothing manufacturers. My grandfather was one of these and, for a time, he did very well. In 1919 my father was writing his fiancée shy, laboured love letters on business notepaper inscribed:

> Alfred Alvarez: Wholesale Clothier and Warehouser.
> Head Office and Warehouse, 34–38 Stoney Lane, E.1.
> Branches: New Cross, Hammersmith, Victoria.

By the end of the twenties the Alvarez dress shops – 'Everything you want from A to Z' – had spread around London and into the provinces, and my grandfather made his tours of inspection regally, in a chauffeur-driven Rolls-Royce.

Because they were Spanish Jews – Sephardim – the Alvarezes considered themselves superior, especially to other Jews. They were educated as well as affluent – my grandfather at the City of London School, my father at Dulwich College – and highly musical. My grandfather could play whole operas by ear on the piano, and two of his five daughters studied at the Royal Academy of Music and played the piano well enough to win Gold Medals. My father did not play an instrument – he had been forced to learn the violin when he was a child, though he had no aptitude for the instrument and he hated it – but music was his great passion and solace. He spent every spare penny on records and claimed to have the largest private collection in the country. I'm sure he was exaggerating but, even so, he had a vast number of 78s – stacked in a built-in cupboard which occupied half of one bedroom wall – and, as a child, I fervently wanted to believe him because it made him seem important.

There was not much else that did, and what there was had mostly to do with music: as a teenager, in 1908, he had queued for 36 hours outside Covent Garden for the first performance in English of *Siegfried*; he had also been there on the famous night, in 1914, when Nijinsky first danced *L'Après Midi d'un Faune* and was encored so many times that the performance did not end until well past midnight. He made it sound as if he had been present at the creation. But it was tone that got to me more than the occasions. When he talked about music he seemed to shed years: his voice quickened, he sat up straight, he was convinced and knowledgeable and enthusiastic. All through my teens, whenever I was home from school or university, my father and I used to sit together every evening and play records. Sometimes he dozed off and the ash from his cigarette would drop on to the lapels of his suit. But mostly he listened intently, head cocked, gently beating time with his foot, filling himself with order, harmony, sweetness, excitement – with everything he didn't get in the rag trade or his unsatisfactory marriage. Or that is how it seemed. For all I knew, he was thinking about his overdraft or his mistresses. But he looked happy. We often argued about what we heard – I hated his Wagner, he hated my Bartók – but the arguing and the listening together were our closest forms of communication. For me, they were my sentimental education.

They were also a source of private jokes and references. My father had five sisters, all younger than he was, and was close to only one of them – Nancy, the most gifted of the two pianists, who died the year I was born. He didn't see much of the others, perhaps because his (to him) tyrannical father shamelessly preferred his daughters to his only son, indulging their whims and financing their divorces. Renée, the liveliest of the gang, was a scandalous redhead, full of jokes, who went through a series of husbands and lovers and cost him a fortune. Vicky, the other Gold Medallist, was pale and artistic; she had a long-standing, curiously public affair with the conductor of the Royal Air Force band, whom she married after her docile husband died. Madge was a skinny, bitter little woman who retired to Brighton and devoted herself to good works after her only son was killed early in the Second World War. Sophie was the soulful one, who wrote romantic novels in secret. My father resented them all, but one sister and her brood in particular set his teeth on edge; they smirked, they were overdressed and self-satisfied, and they moved together in a kind of simpering quickstep. They didn't come often, but whenever they trotted into our house the old boy would wink at me and hum a snatch of what he called 'tiddly-push music', Gabriel Pierné's 'Entry of the Little Fauns'. He hummed it just loud enough for me to hear and it always made me giggle. I loved the irony and was flattered to be the only person who got the joke. Now I'm not so sure. All the wit in the world couldn't disguise the fact that the Alvarez family was drowning in bad blood.

Music also gave me odd glimpses into the life my father had led when he was young, before he was anybody's father, when he was just starting out, like me. Whenever he played Brahms's Fourth Symphony on the gramophone, he used to sing along with the Scherzo:

Shall we go to Wilkins?
Let us go to Wilkins,
Ye-e-e-s.

Wilkins was a fashionable teashop where he and his pals used to go before the First World War. The place has long gone but it remains, in my imagination, as glamorous as the Paris Ritz. Maybe it was the same for him. He had served in the Navy during the war – land-based, not at sea – but I never once heard him talk about that. It seemed to matter to him far less than concert-going and tea at Wilkins. Music was where everything that was important to him happened.

Those evening sessions in front of the gramophone began after dinner, rarely ended before midnight and had been running for as long as I can remember, long before I joined in. Almost every evening of my childhood the house was full of the sound of classical music, played very loud, rising up the stairwell to the night nursery at the top of the house, and echoing through my first sleep. My mother was not part of the deal. Music didn't interest her and my father played his records as a way of shutting her out – her and their mutual unhappiness. But when I showed willing, after my first term away at boarding school, he allowed me into his club of one, suspiciously at first, then almost with relief, as though glad finally to have found someone in the family he could talk to.

The ritual never changed and it was all about feelings. While my mother and I cleared the dinner-table, the old boy would pad upstairs and return with an armful of 78s – symphonies and chamber music, choral works and *Lieder*, the long works in stiff brown cases, singles in carrier bags from Imhof's or HMV or the Gramophone Exchange – whatever it took to match his mood. He never thought of himself as able to teach anyone anything (though what did I know about music in those days?), but he fancied himself in the role of impresario. He didn't look the part, however, and that now makes those evenings seem strange. He was an elegant dresser – the matching cupboard in the bedroom wall that housed his collection of records was full of suits, all of them hand-made – and he always wore the regulation business uniform of the time: three-piece suit, stiff white collar, Windsor-knotted tie. But no matter how late it got or how tired he was, he never loosened his tie or undid the stud that held his starched collar in place. The suits were fine, the ties lively; I admired his determination to cut a figure. It was the collars that were wrong: stiff as rings of high-tensile steel, and seemingly one size too small because they were always overhung by a small cornice of well-shaved neck. He himself never seemed bothered by them; he was too taken up in the music. But they bothered me. They made him look like a man who was being throttled. And that was probably what he felt himself to be when the records weren't playing: suffocated by work he disliked, throttled by his father.

My grandfather Alvarez died of a heart attack at the age of 86, alone in his suite at the Welbeck Hotel. That was in 1957. His son was almost 65 by then, about to qualify for his old-age pension, and up until the moment when the old man keeled over in the middle of his morning exercises, every breath he had taken had been monitored and controlled and constricted by his father. Old man Alvarez, of course, was a Victorian and the Victorians took it for granted that the head of the household should rule the roost unchallenged. But not all of them were bullies and my grandfather, even by Victorian standards, was unusually vindictive towards his only son. For example, my father loved cricket and played well enough to be selected for the Dulwich First XI when he was 15. For a schoolboy, particularly for a Jewish schoolboy at a Gentile school, this was heady stuff. Or rather, it would have been if there hadn't been a catch: the important school matches were played on Saturdays and good Jews don't play games on the sabbath. My father was not a good Jew, even then, and he became less good when his father vetoed Saturday cricket; but he was much too scared to argue and he kept his outrage to himself. (Eventually he learned to shout at his wife, but that was easy because she, too, was a cowed child. When she finally began to shout back both of them seemed happier. It was their way of keeping up their morale, like whistling in the dark.)

Soon after his son was 16 my grandfather decided that he had had as much education as he needed, took him abruptly out of school and forced him into the family business. He started in a menial job – 'to learn the trade' – and he remained a menial, chronically short of money, even when he was nominally a director of the firm. His many sisters' many husbands were brought into the company in various capacities and always did better than he did. Prosperity eluded him, happiness eluded him, freedom eluded him, and he blamed it all on his castrating dad.

He also blamed the old man when the firm began to slide. It had made money catering for the dowdy end of the women's fashion market – dresses for working-class wives whose husbands made £2–3 a week, for parlour-maids who earned half as much. But the dowdy end did badly during the Great Depression and even worse when C&A opened a big store in Oxford Street which sold fashionable clothes for the same price as the Alvarez shops sold tat. My father had no talent for business, but he loved women and he understood what made them look good. The old man, however, was too arrogant to listen to his son's advice, too pig-headed to change, and too besotted with his own importance to imagine that the firm could survive without him. So he stayed in command until death retired him. By that time, the factory and provincial branches were long gone and the shops that remained scarcely made enough to maintain the old boy in his West End hotel.

His final gesture of contempt for his son was a will that shared what was left equally between his five surviving children. My aunts ganged together and insisted that everything be sold, and my father, who had spent his life in work he despised, was left with just enough to buy a poky little shop in Praed Street and start all over again. By then he too had lost touch with fashion and the shop barely kept him in pocket money. When I asked him why he bothered, he gave me the epitaph on a wasted life: 'What else do I know at this age? Anyway, you know what your mother's like to live with. I've got to get out of the house.'

I heard stories about how my grandfather systematically humiliated his only son, but I only witnessed it once. I was in my teens by then and had gone with my father to collect the old boy from his hotel and bring him home for Sunday lunch. On the way back we passed a newspaper stand. 'Get me the *Sunday Times*,' the old man barked. A brisk command: no 'Would you mind?', no 'Please', no 'Thank you'. He might have been talking to a dog: 'Stay', 'Sit', 'Fetch'. If that was how he behaved on a Sunday, I wondered what he was like during the working week.

The major humiliation, however, had occurred 10 years earlier, during the Great Depression. My father was always short of money – insolvency was the element he swam in – but when I was about six years old he hit a rock and his father refused to help. So did my mother's family, so did his friends in the rag trade. In the end he was forced to sell his beloved collection of records. I knew nothing about his troubles, of course, until one afternoon when I wandered into my parents' bedroom and found the record cupboard gaping open and empty. The big double bed and the floor around it were piled high with records – tottering stacks of albums, cardboard boxes and brown paper bags, a lifetime of listening. I couldn't believe there was so much music in the world. A stranger was sorting through them contemptuously. He was a ferrety little man, dark and sleek, with a pointed face and quick, furtive movements. My father was standing silently at the window, crying his eyes out. In those days he was still a remote figure to me, someone I was brought down to see at bedtime, when I was bathed and combed and in my pyjamas. The sight of him weeping was my first true glimpse of what the adult world might hold in store and I was appalled. I was also outraged when the ferrety stranger called in a henchman, who had been waiting in a van outside, and carried the records away. For weeks afterwards my father seemed on the edge of tears and the house was unnaturally quiet without the evening concerts. Then the storm passed, the good ship Bertie Alvarez floated free, he started buying records again, and it was my mother who did the weeping. To me, it seemed like a victory.

It seems odd to be rehearsing the wrongs and resentments of people who have been dead for decades. What business is it of mine that my father was a weak man cowed by his bullying father? The answer is that the voices, in one form or another, go on echoing long after the players have departed. Mostly I take my father's side, but secretly I also admire my grandfather, and none of it matters because they are both dead. What does matter is that fantasies are contagious and the voices go on speaking – not to you, but through you. For example, the only piece of advice my diffident father ever gave me was, 'Whatever else you do, don't go into the family business.' As it happened, I never went into any form of business – not even academia – and so never had the comfort of earning a regular salary. I have spent my life self-employed – wobbling permanently, like my father, on a financial high wire – just to show him that it can be done. Similarly, he loved travel books, daydreamed constantly about chucking everything and getting out, Gauguin-style, and yet he never left home. His passport, which I still have, is as unmarked as it was the day it dropped through the letter-box. It was left to me to bum around the globe, climb mountains, go out to oil installations in the North Sea and, generally, live by my wits. I thought I wanted to be independent, but maybe all I've ever done is try to show him – long after it had ceased to matter – that it is possible to live a life on your own terms.

For my father, who had to work with him, my grandfather Alvarez was a log jammed across his life. All I knew was that he was a permanent presence in the household because he ruled my parents by proxy. Until the outbreak of the Second World War, just after my tenth birthday, I scarcely registered his existence, because the house was full of servants and my life was lived upstairs in the nursery, well away from the adults and their troubles. I finally got to know the old man in my teens, around the time I got to know my father by listening to his records, and I came to dread Sundays because that was the day he put in an appearance. He came for lunch, ate heroically, slept through the afternoon, then played a bad-tempered game of bridge with my parents and a mournful widow who lived nearby. The widow's name was Doris and she seemed to be in permanent mourning for her late husband. She squeezed out a tear whenever his name was mentioned and, apart from her corpse-white face powder and her ill-tempered, tubular pet Sealyham terrier that snapped at everyone, everything about her was black: her clothes, her shoes, her patent-leather handbag; even her thin, wiry hair was dyed black. My father called her Black Bess and my mother plotted obscurely to marry her off to her father-in-law. ('Kill two birds with one stone,' she said. 'Wouldn't that be nice?') Around nine in the evening, the bridge game would finish with a burst of recrimination and they all trooped back into the dining-room and lashed into a cold supper. My grandfather drank a whisky-and-soda nightcap while he explained to my parents how badly they played cards, then was driven home in silence by my father. Apart from the whisky and soda, none of them drank alcohol; instead, they stupefied themselves with food. *Les enfants s'ennuient les dimanches*, but it's not boredom that makes me hate Sunday lunch. I think of it as a Circe's potion which transforms the eaters into truculent swine.

Apart from bullying my father and overeating on Sundays – hard to avoid with my mother at the helm – I have no real reason to demonize my grandfather Alvarez. He was widowed when I was very small, so I never knew him in his glory days – the 12-room apartment overlooking Regent's

Park, the servants, the Rolls – but I have a photograph of him and his wife in their prime. The grandmother I never knew is a podgy little woman; her expression is cynical; she is swaddled in mink. He is standing behind her, looking pleased with himself, top-hatted and beautifully turned out: there is a handkerchief in the breast pocket of his Crombie overcoat; a grey silk tie, hitched up by a tie-pin, nestles below his wing collar; his top hat is brushed and shiny and covers his high forehead. He has a grey moustache, a witty mouth, an amused unfooled level gaze. He is face-on to the photographer, so his profile can't be seen, but I know what it is like because mine is identical, and so was my father's: the three of us look like Mr Punch, all nose and chin and forehead. In fact, if it weren't for the top hat and elegant clothes, I might be looking at a picture of myself – even the moustache is cut the same way – except that the photograph must have been taken in the twenties (there are cloche hats in the background), so he was younger than I am now. He certainly looks more impressive than I have ever been. I wish I could meet him again now the battles are all over and his spell is broken. Better still, I wish I could have seen him as the person he really was while he was still alive – undemonized, uncathected, uncoloured by my parents' fears and resentments.

I know, for example, that my grandfather was strong on moral responsibility. He gave lavishly to worthy causes, believed in good works and spent unpaid hours dispensing justice at the Marylebone Magistrates' Court. He even believed that it was his moral responsibility, as a pillar of the Anglo-Jewish establishment, to pay every last penny of income tax, on the grounds that employing clever accountants to avoid taxes was the kind of thing that gave the Jews a bad name. Not everyone in the rag trade was so particular and, for my father, the easy money flaunted by his friends was yet another source of bitterness. As he saw it, even the old man's rectitude worked against him, keeping him permanently shut out from the good life. I suspect now that my grandfather was a genuinely honourable man, but because his moral responsibility didn't extend to his son and didn't seem to include much kindness, I assumed it was hypocrisy and thought of him simply as self-righteous.

The will that deprived my father of the company he had unwillingly devoted his life to didn't do much to sweeten my grandfather's memory. He seemed as vindictive in death as he had been in life and it was not until 16 years after he died that I finally got an outsider's take on him. In

October 1973 I had a telephone call from Anthony Rudolph, a translator and the publisher of the Menard Press, which specializes in Jewish literature. Did I remember Sam Dreen? He might as well have asked me if I remembered being young. Dreen was the master tailor at the Alvarez factory in Stoney Lane and, although my father was careful to keep me away from the place in case I got interested, Dreen was a figure in my childhood. He used to come regularly to Glenilla Road, two or three times a year, to measure my mother for the dresses he made her – special one-off jobs that had nothing to do with the dowdy line of goods peddled in the family shops. I remembered a peppy little man with ginger hair and a powerful London-Yiddish accent, who always wore a tape-measure around his neck and carried a biscuit of chalk in his pocket. Whenever he said, 'I must take the measures', my mother dissolved mysteriously into giggles. Because I was little, I assumed she was giggling at the twinkling Chaplinesque ballet he staged for her benefit – the flying tape-measure and flashing chalk, the figures he muttered to himself and scribbled on a pad: 'Hips, this much', 'Vaist, that much', 'Bosom, so much.' Or maybe she giggled because she was ticklish. But if so, why did the parlour-maids also giggle when they came within his range? The truth was, Mr Dreen was notorious for his wandering hands and 'taking the measures' gave him the chance to squeeze the boss's wife's breasts and pinch her backside. My father used to imitate him con brio, which made my mother giggle all over again.

'It's been 35 years,' I said.

'He's in town,' Rudolph replied. 'He wants to see you.'

Sam Dreen was born in Vitebsk, the same *shtetl* as Chagall, and I was expecting a figure from a Chagall painting, folksy and vaguely comical. What I got was a white-haired, ruddy-faced old gent in a beautifully cut mohair suit, a white shirt and the kind of soberly patterned heavy silk tie my father used to buy at Sulka's in Bond Street. It wasn't Dreen's elegance that surprised me, it was his energy. He was 89 but looked as trim and feisty as a bantamweight boxer, and he talked like a young man.

And talk was what he did, mostly about himself and his past, unstoppably, rapid-fire, in a clipped sing-song, 'v's for 'w's. He told me he had emigrated to England around the time of the Boer War, had gone to work at Stoney Lane in 1918 and stayed on until the firm was wound up in 1960. Now he was living with his son and younger daughter in

Milwaukee and travelled to England every six months to see his elder daughter. Also present that evening was a bland and overweight American poet called Sam Menashe. When Dreen mentioned Milwaukee, Menashe announced, 'I've never been west of Chicago.' He seemed to think it was something to be proud of. Dreen looked at him with scorn. 'Chicago to Milwaukee is 60 miles,' he said. 'You could valk it.'

Dreen talked a lot about his dirt-poor beginnings in Vitebsk. He had first gone out to work at the age of nine, laying out skins to dry on the roof of a furrier's factory, but his mother took him away because she thought it was dangerous. Next he took a job in a boot factory, making uppers, but quit because he did not like the work, and became apprenticed to a tailor. His elder brother had left Russia for England to avoid conscription in the Tsar's army, and when the rest of the family joined him in Whitechapel Dreen went to work for a rag-trade firm called Jacobs. He stayed there for 12 years, and somewhere along the way he got involved in radical politics. He hung out with the early anarchists and witnessed the Sidney Street siege in January 1911, when two foreign radicals, much like him, held the police at bay in a barricaded house and Winston Churchill, who was then the Home Secretary, brought in troops and artillery to storm the place. (The house was burned to the ground and the 'criminals' died in it.)

After moving from the anarchists to the socialists, Dreen became a prime organizer of one of the women's garment workers unions. That was enough to get him known in the trade as a troublemaker, so when the tailors came out on strike towards the end of the First World War the Jacobs company fired him. He tried working with a brother-in-law as a gentleman's tailor, but 'it was women's clothes I knew', so he gave it up. After 18 months without a job, he applied for work at Stoney Lane and old man Alvarez took him on. 'I brought him a sample,' Dreen said. 'Maybe he liked my work, maybe he liked me. I think he liked me.' My grandfather must have liked him very much because the first thing Dreen did was organize the workforce.

It had never occurred to me that the Alvarez factory had been unionized, still less that my Tory grandfather would have allowed it. For him, left-wing politics were not misguided, they were treasonous, a betrayal of everything he believed in. 'He didn't try to stop you?' I asked Dreen.

'He said vot I did in my spare time was my affair. If the vorkers wanted to be unionized, that was fine by him – just as long as it didn't interfere with business. He was a decent man, very straight, very honest. If he promised you something, he kept his vord.'

I gave him the reply I had heard countless times from my mother: 'And kept us all poor by doing so.'

Dreen was not impressed. 'First things first,' he said.

'Even in the rag trade?'

'Especially in the rag trade.'

Honour before profit, he meant. I wondered what my mother would have thought of that when she nagged my father about his lack of success and muttered about her father-in-law's self-righteousness. Sam Dreen obviously assumed that he and my grandfather were two of a kind – men of principle who happened to have spent their lives working with grifters and opportunists. For the first time I could see my grandfather not as a reactionary bully but as a decent old-style Conservative – the kind who believed that wealth entailed responsibilities – just as Dreen was a decent old-style radical – the kind who believed in 'from each according to his ability, to each according to his needs'. They were equals, two opinionated men who ran the factory between them and respected each other. And because Dreen was not intimidated by the old man's iron rectitude, he must have been closer to him than my father and his co-directors, my loud-mouthed uncles, ever were.

I don't know how long Dreen had been living in America by the time I met him again, but his accent hadn't changed. Earlier in the evening he had said, 'Last year I joined a student demonstration in medicine.'

'Against the AMA?' I asked.

'No, Medicine, Visconsin, the university town.' Then he added, 'I used to sit on the floor and try and teach you Yiddish. You veren't a good learner.' He smiled indulgently. I was still a hopeless case.

I wouldn't have dared to be anything else. Not knowing Yiddish was a matter of principle; it defined the kind of Jews we were. The only Yiddish word I heard regularly was 'shiksa' and even that I misunderstood; until I heard my mother's dashing brother Teddy whispering to my father about this beautiful blonde shiksa he'd met in the Members' Enclosure at Ascot, I thought it meant servant (as in 'Not in front of the shiksa'). What passed for Yiddish in our house was a joke language my scatty mother made up when she needed something expressive – nonsense words with an sch-prefix, like 'schakaboodle', meaning a hullabaloo, or 'schnippy', a combination of snippy and picky, signifying someone small-minded and argumentative. The few real Yiddish words I know I picked up in New York, when I was in my twenties.

Mr Dreen may have spent 70 years in England, but he still didn't understand the snobbery of the English Jews. There was no reason why he, as a Marxist, should have understood it since it was snobbery of a special kind – one that Marx himself suffered from – and it had little to do with conventional class distinctions.

As it happens, none of my immediate family was a social snob, which in itself was curious, considering the upstairs-downstairs world they inhabited. My parents had been brought up rich – or, at least, comfortably middle-class – and in those days, before there were labour-saving devices, when around 30 per cent of England's population was in domestic service, that meant they had spent their childhoods in households where the servants took care of everything. Literally everything. For example, on a cold day soon after my mother was married she went to tea with her mother at Harley House, the block of grand mansion flats overlooking Regent's Park, where both sets of my grandparents lived in the twenties. Late in the afternoon, when one of the parlour-maids had cleared away the tea things, my mother got up to put coal on the drawing-room fire. My grandmother stopped her short. 'Ring the bell for Violet,' she said sternly. 'Let her do it. That's what she's paid for.'

The servants did everything but – probably because of that – they were taken seriously and treated as equals, often as friends. At my parents' lavish wedding reception at the Hyde Park Hotel in 1919, my great-aunt Lily Franks, who had married into the family and had less democratic ideas about class distinctions, remarked haughtily, 'I've never been to a party where so many servants were guests!'

But no one survives in England without being snobbish about something. Neither the Alvarezes nor the Levys were social snobs, but they were intensely snobbish about their fellow-Jews. The Jews from the Iberian peninsula, the Sephardim, have always considered themselves superior to the Ashkenazi Jews. (Stephen Birmingham's two books on the American-Jewish élite perpetuates that distinction. The volume on the Sephardic families is called *The Grandees*; that on the Ashkenazi founding families, who were no less grand and wealthy, is called *Our Crowd*.) And all over western Europe both lots of Jews, once they had been in the country of their adoption long enough and had made it into the middle class, were snobbish about the newly arrived Jews, especially the poor Yiddish-speaking Ost-Juden from the ghettos of the Russian Pale of Settlement, with their beards and curls and skullcaps and funny accents, the Jews who looked like every anti-Semite's caricature of a Jew.

The established Jews were snobbish about the newcomers' religious orthodoxy in the same way and for much the same reasons as American White Anglo-Saxon Protestants are snobbish about fundamentalist or born-again Christians; it had nothing to do with belief and everything to do with style; their fervour seemed exaggerated, unnecessary, in bad taste. They were also appalled by the aggressive difference, the foreignness, of the newcomers, as though it were some kind of contagion which might ultimately spread to them. Because of that alien stereotype, all foreign Jews became a source of anxiety for the English community.

In other words, their snobbery was attuned to a separate system of class distinctions. It wasn't based on religion; even my non-religious, bacon-eating parents never pretended they weren't Jews. It wasn't even based on wealth; the fact that most of the people my father knew in the rag trade had money to burn and he was permanently strapped for cash never stopped him looking down on them. The snobbery was a question of Englishness, of historical rights based on the fact that both our families had been in England longer than any of them properly knew. They had the right accent, the right degree of discretion, the right tailors, and compared to them most other Jews were newcomers. One evening, for instance, my parents went to a particularly elaborate dinner party at the house of some vastly rich, newly crowned king of *shmattes*. On the way home my father said to my mother, 'I knew they were Polacks.' 'How on earth did you work that out?' she asked. 'Rice in the soup,' he answered grimly.

'Our relationship to Germany is one of unrequited love,' Moritz Goldstein wrote in 1912 of the German-Jewish bourgeoisie. When I was a child, the English Jews were similarly lovelorn. They pretended to themselves that it was the foreign Jews who provoked anti-Semitism in order to deny that they themselves were the cause of it. They preferred not to admit that their apparently polite British neighbours despised them in their hearts. The house next door to ours, for example, was occupied by an elderly couple called Noel. He was a retired Army officer and both of them were military in their bearing – upright, scrubbed and tight-lipped. They were also serious drinkers, though the booze never fractured their icy politeness. Although they were not my parents' style, my mother occasionally invited them in because it was the neighbourly thing to do, and they seemed to have no problem about lashing into her gin. But they did so condescendingly and never once returned the invitation. No doubt my parents were glad to be spared, but I was baffled by the way they took the snub as a matter of course.

Isaiah Berlin once told me that he was a Zionist because he wanted the Jews to have a place where they could be themselves without having to apologize all the time. Berlin himself was brought up in London, and apologizing is a very English habit. But apologetic is exactly how it felt to be an English Jew when I was growing up. Because the British are fundamentally a tolerant people, their anti-Semitism took a peculiarly English form. They weren't racist in any crude way. The first 'Jews Out' I ever saw was scribbled on the tiled wall of a gents' toilet in New York, that most Jewish of cities. The British approach was more cagey and underhand and it was based on the assumption that Jews were cowardly and sly: 'Gentiles in the Army, Jews in the ARP' was one of the graffiti chalked on the walls during the Phoney War of 1939–40. (The ARP was a Dad's Army which patrolled the streets during the Blitz to report damage and help out.) Further up the scale, the anti-Semitism was subtler still: they simply made you feel as if you had committed an unforgivable social gaffe by being born into an alien religion. It didn't matter how well-mannered or cultured they might be, Jews, by definition, weren't gentlemen and never could be. The Alvarezes, who had all the trappings of gentlemanliness as well as an in-built Sephardic sense of superiority, found this particularly galling. After all, the family had been in England for generations; what else did they have to do to be English?

Even assimilation wasn't the answer – at least, not the immediate answer – because what was at stake ultimately had little to do with religion. My own religious upbringing was minimal. I learned just enough Hebrew to rattle off what was necessary for my bar mitzvah and, after that, I never went near a synagogue again, except for weddings and funerals. As for religious belief, I seem to have been born without it, like some people are born colour-blind. I have never managed to believe in any god, divine or political or even, after my unnaturally prolonged adolescence, in any of the little local deities that govern intellectual life – Marx, Freud, Klein, Leavis, Derrida. Ideologies interest me, but only as starting-points, as ways of finding out where I stand. There are principles I believe in strongly – generosity, decency – but principles are about how you behave towards other people and towards the work you do. They are a matter of moral and intellectual tone, not ideology.

Principles are also what Judaism is about. The tablets of the law which Moses brought down from the mountain were a strange and sophisticated package. The religion they propounded had no afterlife – no heaven for the good, no damnation for the evil – and its god was an abstraction, not an idol before which the worshipper prostrated himself but a stern inner voice whose laws were mostly about how to behave in this world. Only the first commandment – 'Thou shalt have no other gods before me' – is strictly religious. The rest are a code of behaviour: honour your parents, rest one day a week, do not blaspheme, kill, commit adultery, steal, bear false witness or envy your neighbour. Even the second commandment – 'Thou shalt not make unto thee any graven image . . . [or] bow down thyself unto them' – is about human dignity; for a people subtle enough to believe in an abstract deity, idolatry is childish. For me, the strength of Judaism is that it is a secular religion and, for that reason, I suppose I will never be free of it. Occasionally, I have to fill in a form which requires you to state your religion. For convenience, I write 'Nil', but what I should write is 'Atheist-Jew'. It doesn't seem to me to be a contradiction in terms.

As for unrequited love: Auden once wrote, 'America can break your heart', but that was a typically English response to the overwhelming size and ruthlessness of his adopted country. Mild and cosy England can be no less heartbreaking if you happen to be an Englishman born with a foreign-sounding name.

2

A DAY AT THE RACES

————➤——

On the Marx Brothers' scale of values the cultured and righteous Alvarezes were strictly *A Night at the Opera* and the Levys were *A Day at the Races*. For all their splendour the Levys weren't quite respectable and didn't want to be. The menfolk were raffish and glamorous; they gambled and chased women and lived it up; they were also, during my childhood, very rich. No prizes for guessing which family appealed to me more.

Abraham Levy, the one who looked like a farmer, made a comfortable living but he never got out of the East End. He died at the same address as he was living at when he married – 21 Bell Lane, Spitalfields – at the age of 94. That was in 1894, and by then his son Isaac, my maternal great-grandfather, was well on the way to serious money. In 1931, when Isaac was 87 years old, he dictated a brief memoir about his climb to the top of the tree. The memory of old people, even if they are spared Alzheimer's, is tricky and selective, but usually it is like an archaeological site; the top layers fall away and the foundations become more sharply defined; they forget what happened yesterday but remember, in vivid detail, how things were when they were young. When my grandpa Dick hit 90 – nearly all the Levys were disgracefully long-lived – he could remember an uncle who had served in the Crimean War and returned so toughened up that he was impervious to cold. 'Never wore a waistcoat,' he'd say. 'Not even when the snow was on the ground. Went about in a cotton shirt, with his suit jacket open. No vest, no long johns, no waistcoat. I've never seen a man like him.' He sounded part exasperated, part proud, as though the uncle, who had been dead for 70 years, was still out there, marching around the streets, making a spectacle of himself. He could also remember, word for word, the cries and jingles of the street vendors in his childhood: the men who sold hot pies and muffins and fish, the knife-sharpeners and the chair-caners, the lavender ladies and the rag-and-bone men who collected junk. But he sometimes had difficulty remembering my name.

My great-grandfather's memoirs are like that: he is more interested in his shaky start than in the triumphs with which he ended. He remembers the man he did his first hard deal with and even the maiden name of the man's wife ('Miss Shorter of Crisp Street. Her parents were in the Glass and China trade'), but the details gradually become blurred and scarce, until what remains is mostly a record of his uncanny flair for business.

Like his father, Isaac Levy began in the west country, buying up pawnbrokers' unredeemed pledges, dealing, he writes, 'in metal, rags, jewellery and anything that I thought would realize a profit'. He spent nine months of each year in Bristol and South Wales, scouring the countryside for unconsidered trifles and soon he'd done well enough to settle in London, find himself a wife and open a little emporium which sold 'clothing, furniture and all the latest appliances'. That, too, coined money – so much that he sold up and decided to take his ease. But he was still a young man – not yet 30 – and idleness didn't suit him. He also had a passion for horse-racing, so when a bookmaking friend suggested they should become partners he jumped at it, reckoning that if he was going to spend most of his days at the racecourse, he would do better taking bets than making them. Once more the money rolled in, but his wife hated his being a bookie – it was not a genteel profession – so, once again, he sold out. This time he bought a pub with the proceeds – the Pitt's Head in Old Street, on the edge of the City of London.

That was in 1887. The Pitt's Head prospered, like everything else the old boy touched. He went into partnership with his 18-year-old son, my grandpa Dick, and Harry Franks, his son-in-law, and went on buying pubs. By the time he finished they were all over London and, he writes, 'too numerous to mention'. The first jewel in his company's crown was the King Lud, a famous pub at Ludgate Circus, just below St Paul's. He bought it in 1894 and, from then on, he used to throw a family party there every year on the day of the Lord Mayor's Show. Forty years later, when I was a small child, this was the big annual treat I always looked forward to, though I don't know which impressed me more: our grandstand view of the procession from the first-floor balcony or the feast that went with it. In the room behind the balcony was a long table piled with chickens and turkeys and ducks, sides of salmon, sirloins of beef, breaded lamb cutlets with frilly white paper crowns, cheeses, fruit salads, jellies, trifles, blancmanges and plates of chocolate truffles. By the time I got to join in, the lavishness of the spread was already exotic, a throwback to England's great days of power and plenty at the turn of the century. But maybe this was what my great-grandfather intended, because the King Lud was the starting-point for an operation that eventually changed the nature of English public houses.

Selling booze was a paradoxical way for him to have made a fortune since he was, he wrote, 'an abstemious man, which has been the cause of my success'. This isn't strictly true. He didn't much like drink, but he loved food and the secret of his phenomenal rise to fortune is in the name of one of the major companies under the Levy & Franks umbrella. It was called Chef & Brewer and its trademark was a white-clad chef shaking hands with a brewer in a leather apron; the chef is holding up a great sirloin of roast beef on a platter and the brewer is toasting him with a tankard of beer.

Before Isaac Levy came on the scene, city pubs were not like the old rural coaching inns, which provided food and cheer to travellers. They were direct descendants of the sordid dens of Gin Lane and all they sold was beer and wines and spirits. Some of them kept a glass jar of big arrowroot biscuits, usually stale, which they sold for a penny each, and a few would grudgingly serve bread and cheese if the customer insisted strenuously enough. My great-grandfather's idea, like all ideas of genius, was blindingly simple: pubs should be pleasant places which sold hot food as well as drink, and displayed it prominently on the counter. This seems obvious now, when pub food is a subdivision of gastronomy all of its own and a major source of profit for the owners, but a century ago publicans were doing very nicely on drink alone and they didn't want to bother with anything as time-consuming and troublesome as preparing food. Isaac Levy set out to change all that.

It started at the King Lud, where a penny would buy you a hot Welsh rarebit instead of a dry biscuit, and it took off from there. Most of the early Levy & Franks pubs were in the City and the old man was shrewd enough to see that the area's population had changed. As public transport improved, more and more City workers commuted from distant suburbs and they wanted somewhere congenial near their offices where they could eat a quick hot lunch. In 1905 the *Daily Telegraph* ran a long feature on Levy & Franks pubs. They called it 'Lunch for the Million' and they made it sound like a vision of the future. At that time – in fact, until long after the end of the Second World War – British public houses, like British society, were divided according to class, and Levy & Franks houses catered accordingly. In the public bars, workmen paid tuppence for 'a pint and a buster' – a glass of beer and a ham or cheese roll. A hot saveloy sausage cost a penny, as did a cup of coffee. In the private bars, clerks paid three halfpence for a pint, a penny for a Welsh rarebit or a Cornish pasty, and threepence for a sausage and tomato with a roll. The toffs in the saloon bars paid threepence for a hot steak and kidney pie and fourpence for a plate of beef.

It was an unbeatable formula and, in its way, it changed the quality of London life. This somehow fits with my image of the Levys. Isaac's parents-in-law, the Harts, had owned a fish restaurant in Drury Lane. When my great-grandmother was a child she used to trot down the road every evening to the Lyceum Theatre, carrying Sir Henry Irving's supper in a wicker basket covered with a white linen napkin. Nearby was a little grocer's shop, which did an excellent line in bacon, cheese and ham, and was owned by a family called Sainsbury. For a time Levy & Franks were up there with Henry Irving and Sainsbury's. Advertisements for their pubs were carried on the sides of London buses and they became so much a feature of London life that the name was eventually co-opted into the vernacular. According to Eric Partridge's *Dictionary of Slang and Unconventional English*, 'a Levy and Frank' – 'a Levy' for short – was cockney rhyming slang for 'male masturbation'. If I feel now more a Londoner than an Englishman, maybe it is because my families' lives are woven into the fabric and language of the city. The Alvarezes gave me my feeling for the arts, especially music, and I am grateful to them for that; but the way they behaved made me permanently suspicious of the high moral tone that often goes with cultural pretension. The Levys were not strong on the life of the mind, but they were lavish and generous and slightly disreputable, and their cheerful, noisy pubs plugged me into the energy of cockney London.

Despite their success, the Levy & Franks formula was not immediately accepted. The firm was a major customer of Whitbread and Bass, the brewers. Their houses sold Whitbread beers and they also managed many Whitbread pubs and hotels, including grand establishments like the Imperial in Margate. Isaac was proud of the fact that 'Lord Burton used to call me "Friend Levy"' (through gritted teeth, I assume), and he set up a licensed catering company in Theobald's Road to supply their numerous joint outlets. The licensed catering company was large and efficient; they had buyers in all the food markets – Smithfields, Billingsgate and Covent Garden – and they made their own sausages and pies. (The posher pubs had their own chefs.) But the Whitbread publicans were not interested in selling food and Lord Burton was 'nervous' – my great-grandfather's word – about allowing the old man to lean on them. The two men argued, then tried to compromise, but in the end the contract was terminated and the thriving Theobald's Road outfit was sold to Whitbread (who mis-managed it and closed it down after six months). Isaac Levy was then called in to take over the pubs of another brewer, Meux. But Lady Meux had fallen on hard times, she needed him more than he needed her, and she had no intention of telling him how to do his job. In no time at all, the Meux pubs were selling food and coining money. By the time Levy & Franks went public, in 1946, the company claimed to be the largest licensed caterers in London; they owned or managed public houses all over town, as well as a string of hotels on the south coast and a major chain of London grocery stores.

My great-grandfather lived to be 97, but the only memory I have of him dates from 1941, shortly before he died. He called my mother at 10 in the morning to announce that he was coming to lunch and all he wanted was 'a little piece of fish'. This was during the London Blitz, when 'a little piece of fish' was hard to find. My mother, however, was well in with a fish-monger called Knockles, whose shop was in Heath Street, next to Hampstead tube station. I was promptly sent off to Mr Knockles on my bicycle, with my tin hat on my head and my gas mask slung over my shoulder. The air-raid warning sounded while I was slogging up Haverstock Hill, and by the time I was free-wheeling down again bombs were falling and shrapnel was rattling around the streets. My mother seemed not to notice. She was her family's scapegoat, the one who could never do anything right, and she was too flustered by the prospect of giving her formidable grandfather lunch to bother about anything else.

I was expecting an emperor. What I got, when the regal Daimler drew up and the chauffeur shot out to open its door, was an ancient, rather crumpled little man, with bright eyes and a nicotine-stained moustache. He didn't talk much and he certainly wasn't interested in me, but my mother glowed for weeks after.

While he and Katie were eating their fish in the dining-room, I was in the kitchen with Tom Olive, the chauffeur. Olive and his predecessor, a giant with ginger hair called Pickard, were my heroes when I was a child. (Pickard had auditioned for the role of the gong-beater, J. Arthur Rank's equivalent of MGM's snarling lion.) I loved the beautiful cars they drove (the giant Daimler had swivelling jump seats in the back and a tiger skin on the floor, complete with head, glass eyes and fanged mouth), but I loved their competence and solidity and jokes even more. Compared with my temperamental parents and their dubious high feelings, they seemed to inhabit a sane and stable world.

Not long ago I met up with Olive again, just before he died. By then he was in his nineties, but he still carried himself like a soldier (he had fought in the first battle of the First World War), trim and straight-backed, and he was full of stories, mostly scurrilous, about his life and times with the Levys and the Frankses. He had driven my great-grandfather and his son-in-law Harry (the original Levy & Franks), before he drove my grandfather, and in their democratic way, they all treated him as a family friend. He not only drove them, he bathed them, dressed them, ferried their lady friends around London and answered them back when they got out of line. When my grandfather's only son, my uncle Teddy, died suddenly, it was Olive who drove down from London to make sure the corpse was properly taken care of. When my great-great uncle Harry Franks wanted to go on holiday with his current mistress and conned his doctor into prescribing a therapeutic trip to Canada and America (without his wife, in case she upset him), Olive left his chauffeur's uniform behind and went with him as his valet. When a rich American widow left her artificial hand on the sofa after a strenuous evening with my grandfather, who was then 86, it was Olive who drove it back to the Savoy in the Daimler.

The bosses also used Olive when they went pub-spotting. When they saw a property they fancied, Olive would drive one of them to it, then go inside – without his chauffeur's cap – to chat up the manager and case the joint on the sly. While he sipped his pint he'd check out the fittings, the drinks display, the cleanliness; he'd see if there was food to be had and ask about trade. Then he'd go back to the car, put his uniform cap on again and make his report. 'Very good,' old man Levy would say. 'Now let's count the chimney pots.' The more chimneys smoking in the area, the more local customers there would be for the pub. It was a simple formula, but it worked. As soon as the property was theirs the firm would send their men in to brighten up the place and alter the counters to take hot food. The work was done in-house: Levy & Franks had their own painters, plumbers and electricians, all of them relatives of people who worked for the head office. 'They got on marvellous,' Olive said.

Unlike the Alvarezes, the Levys were not Spanish Jews – they said they came to England from France, probably because all of them had a passion for everything French – and they were not well educated. Isaac Levy briefly attended the Jews' Free School in Bell Lane, the street where his family lived. (He left the school a bequest for an annual prize in his name.) My grandfather went there, too, and used to boast about his lack of education, particularly when any public-school-educated, musical Alvarezes were around. He could afford to boast, given the grand style in which he lived: the great house in Tavistock Square, where my mother was born, the armies of servants, the closets full of Savile Row suits, the gold-topped canes and jewelled snuffboxes.

He was a tiny man but a great dandy and the women loved him. When he swept out of the Savoy, Olive told me, women often used to come up to him and say, 'You lovely, cuddly little man!', although whether they were attracted by his miniature charms or by the waiting Daimler and the diamond-set cabochon sapphire stick-pin in his tie, Olive never said. What is certain is that he adored women and behaved very foolishly with them whenever he got the chance. About 10 years before he died he had a heart attack and his doctor, who was also the Queen's physician, called the senior members of the family together to warn them that the old man's prognosis was grim. Three weeks later there was another family conference – this time to stop him marrying his night nurse. After that a permanent nurse-companion moved in and the usual problems began again. He gave her jewellery, God knows how much cash and a house – 'with roses around the door,' Olive said – and she responded by turning him against Olive, Minnie the cook, Lettie the parlour-maid and as many of the family as she dared.

Olive was a forgiving man and he dismissed my grandfather's bad behaviour as 'mere silliness'. He also loved the old boy for his wild disruptive sense of humour. One day, for example, the two of them arrived in the Daimler at the member's entrance of Sandown Park racecourse. My grandfather lowered the window for the policeman at the gate to inspect his badge and asked sweetly, 'Would you like a tiddly?'

'Thank you very much, sir,' the policeman replied and stretched out his hand. The old man promptly tickled his armpit. But when Olive drove off in disgust, he cried, 'Stop', beckoned to the bewildered copper and gave him a handsome tip. Years later, after the death of my good-humoured grandmother, he married a woman half his age (that provoked another family crisis, but he outlived her, too, by many years), and Olive drove them to the Côte d'Azur for their honeymoon. One afternoon they stopped for an ice-cream on the Grande Corniche. But the ice-cream was not to the old man's taste, so he stuck the cone, head down, on the wall of the café. He was 78 at the time.

I think these outbursts were the secret of his charm for Olive. He loved my grandfather because they shared a cockney one-in-yer-eye subversiveness. Every so often the old boy stopped believing in the way the world saw him – the beautifully dressed toff in the shining limo – and became a stroppy schoolboy again, stirring up trouble, thumbing his nose at the teacher and making his pals giggle.

I never properly knew this clownish side because I saw him mostly through my mother's eyes and she was terrified of him. To his high-rolling cronies Grandpa Dick was a dashing figure, generous and full of fun, but at home he was a martinet, a Victorian tyrant who felt that it was his duty to terrorize the whole household, especially his children. How real his reign of terror was I'm not sure. He certainly had an explosive temper, but most people seemed to assume that was because he was small and excitable and determined to be heard. His patient wife never seemed put out by his tantrums and the servants can't have taken them seriously because three of them – Olive, Minnie and Lettie – stuck with him for most of their working lives and were still with him when he died. His rages were all wind and very little substance; he shouted and roared, then promptly forgot what he'd been shouting about. Even his two older children, Teddy and Lulu, shrugged off his bullying and learned to fight back. The old man believed fervently in the Victorians' foremost child-raising principle, 'spare the rod and spoil the child', and when Teddy was small he bore the full brunt of this conviction. But Teddy was a far shrewder businessman than his father and he turned the tables on him in the end, running the company as he wanted while the deposed tyrant fretted impotently on the sidelines.

Katie, my mother, was the youngest child and the least confident, and the old man made her life a misery. She was a profoundly unhappy little girl and at one point her unhappiness kept her awake most of most nights. This was in the 1890s, when children were considered fair game for sadistic experiments in the name of good upbringing. Edith Sitwell's father made her wear an iron mask in order to improve the shape of her nose, which displeased him.

The Dr Spock of pedagogy at that time was Dr Daniel Gottlieb Moritz Schreber, who specialized in instruments of child torture. One of the mildest of his many inventions was the *Geradehalter*, an iron crossbar designed to discourage masturbation and teach children to sit up straight. The device was fastened to the table or desk at which a child was sitting; the upright extended down to the crotch to prevent the victim from crossing his legs; the crossbar pressed painfully against the chest and shoulders. He had other, more savage inventions – a halter of springs that compressed the chest unless the shoulders were guardsman-straight, straps that bound the child to his bed so that he slept supine and straight, a head halter that compressed the skull to stop it nodding or lolling – and the purpose of them all was a form of primitive aversion therapy – to teach through pain.

Schreber called his devices 'miracles' and we know about them because he tested them on his own children. One of his sons, David Paul Schreber, who became an eminent judge but suffered intermittent paranoid breakdowns and died in a lunatic asylum, wrote an autobiography, *Memoirs of My Nervous Illness*, in which he described in shocking detail the pain and terror his father's 'miracles' caused him. (Schreber's *Memoirs* provoked Freud's influential paper on paranoia and homosexuality and are the subject of Morton Schatzman's chilling book *Soul Murder*.)

My grandfather's solution to his daughter's night fears – presumably, he consulted an expensive Schreberesque quack – was an isolation cell within the night nursery: a cot with high walls of pierced steel that let in glimmers of light and a little air but effectively shut out the rest of the world – her brother and sister and nanny. I suppose the idea was to teach her to make the most of her unhappiness because there was truly no help at hand. It was a hard lesson to learn so young and it had dire side-effects: she was chronically claustrophobic for the rest of her life.

Yet, in its dreadful way, the brutality worked. She was so conditioned not to make a fuss that ordinary physical catastrophes left her cold. She never voluntarily went to a doctor, ignored every illness, and when she cut or burned herself, which she often did as she got older, she stuck a plaster on the wound and forgot about it. She was also impervious to the dangers of big-city life; it never occurred to her to lock the house doors or close the downstairs windows against intruders, and, after she was widowed, she lived alone in her spooky old house utterly unperturbed by the shrouded upper floors and dank cellars. Maybe there was no danger in the real world that could match her private terrors, or maybe she was fundamentally sane despite her florid anxieties. She had her troubles, of course, and complained about them vociferously; but mostly they had to do with her family and what they thought of us – 'desperate but not serious', as the Viennese say. Even so, she never quite got over that terrible steel cot. She mentioned the contraption to me only once, when she was an old lady, and it still made her shudder.

So did her father most of the time. I've written elsewhere that one of her earliest memories was of leaning out of the nursery window at the top of their tall house in Tavistock Square and hearing the paper-boys shouting in the foggy streets below, 'Crippen caught! Crippen caught!' Crippen was a famous murderer, the current bogeyman for small children, and this occurred around bedtime. But what she felt was not excitement, she said, nor even, for once, fear; instead, she was filled with a profound relief: one monster less on the loose.

Although she never properly got over her fear of the old boy, she never held it against him. That would have been hard to do with such a stylish, lively figure, but it would also have been against her nature. She was not a person who bore grudges and she was generous to a degree that baffled all comers. Anyone who entered her house and was rash enough to admire one of her possessions either walked out with it under their arm or spent the rest of the visit fending off her offers. Although she was a woman without politics, she was tormented by the down-and-outs who were every-where during the Great Depression and she was unable to pass a beggar without handing over her small change. She also maintained a small private army of tramps in Hampstead. Most of them were bearded and looked like Santa Claus, not because they were corpulent but because they wore every rag they possessed in order to keep out the cold. My mother knew their names and which public bench each of them had staked out as his own, and she toured them once a week, doling out 10-shilling notes.

Above all, she was convinced that the world's problems could be solved if only people would eat properly. She was a brilliant cook, despite the fact that she had scarcely entered the kitchen until she was almost 50 and the family cook left. The cook's name was Minnie, like my grandfather's cook, and, like my grandfather, she was a tyrant who ruled the roost and kept my mother out. The household ate whatever Minnie felt like cooking and my mother's only responsibility was to telephone Levy & Franks's central catering office every day with a list Minnie had dictated. The first two items on the list were always the same: one dozen eggs and two pounds of butter on weekdays, two dozen eggs and four pounds of butter at weekends. Admittedly there were never fewer than nine people in the house – my parents, three children, Minnie, Nanny and two parlour-maids – and Minnie made a lot of cakes; but where all those eggs and pounds of butter went is still a mystery to me.

Then the war came, the Alvarez business went on the skids, food was rationed and Minnie went off to work for two famous American radio stars, Bebe Daniels and Ben Lyon, who had better access to the black market than we did. Once she was gone, my mother blossomed.

She was an unquiet, unresolved woman who had never known what to do with her life. She couldn't concentrate long enough to listen to music or read books (not even mine, although she handled them with mystified pride). She had been brought up at a time when middle-class girls didn't get educated; they got married. But she had painted quite well when she was a girl and because painting, in those days, was considered a becoming talent in young ladies, she was sent to the Slade School of Art. She lasted just one term – my grandfather used to say, 'She met the scholars coming out' – then resigned herself to the marriage market, although marriage and motherhood were also vocations she had no talent for. Then, suddenly, with more than half her life gone, she discovered she had a genius for food. It was an instinctive talent – she was incapable of following written instructions – but it suited her natural extravagance. Her food was not only delicious, it was also absurdly lavish. She believed there was no point in cooking one meal when you could as easily cook two; if the oven was on to roast a chicken, she might as well roast a leg of lamb at the same time. Maybe someone didn't like chicken. Maybe someone unexpected would turn up. How could you ever tell? But the real point of it all was excess. If you got up from her table thinking you could eat another mouthful, she had failed.

Strangers were enchanted by her innocent generosity – I have friends who still talk, with awe, of dinner *chez* Katie Alvarez – but for us kids it was an ambiguous blessing. Apart from stuffing them with chocolates, she had no understanding of children and their needs. It wasn't even her fault. She had been brought up by a series of iron-clad nannies, and, when her own children came, she did what she had been taught to do: she handed them over to nannies and hoped for the best. And the nannies kept her out of the nursery, just as Minnie kept her out of the kitchen. She was an outsider in her own house; that though, was how the world was ordered at that time and most of her cousins and sisters-in-law lived the same way until the war came, the servants trooped off to well-paid jobs in munitions factories and a generation of confused mothers was left face to face with strangers who happened to be their children.

Up close, I suppose, her children were a disappointment and, even if we hadn't been, she didn't know what to do with her feelings. So she lavished her affection on a series of surly terriers and spaniels, acted Lady Bountiful to strangers – her reputation spread fast among the free-loading widows and spinsters of Belsize Park – and left us kids feeling that we were living off scraps the others had disdained. Physical tenderness was never part of her repertoire – the best she could manage was a nervous peck on the cheek – and when you are young it is hard to understand that great meals may be an expression of love.

It must have been worse for my father. The saddest thing he ever said was, 'I may be a foolish man, but I'm full of feeling.' He loved being in love and went to other women for the affection his wife couldn't give him. Yet he loved music even more than women and my mother was incapable of sharing even that pleasure with him. Maybe she couldn't listen to anything – not to music, not to her husband, not to her children – because she was besieged by her own inner voices, the loudest of which was her father's, who seemed to be telling her relentlessly that nothing she could do was right, that the man she had married was a failure, that her children were failures, that it was shameful for a girl brought up so rich to finish so hard-pressed for cash.

Even her brother joined in the chorus. While my father served in the Navy without ever going to sea, my dashing uncle Teddy was flying

Sopwith Camels on the Western Front. (He gave my mother a gold brooch modelled on his Royal Flying Corps pilot's wings; occasionally, she let me wear it when I played war games.)

While the Alvarez clothing business slid towards extinction during the Great Depression, the Levy & Franks empire grew steadily more prosperous. (People drink more when times are hard.) While my parents' marriage soured, Teddy lived it up as a wealthy man-about-town, surrounded by glamorous women, touring the continent in his Rolls-Royce, eating at all the best restaurants, and sampling all the great vintages (he was a Chevalier du Tastevin). Between the wars, he sent his forlorn sister a steady stream of postcards from all the fashionable places – from the Negresco at Nice, from Antibes, Biarritz, Paris. He boasted to her about his runs of luck at the roulette table in Monte Carlo and the pleasures of taking the cure. 'You and Bertie should try it,' he wrote from Carlsbad. 'Do you the world of good. Cure your blues, get rid of his pimples and put lead in his pencil.' My poor father never suffered from pimples and always had too much lead in his pencil for my mother's liking. Worse still, this was at a time when the Alvarez summer holidays were spent, courtesy of Grandpa Dick, at the Metropole Hotel in Bournemouth, which was owned by Levy & Franks.

To my mother, Teddy's postcards must have seemed like just another not-so-sly humiliation, another excuse for squabbling with her ineffectual husband. Yet she kept them until she died and I can understand why she was dazzled. In his bull-headed way, Teddy was a free spirit, clever, energetic, full of appetites, and had his grandfather Isaac's flair for business. He master-minded the company's post-war expansion and the rebuilding of the pubs that had been destroyed in the Blitz; he understood the market and made sure the firm kept up with changing styles and tastes. He also accumulated a personal fortune along the way, even though, like all the Levy men, he seemed to spend more time at the racecourse than he did in the office.

In the end his passion for horses did for him and, indirectly, for the family money. In 1952 he retired to Dublin, where income taxes were lower than in England, and bought himself a string of racehorses. He was married by then to a young woman called Sandy, who had worked behind the cash desk at Prunier, his favourite London restaurant. She was tall and slim and boyish, with small features and very short hair. When he married her he gave her a diamond as big as the Ritz and an Aston Martin convertible. Naturally this conspicuous consumption of the Levy fortune set the family's teeth on edge, although my father had the grace to make a joke of it. 'Every time she drives up to Lincoln to see her family, the local kids gather round that bloody car to gawp,' he used to say. 'And there's always one who whispers proudly, "That's my ruined sister."' Sandy was pathologically tight-fisted – what she had she kept – but she was also full of life and tough enough to handle my rip-roaring uncle. They seemed to have a lot of fun together but because they had no children he devoted himself to his beautiful horses.

Life in Ireland was not a success. In those days, no amount of classy horseflesh could make a rich Jew called Levy acceptable in Dublin high society. So he kept the stable and moved back to England. The horse he loved best was a wonderful steeplechaser called Coneyburrow. For two seasons, from 1952 to 1954, Coneyburrow won or placed so consistently that Teddy became convinced it could fulfil his last great ambition: to win one of the classic races. The bookies thought so too, and Coneyburrow started the 1954 Grand National as second favourite. But the jockey made a foolish mistake at the first fence and the horse fell, broke its leg and had to be put down. Teddy grieved over Coneyburrow as though it were his only child. A few months later he was found dead at the wheel of his maroon Rolls-Royce beside a road not far from his country house in Sussex. According to the autopsy, he had had a heart attack, but all the family knew he had died of a broken heart.

The family fortune died with him. A year or two earlier Grandpa Dick, who was already very old, had been advised by his accountants that the best way to avoid punitive inheritance taxes was to transfer the bulk of his money to his young and vigorous son, who would then create a trust fund for his sisters and wife. The old boy did as he was told, a trust fund was set up, but when Teddy died prematurely a great chunk of money was still sitting, mysteriously, in his bank account. The tax man got most of it and the rest went to Sandy, who promptly emigrated to Cape Town with her Aston Martin and her dogs.

After Teddy's death things began to go wrong with Levy & Franks. One of the secrets of the firm's success had been that it kept the trappings of a family concern, no matter how big it grew. For years its head offices were in Gordon Square, one square north of the house where my mother lived as a child, and very similar to it. When the house in Gordon Square was sold to London University, in 1951, the offices were moved a few hundred yards west to another stately but modest building in Fitzroy Square. Both houses had originally been designed for domestic use and that seemed appropriate since the whole enterprise was run like an extended family; most of the directors were related to each other and everyone else had been around so long that they behaved like family. The atmosphere was comfortable, informal, low-key.

My great-grandfather Isaac had always refused to turn Levy & Franks into a public company, on the grounds that it was doing nicely as a family concern and he didn't want pressure from outsiders. In 1946, five years after the old boy's death, Teddy floated the company on the London Stock Exchange and, for a time, it flourished sensationally – so sensationally, in fact, that the cosy offices in Fitzroy Square began to seem out of keeping with its glamorous corporate image. In 1963, when Teddy and Grandpa Dick were no longer around to stop them, the directors lashed out on a fancy glass tower in Oxgate Lane, near Staples Corner, and kitted it out with all the latest business equipment, including a big computer housed in a specially designed, temperature-controlled room. It was a grandiose gesture, though they excused it in the name of improved efficiency: bringing management and catering supplies together under one roof, they said, would streamline the operation and cut overheads.

But the market for the catering company was already beginning to shrink; Meux had been taken over by another brewery, Friary, which got its supplies elsewhere, and independent pub owners were buying their food cheap from the new cash-and-carry outlets. Then, within months of the move to Oxgate Lane, the Government initiated the first of its many post-war credit squeezes. The banks called in their loans, the shares dropped dramatically and the company was taken over by its great post-war rival, Maxwell Joseph's Grand Metropolitan Company.

Levy & Franks had been incorporated as a private limited company in 1911, the year George V was crowned and 14 years after Isaac Levy bought his first pub. A little over half a century later the Levys and the Frankses were out of jobs and the party was over. It was a classic case of clogs to clogs in three generations.

3

BERTIE AND KATIE

The Levy fortune was a great problem for my parents and I'm glad they lived to see it squandered. Neither of them cared much about money for its own sake. When my father had any he spent it on himself – all those records and Savile Row suits – and my mother was the least grasping of women; what she had she gave away. But the lack of money drove them to distraction. It was their mutual excuse for not getting on well together and to my mother, who had been brought up to measure success solely in terms of worldly goods, it was a permanent source of bitterness. It confirmed her image of herself as the girl who could do nothing right.

In their teens the Levy girls were known as 'the Jewish Miss Guinnesses'. Lulu was the clever older sister, the one who read books, and Katie was the pretty one. In fact, 'pretty' doesn't do her justice. With her brown curls and expressive mouth and eyes so dark they seemed black, she was beautiful when she was young; her girl's face trembled with emotion, waiting for someone to mould it, and it appealed especially to aesthetes. Clive Bell, the art critic and her neighbour in Bloomsbury, used to pinch her bottom when she walked in Tavistock Square with her governess; Henry Kendall, a famous theatrical queen, was so smitten by her that he forgot his sexual preferences and asked her to elope with him; her voluntary work at the American Officers' Club, during the First World War, was abruptly terminated – by her father – when a photographer offered to take her back to Hollywood and turn her into 'a second Mary Pickford'.

She herself seemed not to notice her charms. She was so overwhelmed by anxieties and phobias and late-Victorian prudery that she thought it shameful to be attractive. Yet she must have been full of appetite; how else could she have evolved into a wonderful cook? She also yearned for affection, though she could only recognize and accept it in her surly, overfed dogs. But she had been raised in a world in which nice girls weren't sexy and, as a result, she was oblivious to her looks. She slapped on make-up any old how, didn't care much for clothes and came into her own only when she was old and the mating game was long over and she could become a character, famous for her great meals and insane generosity. In order for that to happen she had to free herself not just of appearances, but of her bullying father and disappointing husband. Nothing became her in her life like their leaving of it. She perked up disgracefully once they were gone.

The marriage of Bertie Alvarez and Katie Levy was the Jewish social event of 1919. The wedding reception was held at the Hyde Park Hotel and 500 guests – including all those servants whom my great-aunt Lily objected to so strenuously – tucked into a seven-course meal. I found the menu among my mother's papers after she died: Hors d'Oeuvres Parisienne; Consommé Dame Blanche; Saumon d'Ecosse, Sauce Gourmets; Selle d'Agneau Renaissance, Pommes Mignon; Poularde en Casserole Périgordine, Salade Alexandre; Asperges Sauce Divine; Poire Milady; Friandises; Café. It was the full Levy treatment, even though the Hyde Park was not one of their hotels.

I don't really know how much choice my parents had in their union. Those were the days when children did as they were told and marriages were arranged. Young Bertie Alvarez had all the right credentials: he was handsome, cultivated, sensitive and witty, the Alvarez business was thriving, and the fact that he came from an established Sephardic family meant a lot to the Levys. At the start it seemed like a step up socially; later they got a malicious kick out of his inability to keep pace with their high living. The Levy men were a tough bunch; they loved making deals in business and working out the odds when they gambled. Compared to their earthiness, my father was unrooted and unrealistic. What I remember about him, above all, is a certain lightness of presence: light hair, light hazel eyes, light touch, a man with a flair for charming ladies and telling funny stories. He should have stayed longer at school, finished his education and then, perhaps, done something in the world of music. (He knew the classical repertoire inside out and, as I've mentioned, the gramophone concerts he arranged nightly were brilliantly chosen.) He should have married someone who responded to his charm and enjoyed being flirted with. Above all, he should have married someone who knew how to listen.

Maybe he chose the wrong sister, although Lulu was already married when Bertie and Katie met, and she never much liked my father because she thought he mistreated her beloved younger sister. But at least they had interests in common. Aunt Lou wasn't musical but she was a great reader; with her, the Levy passion for everything French included Baudelaire, Anatole France, Proust and Camus, as well as *haute cuisine* and fine wines. She also had a very English passion for cricket, like my father, and sometimes she took me with her to the Middlesex members' stand at Lord's. Cricket was never my game, but that didn't matter because, while Denis Compton was racking up another elegant century for his county, we would spend the day talking about books. Lulu was well read, in her diffident way, and she helped educate me. She gave me literary magazines she had acquired over the years – the *London Mercury*, the *Little Review*, Wyndham Lewis's *Blast*; she also gave me Scott Moncrieff's translation of Proust (which I failed to finish). I loved her for that, and for her odd mixture of shyness and acerbity, and because she was the only member of the Levy family who didn't think me unhinged because I preferred books to business. Lulu's two sons, Dick and Teddy, were similarly devoted to their lavish and scatty aunt Katie, and she adored them because, among other reasons, they were everything I was not: sweet natured, well mannered and successful in what she considered was the real world. (Dick was a director of Levy & Franks; Teddy was a high-powered accountant.)

I am sure my father was at first entranced by his bride's dark eyes, sweet confusion and absurd innocence, and I think he stayed entranced long after he realized that he was never really going to get through to her. But in the end what Bertie and Katie had most in common was a weakness they bitterly resented: they were both in thrall to their powerful fathers. Maybe they couldn't help themselves when they were young – Victorian children were brought up to be obedient – but somehow they never managed to acquire much authority or self-possession of their own, and this made them woefully inadequate parents. They were good-hearted, they were funny, they were utterly lacking in pomposity or self-importance, but they weren't people a child could rely on. When things went wrong they tended to come to us, rather than we to them.

In some curious way this habit of dependence kept my father young and was part of his charm. Even when he put on weight and his hair turned white, he had the hopeful, vulnerable face of a young man. He looked like a boy who had stuffed a cushion under his shirt and dressed himself up in his father's sedate suit only to find himself stuck with this stupid disguise. He seemed astounded by his bulk and his wrinkles – astounded and injured, as though he had been mugged by old age. He was never sloppy in his appearance; his beautiful suits were always perfectly pressed, his shirts freshly laundered, his fingernails clean. At the bottom of the cupboard where he kept his shirts and underwear was a drawer full of smoking materials: packets of cigarettes from Freybourg & Treyer, boxes of Romeo y Julieta cigars, tins of pipe tobacco with bizarre names like Royal Yacht, Baby's Bottom and Presbyterian. Their smell permeated the clothes above so that he moved in the faint, clean, aromatic scent of unsmoked tobacco. Even when he was old he seemed to smell young. When he died suddenly in his sleep at the age of 76, I am sure he was still waiting for his life to get going.

I never really knew much about that life, except that it was elsewhere – with his friends in the rag trade and on the golf course, and with the girlfriends who, unlike his disillusioned wife, thought he was wonderful. Even when he was at home he seemed to spend most of his time in a closed and private world, listening to his records. I could hear the music, but only at night and from a distance, when I was already tucked up in bed in the night nursery at the top of the house. And it was years before I was invited down to share it with him.

The truth is, I didn't have much to do with either of my parents until one month after my tenth birthday. On 3 September 1939, Great Britain and France declared war on Nazi Germany; three weeks later Grandpa Dick decreed that London was not a safe place for his daughter and grandchildren to be and rented a house for us in Hove, a dreary suburb of Brighton. (My father was not consulted.) The house was cosy and semi-detached, with a neat little front garden behind a neat little privet hedge and a neat little iron gate – everything I had been brought up to despise – and it had just enough room for my parents, the cook, my sister Sally and myself. (My elder sister, Anne, was already married.) For the first time in my life the family was thrust together without a comforting buffer zone of servants to protect us from each other. It was a dreadful time for all of us. We stuck it out for six months, then scuttled back to London in time for the Blitz.

Before Hove my parents were remote figures who inhabited a separate world. While we children ate our meals upstairs in the day nursery, our every mouthful rigorously monitored by Nanny, they ate in state in the dining-room, waited on by the two parlour-maids. Their bathroom was on the first floor and exclusive to them; ours was at the top of the house, next to the night nursery, and we shared it with Nanny, Minnie and the maids. Their domain also included an elegant drawing-room, with a glass-fronted satinwood cabinet full of porcelain knick-knacks, which I assumed (incorrectly) were treasures, and a white silk carpet on which we children were forbidden to tread. This was the land of adults, and when I visited it at bedtime for a formal goodnight kiss I felt like a tourist in Wonderland.

Yet there was nothing formal or distant about my father. He may have been unhappy and dissatisfied in private, but he coped with his troubles by trying to make people laugh. He could never enter the nursery without going into an elaborate slapstick routine: his smiling face would appear at the door, then his hidden arm would hook over his head, grab his ear and try to pull him back. That arm seemed to represent all the Victorian rules that kept him out of our lives; he struggled with it fiercely and always won. I thought it the funniest act I had ever seen.

He also had a disconcerting knack – rare in those days – of treating us children as equals. One winter night, when I had been kissed goodnight and was on my way back upstairs to bed, he went out to the car, leaving the front door open. I paused on the landing and shouted, 'Shut the bloody door! It's freezing.' This was in the thirties, when polite people, especially polite seven-year-olds, never swore and audiences still tittered uncomfortably when Eliza Doolittle said, 'Not bloody likely!' I don't know if I was showing off or trying to provoke him but, either way, I seemed to have succeeded. He stopped dead at the open door and stared up at me outraged. 'I will not have you saying "bloody", Alfred,' he said sternly. 'How many times must I tell you the correct word is "bleeding"?' At that moment, the taboo on swearing vanished from my life.

I loved his lightness of touch, his diffidence and his jokes. (He saved me from a lifetime of health foods and salads by remarking, apropos of nothing in particular, 'I can't stand eating lettuce. It's so boring. It's like talking to yourself.') The trouble was, he was never much around and, even when he was around, there was something transitory about him, as though he didn't quite belong, as though he were just passing through, like a bird of passage yearning to be off to somewhere warmer and more interesting. All he left in the air behind him was the sound of music – not just the great classics but also composers like Janácek and Webern, who were considered exotic at the time. Above all, he left me his passion for Sibelius – he was one of the founder members of the Sibelius Society, which sponsored Beecham's first recordings of the symphonies – and I can never hear that spare, stern, heartbroken music without feeling that he is there, in the room, listening with me.

But he wasn't interested in being a father and had no talent for it. He wanted to be fathered, and this gave him an air of permanent vulnerability, which was part of his charm, despite the absurd role reversals it caused. If things went wrong I would never have dreamed of going to him for advice, but after I joined his evening music club he often came to me. Usually all he wanted to do was complain about my mother – a topic on which I sympathized and had plenty of opinions. On one occasion, however, he was so upset and his troubles were so far out of my range – another girlfriend had ditched him – that I could think of nothing to say. I was at a monastic boarding school by then and the only girls I knew were in the centrefolds of *Esquire*, but I had just read *The Psychopathology of Everyday Life*, so I thought I knew about that stuff. 'Why don't you go and talk to a psychoanalyst?' I said. Then I went back to school and forgot about it. When I came home for Christmas, three months later, the first thing my father said was, 'I went to that shrink. A fat lot of good he was.' I don't know where he had found his analyst but the man he picked must have been a classical Freudian and not very experienced because, the moment the old boy paused for breath, he told him he had an Oedipal fixation on his mother. As an interpretation it may have been accurate, but it was hopelessly premature. My father was outraged and the consultation degenerated into the kind of stormy, pointless argument my parents practised every evening over dinner. In the end the analyst ran out of patience. 'You don't need me,' he said. 'Why don't you just go away and read *Madame Bovary*?' 'I did,' my father told me solemnly. 'A wonderful book. But I don't see what it has to do with me. And for that he had the nerve to charge me 10 guineas.'

Another example: Shortly before he died I moved into one of the beautiful old studios behind the Sir Richard Steele pub on Haverstock

Hill. One evening my father dropped by unannounced, 'just to see the new place,' he said. He peered dutifully around, but his mind, as usual, was clearly elsewhere. So I sat him down, gave him a drink and asked what was up.

He looked shiftily around the room – at the books, at the pictures, at the glowing Pither stove – everywhere except at me. Finally he said, 'I need the name of a doctor.'

'You've got a doctor. What's wrong with butcher Kennedy all of a sudden?'

'No, I mean a *doctor*.'

I stared at him in amazement. This was in 1964, when an illegal operation was hard to find. He was 75 years old. 'She's having you on,' I said.

He looked me in the eye for the first time that evening. He seemed offended. 'She's not that sort of a girl.'

'You mean it still goes on?' I asked admiringly. 'Even at your age?'

'It gets better,' he said. 'It's the nicest thing about growing old. The only trouble is, it makes you awfully puffed.'

A year later my father died suddenly in his sleep. Although I lived nearby, I was not seeing much of my parents at the time, but that evening, by some miracle, I had stopped by the house in Glenilla Road to say hello. He was tucked up in bed. The covers were pulled up to his chin, making him seem more like a little boy than ever.

'I feel rotten,' he said. 'Truly rotten.'

I stroked his forehead. It was cold and damp. Yet somehow I didn't take him seriously. He was always complaining about feeling rotten and, anyway, with his face peeping over the eiderdown and the hot drink on the table by his side, he looked ridiculously young.

'It'll be all right. Get some sleep. You'll feel better in the morning,' I said.

My mother was downstairs, cooking dinner. When I asked her what she thought she rolled her eyes to heaven and said, 'Another fuss about nothing.'

He died of a massive heart attack a few hours later. When my mother realized that the man lying next to her was dead she didn't call me immediately. She knew I was busy, she said; she knew I needed my sleep. So she got out of bed, wrapped herself in the eiderdown and spent the rest of the night on the floor in front of the electric fire. She waited until what she thought was a decent hour – 7.30 – before she phoned me. Her first words were, 'I hope I didn't wake you.' I don't know which upset me more: the fact that my father had died without saying goodbye or that her dread of being a nuisance made her spend the night alone with his corpse. But how else do you behave when you have spent your whole life assuming everything you do is wrong?

Once he was gone she began to flourish. Her father had died a couple of years earlier, her children had left home and, finally, she was free. She walked her dog, touring her standing army of hobos and doling out largesse, she cooked lavish meals, stuffed her grandchildren with chocolates and even acquired a few friends who weren't related to her. She finally had what she had wanted all along – a life on her own terms, with no one leaning on her and no one to apologize to. Out of habit she still went through her neglected-mother routine – whenever I called or dropped by, her first words were 'I thought you'd forgotten me' – but her heart was no longer in it and I could tell she was always glad to see the back of me.

Her natural Levy cynicism also began to blossom. When the family was still around her neck she and I had an unspoken pact: I would make outrageous comments about them and she would giggle and pretend to be shocked. Once she was on her own, however, she seemed to have everyone's number, despite her carefully nurtured air of permanent distraction.

She and my first wife had never had much to say to each other but she adored my second wife, Anne, and Anne adored her – for her reckless generosity, her scattiness, her shrewdness, her great cooking. She even put on weight out of sheer affection, because she knew it gave my mother pleasure to see people enjoying her food. But Anne, too, is a generous woman and my mother recognized her as a soul mate as well as the dutiful, appreciative child she had never had. So when I told the old lady we were going to be married, after three years of dithering, I assumed she would be overjoyed. Instead she gave me what she used to call an 'old-fashioned look' – amused, sceptical, out of the corners of her eyes. All she said was, 'Well, dear, since you don't seem able to marry money, at least this time you're marrying earning power!' I burst out laughing and she twinkled back, pretending she'd made a joke, but both of us knew that this was a conditioned response and she was deadly serious. In the world she inhabited, love and happiness and all the other things she hankered after and didn't have took second place to earning power.

Yet now her father and brother weren't around, her children's failure to strike it rich was no longer a torment. She even had some money of her own, although the trust fund she had inherited was cunningly drawn up so that no one could touch the capital. Or rather, no one her father knew. It had to be passed on intact from his children to their children to the children's children. The great-grandchildren were allowed to sell their shares when they reached the age of 21, though I don't know whether Grandpa Dick permitted this indulgence because he hoped that the fecklessness of all around him would have subsided in three generations or because he knew that the funds would be so fragmented by the time the toddlers and the unborn got their hands on them that it wouldn't matter what they did with the money.

My mother also got a share of the little that was left of the old boy's personal estate, but she used a big chunk of that to fulfil one of her husband's wildest dreams: she paid off his overdraft. Even so, the shop in Praed Street was bankrupt by the time he died and the creditors gave her a hard time. The house in Glenilla Road was hers – a present from her father – so they couldn't get at that, but they all knew about her soft heart and did their best to wring it. For someone who couldn't say no, she was astonishingly resistant.

'There was another one of them on the phone this morning,' she'd say. 'Pretending he'd met me, pretending he and poor Bertie were the best of friends, pretending this was a personal debt and nothing to do with the dreadful dresses he peddles.'

'What did you say?'

'What do you think I said? I told him I didn't understand about business and he should talk to the lawyers. You see, darling, he thinks I'm a fool anyway, so it doesn't matter if I sound stupid.'

I couldn't believe what I was hearing. Either breaking free at last had turned her into a realist or her distracted manner had been a strategy all along, a way of keeping the world at arm's length.

I still don't know who my mother was, but Anne was never in doubt; for her, the old lady was a permanent, cheerful source of life. The day after our son Luke was born in the old Charing Cross Hospital in Chandos Place, a blizzard hit London. This was in 1968, when the English still chose to believe that they lived in a temperate climate and were indignantly laid low by every freeze-up. The city was almost immobilized, apart from the tube, which ran so irregularly that, when I went to see Anne and the new baby, the 20-minute journey took more than an hour. But my mother never used the tube; being underground exacerbated her claustrophobia and the din terrified her. She took what buses she could find, but mostly she made the long journey from Hampstead to Charing Cross on foot.

Anne was half asleep when her mother-in-law arrived and everything in the maternity ward seemed as washed out as she felt: white walls, white bedclothes, white faces, hushed voices; outside the windows, the snow made the light seem unnaturally pale and muffled the noises from the street. Katie marched into this muted world in a blaze of colour. She wore too much rouge, her lipstick was on wrong, her hat was at a wonky angle, and she was toting a great basket full of presents – flowers, fruit, smoked salmon sandwiches and chocolates for the new mother, clothes and toys for the baby. 'She was like a walking cornucopia in all that pallor,' Anne says. And that is how she still remembers her.

I wish I could remember her as warmly as that, but it can't be done. The truth is, we were never much of a family. In the good old days before the war, when there was still money around, the household worked on the principle of divide and rule and we children were pawns in the game. Nanny and Minnie the cook were constantly at each other's throats. Minnie terrorized me because I was Nanny's creature and Nanny terrorized my sisters because they were Minnie's. Both of them combined to outflank my mother and to set her children against her. We didn't need much encouragement. Because she had abdicated from our lives, on the rare occasions when we saw her we made her life hell. I have a holiday snapshot, taken by my father, of my sister Sally and me sitting with her in a rowing boat in Lulworth Cove. It is not a pretty picture and I can still remember what happened. Mother said, 'Smile at Daddy, children', and we, as one, turned our backs. Six decades later our childish backs are still in focus – Sally's slumped and depressed, mine skinny and stiff and angry – and Katie is still smiling glassily at the camera. Then and always she must have been glad to hand us back to Nanny.

My sisters and I were no more loving towards one another than we were to her because Nanny and Minnie worked hard to stir up trouble between us. I was the only son, which was already a privileged position, but I was an afterthought and my two sisters were so much older than I was that I might as well have been an only child. I don't even remember, and never properly knew, how much older they were: was it six years and eight or eight years and ten? All I knew was that, despite the fact that we ate our meals together, Anne and Sally, like my parents, inhabited a different, mysterious world and there was not much communication between us in the beginning.

Anne was the first-born, beautiful, clever and sensitive, and she started out without any intention of being a loser. When she came back from her Swiss finishing school she seemed to me unimaginably sophisticated. She rode horses, skied, spoke French and German and seemed to know about what was happening in the great wide world beyond NW3; she had even shaken hands with Marlene Dietrich, whose daughter was at the same school. I thought she was wonderful, especially when she defied the family rules by falling passionately in love with a Roman Catholic. But in those days nice Jewish girls didn't marry out of the faith and my parents were terrified of what their hidebound fathers would say – Grandpa Alvarez because he was a warden of his synagogue, Grandpa Dick because he had paid the Swiss school fees. Her great romance fizzled out in family rows and tears and recrimination and she spent hours in front of the gramophone, listening to Tchaikovsky's *Romeo and Juliet* and weeping desolately. Then she made a proper marriage and, directly the war ended, she and her husband moved to Eastbourne to get away from the lot of us.

The man she married adored her, though he was her opposite in most ways – steady, reticent, shy. He had served in the Navy during the war, as a decoder on Murmansk and Atlantic convoys, dangerous work which he chose not to mention. He loved Dickens and Mozart and enjoyed tinkering with things, finding out how they worked, fixing them. (When he was in his eighties he taught himself to use a computer.) Maybe he adored my sister because she was everything he was not, but apart from his chronic infatuation, he was utterly unromantic and I suspect she gave him a hard time.

Anne was Bertie Alvarez's true child, full of unresolved fantasies and unfulfilled hopes, a charter member of the Madame Bovary Club. She'd had her brief run-in with a glamorous world as a teenager at school by Lake Lucerne, then with thwarted passion when she came home and fell in love, and she didn't want to let either go. She kept the Swiss connection alive by giving French lessons to aspiring Eastbourne mums and their children, and she went on nurturing her broken heart not because she thought she would have lived happily ever after with anyone else but because being broken-hearted and doomed was the role she liked best. She became sporadically depressed as she grew older and the local know-nothing doctor put her on a daily cocktail of increasingly powerful anti-depressants and sleeping pills. They did nothing for her depression but her fantasies grew more florid and she sometimes found it hard to separate them from the real world. All of us were hit hard by our father's sudden death but Anne transformed her shock into a nightmare Victorian melodrama; she went around telling anyone who would listen that he had died cursing her. When she repeated this at Glenilla Road the old lady was outraged. 'What does she mean, cursing her?' she asked me. 'The poor soul was gone so fast he didn't even say goodbye to me.'

His death knocked my sister out of orbit but cancer brought her back. I went down to see her in Eastbourne on an iron-cold day in February, a few weeks before she died. The nursing home was a mock-Tudor villa in a street of mock-Tudor villas, a nondescript suburban house except for the uniformed nurses, the white-coated doctors and the hush. In Anne's room at the back of the house, the only sounds were from the builders working on a site at the end of the garden and the seagulls squabbling overhead. The last time we had met, months before, we hadn't had much to say to each other. Her daily intake of pills made her seem not quite present and I was appalled by what they had done to her lovely face. It was like a mask, with gaunt cheeks and a twisted mouth. Now she was off the pills, the mask was gone and the ghost of her beauty was visible again – nervous and alert, with fine features and haunted eyes. She was almost young again; her face was clear, her eyes were bright and she had her witty smile back. I was leaving soon for the States and would be gone for a month, so I knew I wouldn't see her again, but somehow everything was all right. My beautiful, clever sister and I were back as we had started in Glenilla Road, all passion spent.

Maybe that is what a slow death does to you: the present drops away, your features clarify and you travel back to where you began. Anne, in fact, went on travelling; the last thing she said to her son, before she lapsed into her final coma, was, 'They're doing up Gordon Mansions.' Gordon Mansions, just around the corner from the Levy & Franks head office, was where my parents had lived when they were first married and where all three of us children were born.

Sally was the family scapegoat. She was the one in the middle, the one who could never do anything right, who was no good at school and hated games, the unglamorous daughter, always a little overweight, who took her time about getting married. She fell ill soon after I was born and the usual incompetent family doctor – my parents had a genius for smelling them out – was unable to diagnose the trouble. So he ordered her to spend 12 months on her back in a wickerwork coffin on wheels. At the end of the year nothing had changed but she wasn't any worse, so she got out of her coffin and went on as before.

The war gave her a shot at freedom. She joined the WRAF – even my mother couldn't argue against patriotic duty – but that, too, ended badly. Cycling back to camp late at night with no lights on her bike, she was hit by a car and flung 50 feet over a hedge. She fractured her skull and spent three weeks in a coma. Although the car was almost certainly being driven too fast – the driver was a fighter pilot – it was universally agreed that Sally was to blame. Why was she out after hours? Why did her bike have no lights? Anyway, she was WRAF 2nd-class and he was a Flight Lieutenant, so it had to be her fault. The driver was exonerated and I am willing to bet that she apologized to everyone directly she came to.

Sally was the child my mother picked on to bear the brunt of her own inadequacy and, because she was biddable and passive and seemingly not as smart as Anne and I, she accepted the role, never argued back, acted stupid and let everyone walk over her. Naturally I hunted with the family pack when I was a child, although later her even temper and unshakeable patience made me see it was a cruel charade. Her docility wasn't a sign of weakness; it was the way she chose to meet the world, because she was a good-hearted woman who wished people well and genuinely wanted to please. Above all, she wanted to please her mother. Maybe that's what all three of us wanted, in our different ways, and part of the old lady's hold over us was that, since she was incapable of listening, nothing we could do would ever satisfy her. So Anne turned her back on the whole sorry show and I became a writer, a profession my mother knew nothing about and didn't care for, although she of all people should have understood the frustrations of trying to get through to an obdurate audience

Sally, however, was determined to do the right thing and wanted to be recognized for it. She married a good Jewish businessman who made her happy and she visited Glenilla Road regularly each week, placidly eating bacon and eggs (her husband wouldn't allow pork in the house), while the old lady's aimless, relentless criticism washed over her. Sally's daughter finally vindicated her by making an eminently successful marriage: the man was charming and kind and rich, and the reception was held at the Savoy, Grandpa Dick's old watering-hole. But by then Katie had been dead for two years and Sally herself did not live to see the wedding because her terrible wartime accident had already caught up with her. She spent her last years in a wheelchair, throttled by a neck-brace, and died of a catalogue of illnesses, including the same vicious form of arthritis that eventually crippled our mother. I never once heard her complain. Yet even at the end, she was still under the old lady's spell. While she lay dying in hospital she kept repeating, 'I wish Ma could be here for the wedding.'

Neither of my sisters made it beyond 60 and it seems ironic that I, who started out as the delicate one, should have outlasted them. Maybe I was helped by my having had to fight for survival when I was a baby or maybe they were more vulnerable because they belonged to a generation of women who were brought up to be dutiful and compliant. Maybe. The more likely explanation is that the strain of being daughters of my unreliable parents was too much for them; it sucked them dry, physically as well as mentally. There is an eloquent passage in *The Adventures of Huckleberry Finn* about the books Huck read while he was staying with the kindly Grangerfords: 'One was *Pilgrim's Progress*, about a man that left his family it didn't say why. I read considerable in it now and then. The statements was interesting, but tough.' Life with Bertie and Katie was also interesting, but tough, and it did for both my sisters in the end. As for me, I left my family as soon as I could, but I always knew why.

4

MYSELF WHEN YOUNG

———————➤━

The mysterious illness which confined Sally to her wickerwork coffin was just one of the tribulations my mother had to bear. I was another. According to the tribal prejudices of her family, good wives produced sons to carry on the family name and, eventually, the family business. But poor Katie could never do anything right and the best she could manage was two daughters. Then, when everyone had given up on her and the girls were already at school, I arrived. She was triumphant, even though she got the timing wrong, of course, and ruined everybody's long weekend by giving birth on an August Bank Holiday Monday.

Her elation didn't last. The long-awaited son was born with an ominous growth at the base of his left leg. It was later diagnosed as 'a congenital abnormality of the lymph-vascular system' – nasty but not dangerous – but at first the doctors didn't know what was wrong and suspected the thing might be cancerous and malign. So, when I was between 12 and 18 months old, the front of my leg was opened up from the bottom of the knee to the top of the foot and the growth was cut away. (The scars left by the incision and the stitches looked like a giant zipper and took 30 years to fade.) But the operation was not a success and, as a tree flourishes when it is pruned, the cyst grew back immediately, even larger than before. This was at the beginning of the thirties, when radium was the fashionable cure for cancer. My leg was duly packed around with radium and enclosed in a miniature riding boot made of lead. That didn't work either: instead of dispersing the growth, the deep X-rays solidified it, making it seem permanent.

Naturally I remember nothing of the operation or the lead boot, but it must have been a bad time and I think I survived it more or less intact only because of Nanny. She had come to look after me when I was born and when I went into hospital for the operation she went with me, sleeping in the same room, feeding me, playing with me, singing me to sleep. I think her presence saved my sanity, though why she was allowed to stay with me I will never know, since it was an extremely rare procedure at that period; it was another quarter of a century before the medical profession accepted that children in hospital fare better when a 'care-giver' is with them.

My mother came to visit me every day, laden with presents and full of anxious goodwill, but she hated every minute of it. Hospitals scared her and she couldn't handle any sickness she couldn't cure with large meals or an overdose of chocolate. Then one afternoon, she told me, it finally became too much for her. I was crying and miserable and so restless that the bandages around my leg worked loose and the dressing fell off. When she saw the wound up the front of my leg and the dreadful mess around the ankle she burst into tears and fled in horror.

That, at least, is what she told me, but it is a story hedged around with doubts. Of course, she didn't tell me until years later. Of course, I remember nothing about it. Of course, it was sadder for her than for me at the time. She must have been upset not just by what my leg looked like but what she imagined was her responsibility for it. She couldn't cope with all that gore and she couldn't cope with whatever fatal deficiency in her had produced the deformity. But the extenuating circumstances and the doubts aren't enough. It was my mother who told me the story and I grasped at it because it fitted precisely with how she always seemed to me during my childhood: she wasn't there when I needed her.

Nanny was always there – rock-steady, sensible, calming, affectionate. For my mother, I was a terrible proof of her inadequacy, an only son with something monstrously wrong with him. For Nanny, I was a baby in trouble and it was her duty to take care of me. She was a handsome, vigorous woman, with soft cheeks, a strong jaw and eyes as blue as nursery china. Because she was a country girl, practical and stern, she had no patience at all with anything fancy – and that included my parents' temperamental behaviour as well as the music my father played at full blast on the gramophone every night. Yet she herself had a weakness for poetry and knew reams of it by heart. The poems she loved were not the kind that get into anthologies. Sentimental Victorian ballads and narrative poems were her speciality, high-toned versions of the music-hall classics, like 'Albert and the Lion', which first made Stanley Holloway famous. Her recitations were a big hit at social evenings of the Baptist church she attended and sometimes, if I was good, she would roll them out for me. Her voice was strong and full of feeling, but softened at the edges by a muted west-country burr and always faintly overlaid by the sound of my father's records filtering up from downstairs. Because I loved her and I loved my father, that mixture of ringing couplets and mysterious classical music is where, I suppose, my love of poetry began.

The arts are the subtlest form of communication and Nanny had an uncanny gift for communicating with babies. I discovered this all over again, many years later, when she invited herself to tea at Glenilla Road a few weeks after my daughter Kate was born and we took the baby down to see her there. The two old ladies were glowering at each other when we arrived. My mother had never forgiven Nanny for pre-empting her only son's affections and now she was a free agent – husbandless and fatherless – she made no effort to disguise her resentment. She beamed at us as we came in, offered a cheek to be kissed – her face carefully averted, as always – and said, as always, 'Have a chocolate.' Then she glanced distractedly at her new granddaughter and made what she thought were baby-friendly noises. When Kate looked baffled she turned to me accusingly. 'She's just like you,' she said, then hobbled out to the kitchen to make the tea. All Nanny said was, 'Let me hold her a minute.' She propped the baby against her forearm, cupped its head in her hand, and gazed into its eyes, murmuring softly. Kate gazed back and the two of them stayed like that until we left.

'Did you see that?' Anne asked, as we drove home.

'The story of my childhood,' I replied.

'It makes me sorry for your mother,' Anne said.

Because of what everyone called my 'bad leg', I was often ill as a child and Nanny provided what my parents lacked – common sense and a calming presence. The bad leg was my weak point, a fuse that blew at every trivial childhood sickness – measles, chickenpox, mumps, flu – or whenever I was under serious pressure. The skin over the growth was also abnormally thin and, although it was always bandaged for protection, it cracked easily and became infected. When that happened, the thing became inflamed and painful, it oozed lymph copiously and I ran a high temperature. So I was prone to fevers, as well as to whatever nightmares had been left over by the surgery I could no longer remember. I was terrified of the dark, I was terrified of spiders, I was terrified of whatever lurked in the cellars and the attics and the half-opened cupboards in the night nursery. But apart from the spiders, I was only scared of what I couldn't see. My fear ceased once I could put a face on it and, perhaps because my bad leg inured me to pain, I had almost no physical fear at all.

As a schoolboy in the boxing ring I just kept on coming, no matter what my opponent was dishing out, and on the rugger field, where I was invariably the smallest player, I used to hurl myself into tackles like a kamikaze pilot. Perhaps I owe that, too, to Nanny. Although she nursed me tenderly when I was ill or feverish, she was a tough old bird who was never sick and had stern views about making a fuss. And because she was always healthy, health and strength were what I longed for most. Maybe the operations gave me a head start: if I could survive them I could survive anything.

My mother and Nanny were both women with appetites but, as with everything else, they were at loggerheads even there. Katie loved food but disliked physical contact and had been brought up to think of sex as 'a dirty little secret'. Nanny wasn't much interested in food, although she was tyrannical about making us children eat everything on our plates; but she had no problems with sex.

When I was small I had pretty golden curls, like one of Gainsborough's syrupy, bubble-blowing children, but I lost them prematurely when she started an affair with Mr Featherstone, the local barber. Mr Featherstone was a cadaverous man with a waxy face and thin black hair so highly brilliantined that it shone like patent leather. He owned a sweet shop in Belsize Lane, which I used to visit on my way back from nursery school with Nanny. At the back of the shop, behind the rows of giant sweet jars and tilted boxes of chocolate bars, was a little barber's shop: two wooden armchairs in front of two hand basins and two big mirrors above a shelf of glass bottles filled with violently coloured, violently smelling hair tonics and colognes. At the far end of the shelf was a very small cardboard placard inscribed, enigmatically, 'Durex'. There were a couple more wooden chairs at the back of the room, and a table piled with back issues of *Titbits* and *Lilliput*. In the corner was a door to the back of the house, through which Nanny and Mr Featherstone disappeared as soon as the assistant barber began to snip at my curls. The door had stained-glass panels which caught the sun and Nanny and Mr Featherstone also seemed to glow when they came back downstairs.

1. Great-great-grandfather Abraham Levy (*author's collection*)

2. The Levy grandparents (*author's collection*)

3. The Alvarez grandparents (*author's collection*)

4. My father, Bertie, *c.* 1963
(*author's collection*)

5. My mother, Katie Levy, *c.* 1917
(*author's collection*)

6. With my mother, Bournemouth,
1936 (*author's collection*)

7. Father and son,
Deal, *c.* 1946
(*author's collection*)

8. Oundle Boxing Team, about a year later (*author's collection*)

9. Frank Kermode (*Sir Frank Kermode's collection*)

10. Zero Mostel (*Robert Frank*)

11. Samuel Beckett (*by Avigdor Arikha, National Portrait Gallery*)

12. John Donne, in the pose of a melancholy lover, *c.* 1595 (*in a private Scottish collection*)

13. Zbigniew Herbert
and Adam Alvarez,
c. 1962 (*author's collection*)

14. With Miroslav
Holub, 1992 (*Blanka
Lamrova*)

15. Ted Hughes and Sylvia Plath, 1961 (*David Bailey*)

16. Alfred Brendel reading Ionesco's *The Chairs* (*Marzena Pogorzaly*)

The assistant barber was a pernickety little man who seemed to take forever over my small head of hair, but I learned that if I was patient and didn't make a fuss I got a free bag of sweets as a reward. First, my innocent golden curls were trimmed, then they were shorn. 'Can't have you looking like a little girl,' Nanny explained. Soon I was going to the barber's once a week, 'Just to keep him looking tidy,' she told my mother.

There was a Mrs Featherstone somewhere, so they were discreet, and my mother was too naive to guess what was going on. All she knew was that I was losing my pretty head of curls and she hated it. She complained, she wept, she even threatened vaguely to fire Nanny. But Nanny took no notice. She knew Katie was incapable of following through on her threats and, anyway, she had me on her side, paid for weekly in wine gums and gobstoppers and bars of Cadbury's Milk and Nut Chocolate.

I stuffed myself with sweets but it was Nanny who put on weight – slowly at first, then dramatically. Then she disappeared for two weeks – to see her sister in Lewes, who was ill, she claimed. When she returned her figure was back to normal. 'She can't control her eating,' my mother hissed to my father one evening when Nanny brought me downstairs for the ritual goodnight kiss. 'She goes up and down like a balloon.' Nanny pretended not to hear. My father merely shrugged and gave Katie one of those 'old-fashioned looks', as if to say, 'What she doesn't know won't hurt her.' It was years before my innocent mother caught on. It must have been Minnie who told her because, then or later, Nanny never spoke of what had happened to any of us. In those days, when good jobs were hard to find, nursemaids devoted their lives to other people's children. She put her baby out to adoption at birth and never saw it again.

Nanny was the most important figure in my childhood, but most of the memories I have of her are fragmentary and scattered. I associate her with the smell of the sweet peas in her sister's garden in Lewes and with the piercing, heady scent of hawthorn when we walked on Hampstead Heath in May. I remember waking up when my leg was giving me trouble and seeing the night nursery we shared at the top of the house infused with the orange glow of the gas fire and Nanny beside it in her rocking-chair, reading and knitting in a pool of lamplight. She was a champion knitter and, before I started wearing school uniforms, all my pullovers and cardigans were her creations.

We spent most summers in Bournemouth, as guests of Levy & Franks, in a red-brick Victorian palace called the Metropole Hotel. It had a cupola on its roof, chimneys built like Corinthian columns, marble pillars at the entrance, a huge dining-room with stiff white linen on the tables and a conservatory opening on to a garden. It seemed to me immeasurably grand. (The place was hit by a bomb during the war and replaced later by a hideous wedge of concrete and glass, with a fast-food joint at its base, a jazzy pub, a kebab take-away and a used-car showroom.)

The annual month in Bournemouth was supposed to be a family holiday, but that is not how I remember it. My father stayed in London with his business and his records and his girlfriends, and appeared reluctantly at weekends. Mother spent her time gossiping with the same cousins she saw in town – Eva, Kitty, Queenie – lively women who wore big diamond rings and too much make-up. They, too, were guests of L & F and had husbands who visited only at weekends. My days were spent on the beach with Nanny and my sisters. There were donkey rides and cones of soft ice-cream from a kiosk called Nottiano's. On the promenade, just along from the Westover and Bournemouth Rowing Club, 'founded 1865', was a red-brick Victorian public toilet, almost as ornate as the Hotel Metropole. The beach was lined with bathing chalets with pointed tar-paper roofs, eaves painted red and blue and yellow, and faded curtains in their windowed fronts. I remember how they smelled – of wood and salt and tar paper – and the feel of my dank woollen swimming costume that never dried properly and made me shiver when I put it on every morning. In most of the snapshots that have survived I am with Nanny, but there are some of my mother and me hand in hand. She always looks uneasy, I always look truculent.

At some point, however, Nanny did get her marching orders, and that was when I discovered the power of true grief. It happened when I was about six years old and had started at prep school. Perhaps my parents thought, rightly, that I was too old to have a Nanny or perhaps my mother saw her chance to get rid of her rival. All I remember is coming home one day after school and finding Nanny gone. I also remember sitting at the window of the deserted nursery, howling at the sunset like an abandoned puppy. I kept up my inconsolable weeping for 48 hours, with pauses for sleep. When I woke on the third day, Nanny was back, just as mysteriously as she had left. She stayed for another two years, until even I was embarrassed for my school friends to know I still had a Nanny to look after me.

When Nanny finally left, in 1938, my mother did not take charge of the nursery; it wasn't a proper thing for the mistress of the house to do and, anyway, she wouldn't have known how. Instead she hired a governess, a brisk young woman from Lancashire who looked like Popeye's girlfriend, Olive Oyl – tall and bony, with a head too small for her body and hair tightly scraped back in a bun. Her name was Lowie and she and I didn't much like each other. She preferred my sister Sally – a healthy change in the family balance of power, but not one that I could appreciate at the time. That summer, instead of going to Bournemouth, Lowie took Sally and me for a fortnight's holiday in Southport, her home town. We stayed in a boarding house which belonged to her sister, a mean little place where the food was worse and less plentiful than at school. Although Southport is a seaside town, I couldn't even splash around in the waves. At low tide the sea seemed to disappear entirely, leaving a plain of greyish wet sand, spotted by the casts of sandworms. I hated every moment there. At that safe distance from London, Lowie did not even have to pretend to tolerate me, but she made sure there was never a pen or pencil in the house when I wanted to write a postcard home. She left us at the outbreak of war, along with the rest of our middle-class pomp – the parlour-maids and my father's chauffeur. I couldn't wait to see the back of her.

Nanny remained a slightly bossy presence in my life even after she had gone. Early in the war she moved into a little flat in Swiss Cottage, not far from Glenilla Road, and I saw her regularly, though mostly on the sly, to avoid offending my mother. Although we drifted apart when I went off to boarding school, I visited her most holidays, sent her postcards when I started moving around the world, exchanged birthday cards every year and kept in touch for the rest of her very long life. I wasn't the only one of her proxy children to remain devoted. Before she came to the Alvarezes she had looked after two little girls in Kew. It was a rich family and the younger of the girls made sure Nanny lived comfortably until she died, setting her up in a big, bright flat in Barnes, taking her on holidays and making sure her bank balance was always topped up. I used to visit the old lady in Barnes – but only when she could fit me into her schedule of recitations, whist-drives and dances at the chapel and old people's centre. Her energy was unnerving. She had walked me on Hampstead Heath or Primrose Hill every day of my childhood, whatever the weather; then, when I was a father and she came to tea in Hampstead, she and I would walk my children on the Heath. In those days I was playing squash three times a week and climbing rocks every weekend and she was in her eighties, but I still found it hard to keep up with her. The last time she came to see us she was 90-something and had just had a hip replacement. When I asked her how she was she said, 'Right as two trivets', and danced a jig to prove it.

Nanny was in no way a subtle woman; she didn't much care for the things I came to care about, including poetry (although she was passionate about her Victorian junk, she dismissed everything else as highbrow nonsense); she was contemptuous of my mother and rude to her; she bullied my sisters and was strict with all of us. But she got me through my nightmare operations and the terrors that followed them – and not just with love. Her gruff common sense, resilience and unbeatable good health probably gave me something sane and healthy to aim for.

What she had to teach me is encapsulated in the first and more or less only memory I have of my earliest childhood. Naturally I remember nothing about the surgery on my ankle, but what I do remember, vividly, is relearning to walk. Relearning, because my first steps were presumably taken indoors and very young, whereas the scene I remember takes place at the King Henry's Road entrance to Primrose Hill. I assume I must be two or three years old. Nanny is kneeling a few yards away, beckoning. There is a dangerous stretch of gravel between her and me. 'Come on,' she says. 'There's a good boy.' I start forward unsteadily, half expecting her to move towards me. She doesn't, and I make it all the way on my own. Triumph and elation. I now think I was learning a simple lesson: either I could be a cripple, dependent on other people to wheel me around, or I could become an active, upright, paid-up member of the human race. But in order to do so I had to take risks.

There was a second lesson involved and it had to do with the wild elation I felt when I made it to her waiting arms. What I was experiencing, prematurely, was the adrenalin rush, the great surge of hormone that increases heart activity and muscular action, and generally prepares the body for 'fright, flight or fight'. The adrenalin rush is notoriously addictive; it induces the kind of glow and happiness which a junkie, I imagine, must get from a fix and it alters the psyche's chemistry as surely as heroin alters the body's. I was hooked from that moment on, and since then I seem to have spent a great deal of effort trying, by one means or another, to reproduce that overwhelming sense of elation and well-being.

I was 10 the next time I remember getting that high. It happened in the old Finchley Road swimming baths, which have since been demolished. Up until that time swimming baths were forbidden territory for me. The doctors said the chlorine in the water was bad for the fragile skin on my troublesome ankle. But then the doctors said everything was bad for my ankle and, anyway, this was 1940, the war was on and there was no Nanny to keep me in line. So when the school went swimming I went along with them. I splashed around in the shallow end, learning how to swim, but all that really interested me was the high board at the far end of the pool. There was one man using it who knew what he was doing – swallow dives, somersaults, dead-man's dives, back flips, the whole bag of tricks – and I couldn't take my eyes off him. It was the most graceful thing I had ever seen.

The school's swimming instructor was an ex-drill sergeant, small and muscle-bound, with tattooed arms. When I asked him to teach me how to dive, he told me to sit on the pool's edge, put my hands above my head and roll forwards, pushing myself off with my feet. I practised that manoeuvre until the hour was up. The next visit, a week later, he got me standing upright and diving off the edge. The instructor was a martinet and every time I surfaced he looked at me with distaste: 'Point your toes!' 'Don't look down, look up!' 'Keep your legs straight!' 'Point your bloody toes, I said!' The next week I went up on to the high board. It was a fixed board, covered with coconut matting, and its front edge bent slightly downward. It seemed outrageously high – much higher than it had looked from below – and I stood there a long time, trying to work up my courage. Gradually the echoing voices disappeared and I felt as if I were cocooned in silence. I waved my arms vaguely in the way I'd been taught, tried to look up, not down, and launched myself into space. For a brief moment, I was flying. When I hit the water I crumpled ignominiously and my legs were all over the place. The instructor looked at me with contempt and shook his head. But even he could not diminish my elation. That's what they mean by 'free as a bird', I thought.

A sense of danger was an essential part of the thrill and, because of my bad leg, danger was something I had learned to live with early. I was first made aware of it at the age of five or six, when I started at prep school. I wanted to play football, like all the other little boys, but the family doctor forbade it, on the ground that my ankle was too delicate and vulnerable. So my mother took me to see a famous specialist in Harley Street. I have described what happened there in another book: Mr Cumberbatch was plump and reassuring, a jolly Pickwickian figure, with a florid face and grey curls. He sat me on a high padded stool in an office full of gleaming medical machinery and examined my leg gently for a considerable time. Then he said, quite tenderly, 'You can play games if you really want, but if you get that ankle of yours kicked you might have to have your leg off.' I suppose I was terrified, but I was also outraged, and the practical effect of his warning was to make me almost insanely reckless on the sports field. I was used to wearing protection on my bad leg; wherever I went, it was always covered by a pad of cotton wool and swathed in bandages; I even wore them to bed. As a sop to Mr Cumberbatch, I added a shin-guard when I played games. It was a bulky package and not particularly comfortable, but it was enough to keep the heebie-jeebies away. Yet secretly I must have believed that I was carrying a time bomb around on my ankle. And that increased my defiance.

With hindsight, it seems an appropriate response. There was something dangerous in the air at home which not even Nanny's common sense could disguise. My parents were good-hearted people, but they were fatally mismatched and sometimes at night, when my father's music stopped, I would hear them shouting at each other. I couldn't hear the words, but I recognized the unhappiness and I used to wonder how long they could go on tolerating it and what else would disintegrate with them.

> When the green field comes off like a lid,
> Revealing what was much better hid –
> > Unpleasant:
> And look, behind you without a sound
> The woods have come up and are standing round
> > In deadly crescent.

Danger was in the air during the thirties and what was happening between my parents seemed like an intimate, chamber version of the troubles brewing everywhere: mass unemployment and hunger marches, totalitarian systems in Germany and the Soviet Union, fascist dictatorships in Italy, Spain, Portugal, Hungary and Romania, war clouds gathering on the horizon. I was aware of none of this, of course. Nobody talked politics at Glenilla Road, but they knew about anti-Semitism and had fresh evidence of it right under their noses.

E. M. Forster called Hampstead, patronizingly, 'an artistic and thoughtful little suburb'. The intellectual German refugees who moved there during the thirties made it more artistic, more thoughtful and a great deal more cosmopolitan. They brought with them their own atmosphere and tastes and customs as well as their own language and their faltering English. They opened delicatessens which sold food that seemed, in those days, impossibly exotic: all sorts of pickled and marinated herrings, rye bread and pumpernickel, smoked meats and sausages. They set up their own restaurants, like the Cosmo, in Swiss Cottage, which survived for 60 years, its menu and décor seemingly unchanged. Its clientele, too, remained unchanged; in the seventies it was still frequented by silver-haired gentlemen in worsted suits, once sharply cut by long-dead Berlin tailors, flirting courteously with old ladies in tired furs, while they tucked into *Kasseler*, *Zwiebelröstbraten* and great dishes of boiled meat with dumplings and heavy sauces.

Hampstead has always been home for artists and writers – Romney, Fuseli, Constable, Rossetti, Sickert, Mondrian, Henry Moore, Ben Nicholson, Keats, Stevenson, Mansfield, Lawrence – so what in Kensington or Chelsea would have been merely alien seemed to fit the borough's comfortable tolerance of bohemian oddity. As I said, my family reacted with dismay to the flood of refugees from Hitler, worried by what this sudden influx of foreigners would do to the always fragile situation of the established Anglo-Jewish community. Although I am sure I picked up my parents' snobbery and anxiety, I also remember the foreigners as somehow sympathetic and illuminating. They moved in a more complex world than the one I knew, their frame of reference was larger. But, like my parents, I must have smelt their fear and the sense of threat they brought with them, and it seemed to fit my own anxieties.

Then war was declared and everything became clear. I was on the sea front when it began. I don't know which sea front – Bournemouth or Brighton? – and I've forgotten whom I was with, though it was probably Lowie. All I remember is joining a crowd of people at an open door and hearing Neville Chamberlain's sad thin voice on the wireless: 'No such undertaking has been received and we are now at war with Germany.' I also remember the familiar flicker of wild excitement as I was hurried back to the hotel. My mother was in tears and my father – he must have been there because it was a Sunday – was trying to reassure her. 'It'll all be over by Christmas,' he was saying confidently, like a man in the know with friends in high places. I hoped he was wrong, but reluctantly believed him. I had seen pictures of Chamberlain in the newspapers and there was nothing warlike about him. Wars were fought by heroes, by dashing figures like Douglas Fairbanks Jr and Errol Flynn, and sometimes by my favourite, the laconic George Sanders. There was nothing dashing about Chamberlain. He wore a Homburg hat and a wing collar and he wielded a brolly. He looked like a bank manager, just the type to cut a deal with the enemy.

And that is precisely what seemed to be happening during the first few months of the Phoney War, while the Germans were busy in the east, decimating the Poles. I was issued with a buff-coloured identity card, a gas mask and a tin hat, which seemed like a uniform of a kind, but the closest I got to warfare was the experience of living eyeball to eyeball with my mother for the first time in my life in the poky little house Grandpa Dick had rented for us in Hove. The air-raid sirens sounded occasionally, but nothing happened to set the pulse racing: no bombs, no landing-craft creeping towards Brighton Pier or secret agents floating down by parachute, not even a glimpse of a distant reconnaissance plane. Just life with Katie in a blacked-out semi-detached, with air-raid wardens patrolling the streets outside, shouting, 'Put that light out!' The gravest danger in my life was my form master at Hove College, where I spent a term. He was a death's-head figure who liked caning small boys and knew how to lounge in front of the blackboard in such a way that the sun reflected off his thick glasses, making it impossible to see whom he was about to pounce on next. I was far more frightened of him than of the Germans.

After six miserable months we went back to London. The house in Glenilla Road was shudderingly cold, the roof was leaking, there were damp patches on the walls and the woman who had been paid to check the place out once a week had helped herself to most of the family silver. But at least there was space for us to get away from each other. Endless space. The parlour-maids had gone, Lowie had gone, my sister Anne was married. Then Sally joined the WRAF and Minnie went off to cook for her American radio stars, who had access to PX supplies.

That left three of us: my mother in the kitchen, teaching herself how to cook and communing with the surly dog, my father in the dining-room listening to his records, and me upstairs, pretending to do my homework. The top floor of the house was no longer used, in case of air raids, so my bed was brought downstairs and I turned the day nursery into a bedsitter world of my own. One end of the silvery oak table on which my sisters and Nanny and I had eaten our meals became my desk, the other was a workbench on which I made balsa-wood aeroplanes and fretwork knick-knacks. I hung my planes from the ceiling and my fretwork bits and pieces on the walls, along with an air-rifle, my scout knife, a moth-eaten stag's head and a pair of antelope horns some neighbours had thrown out when they left town. I wanted the room to look like a ranchers' den, the kind of place where the boss gives the cowhands their orders before a round-up: 'Head 'em up and move 'em out.' What I also wanted was my own private space with a door I could close on my parents' troubles. I was just beginning to get it into shape when the Blitz began.

When we returned to London, early in 1940, I had gone back to Peterborough Lodge, the prep school I had been at before we were exiled to Hove. Peterborough Lodge was in Maresfield Gardens, a red-brick Victorian mansion right opposite the house where Freud lived when he moved to London. It was a tall building and the classes were arranged on a vertical scale: the youngest boys started at the top in what had once been the servants' bedrooms and worked their way down, year by year, until they reached the *piano nobile*, where the walls were covered with polished wooden boards carved with the names of old boys who had brought glory to the school by dying in the Great War or gaining scholarships to posh public schools. By the time I went back the pupils had been evacuated to the country, the classrooms were empty and only the elderly headmistress was left. She was a large, sweet-tempered old lady with grey curls and she liked me because I was clever – clever enough, she thought, to win what was then considered one of the great academic prizes, a scholarship to Winchester. So she took me on while she was deciding what to do with the rest of her life. She gave me my lessons in her study – just her and me and her mangy old Airedale which never took its eyes off her. Like her, the Airedale was large and sweet-tempered, and the expression in its eyes was very English – soulful and devoted, as though it were listening to Elgar. The three of us stuck it out until Easter, then she closed the place down and I was moved to The Hall, the only prep school in the area that stayed open for the whole of the war.

The Blitz must have been a dreadful time for adults. The good life had already sunk without trace, scuttled by Hitler's submarines. Food was rationed – four ounces of butter and tenpence worth of meat a week, one egg a fortnight – clothes were rationed, petrol was rationed and there were shortages of everything else that made adult life tolerable – entertainment, whisky, even watery beer. The town was blacked-out, death rained down from the sky every night and life generally was pinched, disrupted and squalid. But children are more adaptable and I only registered how dreadful the grown-up world had become when my beloved aunt Lou's house was bombed. The house was empty when the bomb fell. Aunt Lou had been out, thank God, and her children were long gone – her daughter was married and living elsewhere and both her sons were serving in the RAF. (There was no husband; he had died before I was born and she never remarried.)

I cycled over the next morning to try to help. Aunt Lou was standing in what was left of her elegant drawing-room, weeping and weeping. The place smelt of burnt timber and the brick dust made us cough. She went on weeping while we scrabbled among the debris, searching for her French trinkets and shattered antique furniture. Then an elderly police-man peddled up on a bicycle and told us we'd have to leave, the building wasn't safe. Aunt Lou was still crying when I said goodbye. It was like the day my father sold his record collection, but much, much worse.

By the time I got home I was already gearing up for the nightly air raid and had forgotten all about her. The grown-ups may have been scared and miserable but for schoolboys, who don't believe that death is something that will ever happen to them, the Blitz was a period of wild excitement, a time when all the war games became real. And for an addict like me, it was adrenalin paradise. I couldn't wait for the sirens to wail and the first faint drone of the incoming bombers on the edge of the darkness, announcing my nightly fix. They sounded like the sea, wave upon wave of them rolling in, and sometimes you could see them, caught in the latticework of search-lights, fragile and far up, eerily beautiful, with the exploding anti-aircraft shells blossoming around them. The grove of trees on the top of Primrose Hill, half a mile from Glenilla Road, had been chopped down to make way for a battery of big naval anti-aircraft guns which made our house shake for hours on end. An open space at the south-east edge of Hampstead Heath, close to the area where the fair was pitched in better years, was filled with makeshift rocket-launchers that shrieked and whistled like fireworks. The din was stupefying. It was like a Guy Fawkes Day from heaven.

But the true thrill was in the sound of the bombs. I would lie in bed listening intently, hooked on the way the whistle of the incoming bomb gathered slowly to a scream and the shock waves of its fall made the windows tremble. Then the great thump and bang as it hit. Three of us at The Hall – wolf-faced Williams, who looked as if he were permanently starving, Howells, who was plump and genial but had his father's battered boozer's face, and myself – used to compete in our expertise in judging how close the bombs would fall. We also had a running competition on how near they fell to where we lived. I led the field for a time when a bomb sliced the wall off the house directly opposite ours. The occupants got out of bed, pulled on their dressing-gowns and went downstairs, grumbling. No one was hurt. A few weeks later Howells won outright. A bomb had landed directly outside his parents' shop, blasting out the windows and ripping the shelves from the walls. It also sprang the lock on the shop door. Before she went back to bed, Mrs Howells waded through the broken glass and debris and carefully re-locked the door.

As for air-raid shelters, it was a matter of pride not to use them. The platforms of Belsize Park tube station were lined with tiers of metal bunks and a concrete air-raid shelter was hurriedly built halfway along Glenilla Road. Mr and Mrs Voss, the pompous German refugees who had moved into the house next to ours, dug an Anderson shelter in their garden and spent every night in it, but when my mother wanted to do the same, my father and I ganged up on her. 'Why catch my death of cold when I can die in comfort in my bed?' my father said. As a compromise, one of the cellars was scrubbed out and given a coat of distemper, an old armchair and an ottoman from the kitchen were dragged down into it, and we spent two miserable nights there, shivering with cold. After that only my mother crept down there when the raids were particularly bad. My father lay in state in the walnut marriage bed with the lumpy mattress and read travel books, while I lurked in my ranchers' den, contentedly monitoring the bombs. I was less frightened of them than of the spiders in the cellar.

My father was too old to be called up for military service, so he joined the ARP. Being an air-raid warden gave him what he was always looking for – a cast-iron excuse for getting out of the house at night. My mother, of course, suspected he had girlfriends in the neighbourhood, but whenever she complained – Why was he gone longer than other wardens? Why didn't he come back after the all-clear sounded? – he'd square his shoulders and announce ambiguously, 'I was doing my duty.'

Yet even my disreputable dad had his moment of glory. On the night of the great air raid on the City the police called in the middle of dinner to say that the factory in Stoney Lane was on fire. He hurried out, trotting up the hill to the tube in his navy-blue worsted suit, stiff white collar, silk tie and bowler, while I gobbled my meal, then crept upstairs to the now-out-of-bounds night nursery and sat by the window to watch the show. The night sky was studded with exploding anti-aircraft shells, searchlights were sweeping to and fro, and the whole horizon seemed to be on fire. Although it was a long way off, I could hear the muffled din of the bombs and the wailing sirens of fire engines and ambulances moving in from all over London. I stayed there a long time, entranced, until my distraught mother found me and bustled me downstairs. Then I sat at the top of the cellar steps while she wept on the ottoman below. Her sobs were so racked and desolate that, in the end, I swallowed my fear of the spiders and went down to sit beside her. The explosions moved closer after midnight as the bombers jettisoned their loads and turned for home. The closer they came, the more distraught my terrified mother sounded.

Around three in the morning a key scraped at the front door and my father stumbled in. His suit was torn, his collar was black, his tie was askew, his hands and face were scratched and bleeding and his bowler was gone.

'For God's sake, what have you been up to?' my mother asked accusingly.

'The factory's done for,' he said. 'The place next door got a direct hit. The firemen were trying to stop the blaze spreading, but it looks like the foundations have gone.'

'And you tried to help them dressed like that?'

'Don't be absurd,' said my father, on his dignity. 'I wanted to, of course, but they wouldn't let me.'

'Then how did you get into that dreadful state?'

'Don't blame me, blame the blackout. I was walking back from the tube, minding my own business, and I fell into a bomb crater. Fifty yards away, up Glenmore Road. It wasn't there when I left.'

My mother was weeping again, though more in anger than in sorrow. 'Why can't you ever do anything right?'

'Bloody Nazis,' said my father. 'They've ruined my beautiful suit.'

London was a good place to be during the Blitz. Peace and prosperity bring out the worst in the British – their snobbishness, their complacency, their inertia. When there is nothing at stake the famous sang-froid is often hard to distinguish from a cold-blooded inability to feel anything at all, apart from envy. But they thrive on trouble and deprivation. 'London can take it,' was the slogan of the day and it wasn't an empty boast. London took it – and stylishly – because everyone agreed on how they should behave: with good humour, good manners and a dogged refusal to fuss. Even the sybaritic Cyril Connolly managed to make a joke out of his cowardice. When a bomb interrupted his lovemaking he leapt out of bed and burrowed under it, crying, 'Perfect fear casteth out love!'

It might have been different in London's docklands, where the damage was heaviest, and it would certainly have been different later in the war. Good behaviour wouldn't have counted for much during the saturation bombing of Hamburg or the fire-storms in Dresden. But in 1940–41 the Germans were still amateurs in the art of terrorizing civilian populations from the air, despite the practice they'd had in the Spanish Civil War. In north-west London, the bombing was haphazard, the bombs were comparatively small and it was possible for us kids to make believe we were in the front line and still get on with our lives. All the pleasures of war and 'only five-and-twenty per cent of its danger', as Mr Jorrocks said of hunting. And when the worst happened – when a boy stopped coming to school in the middle of the week and never appeared again – we chose not to mention it. That, too, was part of the code. Since we kids had been enrolled, as a special treat, into this easy-going army of adults, we had to follow the rules and keep quiet.

Williams, Howells and I had other ways of joining in the war games. We collected chunks of shrapnel, searching our gardens for them every morning and cycling to school slowly, heads down, so as not to miss the bits that littered the streets. What these lumps of jagged metal might have done if they had hit us never crossed our minds. We treasured them because they made us feel we were in the firing-line. So did the bombed houses. There was an imposing clutch of them at the Swiss Cottage end of Avenue Road – great Victorian mansions, their flock wallpaper in tatters and marble fireplaces shattered. We crept into them after school, with our tin hats on our heads and our gas masks at the ready, pretending we were flushing out invading Germans, until a policeman flushed us out and sent us running. That, too, was part of the wild excitement of the time. School work, in comparison, didn't offer much. The studious star pupil of Peterborough Lodge became just another delinquent at The Hall. But I was happier than I had ever been.

The happiness peaked during the Battle of Britain. It must have taken place during a particularly lovely Indian summer because I remember long, hot afternoons after school, lying on my back under the four poplars in the garden, watching the planes spin and loop and weave and soar in a cloudless sky. Our Spitfires and Hurricanes, their Messerschmitts and Heinkels. I knew all the official details of every make – horsepower, fire-power, turning circle, top speed – and I followed the day's tally each evening on the radio. I also knew from the newsreels at the cinema what the pilots looked like and how they sounded. They wore leather helmets, fur-lined leather flying jackets and white silk evening scarves around their throats, but they seemed not much older than my friends and I. (They weren't. Most of them were 18, straight from school, and some had faked their age.) We were stuck with pink school blazers and caps, but we adopted their bright, clipped accents, their breezy modesty and, when the bombs fell, their casual indifference to danger. All I wanted was for the war to go on until I could be up there with them.

The dogfights were heroic and school kids, of course, are suckers for hero-worship. But there was something else going on in the sky above my head that summer. It wasn't just a battle, it was a ballet in three dimensions, as graceful and free as the expert diver on the high board. I think I never really got over that eerie combination of beauty and risk. 'Beauty takes courage. Courage itself/Is beautiful.' When I wrote those lines in a poem called 'The Flowers', half a century after the Battle of Britain, I was thinking mostly of my wife and daughter. But I was also remembering the mesmerizing, deadly ballet in the sky and how it hooked me for ever on the adrenalin high.

5

SCHOOL

———▶ ◀———

While the Battle of Britain was on it never occurred to me that I would end up writing for a living. All I wanted to do was fly, like the schoolboy fighter pilots overhead, like Biggles, like my glamorous uncle Teddy in his Sopwith Camel. Until I got my chance with the real thing I consoled myself by making model aeroplanes. I spent hours on them every day when I should have been doing my homework, cutting out the aerofoils from sheets of balsawood with my father's discarded razors, glueing and doping the rice paper on the wings.

My masterpiece was a glider with a wing-span almost as wide as I was high and a fuselage cunningly designed as a lattice of diagonal T-shaped struts, each of which had to be put together separately. I laboured on it for six months, then carried it proudly to the top of Parliament Hill for its maiden flight. But the trim wasn't right and the wind was too strong. The masterpiece careered 50 yards, wobbled, stalled, then nosedived to the ground and smashed to splinters. I carried the pieces home but never had the heart to try to repair it.

The model-making gave me something to aim for in life: if the war was over before I was old enough to fly fighter planes, then I would design aircraft. There was another boy at The Hall who was plane-mad, like me, and had the same ambition. His name was Miller and he was a year ahead of me. He was a gangly child who spent most of his time doodling aircraft of his own design in his exercise books and filling the margins with obscure calculations of wing elevation and drag. His dark hair fell untidily forward over his high forehead, his shirt buttons were always coming undone, his tie was always askew, his manner was permanently abstracted and he was a very good mathematician. Unlike mine, all the planes he made flew. By the age of 12 he was already a true boffin, the type immortalized later by Alec Guinness in *The Man in the White Suit*, and in those days the back-room boys who were using their brainpower and ingenuity to beat the Huns had a glamour all of their own. I wanted to be like Miller, with a slide-rule concealed about my person and a row of pens and pencils in the breast pocket of my pink school blazer, just above the black Maltese cross. I followed him doggedly around for a year, although he was too wrapped up in his projects to notice.

Then he left for Oundle, the school you went to if you wanted to be a scientist. Most of my other friends went on to Harrow or Charterhouse, but Harrow was too close to home for my liking and I had cousins at Charterhouse, so when the time came for me to choose I persuaded my parents to let me follow my hero to Oundle. But Miller was in a different house, public schools are intensely hierarchical institutions and a year makes a lot of difference at that age. The only time I ran into him, during my first term, he barely deigned to notice me and I don't recall ever speaking to him again.

The excitement of the Blitz played hell with my school work, but learning was no longer my priority. I was far more interested in games. Boxing had been permitted from the start – you can't hurt your ankle in the ring – but my bad leg had kept me off the sports field. So as soon as Mr Cumberbatch gave me the nod, I began to play football and cricket as though my survival depended on them – which, in some ways, it did. I was small for my age and skinny and I had no natural gift for ball games, but I was aggressive and determined and, thanks to the surgeons, the prospect of being hurt didn't scare me; I'd been there before. Above all, I loved the wild animal pleasure of hard exercise – the running around, the exhilaration of violent contact, the exhaustion at the end. It made up for all those years when I had been forced to live as though wrapped in tissue paper. William Harvey, who discovered the circulation of the blood, called its movement 'the silent music of the body', and I have always loved music in all its forms. When I failed miserably to get a scholarship to Oundle it hardly seemed to matter because I had already done what I had set out to do at The Hall: I had scraped into the school football and cricket teams. More importantly, I won the diving cup, doing all the things I had seen the expert do on the high board the first time I went to the Finchley Road pool. I have never had a moment of greater glory than that, before or since.

I suspect that my passion for games was also linked with the peculiarly British brand of anti-Semitism that was part of school life in those days. Because The Hall stayed open when thousands of children were evacuated from London and most other private schools had closed, it did great business. As I remember, about two-thirds of the pupils were Jewish. Was that because their parents couldn't bear to be parted from them or because, like mine, they simply couldn't believe that the Nazis meant what they said about the Jews? Or rather, they may have meant what they said about the European Jews, but surely the well-bred, well-mannered, damn-nearly-assimilated English Jews were exempt? Whatever the reason, it was an embarrassment for the headmaster, Mr Wathen. He was one of those tall, silver-haired English autocrats with ice-blue eyes who served the British Raj in its glory days – a former Professor of English at the Government College in Lahore, an Inspector of Schools in the Punjab and Principal of a college in Amritsar – and, frankly, he never seemed to care much for Jews.

But there they were, making a fortune for him while the bombs fell every night and the fair-haired, blue-eyed little boys he would have preferred to teach were safely tucked away in makeshift classrooms in requisitioned country houses in the shires. Although nothing definite was said, we were made to understand that our presence offended Mr Wathen's clubman's sensibilities – he was a member of the Bath Club and the MCC – even while the clever ones were enhancing the school's reputation. When he had to announce at morning prayers that the cleverest of us all, a quiet boy called Goldblatt, had won the top scholarship at Eton, he couldn't keep the dismay out of his voice.

Because we Jews were in the majority at the school, we had nothing harsher to cope with than the headmaster's disdain. Oundle was different. There were very few Jews there in those days and, when I arrived, none at all in Crosby, the house I was assigned to. During my first week there, when all the confused little new boys were still trying to find their way around, Mr Priestman, the housemaster, arrived in our dormitory one evening before lights out, full of good cheer. He joked, he told stories, he tried to get us talking. Suddenly he turned to me in mid-flow and said, 'Of course, you're a Jew, Alvarez, so you see things differently, don't you?' I don't remember what it was that I was supposed to see differently, but that wasn't the point. The point was to make it clear to the other boys that there was an outsider among them. As it happens, Priestman had misjudged his audience. The kids that year were a decent lot and anti-Semitism wasn't on their agenda – God knows why. But he himself disliked Jews and he wanted me to know it. He would also have liked the other boys to give me a hard time.

'Snappy' Priestman was a bouncy man with a meaty face, a lisp and what seemed to be a more than custodial interest in the small boys in his charge. Maybe he just wanted to be young with the young, but he visited the dormitories more than was strictly necessary and always lingered on the beds of the prettiest boys. He acquired his nickname because he was a keen amateur photographer. Parents loved the sensitive portrait studies he made of his charges but the boys were less impressed. The house joke was, 'When he asks you to go into the darkroom with him and see what develops, always say no.' He finished up happily married – but not until he had retired.

Because I had made a hash of the scholarship papers, I was assigned to a lowly form which devoted one English lesson a week to 'general reading'. Mr Chadwick, the elderly form master who taught us Latin as well as English, brought along a selection of light classics – books like *Ivanhoe*, *Kidnapped* and *Tarka the Otter*. We had to pick whatever took our fancy and answer questions about them when the end-of-term exams came around. It was supposed to broaden our minds. By some quirk of choice or maybe as an obscure challenge or maybe simply by mistake, one of the books in the pile was Israel Zangwill's *King of the Schnorrers*. I had never read Zangwill, but I had heard my father mention him dismissively: 'Not bad,' he said, 'if you like that folksy stuff.' It seemed too good a chance to miss and, anyway, I was probably more homesick than I would ever have admitted. When I picked up the book, Mr Chadwick smiled at me conspiratorially and said, 'You know he's one of them, don't you?' I was too embarrassed to reply – for him even more than for me. Mr Chadwick was stern and irritable but a perfectly fair little man, who amused himself by composing Latin-style epigrams on current events, which he pinned to the classroom door or wrote neatly on the blackboard. There was one he was particularly proud of, written in honour of the Allied air raids on Germany:

> Once pale Persephone abhorred the sound
> Of Pluto's chariot whirling her to Enna;
> Now Axis partners shudder underground
> As airborne chariots render earth Gehenna.

'"Axis partners" is rather good, though I say so myself,' he mumbled shyly. I liked his modest, finicky style and he liked me because I was good at the subjects he taught. I knew he would never have said what he did about Zangwill if he'd known I was 'one of them', too. I was ashamed for both of us – too ashamed and too cowardly to set the score straight. Above all, I didn't want him to be one of them, the other thems who thought all Jews were straight out of Zangwill's *shtetl* – clever but shifty, an unaired, weedy, alien lot with funny accents, unalterably different.

What that caricature had to do with my cricketing dad and clubman Grandpa Alvarez and the swashbuckling Levys I had no idea, but secretly I sided with Chadwick. Perhaps because I had been sickly and surrounded by women when I was a small child, I hated the stereotype of the bookish, overprotected Jew who avoided fresh air and exercise. (The Israelis eventually changed the stereotype, but this was 1943, five years before the founding of the state of Israel.) I was at boarding school now, in the gung-ho male world I had hankered for, and a long way from home – not in the cosy Home Counties near my family and friends, but in the bleak agricultural Midlands I had never even seen before. I didn't want to be different and there was no kudos in being clever. In order to survive at Oundle you had to be good at games, so I worked at being good at them. Maybe I thought that if I became good enough I'd cease to be Jewish. So for four years I played rugger and boxed most days of the week. I never had the natural athlete's effortless gifts, but I was already an adrenalin junkie and my recklessness and determination gave me an edge. I had arrived at Oundle looking like Kafka, delicate and haunted. I left with arms like a lumberjack's, a 16½-inch neck and a contempt for anyone who couldn't take the rigours of what passed for education in those days.

Boxing wasn't a problem – I had boxed since I was six years old and knew what had to be done – but rugger was a perpetual frustration. During the forties Oundle was one of the best rugger schools in the country and it intended to stay that way. We played rugger three or four times a week and on the days when we weren't officially playing we were out there practising as soon as school was over – kicking, passing, pounding up and down the field. I loved the game so much that I played club rugger for Wasps during the holidays and for Northampton during the autumn after I left school. (I even got a favourable write-up in the *Northampton Echo*. No review of any of my books has ever given me such pleasure.) Although I was good enough to play for the 'A' team of both clubs, I was never good enough to play for Oundle. I captained the Third XV and turned out occasionally for the Second, but the First XV and the prestige that went with it were beyond me.

My parents never came to any of the rugger games, but they saw me box once. The match was at Dulwich College, my father's old school in south London, which made it especially important for me. But on the long coach journey south Mr Cordukes, the master in charge of boxing, told me my opponent was ill and my fight had been cancelled. Mr Cordukes was a somnolent, kindly man, with a beer belly and a grog-blossom complexion, and he must have known about the cancellation before we left. But since he also knew my parents would be there, he had let me come along for the ride. For me, however, the purpose of the trip was not to see my parents but for them to see me fight. I spent the rest of the journey persuading him to let me take the place of the boy in the weight above mine. (The boy himself didn't need much persuading; he would be getting a day out for doing nothing.)

My parents and Uncle Teddy rolled up grandly in Teddy's Rolls-Royce, then took ringside seats. My mother wore her ocelot coat and an extravagant hat, Teddy and my father puffed cigars and made bets. Between them, they transformed the Dulwich gym into Madison Square Garden. But with growing boys there is a big gap between featherweight and lightweight; the difference in weight is only nine pounds, but the difference in size can be considerable. My opponent was six inches taller than I was and had a long, straight left which he knew how to use. I got under it enough to force a split decision – it went in his favour – but my face was a mess by the end and my boxing vest, with the school crest and coloured ribbon edging I had worked so hard to earn, was soaked in the blood that streamed from my nose.

My father said, 'You should have won and I'm proud of you.'

Uncle Teddy said, 'You did OK, considering.'

My mother said, 'Please, darling, don't get blood all over my nice fur coat.'

When I got back to school that night my nose was the size of a mango and too tender to touch. The hatchet-faced matron gave me an aspirin and told me to soak my face in cold water and not make a fuss. It was not until two weeks later, when the swelling had gone down, that I realized my nose had been broken, but by then it had already set askew. I have snored in my sleep like a hippo ever since.

Oundle had the most sophisticated science laboratories of any school in the country. It also had elaborate engineering workshops where every pupil spent one week a term, with a caramel-coloured dust-coat over his grey flannel suit, learning how to work metal on a lathe and use a micrometer screw-gauge. This made it the favourite school for sons of industrialists, the place where big, hearty men with northern accents who had made their pile in engineering sent their children to learn the basics of the businesses they would eventually take over. For three years I shared a study with John Lyons, a mild, tubby boy whose father had founded Jaguar. Sir William Lyons was tight-lipped and overbearing and John was scared of him, but he had inherited his father's talent for designing exotic cars and couldn't wait to start his apprenticeship. (He never made it beyond the factory floor. Two years out of school, driving one of the new XK120s to Le Mans to help Jaguar win the 24-hour race again, he collided with a US Army truck and was killed.)

Because of its tradition and facilities, the school was full of boys who had a flair for science and maths. It took me a year and a move into a new and more demanding form to understand that I wasn't one of them. The problem was calculus. I loved the sophistication of it and the arcane symbols, which made me feel as if I were penetrating into the mystery of numbers. And because the teacher knew his stuff, I also knew how to apply the rules and get the right answers. But, for the life of me, I couldn't understand how the rules worked or why my answers came out right. It was as though there were a sheet of opaque glass between me and the results.

Hepburn, the maths master, was a saturnine, bored Scot, who had black hair and a hooked nose, so – Oundle being Oundle – everyone called him 'Ikey'. He thought I had promise and I admired his laconic style, yet whenever I asked him to explain the how and why yet again his eyelids drooped with boredom. I might as well have been asking him why one and one made two. He always ended up shaking his head and looking at me wearily from under his bushy eyebrows. I'd let him down again. 'That's how it is,' he'd say. I took his word for it but remained baffled. All I understood was that mathematics was not just a specialized language, it was a separate world in which reality was ordered differently from the world I inhabited. However diligently I obeyed the rules, I would never get through the glass. Directly the School Certificate exams were over, I gave up trying and switched to Modern Languages and English.

One good teacher, they say, can change your life. Mine was changed by Hugo Caudwell, who taught the more senior boys French and English. He was head of the French department, but his true interest was English literature. In those days, however, it was assumed that educated people read great literature in their spare time, so English was a poor relation, not a proper subject for serious academic study, and Oundle had no English department. But Caudwell knew differently; he had studied under I. A. Richards at Cambridge, he loved the subject – Wordsworth was his special passion – he had a subtle understanding of what makes poems work and he went on to publish his own books of literary criticism. He also had a passion for art and was a talented amateur painter. What he was doing at a strenuous science school like Oundle I will never know. Although he was trim and fit-looking, he was not at all sporty. His face was long, his mouth was full and he had good eyes, dark and sharp and deep.

I had begun to read poetry at The Hall. Most of it was kids' stuff – Macaulay's *Lays of Ancient Rome*, Longfellow's *Hiawatha* – but we also used a slim anthology of modern verse compiled by someone called Bebbington. The book was a curious mix of the thirties gang and poets who were beginning to make names for themselves, like George Barker and Dylan Thomas, and poets who later gave up, like Charles Madge. I loved them all because they were new and I was young, but I had fallen especially for the stylishness, guilt and sense of impending doom in Auden's ballads and 'musical pieces' – poems like 'When I walked out one evening', 'O what is that sound which so thrills the ears', and 'Miss Gee'. Maybe that was when I started to write poetry, when I was still a plane-mad little boy wearing a pink blazer and pink school cap. I was certainly writing it very soon after I arrived at Oundle, when I discovered A. E. Housman and fell in love all over again. For a public school boy, even at a school as sporty as Oundle, Housman's mixture of classical restraint, adolescent pessimism and star-crossed homosexual crush was irresistible. I knew the whole of *A Shropshire Lad* by heart.

Each week Mr Caudwell presented us with two or three short poems by different writers for 'comment and appreciation'. The poems were printed in magenta handwriting on mimeographed sheets and they came, in I. A. Richards's best *Practical Criticism* style, without the poets' names attached. One of these anonymous poems was Donne's 'Witchcraft by a picture' and, for me, it was love at first sight:

> I fix mine eye on thine, and there
>   Pity my picture burning in thine eye,
> My picture drowned in a transparent tear,
>   When I look lower I espy;
>   Had'st thou the wicked skill
> By pictures made and marred to kill,
> How many ways might'st thou perform thy will?
>
> But now I have drunk thy sweet salt tears,
>   And though thou pour more I'll depart;
> My picture vanished, vanish fears
>   That I can be endamaged by that art;
>   Though thou retain of me
> One picture more, yet that will be,
> Being in thine own heart, from all malice free.

I had never heard of John Donne, but that didn't matter. I recognized the voice, just as you recognize the face of Miss Right the first time you meet her.

I certainly didn't understand the poem – perhaps I was fascinated because I didn't understand it – but something made me sit up and attend. Maybe it was the dramatic vividness (he was face to face with the girl, looking into her weeping eyes, talking directly to her), or the aroused, casual tone of voice, alive with feeling but wholly unsentimental, that sounded like heightened, subtly charged talk, or the impression that, even in his distress, he was making some sort of logical point, even though I couldn't make out what the point was. I can still remember the smell of that chilly classroom – a mixture of chalk and socks and dank flannel – the afternoon fog outside the window and the curious certainty that I had found what I was looking for, although, until that moment, I hadn't known I was looking for anything.

It didn't even matter that this was happening at sports-mad, scientific Oundle, which, Hugo Caudwell apart, was not a school where there was much room for poetry. Donne seemed to fit in with the laboratories, workshops and muddy playing fields without any trouble. After all, he had a passion for the new sciences and I had the impression that he would have been good at games, too, if schoolboys had played games in his time. Later, when I boned up on his life, I discovered much more to admire, particularly his taste for adventure: he had sailed with the Earl of Essex on expeditions against the Spanish fleet and was famous for his sexual escapades – just the things to make him alluring to a lusty adolescent locked away in a monkish boarding school.

But what I loved above all was his tone of voice, the restless argument and wit, the curious mixture of logic and tenderness, irony and passion – real passion inspired by real women with appetites and sweaty palms and unreliable temperaments. Although there were times when logic got the better of him and he seemed to get trapped by his own ingenuity, there was nothing affected or pretentious about what he had to say or how he said it. He seemed to dislike the plump formality of his duller contemporaries as much as I, a few years later, disliked the complacency of the Movement poets, who were all the rage when I was in my twenties:

> Love's not so pure and abstract as they use
> To say, which have no mistress but their muse.

Donne's message, as I read it, was that life was not only more urgent and messier than other poets made it seem, it was also livelier, more interesting. He was a great poet who was sufficiently at home in the real world to be utterly unimpressed by the pretensions of poetry and, even more, of his fellow-poets.

The more I found out about Donne later, the more sympathetic he became. He was a martyr to depression: 'A Nocturnall upon S. Lucies day' is one of the two great English poems on the subject (the other is Coleridge's 'Dejection: an Ode'); he also wrote the first book in English on suicide, *Biathanatos*. I even liked him for his weaknesses: his tendency to moan, in his letters, about the jobs he didn't get and his chronic ill health and his even more chronic shortage of money. Yet his moaning was always wry and self-deprecating, as though he himself could see the absurdity of it. I loved the poems, but I also loved and admired the personal style and sensibility that shone through them.

I knew nothing of all this at the start. I picked up the details and filled in the picture slowly over the years – a gradual, deepening revelation, which is how it usually is with love. But the recognition was already there that first foggy afternoon.

According to T. S. Eliot, 'Immature poets imitate, mature poets steal.' He meant, I suppose, that most writers get started in their dreadful trade by falling in love with authors, imitating them, then discarding them as they find their own voices. That is what happened to me with Housman, Auden, Empson and D. H. Lawrence. Donne, however, was too remote in time, too difficult and too plain gifted for me ever to imitate. Yet he was a model for everything I would like to have been, both as a writer and as a man. I was 15 when I fell in love with him and I love him still, more than half a century later. It was like the best kind of marriage, where you miraculously meet the right person at the right time, settle down and live happily ever after.

It was also the beginning of a double life. The steps on the Oundle totem pole were finely graded and marked by signs as arcane as those of calculus. Buttons, for example: during the first year, all three buttons on the jacket of your grey flannel suit or blue blazer had to be done up; in the second year it was two buttons, in the third year one; in your last year, you could swagger around with your jacket unbuttoned (and did, whatever the weather). Having two buttons done up when you should have three was a violation of the caste system, a sneaky form of social climbing, a beatable offence. (The beating was done by the house prefects. I thought it a barbaric custom and when I became head of Crosby – against Mr Priestman's better judgement and only because I stayed on two extra terms to sit a university scholarship – I refused to beat anybody, which only exacerbated Snappy's prejudices.) If you were awarded a colour for representing your house or the school at a sport, you got to flaunt a gaudy scarf and were allowed to turn up the collar of your blazer. There were no colours for being clever, and few privileges.

I went along with it willingly, of course. Hence my thwarted yearning to play scrum-half for the First XV and my unseemly pride in my school colour for boxing. I wanted desperately to be one of the boys, tough and fit and good at games, and in the end I more or less succeeded. In fact, I didn't just go along with it, I was besotted by this would-be men's world of stiff upper lips and freezing dormitories. I even had a sneaky affection for the antique plumbing and compulsory cold baths every morning. There were no showers or proper bath tubs in Crosby; instead, we had battered tin hip-baths, God knows how old, which were filled with cold water before lights out, then left to cool further overnight with the bathroom windows open; in winter, the first person in had to break the ice.

When I went home for the holidays my highly strung, unsatisfied parents, who wore their tattered hearts on their sleeves and quarrelled incessantly about nothing in particular, seemed to be inhabiting a messier, overheated creation; it was comfortable and wonderfully well-fed, but it was also unreliable, a quicksand that would swallow me up if I made a false step. I couldn't wait to get away. At school, the rules were absurd, the social distinctions were mean-minded and the food was dreadful, but I knew where I stood. Anyway, that's how life was in the austere, non-Jewish world to which I did not properly belong. I even came to enjoy the morning cold bath.

At least there was music at Oundle. I couldn't sing and it was too late to learn an instrument (my parents had never got around to having me taught when I was young and keen to learn), but each year the whole school pitched into a choral work – Bach's *B Minor Mass*, Handel's *Messiah* or *Samson* – rehearsing the easier choruses after morning prayers in the Great Hall, and belting them out with the choir and orchestra at the end-of-year grand performance. And secretly, at the same time, I was gobbling up poetry – any poetry I could get my hands on. I was also writing it, though I kept that to myself: poetry was not part of the Oundle image.

Maybe they ordered things differently at other schools. Stowe, for instance, which we trounced regularly at rugger and looked down on, seemed more easy-going and cultured. But I doubt it. In those days there was still a fixed divide between the athletes and the aesthetes, the toughies and the wets, a divide that seemed part of English culture and was at least as old as *Tom Brown's Schooldays*. As always, I wanted the best of both worlds and I had John Donne to prove that it was possible to write poetry without being self-consciously poetic, to write and still be one of the boys.

But I didn't really fit in, despite the boxing and rugger in the winter terms, the swimming, diving and inept cricket in the summer, despite the hymn-singing every morning and the chapel services twice on Sundays.

Just before I went to Oundle I had been bar mitzvahed. My irreligious parents didn't much care whether I went through the ceremony or not but the grandparents cared, so Mr Hirschbaum was hired to teach me Hebrew. However, time was short, I wasn't interested in learning the language and Mr Hirschbaum – a grey, patient man with sour breath, who was in perpetual mourning for the family he had left in Germany – was too depressed to bother. I learned my portion of the law by rote, without understanding a word of it, and parroted it with great success to my proud parents and simpering relatives one Saturday morning in the Upper Berkeley Street synagogue. Then I went off to Oundle and forgot all about it. Or rather, I forgot the words but went on hearing their echoes. I enjoyed the boisterous hymn-singing at school and the moment of quiet at the end of the services, after the final blessing, but the enjoyment made me feel ashamed and hypocritical. Who was I trying to fool? When the fruity-voiced chaplain intoned, 'The blessing of God the Father, the Son and the Holy Ghost be with you', I crossed my fingers and hoped he wasn't including me. Then one day I realized that none of it, Jewish or Christian, was my affair; I was only there for the music and brief calm, and because I had to be. After that, I slept easier.

Like the poetry, I kept my atheism to myself. Even so, I began to have trouble with the authorities, especially after the affable old headmaster, Dr Fisher, retired and a new man was brought in to clean the place up. He was a skeletal figure called Stainforth, tall, lantern-jawed, pale-eyed, a dour authoritarian who, like the headmaster of The Hall, had links with the Raj (his father had been a lieutenant colonel in the Indian Army). He came across me first in the English class he taught occasionally – Browning was his speciality – and he did not like what he saw. By the time I was head of my house and a school prefect he disliked me even more. 'He thinks you're a bad influence,' Snappy Priestman told me. 'A subversive.' But Snappy had been having a hard time too, because he was part of the old order, and I think he was impressed that Stainforth had singled me out.

By today's standards my subversiveness seems pathetic as well as pretentious: I went around with a copy of Joyce's *Ulysses* under my arm and displayed it ostentatiously on my desk during Stainforth's lessons. Modernism was subversive by definition, particularly Modernist works which, until recently, had been banned as obscene. Jokes were also not tolerated and I was guilty on that count, too. Stainforth, in his capacity of new broom, had organized the younger masters into a secret police, encouraging them to report crimes directly to him without following protocol and telling the housemasters first. Stainforth's nickname was Gus – his initials were G. H. S. – so I labelled his team of ambitious creeps 'the Gustapo'. The term went around the school instantly and so did its source. When Snappy challenged me about it, he tried to be solemn but found it hard to keep a straight face. For a while, he even forgave me for being a Jew. Stainforth, however, did not like jokes at his expense and he was not a forgiving man.

There were no drugs for adolescents in those days, so we drank when we could to show we didn't care about the rules. That, too, was pathetic by modern standards – small beer in both senses. Although the nearest pub that would serve Oundle boys was four miles out of town and eight miles is a long way to cycle for a pint or two of beer, three of us made the trip regularly, a couple of times a week, as a matter of principle. All of us were 18 and legally entitled to consume alcohol and we intended to exercise our rights.

One rainy evening in my last term, my friends went off to the pub as usual, but I stayed behind to hear a visiting string quartet from London play Beethoven and Mozart in the Great Hall. Stainforth was already there when I arrived, in the front row of the dress circle, surrounded by the Gustapo and their floral wives. He gave me a wintry look when I took my seat in the row behind him reserved for the school prefects; but that was how he always looked at me, so I thought nothing of it.

At the end of the concert, before the applause had died away, Mr Upcott appeared at a side door and began signalling to Stainforth. Upcott was the most zealous member of the Gustapo, a drawling, tweedy figure who taught German and marched up and down the touchline during rugger, bellowing encouragement and brandishing a Leica. No one else at Oundle had a Leica, not even Snappy, who would have known how to use it. Upcott had no particular talent as a photographer, but owning a Leica was part of the dashing image he tried to cut. It went with the tweed suits, the affected speech, the glossy black hair and the slightly thickened matinée-idol profile. That evening, however, he looked a mess. His hair was plastered to his skull, his Burberry was soaked and there was mud all over his cavalry-twill trousers. He stood at the door, whispering excitedly in Stainforth's ear. Both of them glared at me when I went past.

My drinking companions, Phil Ashworth and Carl Heyman, were not in my house, so I didn't find out what had happened until the next day. Upcott had been waiting for them when they came out of the pub, on his knees in the mud in the lashing rain, pointing a big torch at the pub door and poised ready to leap. 'Just like the fucking commando raid on Narvik,' said Phil, who was the first to be dazzled by Upcott's torch. Carl stumbled out next and was duly identified, but Upcott stayed where he was on his knees, with the torch trained on the door. Finally he said, 'Where's Alvarez?' 'Alvarez?' Carl echoed, as though he had never heard the name. 'You tell me, sir.' Upcott got off his knees and shook his muddy trousers. 'I'm reporting you to the headmaster forthwith,' he said. 'Follow me.' Then the three of them got on their bicycles and peddled the four miles back to Oundle in the rain.

The next morning, after prayers in the Great Hall, Stainforth delivered a fire-and-brimstone sermon on the evils of drink and solemnly pronounced sentence. Phil, who was head of his house and a school prefect like me, was reduced to the ranks. Carl, who was lower down the pecking order and had no hierarchical magic to protect him, was summoned to Stainforth's study and thrashed viciously. That evening, Snappy took me aside. 'I have a message to you from the headmaster,' he said. 'He wants you to know that if you had been at the pub you'd have been expelled.' Then he added, quite affectionately, 'I don't think he's ever forgiven you for the Gustapo.'

The Brits are forever congratulating themselves on their invincible sense of humour and condescending to other nations for their lack of it – Americans don't understand irony, they say, and Germans have no humour at all – but even England has its limits. The first rule of the game is 'Thou shalt not make jokes at the Establishment's expense.' After four years at Oundle, where privileges were hard to come by and fiercely defended, I should have known that already, but somehow I never caught on. A couple of decades later, when I should have known better, I reviewed a book by Kingsley Amis. It was not a particularly good book, but it came with a puff by Anthony Powell that was too fulsome to be ignored. In my review I paraphrased Henry James's comment on another old-pal's act, Gautier's preface to Baudelaire's *Les Fleurs du Mal*: 'One must, to some degree, judge a man by the company he keeps. To admire Powell is a mark of excellent taste, but to be admired by him one cannot but regard as somewhat compromising.' Three years after the review appeared, I was introduced to Powell at a party. We talked about nothing in particular for a few minutes. He was icily polite. Then he said, 'That reference you made to me . . .'

'What reference?' It had been, after all, three years.

'In your review of Kingsley.'

'Oh that,' I said. 'It was just a joke.'

The ice thickened. He peered at me closely and seemed appalled by what he saw. 'A joke?' he repeated. Then he turned on his heel and walked away.

I knew what I was doing, of course. The vanity of the Establishment is terrible to behold, but the vanity of Establishment writers is worse, and there was a time when I considered it my duty to provoke the sacred cows and their solemn worshippers. It was dark and lonely work, but somebody had to do it. And it wasn't altogether provocation for provocation's sake. In those days ambitious young literary folk were much more careful than they are now about offending anyone who might eventually help them up the ladder. Dr Leavis thundered away about the metropolitan conspiracy to promote third-rate writers, but Leavis was safe in Cambridge with a regular salary to keep him afloat and I was in London living on my wits and suffering from the writers' affliction C. K. Ogden called 'hand-to-mouth disease'. So I had my own obscure code of bravery, although that was not how I thought of it. My working principle was a line by e. e. cummings which I couldn't get out of my head: 'there is some shit I will not eat.' It seemed particularly wise and grown-up because it implied also that there was some shit I would have to eat, whether I wanted to or not.

I knew what I was doing, then. Even so, it was hard to believe that a passing slight in a forgotten review would still be itching away years later. It surprised me, shocked me a little, that someone of Powell's age and reputation should care so much about the sanctity of his image and bear a grudge for so long.

With Stainforth, the stakes were far higher, though I didn't know it at the time. For me and my friends, drinking a couple of pints of beer a couple of times a week was a mild gesture of defiance; for him, it was a challenge to his precious authority; he held me responsible and he wanted me gone. And gone I would have been without Mozart and Beethoven. If the string quartet hadn't been playing that evening at Oundle my life might have turned out quite differently. There were fewer universities in those days and, with school-leavers competing with older candidates who had served their time in the armed forces, places were short. Being expelled from school would have kept me out, no matter how well I performed in the exams. As it happens, I performed terribly. I had been fasting for three days when I sat the Oxford scholarship papers, living on Horlick's tablets and water, in order to take off weight for a school boxing match. I won the fight but blew the scholarship and had to wait another year to take the college entrance papers. By then, I had left school and my priorities had changed.

I had failed to get a scholarship to Oundle, and now I had failed again at Oxford. My pride was hurt, but instead of blaming myself – what sane person sits an important examination between training bouts and with nothing in his stomach? – I blamed the school: all that worship of games and the boys who were good at them, the tinny patriotism and jolly-good-fellow reticence, the emotional evasiveness masked by a stiff upper lip, the scientists' blithe contempt for anything that couldn't be verified in a laboratory or turned out on a lathe. I had Mr Caudwell to show me that there were other things worth having in this life, but his voice had a hard time getting through the brass-band, middlebrow self-confidence that Oundle instilled in its pupils.

Anyway, I loved the games as well as the competence and ability to cope that seemed to go with them. My father had been a classy cricketer at school, then a keen golfer, but he had given it all up, put on weight and sunk into gloom. He walked up the hill every morning to the garage where he kept his car and back down the hill every evening. Apart from that, he scarcely moved out of his armchair. He was still a ladies' man, so he bothered about his appearance, but he seemed uneasy with his body, as though it were a piece of luggage too clumsy to lug around. I didn't want to go the same way and was grateful to Oundle if only because it instilled in me the habit of regular strenuous exercise. I gave up boxing after the scholarship farce and the rugger only lasted one more term after I left school (playing scrum-half for Northampton in a needle match against Leicester, their local rivals, I was destroyed by the opposing wing-forwards and never played seriously again), but I went on playing squash two or three times a week for 40 straight years, until I was 55 and my back gave out. Rock-climbing lasted even longer and that, too, began while I was at Oundle.

I was 16 when I first went to the mountains in North Wales. The trip was organized by the school, and the master in charge was a gung-ho, old-style, spirit-of-the-hills freak – he had been a reserve on a pre-war Everest expedition – whose idea of fun in the hills was to see how fast we could slog up to the summit of Tryfan and back down to the Ogwen valley. I loathed the boring, remorseless grind as much as I loathed him.

One day he took us up a rock route on the Idwal Slabs. The hard bit – the crux – was a steep little wall, with what seemed like a good deal of empty air below it, and widely spaced holds that looked far too small for my clumsy nailed boots. I studied it a long time, convinced that I was going to fall off. Then I strolled up it without any effort, as easily as if it had been flat. What I felt, as I pulled on to the ledge at the top, was a surge of pure elation and well-being, that old adrenalin magic that I knew so well and cultivated so assiduously. I was hooked and all I wanted to do was repeat the experience. But the weather closed in, we went back to mountain-bashing, and it was not until the end of my first year at Oxford, four years later, that I climbed again.

Later climbing became part of my life; it was what I did with my spare time most weekends, what I thought about when my mind should have been on higher things, a second vocation that I usually found a good deal more absorbing than the drudgery of writing. But for the time being there was just that isolated moment to hold on to, the blissful sense of physical ease and certainty as I moved up the granite wall, an inner silence, nothing on my mind except the next hold and the right balance. I didn't know how to dance back then – there were no girls to dance with at Oundle – but I loved Fred Astaire's movies and this was how I imagined dancing would be: a liquid movement, complex and controlled and precise, and also a little dangerous, like sex seems dangerous to a kid with no experience. You would make a fool of yourself with a girl if you made the wrong moves and if I made the wrong moves on the climb I'd fall and be hurt.

According to Hemingway, who valued danger above everything else, there are only three sports: bullfighting, mountain-climbing and motor-racing. The rest are games. Four years of non-stop games had broadened my shoulders and toughened me up. I was no longer defeated by the body which had given me so much trouble when I was young (although I was almost 30 before the lymphatic growth on my ankle emptied itself out and shrank away until it was a smooth, barely noticeable bump). Yet however strenuously I played games, it was all will-power and defiance and come-and-get-me recklessness. Climbing was different. Briefly, on the Idwal Slabs, in my awkward adolescence, I understood what people meant when they talked about physical grace.

6

AFLOAT

I left Oundle at the end of the spring term with no regrets and very little idea of what I wanted to do with my life. For the moment that didn't matter much because this was 1948 and the next two years would be taken up by compulsory national service. I rather fancied the idea. I had already done four years in the school's Officers' Training Corps (OTC). I knew how to dismantle a Sten gun and shoot a rifle and perform fancy parade-ground drill, and I had certificates to prove it; I had even finished up, improbably, as the Corps' Regimental Sergeant-Major. If I played my cards right I might wangle my way into the RAF and learn to fly. And even if conscription meant what I suspected it meant – forced marches in the rain and two years of prime boredom – at least it would get me away from Glenilla Road and give me time to think about what to do next.

My mother had other ideas. She decided, uncharacteristically, to be motherly and began to fret about my 'poor leg'. 'All that marching,' she said. 'Those awful army boots.'

'What do you think I wore in the OTC?'

'That was different. That was just school. This is for two years.'

My mother was not usually strong on the long-term view and I had never heard her sound so savvy about what went on out there in the real world. I was impressed. When she phoned the family doctor and, through him, made an appointment with a specialist, I went along docilely.

I hadn't seen a specialist since my run-in with the benign but deadly Mr Cumberbatch. This time, the examination was longer and the surgeon more quizzical. The more he implied that I was only there to get out of doing my patriotic duty, the more heatedly I told him I wanted to join up. He listened to me cynically and shook his head. A week later a letter from him arrived for me to present when I went for my medical. It was a two-page, single-spaced analysis of my bad ankle, ending:

It is difficult to say whether or not this young man would be accepted for Service at the present time, but I think almost certainly not, because the conditions in which he could be usefully employed would be very limited and confined to sedentary work in this country. He could not wear Army boots because the upper edge would traumatize the swelling. He could not go on route marches and he would have to wear some kind of protection over the swelling as he does now. He would also be ineligible for Service in the tropics, where Europeans are always prone to contract skin infections.

I think therefore that unless there is some special reason for calling up people for special service in sedentary occupations he is unlikely to be accepted into any branch of the Armed Forces.

The letter was signed by 'Sir Heneage Ogilvie, K.B.E., M.Ch., F.R.C.S., Surgeon to Guy's Hospital, Consulting Surgeon to the Army'.

Though mother was delighted, my own feelings were mixed. It was interesting to know that the monstrosity on my ankle which had given me so much grief was 'a congenital abnormality of the lymph-vascular system, which has probably become more solid in the course of time and as a result of exposure to Deep X-rays', and that the infections that made it weep and brought on fevers 'in theory should eventually lead to its obliteration'. But I was outraged by the man's conclusion that I was only fit for a sedentary life. It was as if all the effort I had put into transforming myself from an overprotected little swot into a rugger-playing tough had been for nothing. My pride was hurt and that made me all the more determined to join up. If I was going to be stuck with a desk job, I'd choose something where, I thought, they couldn't refuse me. Boys who had been cadets in the OTC had a special form to hand in when they went for their medical, along with their Certificate A, Parts 1 and 2, which proved they knew their way around a Sten gun. One of the sections of this form was 'Choice of Arm'. Under 'First Choice' I wrote 'Intelligence Corps', innocently thinking, you don't have to wear boots to be intelligent. Anyway, I didn't have to show them the specialist's letter.

The medical seemed to go pretty well. The doctors tapped and listened and probed and seemed to approve of what they found. Then one of them pointed to the bandage on my ankle. 'What's that?' he asked. I started to explain, but he shook his head impatiently and told me to take off the bandage. The growth at that time was still large and purple and ugly, with an encrusted rim at its base from which lymph oozed when it went wrong. I hated the thing and couldn't bear for it to be touched. He grabbed it roughly and began to probe and squeeze. I bit my lips and looked away, while my anus retreated towards my navel.

Finally I said, 'I've got a letter about it from a specialist. It's in my jacket in the changing room.'

'Get it.'

While he read the letter, very slowly, he kept glancing at my ankle as though to make sure it was still there and not some trick done with mirrors. Then he stuck the letter in his white coat and told me to put my clothes on and wait outside with the other conscripts.

There were about 50 of us in the anteroom, gloomy youths slouched on rows of battered wooden chairs. Most of us wore tweed jackets and flannel trousers, a few wore suits, we all wore ties. We didn't look at one another and we didn't talk. It was a long wait.

When my turn finally came I sat in front of a long table while six white-coated doctors passed Sir Heneage Ogilvie's letter along the line. I sat very straight, shoulders back, trying to look soldierly, but they weren't fooled. Their verdict was: '4F. Unfit for military service.' This was the lowest category. Forget 'unfit for military service': 4F meant you were scarcely fit for human consumption. I felt insulted, particularly since I recognized one of the doctors. He was a member of Wasps' selection committee and I had a card in my pocket inviting me to turn out for the club's 'A' team at the end of the week. As I left he grinned at me and said, 'See you on Saturday.'

So it was back to my future again. My father had repeatedly warned me against coming into the family business with him. 'You'd hate it,' he'd say. 'I always have and you, with your education . . .' He meant what he said, of course, but he was also scared of how his father would react to another Alvarez on the payroll, another hat in the ring. I suspect he was also scared that I'd provoke the old tyrant, who would then take it out on him. He was probably right on all counts.

A couple of weeks after my medical, Uncle Teddy came to dinner at Glenilla Road and I was told to be there. The meal was vast and elaborate, even by my mother's standards, but when it was finished at last Teddy became suddenly business-like. He turned to me abruptly, lowered his bald bull head and said, 'I've got a proposition for you: I want you to come into Levy & Franks. You'll learn the business, then you'll work directly under me. In three years time you'll be earning 10 thousand a year.'

This was in 1948, when £500 a year was a comfortable living and the starting salary for a university lecturer was £350. Ten thousand was several times more than my father earned, an absurd sum, hard for a 19-year-old to comprehend or take seriously.

'But I want to go to Oxford.'

'It's your choice.'

'Couldn't I go to Oxford and then come into the firm?'

'You don't need an Oxford degree to run pubs.'

'L & F's not just pubs.' I pretended to sound indignant on his behalf, thinking flattery might do it. After all, he was a Chevalier du Tastevin, a pal of all the best wine-growers in Burgundy and Bordeaux.

'Pubs, hotels, wines and spirits. What's the difference? It's all catering. You don't need a degree, you need experience.'

'But I'd get that at Oxford.'

'Not the kind I'm looking for. So far as I'm concerned, all you'd do is waste three years and a lot of money.'

My father was sunk in his armchair, his face averted, but my mother was watching us, big-eyed. This was the moment she'd been waiting for, when her only son decided to make good. I think Teddy knew exactly what was going on. He had no son of his own and this was his takeover bid. He resented the Alvarezes and their culture – the music, the books, the intellectual aspirations – and he wanted to recruit me into his tough-minded, high-living world.

'I don't even know if I'll get into Oxford,' I said. 'I've got to take the exams again at Christmas.'

'Christmas is too late. I'm offering you a job now, starting at the end of the month. Take it or leave it.'

'But I want to go to Oxford.'

'That's it, then.'

There was a long silence. Finally, my mother said, 'Oh, Alfred.' She was on the edge of tears, but my father was smiling. 'How about a whisky and soda?' he said to Teddy. 'A little nightcap.'

Teddy ignored him. 'Your parents and I have discussed this,' he said. 'If you can get into Oxford, I'll pay half what it costs.'

I started to mumble thanks, but he cut me off with, 'How much are we talking about? Name a figure.'

I had read *Zuleika Dobson* and *Brideshead Revisited*, but they didn't tell me what it cost to live the Oxford life. They also didn't tell me how to negotiate a deal with a hard-driving businessman. I should have doubled the first figure that came to mind or asked him to let me check it out. Instead, because I admired him and knew I'd let him down, I went for the most modest sum that seemed feasible.

'I don't know,' I said. 'Maybe I could get by on £300 a year.'

'You've got a deal. If you get into Oxford, I'll give you £150 a year for three years. Not a penny more, not a penny less. Shake on it.'

We shook hands solemnly and he left without drinking his nightcap. My mother went upstairs to weep in private. My father and I sat companionably in silence while he played a Mahler symphony at full volume.

When the college bills came in at the end of my first term at Oxford, I realized that I had hopelessly underestimated the cost. But when I told Teddy my mistake, all he said was, 'Tough luck. A deal's a deal. If you get it wrong, you must live with the consequences. Think of it as a valuable lesson.'

At that time each of Teddy's string of racehorses was costing him several times more each year than he was contributing to my education. But a deal's a deal. My poor parents helped out as much as they could, but I was always broke.

The evening Teddy came to dinner, Oxford was still as unreal to me as the £10,000 golden carrot he dangled in front of my nose, but I was fixed on it, and not just because of Zuleika. Cambridge was like Oundle, a dank East Midlands town full of Old Oundelians who went there to study engineering. There was no School of Engineering at Oxford and very few people I knew. I wanted to start afresh, I wanted to do it over again differently. But, even assuming I didn't fail the college entrance exams as I had failed the scholarship papers, the earliest I could hope for a place was the autumn of 1949. That left 18 months to kill.

I put on a suit and went to the offices of Gabbitas Thring in Sackville Street to apply for a job teaching French in a prep school. A chilly young man interviewed me. He was not much older than I was but he wore an Old Etonian tie and didn't seem to think much of Oundle. Nevertheless, I had the necessary qualifications – School Certificate, Higher Certificate – and he reluctantly told me they would find me a job, starting in September. Maybe I was put out by his lofty air or maybe I couldn't cope with the prospect of five months at Glenilla Road, but I left the office knowing the time had come for desperate remedies.

I wandered down Piccadilly, then up the Burlington Arcade, window-shopping, and ended up staring at the goodies on display in the window of Captain Watts's plush ship's chandlers shop in Albemarle Street. For the past four years friends and I had rented a yacht for a week on the Norfolk Broads and had always had ourselves a great time. Maybe that's how to fill the empty months ahead, I thought: I should go to sea. Without giving myself time to think again, I marched in and asked to see the boss. I do not now know why I imagined that a ship's chandlers – even one situated just off Piccadilly – would provide me with a ticket to life afloat. I do not even know why I imagined that I wanted to go to sea. Perhaps I had read too many schoolboy adventure stories. Or perhaps it was simply because I was 18 years old and had never even crossed the Channel. Like most young people in Britain after the war, all I really wanted was to get away from the place.

Whatever the reason, I managed to con my way through the downstairs shop crammed with tackle and ropes and oilskins, up to the Captain's private office. 'Go anywhere, do anything,' I announced, like an advertisement in the agony column of *The Times*.

Captain Watts had a fiery complexion and a fierce stare. 'Any experience?' he barked.

'Four seasons sailing on the Norfolk Broads.' It had seemed like a lot at school, where I had made much of my skill as a yachtsman. With the Captain's framed certificates and photographs around me, I wasn't so sure.

Captain Watts rolled his eyes to the ceiling, then shuffled impatiently through some papers on his desk, waiting for me either to say something or go.

'Anywhere,' I repeated doggedly.

He selected a sheet of paper from the sheaf in front of him and studied it. 'If you can get yourself up to Scotland,' he said grudgingly, 'there's a ship in Port Seton we're bringing south next week. I suppose I could use another deck-hand.'

'Thank you. Thank you very much.' I stared at my shoes, trying to work up my courage. I had never had a job before. 'About the . . . wages . . .'

'No wages. Experience is what you'll get. Valuable experience.'

You should meet my uncle Teddy, I thought. You two would get on like a house on fire. All I said was, 'Thank you. Thank you very much.'

I borrowed some money from my bewildered parents and bought a one-way ticket to Edinburgh.

Port Seton is a few miles east of Edinburgh, on the blowy Firth of Forth. It was low tide when I arrived and only the ship's tall, old-fashioned funnel was visible above the dock. She was an 80-foot steam drifter – I can no longer remember her name – built in Dundee around 1880, battered, rusty, ungainly – a 'dirty British coaster with a salt-caked smoke stack' straight out of Masefield. I climbed down the steel ladder from the dock and called, 'Hullo.' No response. A gull, perched on the seaward rail, peered at me with disdain. I went aft, down some steps, into a corridor, and called again. A muffled voice answered from the end of the passage. I opened the door to a cramped and stuffy saloon where a wolfish, middle-aged man and a heavily made-up woman were sitting at a table, drinking pink gin. They stared at me in amazement. I was wearing a tweed jacket, an Old Oundelian tie and spotless cream-coloured corduroys.

'Captain Watts sent me,' I said.

Silence. They went on staring at me.

'I'm here to work.'

They stirred, blinked, as though coming awake.

'Then you'd better go and see the stoker. The hatch amidships. Leave your gear in the fo'c'sle.'

The forecastle was small and curved, with six bunks and a stained table. The air was stale, pungent and slightly rancid. I dumped my bag, jacket and tie on a top bunk and went back on deck. A hatch was open on the seaward side of the boat. I climbed down into a narrow black hole, full of coal.

The stoker was a tiny, muscular Scot, shirtless, sweating and black with dust. He squinted at me through the gloom and said, 'Fuck me!'

But by then I was getting used to the effect I had on strangers.

For the next three days I worked with the stoker in the hole, shovelling coal as it was dumped, sack after sack, down the hatch. On the second day the wolfish man lit the boilers while the stoker and I laboured, and from then on the hole was like Bombay in a black dust storm. On the third day a line stuck in a block on the forward mast, high up beyond where the ladders gave out. I managed to monkey my way up and free it (any job in the fresh air was preferable to the black hole) and after that the wolfish man looked less depressed when he saw me.

On the fourth day I was given the afternoon off. I washed off most of the coal dust, put on my sports jacket and Oundle tie to offset the now black cords, took a bus into Edinburgh and went straight to a barber. When he rinsed my hair, the water ran like ink down the drain. By the time I got back to Port Seton, Captain Watts had arrived with the rest of the crew – a youth a little older and more experienced than myself, who ignored me, and four purposeful men who were working towards their Master Mariner's Certificate. We sailed the next morning on the dawn tide.

As I remember it, the boat began rolling the moment we slipped our moorings, and did not stop until we tied up again in London.

The 400-mile journey took a week. We crawled down the east coast, always tantalizingly in sight of land. The sun shone but a cold wind blew relentlessly from the east, whipping the waves into white horses and slamming them into the shuddering old ship. 'She's a regular cow,' the stoker had warned me before we left. 'She'll roll in dry dock.' He had also said, of the wolfish man's wife, 'She's so tight-fisted she wouldna gee you a thick ha'penny for a thin un.' On both counts he was right. The old tub rolled all the way down the coast and went on rolling in the milder, more sheltered waters of the Thames estuary. Only when we steamed dead slow into Wapping 19 – 50 square yards of oily green water on which not even the debris stirred – did I seem to feel the uneasy motion slowly fading in her.

It took a day for seasickness to get me, but by that time everyone except the stoker was ill. Even Captain Watts and the trainee Master Mariners were vomiting over the side before we were six hours out of Port Seton. I watched them, amazed that they should have chosen a profession that made them suffer so much, though they had all recovered by the time my turn came.

It was a miserable week, but the night watches were the worst. The ship was so ancient that it had no electricity and was lit, instead, by acetylene lamps. (Hence that pungent, faintly rancid smell that permeated the forecastle and every other closed space.) The most obnoxious of these lamps was in the binnacle housing the compass on the bridge. It was an overhead binnacle, glassed in on three sides, with the compass card at eye-level as you held the brass-bound wooden wheel. But at night the little acetylene jet that illuminated it created confusing reflections in the glass, and in order to read the bearings you had to stick your nose right into the unglassed side, a few inches below the flaring jet. Twice I was up on the bridge on my own from midnight to 4 a.m., inhaling the stink of acetylene and trying to keep the ship on course while the waves thumped monotonously into her port beam and her bows heaved up and down. The first time I left her a mile off course, the second nearer three miles. After that, the Master Mariners got the midnight watch at the helm and I relieved the stoker.

When we finally passed Southend pier, sticking out like a long pencil into the Thames estuary, and London became a smudge of smoke in the distance, I felt like a pilgrim sighting Rome. The rackety Underground branch line from Wapping to Whitechapel was civilization itself – interior-sprung seats, a floor that vibrated but did not pitch or roll, and people, ordinary people, going to ordinary work. London seemed the natural place to be – man-made and, despite its sprawl, scaled to man. In the North Sea I had felt like an intruder, existing precariously and under sufferance. What Delmore Schwartz – another city boy – called 'the fatal, merciless, passionate ocean' is not tolerant of people or their mistakes. The evil white horses walloping unforgivingly into our suffering old ship were a constant reminder who was boss.

Captain Watts had been right when he said I would earn myself experience. I had learned that the sea was not my element, and one week's misery was a cheap enough price to pay.

The North Sea journey freed me in other ways. The pompous middle-class rectitude Oundle instilled in its pupils, the sense of Them and Us which is the basis of the British class system, the conviction that We are always right and They aspire to our condition, had always made me uneasy and it clearly didn't apply on board. Or rather, it applied – Captain Watts and his wolfish first mate were running the show and what they said went – but now I was on the other side. The stoker and I were Them and They had their own set of values. According to Conrad:

> Ships have no ears, and thus they cannot be deceived. I would illustrate my idea of fidelity as between man and ship, between the master and his art, by a statement which, though it might appear shockingly sophisticated, is really very simple. I would say that a racing-yacht skipper who thought of nothing else but the glory of winning the race would never attain to any eminence of reputation. The genuine masters of their craft – I say this confidently from my experience of ships – have thought of nothing but of doing their very best by the vessel under their charge. To forget one's self, to surrender all personal feeling in the service of that fine art, is the only way for a seaman to fulfil the faithful discharge of his trust.

By Conrad's standards the tiny stoker, who was also in charge of the engines, was one of 'the genuine masters'; he understood the old ship and knew how to coax the best out of her at least as well as Captain Watts, and probably better. He also knew how to work and, once my trousers were black and he saw that I was willing to pitch in alongside him, he treated me with respect. And that, to my surprise, seemed to matter more than the School Colours I had lusted after and swanked around in so shamelessly at Oundle.

Maybe this was the beginning of my fascination with how other people function. Later, when I was spending more time than I could decently afford off in the hills climbing rocks or when I hung out with professional poker players in Las Vegas or went offshore to the oil installations in the North Sea and then wrote books about what I had seen, people were continually asking me, in so many words, what a literary guy who knew about poetry was doing in joints like those. They seemed to be implying that the literary-intellectual world was somehow superior to all that practical stuff. Although that is not a belief I have ever shared, I felt I had to give my reasons and make my excuses. 'I went for the pleasure of being there,' I'd say. 'Because I wanted to see it for myself.' The literary intellectuals were not convinced – they assumed it was part of some macho pose – but it happened to be true. Of course, the world of action, the real world where people take real risks with their bodies or machinery or money, is irresistible to the desk-bound writer who lives in his head. Even so, my prime motive was curiosity; I went because I realized very early that I would get only one shot at this planet, so I might as well see for myself what was on offer. But I was curious not just about how the other half lives, but about how it judges itself and its performance. The stoker, the poker players and the climbers were all as demanding in their different ways as any of the writers I have known. So, I suppose, was my uncle Teddy, which is probably where it all began.

A month after my North Sea journey I took the boat I'd been wanting to take all along – the cross-Channel ferry, Dover to Calais – and went to Grenoble, where the university ran a language summer school for foreigners. I loved French, had studied it since I was about six, had passed all the exams with high marks and knew reams of French poetry by heart – Villon, Racine, Lamartine, de Musset, Baudelaire. Yet when I got off the train at the Gare du Nord I was struck dumb. Even 'please' and 'thank you' seemed beyond me and the journey across town to the Gare de Lyons was a major expedition. (I had never seen Paris, so I went by bus.) It wasn't just the way people spoke that bewildered me – the speed and the slang and the accent that were so different from the careful classroom French I knew – it was also their casualness, their assumption that this was the natural language in which to communicate and it was up to everyone else to adjust accordingly.

It was Us and Them again, and again I was on the other side. After 18 years in Fortress Britain, I had become a foreigner, overwhelmed by the foreignness of what was around me: different styles of architecture, different pace, different sounds, different smells (all those clichés about Gauloises and garlic were true). I was still in a daze when I arrived in Grenoble.

Before I left London I had gone with my mother to Simpson's in Piccadilly to buy a new suit. (She paid, but I chose it.) It was Harris tweed, abrasive as a loofah, bright orangey-rust in colour, and built to keep out Highland mists and chills. I was very proud of it. I wore it on my journey across France and was still wearing it when I went for a walk at the end of my first day in Grenoble. The pension I was staying at was on the edge of town, up in the hills, and the streets around it had high embankments overhung by vivid luxuriant flowers I had never seen before. It was late on a sunny July afternoon and I was sweating gently in my carapace of tweed.

Suddenly the sky went black, there was a clang of thunder and rain bucketed down, solid sheets of water, zinging off the paving-stones and overflowing the gutters, as though the second Flood had come and the end of the world was nigh. Ten minutes later the rain stopped as abruptly as it had begun, the sun came out, the roads steamed and the air was heavy with a scent like the perfume one of my rich aunts used to wear. (It was tuberoses; I smelt them later in the market.) But the storm hadn't cleared the air at all. On the contrary, the heat now felt like the rain – violent, tropical, hotter than anything I had known in England. By the time I got back to the pension the sun had dried off the streets, but my suit was soaked again with sweat.

And I couldn't get over the strangeness of it – the violent rain and violent heat, the violent scent of the flowers. A couple of lines by Louis MacNeice stuck in my mind and didn't go away until I got back to London: 'World is crazier and more of it than we think./Incorrigibly plural.' This is what 'foreign' means, I thought. I pictured my father reading travel books in front of the thundering gramophone – Peter Fleming hacking his way through the Amazon forest or Tscheffily and his donkey plodding from Patagonia to Alaska to the accompaniment of Beethoven and Sibelius – and me upstairs, slogging through a fat Victorian history of Livingstone's exploration of Africa, illustrated by stiff, dark engravings, or poring over the atlas, looking for places that were green on the map. This was only France, northern Europe, not even the Mediterranean, but it was a long way from Glenilla Road and I loved it. I wondered what the rest of the world must be like.

There were two other guests staying at the pension, an American called Joe and a young Englishman called Beaumont. (I never knew the American's last name or the Englishman's first, which was par for the course.) Beaumont had blond curls and baleful blue eyes and, like me, was fresh out of public school. He had also been a boxer like me, and was full of the vainglory that comes with that particular skill. We had atheism in common, too, although his was fiercer than mine because he was in the backlash from four years of strict Catholic teaching at Ampleforth. Because of my Spanish name, he assumed that I, too, was Catholic, and because I was certain that his atheism, no matter how strident, would not prevent him disliking Jews, I never put him right. But it was truly strident – strident and relentless – and it made me glad that I had been brought up in a family in which belief or disbelief didn't matter because religion was not an issue. It had been years since my mother last lit a candle on Friday night and synagogue was a place my grandpa Alvarez went to for his own obscure purposes – most of them social.

Beaumont was tormented by disbelief and found proofs for the non-existence of God in everything. He thought of himself as an artist, had a gift for caricature and was always drawing shocking cartoons of the Holy Family and the priests who had made life hard for him at school. The cartoons were genuinely shocking – Jesus had pimples, knobbly knees and gigantic, gnarled feet, the priests were drooling and hook-nosed and always had massive erections – but I think they shocked him more than me. They went with his boxer's swagger, as though he were squaring up to the Almighty in a fight he knew he couldn't win. He planned to go to Paris, find an attic, set up as an artist and have lots of girls. That was something else we had in common: we were both virgins and resented it bitterly. But in the late 1940s that made us no different from most young men of our age and background.

Joe, the American, was a squat, swarthy 25-year-old, with a crew cut and a Brooklyn accent, who was using his grant from the GI Bill of Rights to pick up some French and have some fun. The three of us occasionally went to lectures together and Joe was always blithely out of his depth. We translated for him, we explained the references – 'So who the fuck's this Voltaire guy and why's he so great?' – and we mocked him on the sly, thinking ourselves terribly superior. Yet, mysteriously, the girls flocked around him and ignored Beaumont and me. They even seemed entranced by the way Joe massacred the French language, while our efforts to perfect our accents and pick up the current slang made them giggle. I watched him operate in dumb amazement, but when he tried to help me out I was too shy and awkward to follow his cues. I told myself that the difference between us was nothing personal, that it wasn't his charm that pulled the birds, it was his dollars. It was too humiliating to admit that even teenage girls knew how to separate the men from the boys.

They also knew the difference between English and American, between class-bound and classless, between uptight and easy-going. Although the words were different then, Joe was 'hip' and 'cool'; he'd been around, he'd served in the Army, he was streetwise. Nothing fazed him and he was generous without thinking anything of it, as though money genuinely didn't matter. Francs, dollars, who cared? It was all Monopoly money to him.

I had my nineteenth birthday that August. I mentioned it to no one, but my parents sent me a card and Joe must have seen it. That evening he turned up to dinner at the pension with a bottle of wine. 'A present,' he said. 'Happy birthday. I don't know shit about wine, but the guy at the store said this was the best he had and we should drink it with the dessert.' The wine was a Muscat de Baume de Venise and it tasted nothing like the vinegar served up at the pension or in the student bars. It tasted like I had imagined wine would taste when I was a child and I heard Uncle Teddy and Aunt Lulu talking reverently about great vintages – whatever they were. It seemed to explode in my mouth, rich and subtle and heady. When I tried to thank him, Joe waved me away: 'What the fuck. A birthday's a birthday. You gotta celebrate it because you never know how many you're gonna get.' It was the only reference he ever made to the war.

The Government had imposed severe currency restrictions on travellers after the war. I don't remember how much sterling one was allowed to take out of the country, but it wasn't enough for me to enrol officially at Grenoble University. So I sat in on the lectures, wrote all the required essays and got my landlady to correct them. She was a stickler for grammar and enjoyed putting me right, but she took no notice at all of what I said until, one day, I illustrated some specious argument with a quotation from Anouilh's *Antigone*. Anouilh was the flavour of the month in London as well as Paris and his brand of adolescent self-pity suited me fine. The speech was a florid number on the subject of divine injustice and it must have offended my landlady's good Catholic sensibility. 'Nonsense,' she said. 'How could you possibly say such things? Where do you get these ideas?' I told her the ideas were Anouilh's, not mine, and Anouilh was the latest thing in Paris, very chic, very famous. She didn't believe me, so after that I kept it simple and my French improved. It would have improved more if I had had a French girlfriend, but none of the girls would look at me, not even Joe's cast-offs, and it was years before

I found myself a long-haired dictionary to teach me how the language is really spoken. But by then I was no longer going regularly to France and my fluency didn't last.

My money gave out after five weeks, despite the illegal fivers my mother sent me by mail, hidden in socks and shirts. So I put my tweed suit on and took the train home. I arrived at Glenilla Road with a Gauloise plastered to the corner of my lower lip to show them how much I had changed.

Gabbitas Thring had found me a job at Maidwell Hall, a prep school in Northamptonshire, not far from Oundle. It was an echoing, draughty barn of a country house, surrounded by beautiful gardens which the headmaster tended as assiduously as he tended the little boys in his charge. He was inordinately proud of them both. The gardens were cunningly laid out and full of brilliant, sweet-smelling bushes and flowers so that, in summer, a new scent assaulted you at each turn of the twisting paths. The boys were equally exotic and highly bred. Most of them went on to Eton or Winchester and a number had titles. There was the Earl of This and Lord That and any number of Right Honourables – all of them little kids in short trousers, with runny noses and scabbed knees and a bereft look in their eyes, kids who should have been at home with their mothers, instead of being ordered about and beaten, shuddering with cold and learning irregular verbs.

It was a chilly place in every sense. Most of the senior staff seemed to have spent their whole careers at the school and the grandeur of their little pupils had rubbed off on them. They were a superior lot, who talked wistfully about huntin', shootin' and fishin', and, because I hadn't been to Eton and was closer to the boys' age than to theirs, they took very little notice of me. The exception was the lanky sports master, Mr Brierley, who was looked down on by the others because he had not been to a public school and who liked me because I was playing rugger, briefly, for Northampton. We drank together occasionally at the grim village pub. The locals resented us because none of the other staff went near the place and the staff looked down on us because we did. It was Little England in miniature.

The only people who had any time for me and my airs were the matron and a jolly young woman with a big jaw who taught the bottom class. Both of them did their best to mother the forlorn little children in their care, and once they had seen through my show of punchy independence they tried unobtrusively to do the same for me. The matron and I had outrageous grandfathers in common. Hers was an admiral who, long after his devoted wife died, suddenly married a girl of 22. He was 86 at the time and his memory was not good. He used to confide to his son – also an admiral – that he simply couldn't imagine who this beautiful young woman was who climbed into bed with him every night. But he didn't like to ask in case she went away.

It was a curious time and what I remember most about it is the loneliness. I shared a thatched cottage with the school butler. Or rather, he slept there and I slept there, but we rarely met. The cottage was unheated, except for a small coal fire in my spider-infested sitting-room, but that didn't stop me taking a cold bath every morning, Oundle-style. I did it because I had the habit and it woke me up, but also because it reminded me of a time when I still had an identity. I buzzed around the muddy lanes on my motorbike – a Matchless 350 which cost me the £100 that had been sitting in the bank since my bar mitzvah – but in the days when you wore a duffle-coat instead of leathers there was not much fun to be had on a motorbike in the dead of winter.

Mostly I sat close to the miserable sitting-room fire, kept one eye open for spiders, and read. I had a passion for Aldous Huxley; his know-all cynicism appealed to the budding undergraduate in me, but the know-all part of it was real – he was really knowledgeable and wide-ranging – and his tips led me to all kinds of books I might not otherwise have come across. I also read the complete works of William Shakespeare, thinking I should have that behind me when I went up to Oxford. So I was much better prepared when I sat the college entrance exams. When the letter came from Corpus Christi College saying I had a place for the following October, I got drunk on sweet sherry with the matron and the jolly young woman who taught the nursery class.

Because of the loneliness and all that reading – night after night of it – I began to write a good deal of poetry. Most of it was the usual apprentice stuff, imitations of whomever I was hooked on at the time – Housman, Frost, even Aldous Huxley. I wrote them, then tore them up a few days later. But gradually Maidwell Hall was getting to me – the coldness of the place, the snobbery, the sad children with their beautiful manners. If this was the world I had opted for when I turned my back on Glenilla Road, then I didn't much like it. But my disappointment helped produce a poem, 'Christian Charity', and it was not an imitation of my elders and betters. The poem was the real thing, written in my own voice, a voice I didn't even know I had and could scarcely recognize. It was published in the student paper, *Isis*, during my first term at Oxford, but I no longer have a copy and assume it wasn't much good. Even so, it was as good as I could do at the time and when the last revision was done and the last comma was in place I was happier than I had ever been before.

I knew all about the adrenalin rush and the exhilaration I'd felt on the Idwal Slabs and the high board at the swimming pool, but this was different. This wasn't exhilaration, it was happiness. I'd finally made something as perfect as I could and it had nothing to do with me. It was as though the poem had its own independent life and my job was merely to get it right, like a carpenter making a table.

A few nights later I dreamed I was reading the poem in a book. The book was my *Collected Poems* and I had the impression that it was a posthumous publication, that I was reading it from beyond the grave and was appalled by what had been done to it. All around the page were drawings of flowers – violets and forget-me-nots – pretty, sentimental little watercolours like those ladies of leisure used to paint at the turn of the century. In my dream I was outraged. 'That's not how it should be,' I said. 'It's not a sentimental poem. It's not pretty at all. It's true.' I was weeping with frustration, but I knew there was nothing I could do about it because I was already dead. I woke up sobbing. It seemed to be one of those dreams that foretell the future, though I didn't know if I was weeping for what would be done with my work or with what I myself would do with whatever talent I had.

The master who taught Greek and Latin was a Wykehamist, boyishly handsome – jaunty, dashing, fair-haired – but cursed with a violent facial tic that seemed to reinforce his natural diffidence. He had given up on the classics long ago; they were simply a way of earning a basic wage while he worked on his real interest in life, horse-racing. He pored over *Sporting Life* in the staff common room, knew all the trainers and most of the jockeys, and was constantly on the phone to them and to his bookmaker. At weekends, he put on a houndstooth suit and a brown trilby and drove off to the races in his ancient Austin Seven. When I asked him if he was lucky he seemed offended. 'Actually, luck's got nothing to do with it,' he replied. 'Gambling's like everything else, old boy. You have to work at it. In an average year I reckon to double my salary, but it's got nothing to do with luck.'

To prove his point he took me to the greyhound track at Loughborough, a dingy arena, badly lit and not very full. The crowd was dingy, too. There were very few women and most of the men seemed to have come straight from work. They wore donkey jackets, paint-stained boots and white shirts fastened at the neck with brass studs but without the detachable collar. Most of them looked as if they could barely afford the entrance fee, yet wads of money were changing hands, the bookies were gabbling excitedly and the tick-tack men were waving their arms.

'The dogs are easier than the horses,' explained the Wykehamist, who was not wearing his stylish brown trilby. 'All the races are fixed. You just have to understand what's going on.' The race card printed the track record of each dog. He studied it carefully, then watched the way the odds changed on the bookies' blackboards and the extravagant sign language of the tick-tack men, which he seemed able to decipher. He waited until moments before the traps opened to make his bets and every dog he backed was a winner. I backed them too, though for shillings, not pounds, and at the end of the evening I was five pounds ahead. Unearned money is always sweet, but my salary at Maidwell Hall was only £3 a week, plus board and lodging, so five quid felt like a fortune. On the way home in his wheezing Austin, I asked my colleague about horse-racing and hinted, as delicately as I knew how, that maybe he would take me along with him to the next meeting. He muttered something non-committal, his face twitched galvanically and the subject never came up again. I was not anyone he would want to introduce to his friends.

Towards the end of my year at Maidwell Hall I went to spend Derby weekend with a school friend who lived in Epsom. The Wykehamist had no tips for the big race – 'The Derby's too important,' he said. 'It's always an open race' – but he gave me the name of three horses in the supporting races, names he'd got straight from the trainers, horses that couldn't lose. The hottest of the three was called Summer Lightning and was running in the first race. According to the Wykehamist, who was a fan of Damon Runyon, 'If they start overnight, they still cannot beat him.' I had £5 to spare, the fiver he'd helped me win, and I put three on Summer Lightning. Then my Oundle friend and I burrowed our way through the crowd and found a place on the rails, 20 yards short of the winning-post. Although it was a short race, Summer Lightning was 10 lengths clear of the other horses as it thundered towards us. Then – and this is a true story – at the moment it drew level with me, it burst an artery and dropped dead. The poor creature was so far ahead that it would have won even if it had broken a leg and crawled over. Instead it lay there with its huge, saliva-flecked tongue hanging out of the side of its mouth while the astonished jockey tugged feebly at the reins.

I felt responsible, as though my lousy three quid had killed the beast, as though this was an obscure lesson and the Almighty was tapping me on the shoulder and saying, 'Not for you.' I had been right when I turned down Uncle Teddy's offer. His world was not for me. The other two horses also failed to place, I lost my fiver and the Wykehamist lost a small fortune and never spoke to me again. Since then I have backed horses for fun, but very rarely and only for small sums. Not one of them has ever won.

7

OXFORD

————◄►————

When my daughter was at Oxford in the early nineties – her brother had gone to Cambridge, just to upset me – she came home with a grim joke that was going the rounds among students: Question: 'What do you say to someone with a degree in the humanities?' Answer: 'Big Mac and fries, please.' Now further education is available to everybody and good jobs are hard to find, most young people take for granted that they will be overqualified for whatever work they do and an unreasonable number of them will end up on the dole, doing nothing at all.

This wasn't a problem 50 years ago, when there were more jobs and fewer universities and bright schoolchildren didn't automatically go on to take a degree. University was for budding professionals – academics, scientists, civil servants or diplomats in the making – or for the leisured few who wanted a blue to take with them to the Stock Exchange or the merchant banks. It had nothing to do with the business world. Even my cultured grandpa Alvarez could see no real connection between higher education and making money, and the Levys prided themselves on their lack of schooling, as though it made their wealth more glamorous and deserving. Grandpa Dick picked up the tab when my clever sister Anne went to finishing school, but only because he thought languages, skiing and horse riding would improve her prospects on the marriage market. He would not have considered paying for her to study for a degree.

So I was the first member of my family to go to university and I expected the earth. After all, this was Oxford, not just one choice among many more or less equal choices, as it is now, but the biggest of all possible academic deals. We were the elect, the best and the brightest, with brains as well as youth on our side, and everything conspired to reinforce the illusion – the decorum, the ancient buildings, the church bells answering one another every quarter of an hour, the eccentric, twitching dons weighed down by their learning.

Admittedly Corpus did not offer much in the way of sophisticated high culture and highbrow chatter, Aldous Huxley-style. But Huxley had been at Balliol, a large college, famous for its intellectual swank, while Corpus was studious and small – the smallest college in Oxford – and it specialized in Classics. Classics was a four-year course: two years of Greek and Latin literature and ancient history (called 'Mods') followed by two years of philosophy ('Greats'). Then, if your results were good enough, you sat the Civil Service exams and went on to run the country from the back rooms of Whitehall. It was a demanding course and it didn't leave much time for fun. In fact, it hardly seemed to leave much time for Oxford. Most of the Classics students ground away for their Mods dutifully, as though they were still at school, and once they got going on Greats they behaved as if they were already in the Civil Service. If they were oarsmen they got drunk at Bump Suppers, because that was the conventional thing to do, although little else seemed to brighten their lives. Perhaps Oxford and its irresponsibility hit them during the long vacation between Mods and Greats, but they weren't around in the vacations, so who could ever tell?

When I went up, in 1949, there was another sobering element: about half the college were ex-servicemen and many of them had fought in the war. Now they were making up for lost time and didn't want to waste it on frivolity or chit-chat. As a result they had little to say to us callow knownothings from school and we, in our turn, were shy of them, these bluejawed toughs who had been places and done things we couldn't even imagine.

Anyway, we were too busy enjoying our freedom. For the first time in my life I was being treated as a grown-up with grown-up privileges. My scout, who cleaned my rooms and brought me a jug of hot water every morning to shave in, was old enough to be my father, but I called him by his Christian name, he called me 'sir' and both of us accepted that this was how the world was ordered. I was responsible for my own work and my own behaviour, no longer ordered around and bound by petty rules, coming and going, drinking or not drinking as I pleased, and I organized my own timetable. There were lectures, but my tutor advised me against attending most of them. My only responsibility was to churn out an essay for him every week.

In terms of comfort, life in Oxford after the war was still grim and impoverished. Meat was rationed, the cooking was dreadful, the nearest bathrooms and lavatories were two quads away, and to keep warm you bundled yourself up in sweaters and hurried from one pathetic electric fire to another, like Polynesians island-hopping across an icy Pacific. Even so, it felt like a holiday after Oundle.

Instead of sharing a shoebox study with two other people and sleeping in a dormitory with 20, I had two rooms to myself up a steep staircase under the eaves in the front quad, with a view of the famous Corpus sundial, a painted totem pole crowned with a pelican. The bedroom was monkish – small and narrow and freezing cold – but the sitting-room was large enough and had a pitched roof full of angles and shadows, like the night nursery at Glenilla Road. It also had an outer door, an 'oak', which you 'sported' when you didn't want visitors. I couldn't get over the space and privacy and leisureliness, or the idea that the hours spent drinking coffee and talking about writers was what we were there for. It didn't even matter that much of the talk was word games – quotations, allusions, puns – played out in a lather of pretension and intellectual snobbery. Even that seemed right and proper. It went with being young and falling in love with literature.

I was also falling in love with Oxford, with the graceful stone and lush gardens, with all that silence and history. Whatever the teaching was like, the place itself got to you and you learned from its beauty. It was the college libraries that I fell for most heavily. The Corpus library was very old – Erasmus had worked in it – and was heated only to the bare minimum temperature – 50 degrees Fahrenheit or less – that would keep the books from becoming mildewed. It was a long, high room, with a pitched roof and coconut matting on the floor. The bookshelves were set at right angles to the walls, dividing the space into pews, and each pew was divided down the middle by a high-backed wooden double bench. I worked there every day and, because the benches were hard and the air was frigid, I usually had the place to myself.

When I said I liked it there my friends wrote it off as an affectation, so I covered up by pretending that I needed the discomfort to stay awake. But really I was besotted by the atmosphere. The books in the pews were nothing like the paperbacks we used, with their torn covers and blackened margins. They were massive leather-bound folios, most of them printed in the eighteenth century or earlier, many of them in Latin and none written by anyone I had ever heard of. Each looked like a life's work, packed with learned footnotes and cross-references, years in the making and never read; the pages turned crisply, as though they were fresh from the press. They gave me a sense of the endlessness of learning – there would never be enough time to read more than a fragment of what was on offer – and also of its seductiveness, of the way you could lose yourself in scholarship, wade in over your head and not come up again. Briefly, it seemed like an attractive alternative to the chaos of Glenilla Road.

My tutor, F. W. Bateson, had edited *The Cambridge Bibliography of English Literature* and was prodigiously learned, but he looked like a farmer, heavy, lumbering and red-faced. He also walked with a limp, though it disappeared miraculously when he went on to the tennis court. He was a shy, awkward man, with a voice that squeaked when he was under stress, and he resented the fact that, despite his learning, the other Corpus dons didn't take him seriously. Back then Corpus was still above all a Greats college, although mathematics was acceptable and PPE (Philosophy, Politics and Economics), history and the sciences were tolerated – more or less. But English was not considered to be a serious academic discipline; it was like geology or forestry, a subject you read if you weren't up to anything more demanding.

This attitude was not peculiar to Corpus. The English Faculty itself thought the same and insisted that we acquire a little intellectual rigour by devoting at least a third of our time – three out of the nine papers in the final examinations – to the study of Old and Middle English and modern philology. So far as Corpus was concerned, undergraduates reading English were second-class citizens and their tutor, by definition, was a lightweight and an outsider.

Freddie Bateson was also an outsider in the English Faculty, which in those days was divided into three separate camps: the philologists, whose interest in literature ended before Chaucer; the heavy scholars, whose great ambition was to produce the definitive edition of a very minor poet; and the 'appreciative' critics, who believed, with Wordsworth, that 'we murder to dissect' and preferred not to sully their sensibilities with argument or detail. Freddie had a foot in two of the camps – the last book he published was called *The Scholar Critic* – but it was criticism that interested him most, though he was too intellectually curious to be satisfied with Oxford-style 'appreciation'. Although he could appreciate with the best of them, he wanted to know how poems worked and why one was better than another. He was also a socialist, a man of the thirties who loved Auden and the Pylon poets and never forgave his hero for decamping to New York at the outbreak of war.

He had even written a volume for Gollancz's Left Book Club called *Towards a Socialist Agriculture*, which, in homage to T. S. Eliot, I always referred to as *Notes Towards a Definition of Agriculture* – another joke that fell flat. Although Freddie liked to put a political spin on his reading of literature, he was too good a teacher to try to force his opinions or his methods on his students. He listened to the weekly essay with great concentration, puffing his pipe and making little squeaking noises when provoked, then he told you the vital facts you had missed, the sources, the references, the textual variants – he had them all at his fingertips. And he would argue. The arguments, in fact, are what I remember best of my tutorials. Freddie must have had a high threshold of patience for opinionated undergraduate bullshit because he paid you the compliment of arguing with you seriously.

Towards the end of my first year I still hadn't been able to get to grips with the basic problem of criticism: how to talk accurately about poetry, how to describe my experience of it and reactions to it without using the word 'magic' – then the key term of the Oxford appreciative critics – or taking Freddie's political slant, which didn't appeal to me. I nagged him about what to do until he threw up his hands wearily and said, 'Go away and read Richards and Empson.' I spent the summer reading *Practical Criticism, The Principles of Literary Criticism* and *Seven Types of Ambiguity* and came away feeling I had found the answer. Richards and Empson didn't treat poetry as if it were a religious experience, available only to initiates; they talked about it as part of ordinary life – subtler, more concentrated and pared away, but still part of the life everyone leads, and open to intelligent discussion, like any other intellectual activity. All you had to do was read closely, listen carefully and think.

Empson was even more alluring than Richards and not just because of his cleverness and convoluted wit. What impressed me most was the fact that he had been so damn young when he wrote *Seven Types of Ambiguity*. We were all of us obsessed with the idea of precociousness – the Brilliant First, then the dazzling first book as a marker for future glory. It was an innocent form of snobbery and went with the idea of ourselves as the best and the brightest. Empson, however, had pulled it off, had shown it could be done, and done spectacularly. *Seven Types*, a book that seemed to read literature in a way it had never been read before, was published when he was only 24; more impressive still, it was based on the weekly essays he had written when he was Richards's pupil at Cambridge. Knowing this seemed to change the rules of the game and raise the ante.

Oxford had a tradition of smart-talking, aphoristic high style which went from Oscar Wilde to Aldous Huxley and was still very much in vogue among the bright sparks. (Ken Tynan had gone down the term before I arrived, but his memory lingered on.) Empson made all that seem foppish and trivial. His prose style was mannered and dense and easy to imitate (which I did, of course). But his intelligence was always intensely focused on the text in front of him and that, I realized, was what it was all about. Why else was I there, when I might have been making a fortune working for Uncle Teddy, except to learn how to use my intelligence? It was one of those truths which we hold to be self-evident, though it hadn't occurred to me before. Then, as though to confirm it, I came across a remark in an essay by Eliot, a throwaway comment on somebody's ponderous discussion of Aristotle's 'method': 'The only method,' Eliot wrote, 'is to be very intelligent.' As I remember it, the aside was in parentheses, which made its disdain seem even more enticing and deadly.

I also discovered that the critical word was out everywhere except Oxford. In America there was the 'New Criticism', a whole school of literary critics who had taken their cue from Richards and Empson. It didn't matter that the best known of them at the time, Cleanth Brooks, had simplified 'the only method' into a teaching technique and made it seem mechanical. At least they were reading poetry in the same cool, analytic way, as though taking for granted that brainlessness was not a necessary precondition for a literary sensibility.

I went back to Oxford in the autumn with a light in my eye, determined to spread the good news in the only way available to an undergraduate: I would start a student discussion group and call it the Critical Society. But I was nervous about doing it on my own, so I hijacked two other Corpus men – David Thompson, who later became the art critic of *The Times*, and John Miles, a poet who was reading philosophy – and Graham Martin, a friend from Jesus College who eventually became Professor of English at the Open University. We drew up a fighting manifesto about the deplorable state of Oxford criticism and how the Critical Society was going to set it right, had 2000 copies of it printed in two shades of blue and spread them all over the university. We piled them up in the lecture halls and common rooms, pinned them on all the college notice boards and scattered them through the student cafés.

Freddie Bateson was not impressed. No one will come, he told us; this is Oxford; they don't want to know. I thought his knee-jerk put-down was typically Oxford, too, and resented him for it. But secretly I believed he was right and was astonished when the first meeting was packed out and briefly the Critical Society became the hottest ticket in town. Empson, Leavis and a host of visiting Americans came and talked. Wallace Robson, an English don at Lincoln College who later became a professor at Edinburgh, egged us on; so did Frank Kermode and John Wain, then both at Reading University. We all wrote papers and argued ferociously, and for a time the society was what it was supposed to be – subversive and fun.

Four of the writers at Oxford just after the war became famous – Philip Larkin, Kingsley Amis, Iris Murdoch and John Wain – but in 1950 only Larkin had published a book. In fact, he had already published three – two novels and a book of poems – but they had got nowhere and now he was buried away in Belfast, honing his misanthropy, while Amis taught English in Swansea and Wain was in Reading. Iris Murdoch was the only one of them still in Oxford, teaching at St Anne's, but in those days she was a philosopher, not a novelist, the lone Existentialist among all the Logical Positivists, a handsome young woman, with a bell of blonde hair, a broad face and a gruff, forthright manner, like one of Eisenstein's peasants. I met her, as I met Wain, through Wallace Robson.

Wallace was Oxford's young literary guru, the one they all deferred to, the man who had read everything, the Continentals as well as the British, the philosophers, linguists and psychoanalysts as well as the poets and novelists. He had even had a Kleinian analysis at a time when Melanie Klein was scarcely known outside the feuding psychoanalytic circle in London NW3 and psychoanalysis itself was still considered a self-indulgence, a game for foreigners and Jews that no decent Brit would play unless he was genuinely crazy.

Wallace was anything but crazy, but he was profoundly neurotic. While other English dons dressed in tweed jackets, woollen ties, cavalry-twill trousers and polished brogues, like Army officers on leave, he slopped around tieless in a greasy blue suit with dandruff on the collar. His hair was long and unwashed; his complexion was dreadful; he was prone to anxiety attacks that made him sweat and, although he seemed to have all the talent and insight in the world, he couldn't get anything down on paper.

Yet Wallace was far smarter and better read than Amis and Wain, and before they became famous they deferred to his authority. He was also more humane and available, perhaps because he was too intelligent to need to assert his superiority. He and I once taught at a summer school for foreign students at Oxford. We gave seminars in adjacent rooms and used to meet at the foot of the stairs after each morning session. He always looked dejected, even when – or especially when – he was surrounded by the prettiest students, but one day he looked even more downcast than usual. 'I'm such a bore,' he announced. 'When I talk to people they don't yawn, but tears come into their eyes.'

Wallace had a gift for seeing how absurd his anxieties were and making them outrageous. Kingsley Amis once found him sitting on his bed in Lincoln, stark naked, with a face like a tragic mask.

'What's wrong?' Kingsley asked.

Wallace had the habit of lengthening vowels for emphasis. 'It's my pee-eenis,' he said. He sounded desolate, far too desolate for Kingsley to snigger.

'What's the matter with it?'

'It's so-o-o ugly. It's a-all red and browwwn.'

Even Kingsley, who was working on *Lucky Jim* at the time and considered himself a master of outrage, was impressed.

Wallace had a special talent for using his own florid neuroses to get inside the heads of writers. He talked about Donne's hypochondria or Coleridge's garrulous depression or Keats's social awkwardness as though they were the weaknesses of troubled friends who were there in the room with him. And in a way they were. Wallace knew how to take poems apart as shrewdly as Empson, but because he himself found it almost impossible to write, he had an uncanny understanding of everything that stood between the writer and his work. As a result he made literature come alive, he made it personal at a time when Eliot and the New Critics were insisting on the essential impersonality of art.

Oxford, being full of clever young people competing with each other to see who was cleverest, was obsessed with the idea of intellectual brilliance. It seemed to be part of the fabric of the place. It impregnated the texture of the Portland stone, the dusty smell of the libraries, the air we breathed. Somewhere in *Finnegans Wake* an Oxford don appears, pushing a lawnmower that goes, 'clevercleverclever'. This may have been Joyce's revenge for his difficult life and what he considered to be his own unrecognized genius, but it catches the spirit of the place very accurately. Even the dullest dons seemed convinced of their brilliance, as though it went with the job description. Since only the brightest and the best were allowed into Oxford to study, it stood to reason that those who stayed on to teach them must be the brightest of the brightest.

So far as I was concerned, Empson was the incarnation of brilliance and the Critical Society had been founded in his honour. Naturally he was one of the first guest speakers we invited. This was around 1951, when his reputation as a poet was at its peak and he was, briefly, a cult figure, the man who was going to lead British poetry out of the booming neo-romantic wilderness of Dylan Thomas, George Barker and Edith Sitwell. John Wain had written an influential essay about Empson's verse in John Lehmann's magazine *New Writing*, but Wain, who was a sentimentalist, was besotted by Empson's sonorous villanelles and imitated them repeatedly. I preferred (and imitated repeatedly) Empson's spikier early poems, the ones that sounded like Donne in contemporary disguise: compressed and ironic and full of arcane learning, just the style to appeal to a literary young man with intellectual pretensions.

Empson was only recently back in England. Apart from a wartime stint at the BBC, he had been teaching in Japan and China since 1931, having been thrown out of Cambridge because, they said, he decorated the candles in his room with condoms. When I heard that he was living on Rosslyn Hill, not far from my parents, I wrote to him immediately, saying we'd be honoured etc., unfortunately we couldn't pay etc., but Oxford was full of his admirers and we'd throw a party if he fancied one. To my astonishment, he said yes.

Because of his poems and his brilliance and his alluring precocity, I suppose I was expecting another Donne, as lovingly described by his friend Izaak Walton:

He was of Stature moderately tall, of a strait and equally-proportioned body, to which all his words and actions gave an inexpressible addition of Comeliness.

The melancholy and pleasant humor, were in him so contempered, that each gave advantage to the other, and made his Company one of the delights of Mankind.

His fancy was unimitably high, equalled only by his great wit; both being made useful by a commanding judgment.

His aspect was chearful, and such as gave a silent testimony of a clear knowing soul, and of a Conscience at peace with it self.

His melting eye shewed that he had a soft heart, full of noble compassion . . .

Empson was moderately tall of stature, but his eyes were like ice and he clearly didn't much like what he saw when we all met up in Wallace Robson's rooms. I don't think it was just us, the welcoming committee, whom he disliked, though he made it plain that he couldn't imagine what he was doing in Oxford. The distaste he exuded was beyond that. It was like a spell of bad weather, steady and impartial: he disliked everybody, hated being back in England and seemed to dread the prospect of going to Sheffield, where he was soon to be installed as professor. He didn't cheer up until we started uncorking the wine which I had laid on in great quantities, courtesy of Levy & Franks.

He may have hated being back in England, yet he was a peculiarly English figure, bony and bleak and abrupt, more like a country squire than a poet and intellectual. What set him apart was the strange, Chinese-style beard which grew richly around his neck like a ruff, but stopped short at his carefully shaved chin. He spoke hardly at all and when he did his voice was so squeezed and plunging that it was almost impossible to understand. His talk to the society was a more or less impenetrable section of his book in progress, *The Structure of Complex Words*, which he read without much conviction from a dog-eared manuscript. After it was over we trooped back to Wallace's rooms and clustered around him while he lashed into the Mâcon, waiting for some brilliant remark that would redeem the boredom and disappointment. Empson, after all, was no ordinary academic. *Seven Types* was full of elaborate witticisms which we knew by heart and quoted remorselessly to our bored tutors, and the Critical Society had even been founded in honour of one of them: 'Critics, as "barking dogs" . . . are of two sorts: those who merely relieve themselves against the flower of beauty, and those, less continent, who afterwards scratch it up.' It seemed unjust that he would not deign to throw us some scrap as a reward for our puppyish devotion.

It was a long wait. Around two in the morning, when we were all drunk and exhausted, Empson stretched back on Wallace's sofa and pronounced in his roller-coaster accents: 'When Eliot, in the *Four Quartets*, says, "Time past and time present are both perhaps present in time future", he's making a grammatical statement. What he's really saying is, the future perfect equals the ablative absolute.' There it was, the aphorism we had been waiting for, straight from the horse's mouth and not yet in print. It almost made our misery worthwhile.

The next day, when Empson was safely on the train back to London, I asked Wallace what had gone wrong. Everyone is supposed to know that idols – especially idols who write books – have feet of clay, but this was my first experience of the old truth and I wasn't ready for it. Wallace was a kind man and he must have seen my disappointment. 'It's nothing personal,' he answered. 'He's a Wykehamist and that's what Winchester does to all its boys. It forces them all into the same mould. But the really original ones don't fit, so they get squeezed out of shape.'

It didn't end there and I think it was personal. Empson disapproved of me and my lot for the best possible reason – because he thought we were prigs. In fact, we were less priggish than he imagined, less priggish than they were in Leavis's Cambridge. But he smelt the Leavis contamination on everyone below a certain age and he disliked me because I'd picked up some of the lingo and the disdain that went with it. He was also a true eccentric. Whether or not the story of the condoms on the candles was true, Empson had been a wild man in the thirties and he had stayed that way. He wore that absurd neck beard not just because he had gone native during his spell in China, but as a sign of his difference.

Because I still admired what he wrote, I went on seeing him occasionally in Hampstead, but that didn't work out either. His house on Rosslyn Hill was large and comfortable and seedy, littered with empty bottles and overflowing ashtrays, and there was always a constant stream of cronies dropping by for a drink. Like them, Empson himself seemed to be just passing through, camping out in his own home and ready to move on at a moment's notice. He shared the house with his South African wife Hetta, who was tall and tough and hard-drinking, and her young South African lover, Peter Duval Smith, a pugnacious journalist who eventually died violently in Vietnam, though not in battle; he fell down the stairs of a Saigon brothel and broke his neck.

Hetta was more like a painter's moll than the wife of a professor and Empson seemed as bohemian as she was – a poet who just happened to teach at a university. That suited me fine; by then I, too, was on my way out of academic life. Yet bohemianism didn't stop him being obsessed with academic squabbles, especially with his long-running, savage battle with Helen Gardner, the Donne scholar and Empress of the Oxford English department. I couldn't understand why a man with his gifts should bother to bang on so virulently about all that trivia, and that reinforced my desire to get out. If university life could reduce even Empson to nit-picking and bickering, no one was safe. But I didn't much like his alternative. His version of the bohemian life was too chaotic, too cold, too hard-hearted for my taste and, because he must have known that, I think he held me in contempt. He was probably right. I was 20 when the fifties began and the young in the fifties were a pusillanimous bunch, careful with their emotions, respectful of their elders, and without much sympathy with the messy life. I was on my way out of that, too, though I didn't know it then and by the time I did Empson was no longer part of my life.

It astonishes me now how good young people of my generation were in comparison with the hippies and punks who followed. Naturally my parents didn't see it that way. To them, my sisters were the good ones, docile and biddable, and I was always trouble. I had been a monstrous little child, wilful, provocative, unsteady, as well as prone to bouts of feverish bad temper whenever the growth on my ankle went haywire. But Nanny had been hired to cope with that and Nanny knew how to soothe me down. Then she left, the war broke out, my sisters left home and my parents and I were left eyeball to eyeball with no one to stand between us. I couldn't wait to get away to boarding school and they couldn't wait to see me gone. Hostilities always resumed when I came home for the holidays – I even managed to squabble with my father about the music we listened to together every evening – but Oundle changed the battle orders.

My parents had always been proud of the fact that I was clever at school, and I had used it to shut them out. Whenever they started bickering, I'd say, 'I've got work to do' and march upstairs, knowing they couldn't object. In fairness to myself, I was no longer making model aeroplanes up there in the day nursery that I had transformed into my den; I really was studying, but the books I devoured were made more alluring by the sounds of marital strife filtering up from below. Oundle added games and heartiness to my armoury – squash on weekdays, rugger for Wasps on Saturdays, both followed by gallons of beer. My parents didn't object to drinking – that would have been hard for them to do since the Levy fortune was founded on booze – but they themselves drank very little and they looked down on it. Drink was for goys who knew no better; Jews had other things to do with their money, other things to do to their heads. A games-playing, beer-swilling son was not what they had had in mind when they sent me off to my expensive boarding school. Oxford changed all that, but by then the ropes mooring me to Glenilla Road were loosening and I was moving into a world they knew little about.

In terms of adolescent rebellion, beer, bad temper and bad behaviour don't amount to much, but they were the best that I and most of my contemporaries could manage. The truth is, we were a generation of good children, maybe the last of them, and certainly, according to Joan Didion, 'the last generation to identify with adults'. We may have squabbled with our parents, but we didn't disagree with them fundamentally about how life and society were ordered. Because I had no intention of going into the family business didn't mean that I couldn't see a connection between me and my father and my father's father – in addition to the fact that we all looked so alike. I was determined to live my life in my own way and on my own terms, but it never crossed my mind that I wouldn't finish up as a good citizen, obeying most of the rules, paying my taxes and fathering children who would also turn out to be good citizens, each in his or her different way.

It never occurred to us to do otherwise because, however knowing and sophisticated we tried to be, we were a profoundly innocent bunch, although not quite as innocent as the bunch who went before. Lucky Jim Dixon pulled rude faces and thought rude thoughts and even did rude things, but he ended up getting the nice girl in the conventional romantic fashion, just as Kingsley Amis ended up as a knight of the realm, a fixture at the Garrick Club bar and the author of a shelf full of books in which an increasingly surly hero gets the nice girl in the end. That innocence was killed off in the sixties when kids began to deny their connection with the past and set out to bring the whole edifice of society down around everybody's ears. Even so, *Portnoy's Complaint*, which seemed like the great subversive book of the time when it was published in 1969, is not really in the anarchic spirit of the decade. It was written by a member of my innocent generation and its true subject is the revolt of the good children. It was considered outrageous when it appeared, but the real outrage was Philip Roth's and he was outraged above all because he couldn't help being a good boy however much he wanted to be bad.

Quite simply, he had been born too soon. Like me, he belonged to a generation that didn't take drugs and didn't drop out, that still believed in high culture and high principles, yet was young enough – around 30 when the sixties began – to see that high-mindedness no longer applied and the new freedoms were there for the taking. For Roth and the other writers I think of as my contemporaries – Ted Hughes, Thom Gunn, Sylvia Plath – the war had been a school-time experience, something that was happening around the edges of the picture and, in Britain, it affected us mostly in terms of shortages – not enough to eat, nothing to buy and, because of the blackout, nowhere to go. But it was also exciting; it made life seem risky, adventurous, interesting – particularly since we were too young to fight. The Brits always flourish in adversity, no more so than during the Blitz when everybody behaved well, with unflinching patience and good humour and courtesy.

Unfortunately the wartime mentality lingered on long after the fighting was over and the excitement disappeared. Life in 'the age of austerity' that followed the end of the war, when luxury meant a steak or a banana or a cup of genuine coffee, seemed more pinched and deprived than it had been while the bombs were falling. Also more depressed: the country was exhausted by the battering it had taken and demoralized by the loss both of its empire and of its status as a world power. The hard times and the joylessness that went with them lasted well into the fifties, long past their sell-by date. When the good times finally began to roll, the shops began to fill and London began to swing, it felt like my life was picking up where it had left off during the Blitz and was once again becoming interesting. The sixties may have been mindless and muddled and awash with false sentiment, but at least they were full of possibilities. I was 30 when they began and I had crammed all my twenties with toil, just as Yeats advised. I couldn't wait to have some fun.

Larkin, Amis and the rest didn't see it that way, perhaps because they were older than I was. Only Amis had been in the forces, but all of them had come of age during the war and, for them, being young was not very different from being middle-aged and underprivileged. It meant boredom, routine, stupid orders that had to be obeyed, and the kind of resentment that swept Churchill from power in the 1945 election. (The Labour Party's landslide was not so much a vote for socialism as a vote against the officers by the enlisted men.) They were not interested in 'making it new' or any form of iconoclasm, but they were profoundly interested in class. They cultivated a kind of sergeants' mess touchiness about their rank and rights: condescending to us privates, their juniors, but resentful of anyone or anything, social or cultural, that seemed to pull rank on them.

They loathed Modernism and the things it had done to literature just as they loathed 'abroad' and the things that were done there to good plain cooking. Whenever you mentioned a Modernist writer to Amis, especially an American like Eliot or Pound, he pulled one of his famous faces – lips curling, eyes popping and rolling – to indicate disgust both for their literary pretentiousness and for yours in mentioning them. The first few times he went through this routine were funny; after that it was just depressing. For Amis & Co., Modernism was a plot by foreigners – Americans, Irishmen and Continentals, people with funny accents they could mimic – to divert literature from its true purpose; and their business was to get it back on its traditional track, back to Arnold Bennett and Galsworthy, back to Chesterton, Hardy and Housman.

Maybe this was a failure of imagination on their part or maybe it showed that wartime rules and regulations and deprivation suited them fine, but the effect on writing in general and poetry in particular was deadening. What passed for the latest movement in English verse in the mid-fifties – the nine poets included in Robert Conquest's 1956 anthology *New Lines* were, in fact, labelled 'The Movement' – was glumly unadventurous. In Movement terms the ideal poem was like a well-made essay; it had a beginning, a middle and an end, and it made a point. It was carefully rhymed, rhythmically inert and profoundly complacent.

The one poet in Conquest's anthology who was able to make something original out of the restrictions of the style was Philip Larkin – a master of the wry, self-deprecating put-down and slangy half-rhymes indicating disrespect ('sod all' with 'untransferable'). But, as everyone now knows, Larkin himself was mired in drabness. He seemed truly to have believed that life was as parsimonious with opportunities as he was with his own resources. He was a brilliant craftsman and he had a beady understanding of his own limitations, but generosity was not his style, neither in spirit nor in practice. If he had a philosophy of life – although the very idea of anything so high-flown would have made him cringe – it was summed up in one of his gloomy aphorisms: 'Sex is much too wonderful an experience to share with anybody else.'

Sex, in fact, was precisely what separated the kids of the sixties from their elders and Larkin famously knew it, although he derived his pleasure from the sense of being left out:

> Sexual intercourse began
> In nineteen sixty-three
> (Which was rather late for me) –
> Between the end of the Chatterley ban
> And the Beatles' first L.P.

That is not how it looked by the end of the sixties, when the upheavals had become politicized and were explained in terms of youthful outrage, as the reaction of a post-war generation to the Cold War as it was currently being played out by the Americans troops in Vietnam and the Soviet tanks in Prague. In 1970, when commentators on the sixties took stock of the decade's flaws, they were thinking of student riots and *les événements*, of the middle-class terrorists Jillian Becker called 'Hitler's Children' – the SDS, the Weathermen, the Baader–Meinhof gang and the Brigate Rosse – of a youth movement hijacked by political showmen like Jerry Rubin,

Abbie Hoffman and Danny Cohn-Bendit. But the starting-point for it all was not in the texts of any of the fashionable Marxists – Che or Mao or Fanon or Marcuse. It was in books that promoted the wisdom of madness, like R. D. Laing's *The Divided Self*, and the cutesy, vaguer slogans of love-in showmen like Allen Ginsberg and Timothy Leary: 'flower-power', 'make love not war', 'tune in, turn on, drop out'. And behind all that was a new sense of freedom that had begun with a simple medical breakthrough: the contraceptive pill, which liberated women to sleep around like men, with whomever they wanted whenever they wanted, as the fancy took them, without the fear of finding themselves pregnant, without being coerced into marriage. The first freedom was pharmaceutical; politics was icing on the cake.

Anyway, that is how it appeared to us children of the Cold War who came of age at the beginning of the fifties. Marching solemnly – and peacefully – against the Bomb, from Aldermaston to Trafalgar Square, or demonstrating – also peacefully – against apartheid was as near as we got to political protest. And we distrusted all the ideologues – the Stalinists who ruled the roost behind the Iron Curtain and laid down the law on the Left Bank, Senator McCarthy and his witch-hunters, the spineless grey men in Whitehall. Their squabbles seemed to have very little to do with the personal freedom we were after, the kind that was private and began in the dark and, unluckily for us, wasn't generally on offer until after the end of the Chatterley ban and the Beatles' first LP.

When I was an undergraduate it was impossible to imagine the easy-going sex life that kids took for granted a few years later. People my age had very little practical experience of sex, but we had almost as many theories as fantasies and most of them were derived from D. H. Lawrence. There was also Henry Miller, but he was as near as most of us got to pornography; we had to smuggle his books in from France, wrapped in brown paper and hidden at the bottom of our rucksacks. Lawrence, on the other hand, was literature – great literature, according to F. R. Leavis, the twentieth-century novelist by which all the others were judged and found wanting.

I never quite believed that, even in the days of my infatuation with Lawrence, but I was mesmerized by his independence and fire, and by the romantic life he led: the young genius and the older married woman, the outraged husband and abandoned children, the penniless, footloose life, wandering the globe in search of some primitive Eden where he could come to rest and flourish. He must have known he would never find it, but at least the search took him to wild and beautiful places, the kind of places I wanted to see, the kind of places my father yearned for while he sat in front of his thundering gramophone reading travel books.

Lawrence was the man who got away, who turned his back on 'the stuffy old show' and stayed free. It didn't matter that the great romance was far from romantic or that Frieda was a sexual adventurer, bored with her prim husband and provincial life, who went off with Lawrence expecting a brief fling and then found herself stuck with the consequences. It didn't matter that Lawrence and Frieda fought like dogs and that she was consistently unfaithful to him. He redeemed their turbulent marriage and made their unhappiness worthwhile by using it as the source for all his writing. For a young man with literary ambitions and a longing to break free, it was an irresistible story.

Unfortunately that was not how the gospel according to Lawrence was preached from Cambridge by Leavis. He disapproved of everything I loved about Lawrence. He dismissed the romantic, wandering life as 'homeless and childless vagabondage' and had no time for Frieda and her selfishness and what he considered her intellectual limitations. Nor did he have time for Lawrence's scandalousness; he refused to be a witness for the defence at the trial of *Lady Chatterley's Lover* and was only narrowly dissuaded from appearing for the prosecution. Lawrence had spent his life battling against prudery – his own prudery as well as that of the Mrs Grundys – but Leavis's Lawrence was a puritan, like Leavis himself, a keeper of the moral flame and a defender of the kind of Englishness which, Leavis thought, had been fatally corrupted, first by the industrial revolution, then by mass culture.

In other words, Leavis absorbed Lawrence into the 'Great Tradition' that descended to him via Jane Austen, George Eliot, Henry James and Conrad. But the Great Tradition was part of an intellectual enterprise that had more to do with criticism than creativity. It was the basis of a culture of high seriousness, founded on Matthew Arnold's belief that literature would replace religion as a source of true values and it was up to literary folk to set the tone. Literary critics had responsibilities beyond distinguishing the good from the less good or trying to explain how a poem or a novel worked and what it felt like to read the thing. They were the guardians of the moral and spiritual welfare of society and Leavis provided the catch-phrases by which virtue was measured. It seems absurd now that young prigs fresh out of school should sound off about 'maturity' and 'the quality of felt life', but it was heady stuff at the time.

Literary criticism in the fifties was not the starchy academic discipline, a subdivision of politics or sociology or history, that is now taught in most universities. It wasn't even the hard way to make an uneasy living that it became for me when I was reviewing full-time. It was a vocation, a religious calling, and we gave ourselves up to it in the same spirit as young people had volunteered for missionary work a century earlier.

There was a perverse logic in all this: for us, sex meant Lawrence, but Lawrence meant Leavis, and Leavis's Lawrence was the high priest of marriage. So we fell into marriage as quickly as we could, carelessly, with no idea of what we were getting into, out of an obscure sense of duty, our youthful lustiness railroaded by moral seriousness. All we really lusted after was lust itself, carnal knowledge, experience, but we persuaded ourselves that we were lusting after responsibility and maturity, and the only way to combine the three was marriage. It was a way of showing we were serious, a gesture of cultural solidarity, joining us to the Great Tradition, to Lawrence and the rest, to all those high principles and moral claptrap.

I mean that Leavis exerted a strange power even over those of us who were lucky enough not to be directly under his influence at Cambridge. I met him first when he came to talk to the Critical Society at Oxford, a slight, wiry man, bristling with nervous energy, intensely present, and with what Yeats called 'the terrible gift of intimacy'. Wallace Robson had that gift, too, but in a shuffling, self-deprecating way: he'd shake hands with a stranger at a party and say, 'My name's Robson. I'm impotent' and immediately the stranger, out of sheer embarrassment, would start confessing all his own secrets.

Leavis used his gift in a different way: he made you feel complicit. All through dinner before his talk that evening in Oxford, he denounced the 'metropolitan gang' of book reviewers and their conspiracy against critical standards. It was an extraordinary tirade – wicked, vehement, abusive and utterly spellbinding. We were so flattered to be swept up on the side of moral righteousness that we didn't have time to notice that his contempt for literary hacks and their dreadful trade hadn't stopped him reading and remembering all the reviews. He made us feel knowing: we, too, had the number of those slimy fixers, even though we only dimly recognized their names. We shovelled down our curries convinced that we were being let into the secret of how the literary world was run, that it was him and us against the forces of sleaze.

The subject of his lecture was Shelley, Shelley and his moral and poetic shortcomings – a sinister combination of self-indulgence and flabby thinking that amounted, Leavis said, to 'viciousness and corruption'. Shelley, of course, was an Oxford man and a great favourite with the dons who taught us, so Leavis's swingeing attack went down a treat with his iconoclastic audience. But it was a baffling performance, not least because what he was saying seemed so much at odds with his appearance. In his shabby corduroy jacket, with his shirt wide open at the neck, he looked just like the portraits of Shelley. Like Shelley, too, he seemed weightless, all fire and nerves and literary passion. And the passion made the lecture doubly puzzling. At one point he read Shelley's famous lyric 'When the lamp is shattered' and then explained, in detail, why it was a dreadful poem. But he had read it with such understanding and feeling that the reading made nonsense of the analysis. He made the poem sound beautiful and convincing, he made it sound like a masterpiece, so that when he trampled all over it he seemed to be doing violence to himself. It was a classic example of what Ronnie Laing called 'the double bind'.

Leavis made me glad not to be at Cambridge, glad to be spared the dogma and exclusiveness. Even at Oxford it was hard to escape the sense of moral purpose, but you could like Shelley or Hardy or Milton or Auden without being damned for it. It was the variety and differences, in fact, that made literary criticism interesting. To do the job properly you had to discard your own prejudices and preconceptions and try to get inside the head of each writer to see how his or her sensibility worked. It was a bracing and oddly ascetic discipline, motivated above all by curiosity: you had to be involved and disinterested at the same time; you had to be attentive to the pitch and tone of the voice; you had to listen to the inner movement of the words on the page, because that was how the writer's sensibility expressed itself.

Leavis himself used to claim that that was precisely his method, that all he did was present a text, interpret what he found in it, and then say, 'This is so, is it not?', as though his conclusions were open to debate. But that wasn't how it appeared to the outsider. On his own turf, Leavis was authoritarian and unforgiving, more like Stalin than Matthew Arnold, and he told his followers what they could believe in: the Great Tradition, the Line of Wit, Pope, Wordsworth, T. S. Eliot (intermittently), Dickens (later), the early poems of Ezra Pound and Empson, and very little else. Most of them took his word for law and never ventured beyond the prescribed texts.

A few years after I first met him I was invited to talk to the Doughty Club, the undergraduate literary society of Leavis's college, Downing. At that time I was the poetry critic and editor of the *Observer*, so I suppose they wanted me to talk about the machinations of the London literary world. I chose instead to read them an essay I had just written on *Jude the Obscure*, although I knew of course that Hardy was not included in the Great Tradition. The invitation had come from Leavis's assistant, Morris Shapira, but it was Leavis who gave me dinner on high table before the talk. Or rather, I ate dinner while he sat beside me, eating nothing, crumbling a piece of bread and denouncing the literary world to me and the bemused Master of the college. At the end of the meal he handed me over to Shapira and said he had urgent work to do and wouldn't be able to come to the meeting. He did not apologize. This was a process known as 'placing', a term Leavis had adopted from Henry James and applied rigorously to show where all writers, dead and alive, stood in his critical pecking order. I was supposed to recognize it for what it was (I did) and understand that I was not worth his wasting valuable time on.

I had guessed that this might happen when I told Shapira that I wanted to talk about Hardy, but I assumed that he and at least some of the students might have read the novel – if only to dismiss it. I should have known better. The essay was full of detail – I had written it as an afterword to an American edition of *Jude* – and it was clear that the audience recognized none of it. A cloud of unknowing settled over the room and lifted only when I quoted from the book. Then there would be a brief, disapproving stir that lasted until the extract finished. I'm sure I was boring them, but I'm also sure they were bored because they had no idea what I was talking about – no idea of the plot or the characters or of the tone and feel of the book. All they knew of *Jude the Obscure* was the bits I was reading them.

One of the extracts was the beautiful passage in which Hardy introduces the child nicknamed Father Time:

He was Age masquerading as Juvenility, and doing it so badly that his real self showed through crevices. A ground-swell from ancient years of night seemed now and then to lift the child in this his morning-life, when his face took a back view over some great Atlantic of Time, and appeared not to care about what it saw.

In the discussion after the talk, the students seized on this passage and tossed it around like puppies with a bone, trying to show that the images didn't hang together, didn't work, were overblown and pretentious. I read it again as convincingly as I could, and again they mauled it. Finally a burly young man stood up at the back.

'I think it's gibberish,' he said.

'You mean you don't understand it?'

'That's right. I don't understand it.'

I read it once more, very slowly, enunciating each word with care, as though to a mentally handicapped child.

'You still don't understand it?' I asked.

The young man squared his shoulders. He looked like a ploughboy trying to pick a fight in a pub. The expression on his face was truculent and smug. 'Aye,' he said. 'I still think it's gibberish.'

Shapira, who I knew was a subtle and intelligent man, was nodding approvingly in the front row. The patients had taken over the asylum and I couldn't imagine what I was doing there, pretending to reason with them. I tried to think of the sanest person I knew and came up, unexpectedly, with Mr Dreen. He may have failed to teach me Yiddish, but I had always admired his accent and the way he manhandled the English language. I threw up my hands just like he used to do and said, 'Maybe you don't speak English so good.'

And that was how the evening ended. It was also my last contact with Leavis and his disciples.

The Cambridge English department was famous for its rancorous in-fighting; Oxford was more easy-going and good-humoured, perhaps because nobody there had Leavis's genius for bearing grudges. Anyway, being young meant we didn't have to take the bickering seriously. Or rather, we pretended to take it seriously, we took sides and argued until our lips bled, but it was all a sideshow staged for the benefit of our elders. One of the best things about being young is that solemnity doesn't last. You keep making stabs at being adult, but appetite and the simple pleasure of being alive save you every time.

I'm talking about girls, of course, and girls continued to be a problem. In those days women and men lived in separate colleges and meetings between the sexes were tightly controlled. No women were allowed in Corpus after 6 p.m. and invitations to their colleges were desperately hard to come by. Not that it mattered since the girls mostly came from the same type of segregated, unisex schools as the boys and were equally shy and awkward. I steeled myself to chat to one or two young women I met at lectures and went through the expected motions – sat in a punt on May Day morning listening to the choristers singing on the top of Magdalen tower or poled up the Cherwell while some studious young lady lay back on the cushions and talked about Chaucer – but neither of us knew what to do next and that was as intimate as it ever got.

I kept my tiresome virginity until the beginning of my final year, then lost it to a married woman, the wife of one of the older undergraduates who had come up late to Oxford after national service. Like most married couples, they lived out of town, in a whitewashed Elizabethan cottage in a village straight out of Arnold's 'The Scholar Gipsy'. The cottage had a thatched roof and oak beams, but what I remember most was the cold. The only fire was in the big open hearth downstairs, but downstairs was too public in a small village with prying neighbours and we drew the line at using the marriage bed. So we filled the big iron bath tub with hot water and made love in that, or in the outsized airing cupboard that housed the electric boiler.

Having a married mistress made me feel grown-up and sophisticated. Raymond Radiguet's *Le Diable au Corps* became my favourite novel and when the film was shown at the Phoenix, the Oxford cinema that specialized in foreign movies, I went every day for a week and tried to picture myself as Gérard Philipe. Unfortunately it wasn't like that. When the lovers first go to bed together in the film the camera famously cuts to the fire in the hearth which slowly begins to blaze higher and higher. What we had was nothing like as triumphant. The woman was as nervous as I was and, married or not, she seemed almost as inexperienced. The husband was a shy, retiring man, so perhaps sex didn't figure much in their relationship. Maybe he assumed that I, too, was uninterested in it because he seemed glad to have me around. That made me doubly uneasy. It wasn't much fun.

Or perhaps the husband was too busy preparing for finals. In our last year all of us went a little mad with work. It was a beautiful summer, but I saw nothing of it: no croquet on the college lawn or punting on the Cherwell or beer at the riverside pubs. I spent all my time in the Corpus library – 14 hours a day as the exams got closer – slogging backwards and forwards through *Beowulf*, *Havelock the Dane* and *Gawain and the Green Knight*, trying to memorize inane textual variants and emendations. The narrow wooden benches made my backside sore, my shoulders and arms ached from leaning, the dusty smell clogged my nose and permeated my clothing. And each time I looked up, the great unread leather-bound folios on the shelves seemed to peer at me reproachfully, telling me there was no end to learning and I would never know enough to satisfy the examiners.

Long before we got to university the cult of the Brilliant First had been drummed into us by our schoolmasters, most of whom had failed to get one. It was what I wanted most of all when I went up to Oxford, wanted with the same baffled intensity as I'd wanted to play rugger for the First XV at Oundle. Freddie Bateson didn't approve. Because his socialism set him apart from the other English dons, the pupils he liked best and who followed his political interpretation of literature never got Firsts, no matter how clever they were. So when my results came through he responded with malicious glee, as though I'd tricked the examiners (whom he despised) but he and I knew better.

Sir Richard Livingstone, the President of Corpus, seemed to agree, though for different reasons. He was Oxford's most distinguished Platonist, a willowy old man with wispy white hair, a drooping moustache and an unworldly air, who floated around the quad, smiling benignly but recognizing no one. For him, serious scholars read Greats and English was not a subject worth bothering with, but it was his duty, as president of the college, to congratulate me. His letter was a masterpiece of double-talk: good about the degree, pity about the subject. (Isaiah Berlin told me he had had much the same response when he got Corpus's first First in PPE a couple of decades earlier.)

As usual, it was my mother who put the craziness in perspective. The results were posted late in the afternoon. I had been hanging around in the entrance hall of the Schools building for hours with a group of friends, but once the lists were pinned to the notice board and the babble started I just wanted out. I took a quick swig of someone's champagne, then slipped away and walked north, past the Radcliffe Camera and the Bodleian, past the White Horse pub on the Broad where I drank and played shove-ha'penny every day, past the red-brick Victorian mansions on the Woodstock Road where the married dons lived, on up towards the Woodstock roundabout. I don't know what I was feeling, but it certainly wasn't elation.

Finally I saw a telephone box, empty and in working order, so I called home, reversing the charges. My mother accepted the call grudgingly. As always, the first thing she said was, 'I thought you'd forgotten me.' As always, the second thing she said was, 'Is something wrong?'

'Nothing's wrong,' I said gloomily. 'It's just that the exam results are through. I've got a First. I thought you'd want to know.'

There was a moment of baffled silence, then she said, 'Oh good, dear. Does that mean you're a BA?'

That was exactly what it meant and would also have meant if I'd got a Third or a Fourth. It was the first sane response to the Oxford fever that I'd heard for three years.

By the time I went home a few days later my mother had been briefed about Oxford degrees and was doing her best to appear impressed. My father, of course, was delighted; he seemed to think it was the first step on the road to freedom for him as well as me. To celebrate they brought out a half-bottle of champagne which had been sitting in the little wine rack in the dining-room sideboard since Grandpa Dick had given it to them when I was born. My father uncorked it ceremoniously; after all, it was Moët Chandon '29, a great vintage. But there was no pop. The cork had dried out, the wine was flat and vinegary. And that seemed to sum it all up.

While I was an undergraduate I could think of nothing more desirable than to stay on at Oxford, reading in the ancient libraries. A don's life back then was pleasant and undemanding: a little teaching, a little research, the life of Riley at high table every evening, and maybe a book or a definitive edition to crown it all. The only ticket you needed was a First, but once I had the ticket and a research scholarship from the college to start me off, I was no longer sure that that was what I wanted to do for the rest of my days.

Or rather, I told myself that that was what I wanted, but my body thought otherwise. I was living in an ancient lodging house in Longwall, one of a crumbling row of eighteenth-century slums under what had once been the city wall. My landlady was a little gnome of a woman with a child's rosy cheeks and guileless blue eyes, and an astonishing halo of white hair. Her name was Elsie. Her parents had died when she was a baby and she had been taken in by her aunt who ran what was then – this was at the turn of the century – one of the best lodgings in town. The dark hallway was lined with framed sepia photographs of groups of sturdy, dignified young men with walrus moustaches, wearing boaters and striped blazers, holding cricket bats or oars or footballs – most of them, presumably, slaughtered in the trenches during the First World War.

'Aunty' had been a tyrant who had terrorized Elsie all her life, and though she had been dead for 20 years, Elsie still ducked her head sideways apologetically when she spoke, as though wincing away from her. She spent long hours in the tiny kitchen, tending the coal-fired stove she cooked on and sipping Guinness, but even there she kept her head cocked alertly, as though listening for Aunty's steely voice. And just in case that gaunt figure chose to reappear from wherever it was it had been biding its time, Elsie kept the house just as Aunty had left it – the same shredded carpet on the stairs, the wallpaper roses dark with age, and in the loo at the end of the overgrown garden under the crumbling city wall, an enamelled picture of a simpering child in a frilly dress, advertising Pear's Soap, watched you while you peed. Elsie hardly even dared to change the prices, which meant that I and the other lodger lived absurdly cheap but had to chip in each quarter when the bills came in. She brought up a jug of hot water every morning, a scuttle of coal for the fire and a three-course Edwardian breakfast, the best I have ever eaten.

My rooms were at the top of the house – a bedroom at the back and, across the landing, a sitting-room with a battered armchair, a mahogany table covered with a green baize cloth, and a view of the stately trees and lawns of Magdalen gardens, where the deer grazed. I loved the place – it was like a time capsule I'd stumbled into by sheer good fortune – yet every morning when I opened the door of my sitting-room I felt queasy. However hungry I was for Elsie's magnificent breakfasts, the sight of my books on the shelves each side of the fireplace made me nauseous. I suppose I was in shock from the demented blitzkrieg of work before my final exams, but it expressed itself physically. The mere glimpse of all that learning made me sick.

It seems strange that I can remember Elsie and the Longwall house and the little sitting-room with my pictures on the wall – a Scottie Wilson and a Picasso etching, but I'll come back to them – yet I can remember almost nothing of the work I was supposed to be doing every day in the Bodleian Library. The subject of my thesis was 'The Decline of Metaphysical Poetry' and it was a doctorate, not a B.Litt., because Oxford in those days was not interested in graduate teaching and, by some obscure quirk of academic bureaucracy, there were no formal requirements for a doctoral degree. The D.Phil. was supposed to be 'an original contribution to learning' and you were left to get on with it as originally as you could, whereas candidates for the more lowly B.Litt., who mostly came from other universities whose standards Oxford did not trust, had to take a course of lectures on bibliography and basic research procedures, and then sit an examination. I had no intention of ever sitting another exam or attending another lecture, so a doctorate it had to be. (Two or three years later, my mother finally got around to asking me why I was still at Oxford now I had a degree. When I told her I was working on a doctorate her face brightened. 'Darling,' she said, 'you're going to be a doctor!' 'A doctor of philosophy,' I replied. 'It's a graduate degree.' She shook her head despondently, as though all her worst fears had been confirmed.)

My supervisor was Hugo Dyson, a jolly don with a limp, at Merton College, next door to Corpus. I saw him just once. He gave me sherry, told me, between gales of laughter, that he knew nothing at all about 'Metaphysical pottery' (more laughter), and suggested I went to the resident expert, Helen Gardner. I wrote to her immediately, then wrote again twice, at decent intervals, until she deigned to reply with a letter that began, 'Constant dripping wears down the stone . . .' But it was another two terms before she agreed, reluctantly, to see me and I saw her precisely once more, two years later. At no point did she ever offer to read anything I had written on the subject. Eventually I ditched the doctorate and used my research to write a critical book, *The School of Donne*, which I gave as the Gauss Seminars at Princeton in 1958. Meanwhile, when I wanted to talk about literature I went to Wallace Robson or Freddie Bateson, or I drove down to Reading to see John Wain and Frank Kermode.

Wain was an inspiring figure in those early days, quick-witted and funny, shivering with energy and ambition. He had the 'flashing eyes and floating hair' of someone who had truly drunk the milk of literary paradise and had no intention of sobering up, although the role he had chosen for himself was very different: he saw himself as a mixture of Dr Johnson, George Orwell and J. B. Priestley, a plain man full of common sense, a plain-speaker who had no truck with pretension. He talked about books brilliantly, but only in pubs over a constant stream of pints, and preferably to an admiring audience. Perhaps he had picked up this habit from his mentor at Oxford, C. S. Lewis, whose weekly meetings with his disciples at the Lamb and Flag were celebrated in a villanelle that began: 'Big Jack Lewis is our hub./All around his spokes are we:/Hearty Christians in a pub.'

For a while Wain adopted me as his bright young protégé and even dedicated to me his first book of criticism, *Preliminary Essays*. ('A terrible title,' Wallace Robson said. 'It threatens there'll be more.') But friendship with Wain was a tricky business. He behaved like someone who was, and always would remain, his parents' golden child, the one who could do no wrong and whose every utterance was treasured. It was a childish arrogance, without any malice in it. He simply wanted to be the centre of attention and whenever he imagined he was being taken for granted he flounced out – out of pubs, out of parties, out of his cushy job at Reading University, even out of the Royal Literary Society – and each flounce was always bristling with higher significance. Leaving Reading, he claimed, inspired Larkin's 'Poetry of Departures', the poem that begins: 'Sometimes you hear, fifth-hand/As epitaph:/He chucked up every-thing/And just cleared off . . .'

Wain cleared off to write books, he said, though there were probably other, equally pressing reasons: the break-up of his first marriage, impatience with academia, boredom with Reading (when Oxford offered him a job a few years later he took it immediately). Whatever the reason, he made the act seem freighted with existential meaning, and back then we were all Existentialists, dressing in black, smoking Gauloises and pretending to read Sartre's *L'Etre et le Néant*. By leaving Reading, Wain became a home-grown version of Victor Kravchenko, the renegade Soviet spy whose book, *I Chose Freedom*, was big at this period in the Cold War. Because I myself was on the point of flouncing out of Oxford and freedom was much on my mind, I admired Wain's arrogance and the courage it took to turn his back on security. What I didn't admire was his self-importance – the way, for example, he recorded his resignations in his entry in *Who's Who*, as though the whole world was interested.

Perhaps it was the scholar in him, writing himself into literary history, or perhaps he was what he seemed, a man without much modesty who sincerely believed he was a great genius and would tolerate no one he couldn't patronize. Because he was such fun to be with when he was starting out, I didn't mind being patronized – he was pushing 30, I was 21, and at that age what did I know about anything? – but I never believed his own estimate of his talent. Finally, after 10 years of friendship, I wrote a review of his poetry which he considered disrespectful and I never heard from him again.

But I saw him twice. The first time was a cold, bright January day in 1973, a dozen years after my fatal review, when I drove up to Oxford for the day with my wife and small children to visit friends. I took them to the Trout at Godstow for lunch so that the kids could see the fish circling in the pool below the weir. When we drove out of the car park I saw an elderly figure in a long tweed coat and a flat cap, shambling along the road towards us, swinging a walking-stick. A retired don, I thought, out for his Sunday constitutional on the meadows. As he got nearer I saw that his mouth was twisted to one side and he was chattering dementedly to himself. It was only when I drew level with him that I realized that the mad old man was John Wain. I did not stop.

The last time I saw him was several years later, at a retirement party for Terry Kilmartin, the literary editor of the *Observer*. The room was packed and I was standing at the back, waiting for Clive James's eulogy to end so that I could shake Terry's hand and leave. Wain suddenly shoved his way through the crowd and came and stood beside me. Once again he was hard to recognize. His eyes were rolling and slightly crazy, his face was inflamed and puffy with drink. He looked at me, I looked at him, then he squeezed my shoulder in the way he used to do when I first knew him – part patronizing, part affectionate – and surveyed the room imperiously. 'Orwell said that at 50 every man has the face he deserves,' he announced, without bothering to lower his voice. 'Look at them, Al, just look at their dreadful faces.' Then he walked away as suddenly as he had arrived. I wanted to call after him, 'Who are you talking about? Them? Me? You?' but he had disappeared into the crowd. I never saw him again.

While I was still his protégé, Wain asked me to write a piece about contemporary poetry for *New Soundings,* a literary magazine for radio that he was editing for the BBC's Third Programme. 'Make it a squib,' he said. 'Something to stir them up a bit.' This was at the beginning of the fifties, when the Third Programme was glamorous and influential. Between the classical concerts and experimental music it broadcast talks by intellectual stars like Bertrand Russell, Isaiah Berlin and André Gide (in French, of course, and not translated) as well as the verse plays of Louis MacNeice, Dylan Thomas's *Under Milkwood* and, a little later, Beckett's masterpiece for radio, *All That Fall.* Nobody knew how many people actually listened to the Third Programme – the number was below the threshold at which audience research applies – but no one cared. Lord Reith ran the BBC and the Third Programme was his baby, his personal contribution to the nation's intellectual welfare, and there was no one in authority brave enough to argue with him about the public cost of excellence.

I was still an undergraduate when Wain invited me to say my piece, and very flattered. I laboured on the 10-minute talk like Moses laboured on the tablets of stone he brought down from the mountain, then went to London convinced my contribution would be dropped at the last moment. It wasn't and when the broadcast was safely in the can we all went around the corner to the George to celebrate. The George was the BBC pub (it was also owned by Levy & Franks, though I kept quiet about that) and while we were noisily getting drunk in one corner, Louis MacNeice was doing the same, lugubriously and on his own, at the bar.

I told my parents about the broadcast, although my father was already a Third Programme addict and would have heard it anyway, but I didn't mention it to my friends in Oxford and listened to it alone in my shabby little sitting-room, against a background of heavy static and the noise of the traffic fuming along Longwall. I was not sure I liked what I heard. So when the programme was repeated two weeks later, at six o'clock in the evening, I didn't want to be around. To avoid the temptation of switching on my radio I went to a pub near Corpus for a pre-dinner beer. But it was a hot summer evening, all the windows were open, and as I went along the lane to the Bear I heard my own voice spilling out on to the street. I paused, fatally. Then my voice stopped abruptly in mid-sentence, there was a blur of noise as someone spun the dial on the radio, then another voice said, 'The South Korean delegation . . .' I had been switched off. All that labour, all that expectation had got me nowhere. It was my first lesson in the vanity of human wishes, literary-style, and I never forgot it: nobody really listens.

Sometime during my first year at Oxford I exchanged my quite new motorbike for a sports car that was only a few months younger than I was. It was one of the original MGs, a 1930 M-type, painted British Racing Green and modified in its youth for the 24-hour race at Montlhéry. The louvred bonnet was fastened with leather straps, the windscreen swivelled flat, the petrol tank in the duck's-arse rear was so large that, in the seven years I owned the car, I never once had enough money to fill it up. Instead of side windows it had sheets of heavy celluloid which were inserted or removed according to the weather. The canvas roof kept out the rain only when the car was stationary and was held down by fasteners that popped open in every breeze. But it made a wonderful noise – it had a straight-through exhaust instead of a silencer – and the wind in my face made it seem much faster than it really was. I loved it like a child and kept it until it disintegrated.

I used to drive regularly to Reading, collect Wain and roar off to a country pub to swill beer and talk about poetry. But Wain at home was different from Wain in the pub or on the lecture platform. Even before 'he chucked up everything/And just cleared off', he cultivated a feisty bohemian image and his house on the edge of town didn't fit it at all. It was a neat bungalow with all mod cons, the embodiment of 'Books; china; a life/Reprehensibly perfect' in the Larkin poem he claimed to have inspired. He took great pride in the comfort of the place – the matching suite in the living-room, the fitted kitchen – and I didn't know what to make of that. Each of us had a chosen role; he was the roaring-boy of Reading's English department, I had my superannuated sports car, and both of us were defiantly free spirits. Wain the proud owner of an ideal home upset the balance. I felt I was being let in on a personal secret I preferred not to know.

He was, anyway, a touchy, temperamental friend, and after a while I found I was really going to Reading to see his colleague, Frank Kermode. Unlike Wain, who was always centre stage, Kermode was modest and self-deprecating, ironically gloomy, expecting the worst and responding to praise with 'Who? Me?' surprise. But his baffled incompetence was all a show. He was astonishingly well-read; he knew all the texts, all the facts, all the variants and emendations, and all the scholarly comment on them.

In theory, there was nothing unusual about Kermode's learning, except that he took it for granted and made it look so easy. But universities are full of learned people and, while I was pretending to research my thesis on the Metaphysical poets, I spent hours each day in the Bodleian surrounded by scholars, each one of whom knew – or was in the process of finding out about – everything there was to know about some tiny unaired corner of human knowledge. I used to peer at them over the top of the piles of books on the table in front of me, wondering what they did with themselves when the library closed, wondering if I was becoming like them. I was haunted by four lines from Pope's *Dunciad*:

> There, in dim clouds, the poring scholiasts mark,
> Wits, who, like owls, see only in the dark,
> A lumber-house of books in ev'ry head,
> For ever reading, never to be read!

Frank Kermode's scholarship was altogether different. He showed that it was possible to know everything about, say, a play by Shakespeare or a poem by Donne and still be shaken by the experience of reading it. More importantly, he seemed to have been impelled to find out about it because it had shaken him. He was equally passionate about music and very knowledgeable, but whenever he was presented with a work he hadn't heard before, the first thing he did was read the programme notes, as though he needed to know the historical context in order to listen properly. The scholarship was a habit of mind, but it was secondary to his love of the art itself.

Frank had served in the Navy during the war and the Navy had taken him to places he had probably never dreamed of when he was growing up in the Isle of Man – Iceland, Algeria, Australia, the United States. So he understood that there was a world outside the universities, a world with different priorities which he respected and handled well. That, too, was something I admired in him, although all I knew of the world elsewhere was what I had picked up during my five weeks in Grenoble. But it was enough to make me uneasy with Oxford. Each day I spent in the Bodleian made me more fretful and twitchy, and the knots in my head only began to loosen when I got in my car and drove down to London. The first glimpse of the shabby semis on the fringes of town, the brick tower of the Exide building and Hoover's Art Deco palace, the idea of all those millions of people crammed together and noisily getting on with their business induced in me a kind of peace. The closer I got to home, the more I believed that my scatty, cynical mother had been right all along: the dreaming spires of Oxford were really a dream and the world of learning was a sham. I wanted out, though I would never have admitted that to my parents.

I didn't even admit it to myself. I loved literature – reading it, writing about it and trying to write it myself. I also enjoyed teaching the handful of undergraduates Freddie Bateson had passed on to me to boost my research scholarship. It was the only life I was properly qualified for. But not yet, I told myself, not before I had got out of England and seen what the rest of the world was about.

So I applied for a visiting fellowship to America. Freddie, as usual, assured me I had no chance and urged me to put in for a junior lectureship that was being offered at Reading. Not that I had much chance there, he told me, but the competition would be less fierce. I wasn't up to Kermode's standards, he said, but Wain might put in a word for me. To Freddie's astonishment – and mine – I was offered the job, but by the time the letter from Reading arrived I had already been awarded a Procter Fellowship at Princeton. When I told Freddie the good news he grinned at me conspiratorially and shrugged his shoulders, implying I'd fooled them again but he and I knew better.

America changed my life, and though it didn't immediately end my Oxford career, it put it in perspective. At the end of my year in Princeton, I went back to Corpus to get on with my doctorate. Freddie was away for a year, lecturing in the States, so I took his place, tutoring the undergraduates and dining on high table. Dons did themselves proud in those days and the pomp and circumstance were hard to resist – the elaborate meals and great wines, the priceless silverware that was trundled out every evening, the port and walnuts after dinner in the panelled Senior Common Room. I fell for it all, but I didn't really believe in it. The silverware and six courses, the clarets, burgundies and hocks, the vintage port and the candlelight were an illusion staged for our benefit. I was always waiting for some sly, overweight pagan god to be lowered, creaking, in his chariot and tell us we'd been forgiven. Or tell us to wake up. It was great while it was happening, but it made me restless.

Maybe I was too full of America. Soon after I got back to Oxford, Lord David Cecil invited me to dine with him at New College, where he taught English. Cecil was Oxford's ultimate appreciative critic, all fine feeling and sensibility. His face was long and delicate, like a borzoi's, he wore beautifully cut tweeds and a velvet waistcoat, he spoke in sudden bursts and with a lisp. I got to know him just after I founded the Critical Society, when he invited me to join his weekly seminar in practical criticism, and, to our mutual astonishment and Freddie's scorn, we got along just fine.

Over dinner that evening I told him a long-winded story about a Princeton friend who spent a summer climbing in the Bugaboos, in British Columbia, ran out of money and had to hitch-hike back to New York with $5 in his pocket. It was a difficult trip all the way, but his worst moment was at three in the morning, in the middle of the Panhandle desert, when he had to use his clasp-knife to fight off a homosexual truck driver. It was a good story but I was over-dramatizing it, trying to impress Lord David with this macho new world I had discovered. He listened wide-eyed, as a good host should, until I had finished. Then he said, 'Good heaventh, I would have thuccumbed!'

Cecil was a master of high-table chat, but there were not many like him. I once sat through three courses – soup, fish, meat – listening to two professors of modern languages upstage each other with details of the dreadful boredom poor Stendhal had endured during his years in Civitavecchia. Finally a young physicist sitting opposite them butted in: 'For God's sake, it's only an hour from Rome on the *autostrada*!' They glowered at him, then at me because I had giggled, and that was the end of conversation at our end of the table. Neither of the professors ever spoke to me again.

High-table talk was part of the Oxford ritual; it went with the Latin grace before meals and the silver candlesticks; it was something a gentleman-scholar did well. I knew it was all a game, but the elaborate formality of it gave me no pleasure, the shows of pedantry and inadequately veiled bitchiness got on my nerves and I never properly got the hang of it. It wasn't the talk itself; I'd always enjoyed that and been good at it. What made me despair was the way talk was used as another of those snobbish games the English play in the name of class consciousness. Even the intellectual life was reduced to cleverness and style and facility. And because America had given me a taste of something more open and easy-going and energetic I wanted no part of it. That wasn't what I'd had in mind that evening at Glenilla Road when I told my parents and Uncle Teddy that I wanted to go to Oxford.

8

AMERICA

———◆◆———

'America is a willingness of the heart.'

Scott Fitzgerald

Going to America was a serious business in 1953. These days it takes a few hours and you are transported like any other product, packaged and passive, shifted from one queue to another, crushed in with all the other packages, breathing bottled air and with nothing to look at. Back then there were long railway-station farewells, then the train to Southampton and six days living it up on a stately liner – the elaborate rituals of the dining-room, the hours walking on deck or playing shuffleboard or reading out in the breeze wrapped up in a blanket, bouillon at 11, cocktails at six, shipboard romances – six days in suspension between two lives, between the receding wake and the empty horizon ahead.

I spent a lot of time at the stern, watching the distance grow between me and Glenilla Road, saying goodbye to all that. I was on my way at last. On the final morning I got up early and crowded on to the forward deck with the other hopefuls for a first dazed and dazzling glimpse of Manhattan's downtown skyscrapers hanging like a mirage above the horizon.

Lynn Bartlett was waiting for me behind the Customs shed on the pier. He was a big man – belly, big shoulders, a big, round face and bottle-top glasses. Even so, he seemed constricted, as though he needed even more space to expand into and would burst out of his skin if he didn't find it. Hence his galvanic laughter, his constant fusillade of jokes and a jollity that seemed close to despair. I had met him at Oxford, where he had been studying for a B.Litt. after serving in the US Air Force during the war. According to Wallace Robson, who was one of his examiners, Lynn's thesis was the best he had ever read and should have been published as it stood. But Lynn was a perfectionist. He said the book needed rewriting and did nothing about it, blaming his lowly job at Vassar and a teaching workload that overwhelmed him. He was also overwhelmed by the boredom of trying to drum great literature into the heads of fidgety adolescent girls. I found them shockingly attractive whenever I visited him there, but I was 10 years younger than Lynn, I wasn't married and I hadn't fought in the Second World War. So he published nothing, stayed on at Vassar and – because a B.Litt., however brilliant, is not a doctorate – it took him years to inch his way up the academic ladder.

We piled my trunkful of books and my suitcases into a taxi and set off for Penn Station. But when the driver heard my English accent he decided I should see some New York sights before I caught the train. He stopped at Times Square opposite what was then the city's most spectacular billboard: the statue of a gigantic woman posed against a real waterfall, advertising Bond clothes.

The driver shifted his cigar from one side of his mouth to the other and said, 'How'd you like to tackle her, buster?'

He wise-ass cabby, me wide-eyed tourist. 'Golly!' I exclaimed, in my best Oxford accent. The driver winked heavily at Lynn.

The big surprise he saved for Penn Station. He had been honking his horn and cursing other drivers all the way; then, as he drove off, he grunted resentfully through his cigar, 'Have a nice day!'

I had never heard the expression before. 'Have a what?' It had never crossed my British mind that a nice day could possibly be an option.

The Fulbright Commission had paid my fares from England and given me a voucher for the train journey to Princeton. The clerk at the ticket office looked like a two-bit poker hustler – bow-tie, white shirt, armbands, braces and a green eye-shade. When I handed him the voucher he did not look up. All he said was, 'Jeez-zus, another limey apple-knocker.'

Behind me Lynn was shaking with crazed laughter. He was swollen with pleasure and pride, as though he'd staged the whole show himself. 'Welcome to the U S of A,' he cackled.

For me, it was love at first sight. I loved the rudeness and bustle. No evasions, no duplicity, no false shyness. You could say what the hell you wanted and nobody took offence because that was how the game was played. (In one of the jokes going the rounds at that time, a visiting Brit asks a cab-driver, 'Could you tell me how to get to Union Square, please, or should I just go fuck myself?') This was the high noon of the American century. They had just won the war – with a little help from their friends

– sly old Eisenhower was in command, just as he had been on D-Day, and the economy was booming. Being the son of my foolishly generous mother, I couldn't get over the sense of plenty, the sheer lavishness of the American way of life: steaks as big as the plates they were served on and sandwiches stuffed with more meat than we saw in a fortnight back home. (Question: 'Why are New York deli sandwiches so big?' Answer: 'Two thousand years of guilt.') I loved the gleaming kitchens with their labour-saving appliances (the kitchen at Glenilla Road, like most other British kitchens back then, didn't even have a fridge; the food was kept in a cavernous, stone-flagged pantry). I loved the endless parade of pretty girls, with their dazzling teeth and shampooed hair and neat clothes and deodorized armpits, who seemed so friendly and talkative and at ease with themselves, so unlike the shabby, tongue-tied heavies I'd known at Oxford. Above all, I loved the energy of the place, the busyness and cynicism of New York and the intellectual openness, even in staid Princeton, where any outlandish idea was thought to be worth arguing about and no one had heard of Leavis's moral superiority or the art of the snide put-down.

Princeton in the fifties, however, was truly staid and, superficially, rather English. It reminded me of Oundle: mock Gothic, few Jews, two or three token blacks and no women at all, except at weekends when flocks of chattering blondes in camel-hair coats were shipped in for football matches and fraternity parties. The English faculty was tweedy and pipe-smoking and conservative, but there was a splinter group centred on R. P. Blackmur, and that was where the action was.

Richard Blackmur was one of the first and most original of the New Critics but, unlike the others, he had developed his skills outside the university and it showed. Graduate schools at that time were swarming with young people trying to imitate the brisk simplifications of Cleanth Brooks, but no one in his right mind tried to imitate Blackmur. He was a poet, a man obsessed with the nuances of language, alert to every vibration and pause. He was also in love with European culture and thought of himself as a descendant of America's great Europe-worshipping high-stylists, Henry Adams and Henry James. Blackmur's style was as oblique as theirs, elliptical, full of unexpected analogies and difficult jumps, yet also elegant and sonorous. I suspect he had developed it, in an idiosyncratic way, from Henry James's famously obscure prefaces, though the essay Blackmur wrote on them was itself famous for being even more obscure than its subject. Yet none of this was mannerism or affectation. His talk was as dense and probing as his prose, full of allusions and half-buried quotes, because that was how he was – a private, difficult man with a passion for literature which he had lived out on his own terms.

What he was doing at Princeton was a mystery, though on one level he and the university suited each other fine: Princeton was a conservative establishment and Blackmur liked to call himself a 'Tory anarchist'. The Tory in him expressed itself in a lordly taste for good food and expensive hotels, as well as for great literature, but he made his own rules intellectually. His more conventional colleagues resented the fact that he seemed to know as much about, say, St Augustine or Vico or Montaigne as he did about subjects he was supposed to know about, like modern poetry. I think it induced in them a certain envious frustration which they thinly disguised as disdain: after all, they implied, despite his reputation as a subtle literary critic, despite his poetry, despite even his phenomenally wide reading, the fellow had never attended a university and didn't have a degree.

Blackmur's formal education had ended when he graduated from Cambridge (Massachusetts) High and Latin School. He had continued it in his own time and fashion while working at the Mandrake Bookshop in Cambridge and unofficially sitting in on lectures across the road at Harvard. Back in those days, when he was starting out, he was a bohemian figure, an old-style independent man of letters who wrote poetry and criticism for a living and was even, briefly and in his restrained way, something of a dandy. He was also a regular contributor to and associate editor of *Hound and Horn*, one of the most influential of all American little magazines, and the articles he wrote for it were brilliant examples of what later became the New Criticism. He kept going as a freelance writer for the better part of 20 years. Then, in 1940, when he had published two books of criticism and a collection of poems, Princeton hired him to teach creative writing. Eleven years later they gave him a professorship, but the only degrees he ever received were honorary: a Doctor of Letters from Rutgers in 1958, when he was 54, and an MA from Cambridge University when he went there as Pitt Professor in 1961.

Although Blackmur was Princeton's literary star, he seemed isolated from the bland scholars who ran the English department. Those who rallied around him were younger, livelier and mostly without tenure, people he brought into the creative writing programme for a spell – including the young Saul Bellow, Delmore Schwartz and John Berryman – who then moved on. Apart from them, Blackmur chose most of his friends from other disciplines – music, modern languages, philosophy, the sciences – and from the Institute of Advanced Study, the sanctuary for some of the distinguished refugees from Nazi Germany, such as Erwin Panofsky the art historian and Erich Kahler the social philosopher. As an excuse for bringing together these different friends with their different interests, he thought up and organized the Christian Gauss Seminars in Criticism, which turned out to be the brightest intellectual happenings in Princeton. Attendance was by invitation only and no students were invited. Whatever the topic, there were always fewer specialists in the audience than people who were experts in other fields. The formula was invariable: one hour's lecture followed by one hour's discussion, then back to Blackmur's house to drink and talk into the small hours.

Blackmur was at his best at those impromptu parties. Surrounded by people who liked and admired him, white-haired and round-bellied, a benign and highbrow Father Christmas dispensing whisky in tumblers big enough to wash your hands in, he would relax and expand and argue for hours in fierce, sidelong bursts. He had a curious, attentive way of holding his cigarette – between his third finger and his thumb – which made him seem continually poised to ask some unanswerable question.

Blackmur became a great friend and was my first – and only – patron. In 1955 he engineered a fellowship for me from the Rockefeller Foundation, which gave me a year in America to write my first book, a study of modern poetry which I dedicated to him. Two years after that he invited me back to give the Gauss Seminars – for which I wrote my second book – and that winter, when my first child, Adam, was born in Princeton, Richard became his godfather. Yet in some odd way I never really knew him. Although we talked endlessly, he remained implacably private. He never mentioned his past or his parents or the wife he had divorced a couple of years before I went to Princeton. And when the sweet-tempered woman who was with him for years finally moved out he never mentioned her either. He talked about his garden and the flowers he tended like children, but that was as close as he ever got to discussing his personal life. And – this is what is odd – that is how I felt it should be. He was 25 years older than me, but that wasn't very old; he was a mere 49 when we met, still a middle-aged man in his prime. Yet I always thought of him as an old man, far older than my then 60-something father.

Despite his intense intellectual presence, Blackmur was physically tentative and uncertain, as though he had run out of energy long ago. He drank a great deal but everybody drank a great deal back in the fifties, when bourbon was America's *vin du pays*. Although I don't remember seeing him drunk, the side-effects were not helpful: the booze made him put on weight and exacerbated some illness that affected his legs, so that walking became painful and difficult and slow. That, too, he didn't mention. He kept his troubles to himself, let no one in and left his friends to cope silently with the spectacle of this grim deterioration. He himself seemed to take it for granted as his natural state, as though his defining attribute, like a tortoise's, was great age.

During the last few years of his life, as he got iller, the loneliness tightened around him. His beautiful little house in Princeton never seemed quite full enough, despite the piles of books and papers everywhere and the friends and students continually dropping by. He had always idealized England for all the subtleties Henry James read into the place and which probably never existed, so the year he spent there, in 1961–2, was a terrible let-down. He was the first literary man to hold the Pitt Professorship of American History and Institutions at Cambridge, but the rancorous English Faculty, rapt in its usual in-fighting, ignored him, and the undergraduates stayed away from his lectures because they were too hard. When I saw him in London, in the beige gloom of the old Park Lane Hotel, he seemed bleak and disappointed.

In the end the loneliness got into his writing. His work had always been difficult, but the difficulty of the later essays was radical and profound, whereas that of his earlier work was simply one of adjustment. He had, from the start, the writer's equivalent of absolute pitch: he knew the precise weight and vibration of every word, and his insights into these faint modulations controlled what he had to say. Yet once you had tuned into this very high frequency, the discriminations were clear, graspable and often rather witty. Despite his New Critical principle of never making a statement he couldn't prove from the text, he obstinately used literature for purposes of his own, purposes, as he put it, 'of reaching understanding of the grounds of action and of finding a frame for decision, or alternate decisions' – which is a characteristically roundabout way of saying that he used literature to understand how he lived his own life.

He was also preoccupied with what he saw as the crisis of modern art: the artist's need of a framework of values at a time when the framework was ceasing to exist. So he built up his values bit by bit by his loving, unbiased attention to the work of art and his endless awareness of the resources and reverberations of language. Meticulously, fastidiously, he seemed to re-create each work from the inside out, without ever allowing his judgement to be submerged by the details. He was selfless as a critic but he knew what he knew and wasn't easily fooled.

Even in his early essays Blackmur the critic and Blackmur the poet were never far apart. As he grew older and lonelier the poetry stopped and the prose became more elliptical and gnomic. He ceased to be interested in the everyday business of practical criticism and became absorbed in more general themes: the function of the arts, the function of the intellectual and, above all, the function of reason in an increasingly irrational century. He was happiest lecturing in Japan, where his hosts called him 'Sage' and treated him as a source of wisdom, not as a literary critic.

What he had to say was subtle and original but often it was almost impenetrably difficult. Most of his late essays were delivered as lectures and God knows what the audiences made of them. I suspect Blackmur himself didn't much care by then. At some relatively late point in his career he seems to have come to the conclusion that, however flattered his audiences may have been to be treated as equals, they had never really understood what he was getting at. So he simply wrote in his own way and let the audience go hang. The more his influence seemed indirect and his position marginalized and his loneliness complete, the more opaque his writing became. Perhaps this was what he was getting at when he adopted Montaigne's motto: '*Epecho*: I will not budge, I will suspend judgement.'

The last time I saw Blackmur – in Princeton, in 1965, not long before he died at the age of 61 – he seemed ill and depressed, as though he realized that all that purity and concentration and effort had got him nowhere and what he had been writing all along was an epitaph on a tradition. He belonged to a period of high cosmopolitan sophistication in American culture; his heroes were Henry James and the great Modernists – Eliot,

Yeats, Joyce, Wallace Stevens, Marianne Moore. Now all that was being swept away, the fashion was for what he called 'that easiest of all reservoirs, spontaneity', and the influence was with the tradition of 'the barbarians', Whitman and Pound. He had always been, in his own words, 'a hospitable intellect', but only up to a point, and I think it made him bitter to see everything he believed in swept down the hippie drain.

A dozen years earlier, however, when I first arrived in Princeton, everything still seemed possible. The fifties are written off now as complacent and conformist and timid, and maybe they were. Maybe the Cold War and the constant threat of nuclear destruction lay like an undetonated bomb deep in our collective psyche, sapping our initiative and keeping us in line. Compared with the Dr Spock-reared generation who came of age in the sixties, we were well-behaved and dutiful, but that wasn't how it felt at the time. Up on Goon Hill – the Graduate College – we spent hours each day in front of the college's one television set watching the Army–McCarthy hearings, cheering on Joseph Welch, the Army's lawyer, jeering at Cohn and Schine and the junior senator from Wisconsin. The know-nothings and petty shysters were being given their comeuppance by a master of elegant high style. It was the best show in town. It may have fed our intellectual arrogance but that itself was just part of the intellectual buzz on which we thrived and the Gauss Seminars seemed to be the centre of it all.

All sorts of other subjects were buzzing in Princeton at that time. Einstein and Oppenheimer were at the Institute of Advanced Study (Oppenheimer and Blackmur had lunch together each week at Lahière's Restaurant) and one of the first computers was being built at Princeton. (A boffin called Bigelow, who had designed the electric chimes for the Graduate College bell tower, took me to see it. It occupied a big room filled from floor to ceiling with shelves full of valves and ropes of wires. When he set it in motion to multiply two not very large numbers the whole contraption buzzed and clicked and hissed like a primitive combine harvester.) But physics was too difficult for the uninitiated, and because of the Cold War, the atom bomb and the Alger Hiss scandal, it was also too political. Politics were out and all the squabbling that had occupied the intellectuals during the 1930s – the Stalinists versus the Trotskyites, the Cannonites versus the Shachmanites – had been transferred to what had previously been a non-argumentative, rather amateur field of enquiry – literature and the criticism of it.

This was the period of the great literary quarterlies – the *Partisan, Hudson, Kenyon, Sewanee* – when criticism was the hot topic, not the self-enclosed academic discipline it became 30 years later when The Theory was The Fashion, but something that really mattered because it concerned itself with all the things that no one else seemed eager to discuss – morals and insight and how to live your life. For some critics – especially ex-Marxist New Yorkers like Dwight Macdonald and Philip Rahv – criticism was a continuation of politics by other means; Lionel Trilling, who had already rejected politics in favour of the inner world, used it as an extension of psychoanalysis; Blackmur loved it for its own sake, purely, because literature, for him, was the world and criticism as he practised it was an art form in its own right. But the man who brought everything together was Kenneth Burke and, for him, criticism was a form of intellectual discourse that included all the others – psychology, anthropology, linguistics, Aristotelian philosophy, along with anything else that happened to catch his fancy.

Burke was like everybody's image of the nutty professor: high forehead, a receding mop of electric white hair, a moustache like Einstein's, wild eyes and a distracted manner. He once spent a whole term analysing the first page of *Moby Dick* with a bemused class of students at Bennington and he laboured for years on two fat volumes, *A Grammar of Motives* and *A Rhetoric of Motives*, which used literature as the starting-point for a comprehensive philosophy of language and human conduct. He had spent time at the Institute while he was revising the manuscript of his great work, so naturally Blackmur invited him to the Gauss Seminars to test out some of his ideas. And because Burke was a polymath, a one-man Institute of Advanced Study who knew everything, he embodied the spirit of the Seminars even more comprehensively than Blackmur himself.

Burke's Gauss lectures were before my time but he turned up once to a seminar during my first year at Princeton and afterwards a group of us got into an argument with him. It was still going strong when Blackmur threw us all out, so Burke invited us back to his house to finish it. I don't remember what the argument was about but I remember the drive – 40 minutes on back roads through a dark, snowy landscape with two young,

17. Climbing in Wales, 1962 (*John Cleare*)

18. With Mo Anthoine on the way down from the Comici route on the Cima Grande di Lavaredo, 1964 (*John Cleare*)

19. With Torquil Norman in his Tiger Moth, 1999 (*Anne Alvarez*)

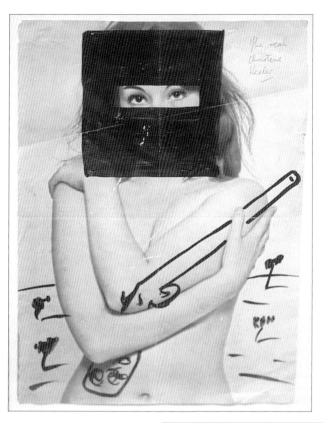

20. Christine Keeler by
Sidney Nolan
(*author's collection*)

21. Christine Keeler
by Charles Blackman
(*author's collection*)

22, 23, 24, 25. John le Carré visits Russia (*author's collection*)

26. At the poker table, 1991
(*R. Paul Miller*)

27. As seen by Mark Boxer
(*author's collection*)

28. Jill Neville (*Anthony Barrell*)

29. Tony Holden and Cindy Blake (*author's collection*)

30. Katie Alvarez in old age
(*author's collection*)

31. Luke and Kate Alvarez, 1998
(*author's collection*)

32. Anne Alvarez, 1968 (*author's collection*)

untenured professors and their even younger wives. In those days most of the academic wives seemed to be much younger than their husbands – trophy second wives, alluring and full of spirit, who had been students at colleges where the husbands had taught before coming to Princeton – and the sexual charge between them made the air crackle. That combination of sex, booze, fierce argument and the suppressed violence of respectable people behaving badly seems now to embody exactly how it felt to be young in the fifties. Edward Albee immortalized it in *Who's Afraid of Virginia Woolf?*, and John Berryman caught it precisely in the poem 'New Year's Eve': 'I set my drink down hard. Somebody slapped / Somebody's second wife somewhere.'

That night the sexual charge and the stimulation of arguing flat out with a man as clever as Kenneth Burke seemed to be one and the same thing, an interchangeable excitement. Burke's house was deep in the countryside, with forest at its back and a winding blacktop in front. When we arrived – it must have been well after one in the morning – his two teenage sons were sitting in front of a wood fire, playing three-dimensional chess. That, too, seemed to fit the scenario. We went on arguing until sun-up, then drove back to Princeton through the icy orange dawn still arguing, while the wives slept sweetly in the back of the car. I wish I could remember what we'd been arguing about but it doesn't matter. All I remember is feeling exhausted and content. That night had been how I imagined the intellectual life would be before I went up to Oxford and saw what they did to it there.

Three years later I met Burke again in the middle of a crosswalk on Fifth Avenue. He was walking west, I was walking east and he scarcely bothered to say hello. He simply picked up the argument – whatever it was – exactly where we had left off in the New Jersey dawn and we kept at it, drinking coffee in a Chock Full O' Nuts, for two hours. Then he hurried off to catch a train. I never saw him again.

> In the chambers of the west we'll meet again
> I will say Randall, he'll say Pussycat
> and all will be as before
> whenas we sought, among the beloved faces,
> eminence and were dissatisfied with that
> and needed more.

John Berryman wrote that about his friend Randall Jarrell. As it happens, Jarrell was not one of the young writers who gathered around Blackmur, though like most of them – Berryman, Schwartz, Lowell, Roethke – he died badly and too soon. But whenever I read Berryman's lines about the beloved faces I always think of Blackmur and Princeton, of being young and ambitious and full of ideas, and of arguing all night with Kenneth Burke. And sometimes the poem makes me wish that I, too, believed in an afterlife – if only because I know that if I ran into Burke up there we'd go on with the argument and all would be as before.

When Blackmur was a young man in Boston he had dressed like a *fin de siècle* poet in a velvet jacket, a flowing tie and, sometimes, a cloak. When he moved to Princeton he put on tweeds and polished his shoes, just like the other faculty members, but that still did not make him an authentic academic and his colleagues never let him forget it. Neither did he. That is why the people he brought in were mostly writers, mavericks with a passion for literature but more interested in doing their own work than in burrowing away at other people's. Because their passion for books was real, some of them were even learned in their quirky ways, but Berryman was the only one who managed to combine his own poetry with a genuine interest in scholarship. It was a difficult balancing act – maybe the strain of maintaining it contributed to his chronic alcoholism – because, on both sides of the Atlantic, there was the same unbridgeable rift between the scholars who knew about textual variants and background detail and the critics who tried to explain what a work of art was doing and how it did it. The scholars looked down on the critics as amateur dabblers while the critics dismissed the scholars as pedants and treated the literary essay as an art form in its own right.

When the New Critics were riding highest, in fact, some of them behaved as if the art they practised was far more demanding than the poet's or the novelist's. The critic was the authority who interpreted the work in elegant prose, rationalized its inconsistencies and generally made it intellectually respectable. The writer was just the poor schmuck who provided the raw material.

Yet, grandiosity apart, good criticism really was a modest kind of art. What I liked about it was that, to do it properly, you needed an odd combination of detachment and attention – an attentive state of detachment. To find out what makes a writer tick or how a poem hangs together you have to let go of your own sensibility and immerse yourself in that of a better writer – watching, thinking, listening and giving yourself up all at the same time. Because I was trying to write poetry of my own, the business of criticism seemed a relief, a welcome current of free air blowing through my murky preoccupations, as well as a constant reminder of how good real poetry could be. Before Princeton, however, I'd always assumed that if I wanted to write criticism I'd have to stay in academia and pretend to be a scholar. Now I was at a university where writing seemed more important and worthwhile than scholarship. It was a paradox: the visiting fellowship at Princeton was my reward for having worked so hard at Oxford; but this entry ticket to academic life had landed me at a university where, thanks to Blackmur, an academic career seemed second-best. And also thanks to Blackmur, I could see that it might be possible to make a living as a writer without teaching.

It was all a matter of luck and timing. The fellowship I had at Princeton – the Procter – was bundled up with a similar fellowship at Yale – the Henry – and candidates had no say in which they were given. Would my life have worked out differently if I'd gone to Yale? Probably not much. When you are starting out everything seems to depend on chance – the places you land up in, the friends you make, the lovers you find – but in the end it's like a poker game: the cards go around, the luck gets distributed pretty evenly and all that really matters is how you use whatever talent you have. That first year in the States I was on a roll.

I had two rooms in the Graduate College – a large study and a tiny bedroom, just like at Oxford – and I shared a bathroom with whoever was in the matching set of rooms across the landing. That fall it happened to be V. S. Pritchett, who was in town to give six lectures on the modern English novel to the Gauss Seminars. Pritchett was the star reviewer of the *New Statesman*, which at that period was the best and most influential magazine in England. Kingsley Martin and his henchmen hammered away at the Government at the front of the paper; the literary pages at the back, edited by Janet Adam Smith, published the classiest reviews in town. Nowadays university dons are constantly reviewing for the London papers or sounding off on television, but back then literary reviews were written by literary people. Dons rarely got a look in and they resented it.

As a result most of them were like Leavis: they viewed all that liveliness with a bilious eye, as though it were a personal insult, and wrote off the metropolitan literary world as an alien planet on which dark forces plotted against literary values.

Being straight out of Oxford, I imagined Pritchett would be one of the aliens: devious, suspect and threatening to my moral purity. In fact, he was garrulous and funny, a small, tweedy man with a pipe, fizzing with energy and utterly lacking in self-importance. He was also a professional writer, the first one I had ever met, a genuine man of letters who made his living entirely by his pen, without moonlighting as a teacher or a journalist or a civil servant or a taxi-driver. Short stories were what he wrote best – he had a genius for the form, like a British Chekhov – but short stories are an unreliable source of income, so he wrote reviews to pay the bills. Pritchett's reviews were not the usual brief résumés and snide put-downs that pass for criticism in most literary pages; they were the real thing, packed with insight and shrewd judgements, even though they were absurdly brief by American standards: a 'Books in General' essay, the lead review in the *New Statesman*, ran to 1800 words, a mere postcard compared to Blackmur's lecture-length meditations. Like John Updike, who, among his many other talents, is also a marvellously perceptive critic, Pritchett was an insider who made other writers' books and inner worlds come alive for the reader because he brought an author's preoccupations to bear on everything he read.

And he had read everything. So had Blackmur, of course, and Frank Kermode and Wallace Robson, but listening to them when they were in full flow often made me uneasy about how little I knew. Pritchett was different. He had begun devouring books as a small child – it was his way of keeping his impossible parents at a safe distance – but he had left school at 15 to be apprenticed in the leather trade and had continued his education in his own time and on his own terms while he scraped a living – first in lowly office jobs and as a commercial traveller, then as a jobbing journalist knocking around France and Spain, Ireland and Appalachia. Literature had kept him going through all this but it was also part of the highly unliterary life he was leading. He talked about books and authors as though they were living presences, people he thought you should meet, with quirks and weaknesses and bad habits, an extended family of aunts and uncles, cousins, in-laws and the usual black sheep. There was nothing self-congratulatory in the way he talked about them. It wasn't even an invitation to read more. Instead he seemed to be encouraging you to keep your eyes open and enjoy life. 'I have always thought of myself – and therefore of my subjects – as being "in life",' he wrote in *Midnight Oil*, the second volume of his autobiography; 'indeed books have always seemed to be a form of life, and not a distraction from it.'

Wherever he went, he created his own microclimate, fizzing with energy and appetite. He was addicted to writing like some people are addicted to the bottle. He wrote every day and seemed able to write anywhere – in the waiting room of Grand Central Station, on the train and, probably, in his head as he walked the last few hundred yards to wherever he was going. He was a masterly stylist, always refining, sharpening, paring away the excrescences. But people interested him more than style and it was their excrescences that interested him most – the little stabs of greed, lust, kindness and hypocrisy, the patter they keep up while the crazy engines whirr away out of sight.

'During the war,' he wrote in *Why Do I Write?*, an exchange of letters with Elizabeth Bowen and Graham Greene, 'when I was collecting material for an official pamphlet, I was obliged to question a number of railwaymen about the work they did, their hours, their pay, their experiences. My questions were dull, the response was dull and one man at the end of it all, a man with a touch of satire, suddenly said, "And put down I have shocking dreams."' That was the kind of illumination he liked best, when the private person suddenly jumped out of hiding, singling himself out from all the anonymous groups people divide themselves into for convenience's sake – political groups, religious groups, and what he called 'the huge jellyfish of deadly, transparent people who believe they belong to no group at all'. He was consumed with curiosity about whatever it is that makes people individuals. 'The world of art,' he wrote, 'is a great secret order with which all human beings have, from time to time, a private relation.'

Pritchett's love of eccentricity was as British as the figure he cut – the pipe, the baggy flannels and rumpled tweeds, the constant stream of witty, off-beat talk. What was not at all British about him was his classlessness. He was always on the lookout for signs of life – the college janitors interested him as much as the professors, or probably more – and he refused to take the high ground with anyone. He was a famous writer

30 years older than I was, but he treated me as an equal from the moment we met and we quickly became good friends. To me, Pritchett's instinctive democracy seemed to be part of the strange new freedom of America. According to a New York friend of mine, the USA is great because it is a 'kidocracy'. If a young person has a bright idea, he meant, there is always someone who will give him or her a chance to try it out.

Blackmur gave me my chance as a literary critic by getting me a Rockefeller Fellowship to write my first book, then making me write my second by inviting me to give the Gauss Seminars. Pritchett gave me my start in London by recommending me to Janet Adam Smith at the *New Statesman*. She sent me a *Partisan* anthology to review, liked what I wrote, and suddenly I was off and running. I am grateful to him for that, but I am far more grateful for the way he made me see that literature is a lively art and it is the business of the critic to write about it in a way that reflects its liveliness. Most important of all, he treated me as a fellow-writer and encouraged me to gamble on whatever talent I had. To an adrenalin junkie like me, the combination of gambling on a chancy way to make a living by doing something I found difficult (I think of myself as an unwilling and indifferent writer but a very good rewriter, which is why everything I write goes through so many versions and takes so long) was an irresistible challenge.

For me, there was another great democratic freedom on offer in America: I no longer had to apologize for being Jewish, or rather, for being whatever 'they' thought Jews were – overwrought, grasping, too clever by half. I discovered this one evening with Blackmur and Borgerhoff, a melancholy professor of French. Borgerhoff mentioned his Danish grandparents and that set Blackmur off on one of his favourite topics: his dour Yankee background. Then he paused in mid-flow and asked me casually if my Spanish name meant I was Jewish. Here we go, I thought; from now on I'll be 'placed', pigeon-holed, dismissed as an insidious alien. But when I shrugged and said, equally casually, 'Of course', Blackmur seemed pleased, more friendly than before, even – though it seemed ridiculous, considering the difference in our ages – respectful. Here in the States it was my Englishness that was alien and being a Jew – even a half-hearted, irreligious English Jew with a Spanish name – was a positive advantage. In intellectual America, everyone either was Jewish or wanted to be. Even the non-Jews in non-Jewish Princeton thought Jewish because that was how the life of the mind was ordered: Marx, Freud, Einstein; the Gentiles scarcely got a look-in. It was only when I realized that I no longer had to apologize or explain or pretend, that I began to comprehend how much of a strain it had been to masquerade as a nice young Englishman. It felt like Kafka's *The Trial* in reverse: I was pardoned for a crime I secretly knew I had committed. I couldn't get over the sense of relief.

Most weekends, while the undergraduates and their blondes were whooping it up in the fraternity houses, I would hitch a ride into New York. In those days, when there was no New Jersey Turnpike, you drove to town on Route One. It was a terrible road, crowded and badly surfaced, the towns it went through were mostly hideous – New Brunswick, Rahway, Elizabeth, Newark – and the landscape was a gas-station culture of car lots, rundown factories, breeze-block diners, oil refineries and polluted rivers. At first I sneered in an English way at the brutality of it all; I missed the greenness of England, the cosiness, the sly way we Brits manage to keep our industries out of sight. But my superiority didn't last. There was something in the arrogance with which the Pulaski Skyway swept high above the industrial swamps of New Jersey – as though they didn't exist, as though there was no challenge that couldn't be met – that touched my heart. The ugliness was the flip side of the American dream and it had a beauty all of its own. I told myself that this was what the true modern world was like – power without excuses, energy without frills, grimy and unrelenting – and all that European prettiness was an illusion – a double illusion, in fact, since, in the early fifties, great tracts of Europe were still an unreconstructed battlefield.

The wasteland beneath the Pulaski Skyway was fascinating for another reason. The Mob dumped its victims in the marshes and the underworld was big news at that time. The Kefauver hearings on organized crime were Washington's longest-running attraction, *On the Waterfront* was movie of the year in 1954, and in 1957 Albert Anastasia, boss of Murder Incorporated, was shot dead in a barber's chair at the Park Sheraton Hotel on Seventh Avenue while having his morning shave. All this seemed part of America's dangerous glamour. I was already addicted to gangster movies and westerns and had a romantic passion for the hard-boiled world where Richard Widmark, Glenn Ford and Lee Marvin were kings.

Now I was in the land where Hollywood fantasy became reality. It was childish thrill, all make-believe on my part, but the romance of toughness and unforgiving ugliness is a make-believe that many Europeans share when they first arrive in the States – witness Fritz Lang's *The Big Heat* and Alexander Mackendrick's *Sweet Smell of Success*.

The other romance was the vastness of America, the freedom and possibilities that went with the sheer scale of the country. I had been reading Hart Crane and my head was full of his poetry, especially when the creaking Chevy or Ford I was riding in left the Princeton turn-off and pulled on to Route One:

> Macadam, gun-grey as the tunny's belt,
> Leaps from Far Rockaway to Golden Gate.

If we turned north and kept going we'd reach the Canadian border in northern Maine; turn south and we'd end up in Key West:

> John, Jake or Charley, hopping the slow freight
> – Memphis to Tallahassee – riding the rods.

For all I knew, Memphis, Tallahassee and Far Rockaway were as grim as Newark and Elizabeth, but in my imagination they were like Samarkand and Timbuktu, mysterious and beckoning.

In other words, I was falling in love. I had discovered the brave new world I had hankered for and there was nothing about it – no ugliness, no brutality, no casual, fuck-you rudeness – that didn't somehow add to its attraction.

For the next dozen years I spent every alternate year back in the States on some excuse or another – writing a book, teaching at Princeton and Brandeis and Buffalo, researching documentaries for the BBC's Third Programme. I went so regularly that I began to think of myself as almost American – an imaginary American, halfway there, a citizen of Rockall. I had more friends in New York than I had in London and each time I arrived at Immigration a weight lifted from my spirit. I felt more energetic, smarter, more interested than I ever felt in England. I felt as if I were coming home.

That first year was the year I got to know New York. Or rather, two New

Yorks. The first was a student New York of Horn & Hardhart Automats and White Castle diners, where hamburgers cost a quarter. (Occasionally, if I was uptown and feeling flush, I'd lash out on a better class of hamburger at Prexy's; they called it 'the hamburger with the college education', which seemed – I was still feeling superior – a good description of most of the undergraduates at Princeton.) I liked drinking in White Rose bars, not just because their booze was cheap but because of the gloom and the smoke and the solitary drinkers waiting to tell you the story of their dreadful lives. Anyone would tell you everything, down to the last chilling detail, if they thought there was a free drink at the end of it. I liked that too, after buttoned-up England.

The final answer to buttoned-up came on my second trip, two years later, when a visiting Leavisite took me to meet Marius Bewley. Bewley was Leavis's most favoured disciple, a subtle critic and also a brave man because, unlike Leavis's other favourite, Morris Shapira, he made no secret of his homosexuality at a time when homosexual activity, even between consenting adults, was still a criminal offence. The visiting Leavisite was a righteous Scot and I suppose Bewley had me pegged, too, as a disapproving moralizer, so he and the man he lived with – he was younger than Bewley and wore pancake make-up – took us on a tour of the gay bars under the El on Third Avenue. We spent the evening talking earnestly about Hawthorne and Henry James while pretending not to notice the Desperate Dan truck drivers in little black cocktail dresses all around. Welcome to America, where anything goes.

Usually my friends and I hung out innocently in Greenwich Village, doing what you do when you are young and short of money: we sat for hours in the coffee shops and cheap Italian restaurants below Washington Square, watching the passing show and talking windily about books, about what we were going to do with our lives or, more often, about the things we most wanted and didn't yet have, like fast cars and girlfriends – especially girlfriends. My married friend wrote regularly from the thatched cottage near Oxford and I at first wrote back – letters with poems in them or snotty, show-off letters about the horrors of American graduate school. But it was all a fake. Both of us knew the affair was over. Her patient husband and his achievements began to figure more and more frequently in her letters until finally I stopped answering them. Anyway, I was in love with America, with the sweep of the Pulaski Skyway and the heart-stopping vision that was always waiting just short of the Lincoln Tunnel whenever I drove into town – the packed, glittering, delicate towers of the Manhattan skyline. I was also entranced by the smiling girls who flocked into all-male Princeton at weekends, but there seemed no way of meeting them up on Goon Hill.

Because I had so far slept with only one woman my knowledge of the other sex was theoretical and blurred. Yet I knew exactly what the girl I was searching for would look like – the repose of her mouth, the tilt of her nose, the swing of her hair. The image in my head was perfectly clear even though it was generated from a confusion of high culture and Hollywood: Cranach's *Eve* and Audrey Hepburn, Petrus Christus's *Portrait of a Young Girl* fresh-minted out of a fifties campus movie, complete with bouncing hair, dazzling teeth and bobby socks.

One evening in the White Horse on Houston Street, where Dylan Thomas had recently drunk himself to death, I got talking to a young couple about my age. He was Jewish, overweight and sad, she was the girl I was looking for – small and blonde and achingly attractive. They had only been married a few months and already loathed each other. Around midnight they invited the whole Princeton car-load of us back for a nightcap in their little cold-water walk-up apartment around the corner. They began fighting as we walked through the door and kept it up until we left. They fought about everything and anything – about his mother and her father, about why the red wine was in the icebox and the beer wasn't, about books and movies, about a pair of lost socks. Because she sat as far from him as she could and wouldn't look at him, and he couldn't take his eyes off her, I supposed they were fighting about sex. And because I couldn't take my eyes off her either and she had flirted absent-mindedly in the bar, I sat there hoping she would glance my way and give me a sign. It never came. She was too caught up in her rage against her husband to bother with anyone else.

Yet they didn't want us to leave and I took that as a sign, though if I'd known more about wedlock I'd have recognized it as a symptom: either they disliked each other so much they were afraid to be left to themselves or they needed an audience and fought more fiercely in company than they did when they were alone. Whatever the reason, it was a long way from the holy cult of matrimony as it was preached in the fifties. I should have taken it as a warning but I was too interested in the girl. I went back to the White Horse often after that evening but never saw either of them again. I couldn't even look them up in the telephone book: I had found the girl I was looking for and had forgotten to ask her name.

When I wasn't mooning around the Village, searching for Juliet and finding Italian cooking, true love of a different kind – my first pizza, in a joint called Henry's on Bleecker Street, was *le coup de foudre* – I was discovering a completely different New York on the Upper East Side – the witty, sophisticated city of Harold Ross's and William Shawn's *New Yorker*. I was introduced to it by Barbara Kerr, a friend of Pritchett, who had come down to Princeton with a clutch of other clever New Yorkers to hear his Gauss Seminars. I met her at one of Blackmur's post-seminar parties and made her laugh. Then Pritchett went back to England and Barbara adopted me.

I adopted her, too, although she was 20 years older than I was and besieged by admirers who were older still. Maybe I adopted her as the kind of mother I would have liked – a woman with my own mother's deep cynicism about the ways of the world but none of her scatty innocence and crippling terrors. But that wasn't how it felt; I never felt filial towards Barbara and I don't think she felt particularly motherly towards me; she was simply a subtle, knowledgeable, older friend who became, over the years, my oldest, dearest friend. Why she bothered with me in the first place I don't know; her friendship was a stroke of luck I never questioned too closely. Maybe she liked me because I made her laugh, or maybe she liked young people because she herself always felt young. (Forty years later, when she was in her eighties, she entertained my children when they were in New York and they fell for her, too.) Most probably she took me on when I was young and brash, and let me stay in her spare room whenever I was in New York, out of sheer generosity – the generosity of spirit that goes with being shrewd and funny and utterly independent.

She had had to work for her independence. Her family were the most proper Bostonians – they had arrived on the ship after the *Mayflower* – and Barbara was brought up in a WASP culture so pure that few Americans outside old Boston could comprehend it: no blacks outside the servants' quarters, no Jews anywhere and certainly no Democrats. One of Barbara's grandmothers had been painted by Sargent and her portrait hung over the fireplace in Barbara's drawing room. But there was another grandmother who had brought disgrace on the family by eloping with her music teacher and thus becoming the first divorcée in Boston high society. This had happened long before Barbara was born and, because her name was never mentioned, Barbara had always assumed that her grandmother was dead. She was 12 before she discovered – by accident – that the old lady was alive and well and still living contentedly with her music teacher in the rue St Honoré. The young girl and the old woman met the next year in Paris and became devoted to each other for ever after.

Outrage at her parents' dishonesty turned Barbara into a rebel, so she outraged them in her turn by going to Washington and working for the New Deal. (Her family considered Roosevelt a traitor and refused to mention his name, too; like the music teacher, he was always 'that man'.) When she arrived in Washington she was 20 years old and had never met a Jew.

When I first met Barbara she was working for Adlai Stevenson, a little later she was editing women's magazines – *Mademoiselle* was one of them – but she hadn't altogether shed her grand Bostonian background. Edith Wharton had written a story about Barbara's scandalous grandmother – it is called 'Autres Temps . . .' – and Barbara, whose name was in the Social Register, still lived partly in an Edith Wharton world where everyone knew everyone who was anyone. They all turned up to her Christmas bash at her brownstone on 92nd Street, between Park and Lex, and her dinner parties were famous. But the Wall Street bankers and lawyers, the elegant couples who seemed to do nothing in particular – or nothing they cared to mention – the visiting Brits who had estates in Scotland and rooms in Albany, where Barbara stayed when she came to London, were always outnumbered by politicians, writers and journalists – people like George Ball, Arthur Schlesinger, Mayor Wagner, Norman Mailer, Mary McCarthy, staff writers for the *New Yorker* and editors from *Time*.

Whatever the company, Barbara was always the most stylish figure in the room, even when she was in her eighties. Her clothes filled the wardrobes in her bedroom and gradually overflowed into the spare room – racks of dresses and coats along the walls, boxes from Bergdorf Goodman piled high on the bed, until finally there were too many to move, the spare room ceased to be spare and I had to find somewhere else to stay. But that took time and for years, whenever I was in New York, I wandered between the glamorous house on 92nd Street and the Village dives without ever registering that they might be two separate worlds. I simply assumed that that was how American democracy worked. When I was uptown, Barbara introduced me as a promising young writer and her friends were too polite to question me closely about what I might have written; all they required of me was that I should keep up my end of the conversation. Down in the Village, nobody gave a damn about who you were or what you did; they had their own style of sophistication – Miles Davis, the MJQ, Dave Brubeck – as well as a peculiarly New York brand of cynicism which culminated, I thought, in the lyrics of Pearl Bailey's song 'Good Enough For Me':

> I don't want no genius for a husband
> Nor a guy who's big financially.
> Give me a simple little fella like Joe Louis,
> That's good enough for me . . .

> And when I finally settle down in marriage
> I want all of my in-laws to be
> Simple country folk, like the Vanderbilts, the Whitneys –
> That ain't no bad bunch to hang out with –
> They're good enough for me.

Uptown and downtown were joined in a mocking, mutual disrespect, untainted by sentimentality. It seemed like an ideal arrangement, a variation on a style of classless personal freedom that didn't exist in Europe and that was, for me, part of America's fatal attraction. It was a country at ease with itself and being there made me feel easy, too. I felt more intelligent and energetic than I did in England and careless in the literal sense: 3000 miles from home and without a care in the world, no longer burdened by the sly condescension and distaste that true Brits believe is the proper reaction to any show of enthusiasm. Only when I went south did I discover that the balance of power I thought of as healthy mutual disrespect became something altogether different. Back in 1954 it meant 'equal but separate'.

In *The Arabian Nights* the password to the treasure-house is 'Open Sesame'; in America, where the greatest of all the many freedoms on offer is to get into an automobile and go, the password is 'Let's drive'. When the academic year ended in May, four of us from the Graduate College – myself, two Chileans whose names I no longer remember, and François Hoffman, a Franco-American who was born and brought up in New York but spoke with a heavy French accent – piled into an ancient, wallowing Ford and headed south to Mexico. But the car was a gas-guzzler and of course we were short of money, so we pinned up notes in the university dormitories asking if anyone wanted a ride in return for a share of the expenses. There was no response. Princeton undergraduates were disdainful of the folk who lived on Goon Hill and most of them had their own cars, far snappier than ours. Then, a day before we were due to leave, a soft-spoken young man called to ask if we were planning to go via Arkansas. We were three foreigners and a New Yorker who had never been south of Princeton, so our idea of North American geography was vague. 'Why not?' we answered. 'We'll pick you up tomorrow morning at seven.'

The student waiting outside the dormitory – call him Paul – was black. He looked like an athlete, not tall but trim, muscular and self-contained, and he didn't seem to think much of our chatter and foreign accents – French-English, Spanish-English, Oxford-English. At that time there were only a handful of black students at Princeton, so few that you rarely saw them, and I think Paul's freshman year must have been hard. He watched us suspiciously as we stowed his gear in the boot, and spoke hardly at all, as though waiting to be snubbed. I wondered if he had put off calling us until the last minute in case we turned him down. Or maybe he wasn't suspicious of us, just full of foreboding because, unlike us, he knew what would happen when we crossed the Mason-Dixon line.

We reckoned to save money before we got to Mexico by staying at colleges along the way. The term was over, the dormitories were empty, so we planned to show up, say we were foreign students, guests in a strange country, and beg for a bed. Our first stop was the University of Virginia at Charlottesville, where the friend of one of the Chileans was studying. The friend had already left for California but he had sent the key of his room and detailed instructions for finding it. He had also said that the place was a southern version of Princeton, stuffy and full of the sons of gentlemen, but he hadn't mentioned that it was totally segregated.

Because it was our first day on the road we had no idea of the distances involved, of the hours of driving between places that seemed close together on the Esso map, so it was near midnight when we arrived at the Charlottesville campus. I had a vague impression of Grecian columns, tall trees, wide lawns and a steaming tropical night full of the sound of crickets. There was no one about. We found the room, tossed a coin to decide who got the bed, who got the sofa and who slept on the floor, and were all asleep within minutes. The next morning we were up early but not quite early enough. As we were walking towards the stairs a door opened and a pale young man stepped into the corridor. He was wearing a white dressing-gown and had a towel around his shoulders. When he saw Paul he stepped back suddenly like a man who has been punched hard for no reason he can think of, more astonished than outraged. I said, 'Good morning' in my most drawling Oxford accent but he didn't reply. At the top of the stairs I looked back. He was standing in the middle of the corridor, arms crossed, pale hair, pale face, pale eyes, a white ghost staring after us.

We stopped for breakfast at a Howard Johnson's on the edge of town. The conversation stopped when we filed in and the waitresses went into a huddle. Finally one of them came over to our table and said, 'Sorry, we can't serve you.' The Chileans and I gaped at her uncomprehendingly and Paul, who knew what was going on, kept his eyes on the tabletop. Hoffman, however, was a New Yorker; he had heard stories about 'down south' but couldn't believe they applied to him, so he exploded into a Gallic harangue – very passionate, very logical – about social justice and legality. The waitress looked bored. She waited until he had finished, then shrugged and said, 'Sorry, but that's how it is.' 'Call the manager,' Hoffman demanded. 'Won't do you no good,' the waitress replied, and she was right. We went through the same performance at three other diners and ended up eating coffee and doughnuts in the car.

And that is how it went for the next three days. We gave up trying to eat in restaurants, bought our food at stores and ate in the car or at the side of the road out of town. At some rural stores they wouldn't even sell us food to take away if Paul got out of the car with us. It was the same at the colleges we tried. First it was 'Sure thing. Welcome to the U S of A. Always glad to help a visitor.' Then they would see Paul and suddenly remember, goddarn it, the whole place is plumb closed for the night, locked up tight as a nut, and the janitor's gone home. On our second night, in Nashville,

Tennessee, we finished up at Fisk, one of the oldest of the all-black universities. The dean seemed astonished to see us, though he made us welcome, but the students jostled us angrily in a bar just off campus and Paul spent long minutes talking urgently to the guys who seemed angriest. We were too innocent and dumb to understand why they should resent us as much as the whites resented Paul. On the third night, in Memphis, we gave up trying. Paul left us at the whites-only YMCA and said he'd come back in the morning. God knows where he spent the night.

We dropped him off the next day at his grandmother's house in Arkansas. She was large and motherly and, like Paul, soft-spoken. She fed us lavishly and thanked us for taking care of her grandson. Paul said nothing. He had become progressively more silent as the journey went on and, like us, he was glad the ordeal was over. Satisfied, too, as though with a job well done: he had taught three ignorant outsiders a lesson in American reality and stilled our pompous chatter.

We shook hands on the porch. 'It's been interesting, all things considered,' he said and smiled for the first time since we left Princeton.

That night we got drunk in a bar full of cowboys in a hick town somewhere in north Texas and got beds at the local college with no problem at all.

9

PUPPY LOVE

━━━━━◆━◆━━━━━

'Twice or thrice had I loved thee,
Before I knew thy face or name.'

John Donne

I spent the next academic year back in Oxford, teaching English at Corpus while Freddie Bateson was off in the States, and pretending to work on my doctorate. What I was really doing was falling in love.

God knows, I'd tried in America. The place was swarming with girls I would like to have met – talkative girls with long legs and dazzling smiles like the ones I'd seen in the movies and glimpsed now across a room or a street or a couple of rows away in the Princeton football stadium when the Tigers were playing at home. But apart from the dream face in the White Horse on Hudson Street, I never managed to get close to any of them.

Barbara put her mind to the problem – it was the kind of social engineering she enjoyed most – and came up with the daughter of a friend who wrote about books for the *New York Times*. The daughter and I put on a show of liking each other – she even paid a chaste visit to Princeton – but there was nothing between us except Barbara's idea that, properly encouraged, we might make an interesting couple. I left for Mexico with no regrets and forgot all about her.

A couple of months later, when I was back in New York, I called her to say goodbye. I was sailing for England the next day and was panicked by the thought of the unfinished business ahead – there had been a pile of letters from the thatched cottage waiting for me at Princeton. I was also curious to hear her voice and see what it did to me. The answer was, nothing at all. She sounded distracted and brittle, anxious to hang up. Well out of that, I thought, and put her out of my mind. Years later, in London, I heard about that telephone call again, casually, in a conversation about something else entirely. The name was mentioned of a man I didn't know. 'You two had a friend in common in New York,' I

was told. 'You called her up one afternoon when he was in bed with her.'
By then I had been married, divorced and was now happily married again.
Even so, I was shocked – not because my untouchable girlfriend had never
gone to bed with me and my pride was hurt, but because she had put me
out of her mind far quicker and more brutally than I had her.

I went back to Oxford in August to teach at a summer school for foreign
students. The other teachers were Wallace Robson, Kingsley Amis, John
Wain and Raymond Williams. Later Williams became the literary guru of
British socialism, the standard-bearer of working-class virtues; back then
he was a dandy, a handsome man, always elegantly dressed, but a dull
lecturer compared with flashy performers like Wain and Amis.

The star of the course, however, was Susi, the German wife of the man
who organized the summer school. They were an odd pair, one of those
mismatches that seem obvious to everyone except the couple involved. He
was ponderous and middle-aged, with a booming voice and a taste for
plonking, Leavis-style moral judgements; she was 20 years younger, slim
and blonde and very subtle, with a clear, tender face and clever blue eyes.
Although she was the mother of two little boys, she herself looked like a
child, a refugee waif from bombed-out Germany, so young that barmen
sometimes refused to serve her in pubs.

Susi was our Zuleika and everyone was after her. They clustered
around her during the breaks, bought her drinks and coffees, took her on
long walks to romantic riverside pubs and tried to stun her with their
cleverness, wrote poems about her, put her in their novels and drove their
own wives crazy. Who would be the lucky man? Wain or Amis or
Robson? It was the one topic everybody was interested in and it might
have been the summer school's running gag if they hadn't all taken it so
seriously.

In fact, Susi chose none of them. She seemed to prefer her dismal
spouse, though nobody understood why or what the two of them could
possibly have in common unless it was power over all those clever young
writers on the make. Did she and her husband make fun of her suitors
behind their backs, when the doors were closed and the lights were out?
Was that what turned them on?

I hung around the edges of these conversations and kept quiet. This was
not only because I was shy and inexperienced and they were all older,
more worldly men with, they claimed, countless scalps on their belts. I

kept quiet because I was in love with Susi – hopelessly, helplessly – and had been from the moment I saw her across the room at the summer school's opening get-together. I had never seen her before yet I recognized her instantly. Delicate features, pale hair, amused blue stare: it was the face I had been looking for all along. I wanted to push through the crowd and say, 'You don't know me and I don't know you, but I've been in love with you all my life.'

She recognized me, too, though for different reasons. I don't know if she was ever really in love with me but, like all of us, she was in love with D. H. Lawrence and saw herself as another Frieda. I was no Lawrence, but I was young and intense and mad for her, so for the time being I fitted the part.

I had never been so besotted or so miserable or so flattered. I was obsessed with every detail of her: with her slender arms and fragile wrists, with the scent she left on the air (4711 Cologne), with her cleverness about people and her wayward treatment of English vowels, with the way her mouth turned down before she smiled, as though every pleasure had first to be salvaged from some kind of disaster. At night I haunted the street where she lived, hoping for nothing more than to catch a glimpse of her when she drew the curtains, and I once spent three hours in the pouring rain outside a restaurant while she and her staid husband ate dinner. That vigil cost me a dose of feverish flu, but even that seemed right since fever was what I was suffering from, a sickness I would have contracted 10 years earlier if I hadn't spent my adolescence playing games at a monastic boarding school.

I think Susi was appalled by the storm she had unwittingly provoked in me. Frieda Lawrence was her idol but she had nothing of Frieda's arrogance or promiscuousness or flamboyance. She had had a bad time during the war and the comfort and stability of her life in Oxford, even the dullness of her dependable husband, were important to her. She showed this in the way she presented herself to the world – always in drab, shapeless clothes that disguised her figure and neutralized her looks, without make-up and with her astonishing sunlit hair scraped back in a bun. She dressed in order not to be noticed, in order to disappear into the anonymous army of harassed young mothers with their shopping baskets and prams, like a spy in deep cover.

She was in no hurry to disrupt her peaceful life and it was weeks before she let me get near her. And even when she finally did – without warning, when I had given up hope – she never allowed us more than an hour or two alone together, as though she believed infidelity was measured in days and anything briefer was a venial sin, easily atoned for, forgiven and forgotten.

Because she was an older woman and the one who was taking all the risks, I didn't dare to complain. Anyway, I was too infatuated, too scared of being dumped. I was also too full of guilt and foreboding. That, too, was according to the book and books were all I knew. 'Romance only comes into existence where love is fatal, frowned upon and doomed by life itself . . .' Denis de Rougemont wrote. 'Passionate love is a misfortune . . . [and] in nine cases out of ten [it] takes the form of adultery.' For us, the guilt and doom of adultery added to the literary thrill – just like Lawrence and Frieda – and were exacerbated by Susi's particular style of unbearable lightness. There was something in her physical presence that both held me back and led me on. Her fragility was part of her sexual appeal, like Mimi's consumption in *La Bohème*. She seemed as translucent as alabaster and as easily broken. It was like making love to an erotic shivering wraith.

But the truth was, she wasn't physically strong – perhaps because she had nearly starved during the war – the dank Oxford climate made her ill and her frailty scared me too much to push my luck. So I hung around her in agonies for the whole academic year, gratefully feeding off whatever scraps she chose to throw me.

When the long summer vacation began she was ill – again or still? I don't remember – so she persuaded her husband to let her go home to Germany for a couple of weeks. He and the au pair could look after the children, she told him, while she lay around in the sun, did nothing and got better. He hated the idea, but her frailty scared him as much as it scared me, so he let her go.

I followed her a couple of days later – a long journey on slow trains with many changes, third class and mostly on wooden benches – to a primitive village in south Germany. The flattened towns where I changed trains were being rebuilt but this village was too small and woebegone to have been worth bombing. It looked like the setting for a fairy story by the Brothers Grimm: ox-carts in the streets, dense forest all around, men in lederhosen, women in dirndls. Susi had booked me a room in the village inn, an echoing gingerbread house made almost entirely of wood –

wooden walls, wooden stairs, wooden bedstead. She herself was staying a mile or two away in a comfortable hotel and visited me only when she chose. It was like Oxford all over again, except that no one spoke English and I spoke no German.

I tried telling myself that this, too, was just like Lawrence and Frieda, but that wasn't how it felt and secretly I knew that our great romantic passion was not working out. Now I supposedly had her to myself I felt I deserved more of her time. Now she had me to herself she realized that I wasn't what she wanted. Her husband was dull and moralistic, but middle age had given him an edge. He knew how the world was run, when to sound off and when to shut up, he knew the limits of what one could reasonably expect. Above all, he knew how to leave her alone and let her come around to him in her own time. In contrast, I was childish in the worst sense – demanding and self-centred – and up close my childishness began to irritate her.

It rained for a week, a heavy, unforgiving rain that seemed as if it would never let up. But one day the sun broke through and Susi relented enough to suggest a bus trip to Rothenburg ob der Tauber, a local beauty spot. She had a passion for Schwabische Barock churches and the Gothic lime-wood carvings of Tilman Riemenschneider, and she wanted to educate me. The road followed the narrow, wooded valley of the River Tauber and even its name seemed to contribute to my lovesickness: it was called the Romantische Strasse. The valley's hills were low and intricately folded, the river itself was barely 10 feet wide, the farmhouses and villages had half-timbered façades. Apart from the metalled road, the twentieth century seemed to have passed the landscape by. I surveyed it all with my Londoner's eye, thinking, If this is the country of her heart, I haven't got a chance.

We wandered the gabled streets of Rothenburg, drank the local wine and admired Riemenschneider's Altar of the Holy Blood in the echoing Church of St Jacob. While we were waiting for the bus back to our muddy village, Susi bought me a little picture book of Riemenschneider's work and showed me a photograph of a group of weeping women he had carved for the church altar in the neighbouring village of Detwang: Mary half-swooning front centre; John on her right tenderly holding her up; Mary Magdalene close in on her other side, just touching her robes; behind them, three other grieving, shrouded heads, one a mere outline; all six mourners strangely fused together, like so many flowers growing from one stem.

'That's how I feel,' Susi said. 'I don't know which person I am any more. I don't know who I belong to.'

It was the most romantic thing I had ever heard, and certainly the most adult. For the first time in my student life I had an insight into the world beyond literature. I felt as if I had come of age. I also knew at that moment that I had lost her.

A few days later she returned abruptly to her husband in Oxford, leaving me with a broken heart and a book of pictures.

In *The Sea and the Mirror*, Auden's variations on *The Tempest*, Prospero, meditating on the young love of Ferdinand and Miranda, concludes: 'I am very glad I shall never/Be twenty and have to go through the business again,/The hours of fuss and fury, the conceit, the expense.' Susi may have fancied herself as Frieda Lawrence, but she was far too grown-up to be anyone's Miranda. In the end the intensity of my infatuation did what it would have done to any woman in her right mind: it bored her.

And she was right to be bored. She was living in the real world with real responsibilities – two small children as well as a husband – and I was living in the land of fever and illusion. Even now, I don't know if I was in love with her or with some fantasy figure which she, to her cost and eventual irritation, embodied. I know what the fantasy wasn't: not my dark-haired, dark-eyed, unreliable, invasive mother. I loved Susi for her blondeness – for her emotional lightness of touch as well as her colouring, for her subtlety and self-containment, for the way she didn't intrude. But that was only after I got to know her and what I am talking about is love at first sight, *le coup de foudre*, the instant recognition of an image I had constructed unaware and knew nothing about until I saw it across the room from me at the summer school in Oxford. Whatever it was, it was the real thing – and it was a long time before I got over it.

I don't know if the trip to Germany cured her of her wish to be another Frieda Lawrence, but it certainly didn't cure her unsatisfactory marriage. Within a couple of years, she had left for Canada with another man, taking her children with her. I never learned who the man was or whether or not they stayed together, but I saw her once more, a dozen years later, in London, soon after I married for the second time.

Susi had always joked about her obdurately youthful looks, as though they were some witch's curse she was fated to live with. 'I'm one of those dreadful women who go on looking the same from 16 to 60. Then the magic goes and their faces just cave in.' She had a sly, self-deprecating way of saying this that only added to my infatuation and left me fumbling for a reply. Now I saw it was true. Although she was in her middle forties, she still looked like a child – untouched, uncanny, as though she had just stepped down from one of Riemenschneider's altars. She was also as subtle and shrewd and alert as I'd remembered, making no claims, presuming on no shared past history that might set a new young wife's teeth on edge. When she left, Anne, who knew all about the affair and had every reason to resent her, said, 'Now there's a classy woman!' I never saw her again.

My Lawrence fever still had a long way to run. A couple of months after Susi ditched me in Germany, I took my heartbreak back to the States, this time with a visiting fellowship from the Rockefeller Foundation, organized for me by Richard Blackmur, to write a book on modern poetry. (In England the book was called *The Shaping Spirit*; its American title was *Stewards of Excellence*.) The Foundation insisted, in the politest possible way, that I spend the first six months at Harvard. But Harvard reminded me of Oxford – Oxford without the architecture and without Susi – and I was too lovelorn to enjoy what it had to offer. My happiest day there was spent snow-shoeing on Mount Washington with I. A. Richards and his wife, Dorothy Pilley. When we stopped below the summit to eat our packed lunches, Richards built a fire. While he shuffled around collecting twigs and laying them carefully in place, he recited his oddly beautiful poem, 'Lighting Fires in Snow':

> Tread out a marble hollow
>> Then lay the sticks athwart,
>> Teepee-wise or wigwam,
> So that the air can follow
>> The match-flame from the start:
>> As we begin a poem
>> And some may win a heart . . .

He recited the words with relish and the fire miraculously blazed.

That was the best moment in the six months, apart from the evenings I spent in a student café near Harvard Yard listening to the singing of a melancholy, unknown girl who had black hair down to her waist, deep eyes, a guitar that seemed several sizes too big for her and an easy, guileless voice, as fresh as the girl's next door. Her name was Joan Baez. I went to hear her every night she was there and by the time she moved on I knew all her songs by heart. I used to sing them to myself, daydreaming about Susi and wallowing in self-pity.

While I was at Harvard, I also got my first glimpse of what the literary life can sometimes do to its practitioners. As part of my research for *The Shaping Spirit*, I went down to Washington to talk to Ezra Pound, who was then incarcerated in St Elizabeth's Hospital for the Criminally Insane. I visited him twice and each time I saw a different person. Our first meeting was in a locked ward and we were alone. Or rather, we sat together by a window in one corner of the ward while the other inmates wandered up and down, muttering and staring. Mostly they kept clear of us and, whenever they came near, Pound shooed them briskly away. He seemed amused by them and faintly contemptuous, as though they were merely a colourful background, nothing to bother about.

We talked about poetry and poets, especially about Eliot. The last time Eliot visited him, Pound said, an inmate had been silently scrubbing the floor of the ward. It was something the poor guy did every day, one of his obsessional rituals. The closer the schizophrenic came with his scrubbing-brush and pail, the more determinedly Eliot ignored him. When he finally reached Eliot's chair and began scrubbing around and under it, the great poet hooked his feet over the front rung and went on talking as though he and Pound were alone. Pound told the story as a joke, but without malice – a tender joke about a man younger than himself, an innocent who needed to be looked after. I was another innocent but he put me slyly in my place. When I asked him (of course) what he thought of Lawrence's novels, he looked me up and down, then shrugged and said, 'I'm not interested in the Russians!'

And that was how Pound was for the two hours we were together while we talked only about literature – witty, courteous, lucid and passionately interested, a devoted master of poetry who, in the locked, evil-smelling ward, full of crazy people and strange noises, looked like becoming a latter-day martyr to the art. We got on so well that he asked me to come back next visiting day.

When I returned a couple of days later Pound was sunning himself outside on the hospital lawn, surrounded by disciples and talking politics. There were about a dozen people around him, most of them burly young men with cropped hair and faces that looked as if they had been cast in iron. They were pumping him on his favourite topics – usury and social credit – as well as 'Commie plots' and the use of drugs for political ends. I had the impression that the questions were more for his benefit than theirs; they already knew all the answers and Pound knew they knew them. But that didn't stop him giving them what they wanted. He held forth on truth drugs and brainwashing, on Manchurian Candidate-style drugs that change the personality, on drugs pumped into the air at political rallies to induce mass hysteria. He appeared completely paranoid – tight-lipped, intense and driven by deranged logic. But every so often he would pause, lean back in his deckchair and glance around quickly to see if any outsiders were listening; at those moments, he seemed faintly embarrassed by his followers' zeal. Then came the next question and off he went again. There seemed no connection between this weary crackpot and the lively man of letters I'd seen a couple of days before.

It was a depressing performance, but also sad. No doubt Pound had wished those young political hoods on himself because he was lonely and had no one else to talk to. Apart from occasional friends and a few would-be scholars like myself, the cranks were the only ones who put themselves out to visit him regularly. But none of them gave a damn about books. They were interested only in politics and politics did to Pound what the lunatics in the locked ward could not: they drove him crazy. For him, I think, politics were the symptom of a nuttiness that had begun not during the war, when he was broadcasting propaganda for the Axis, or after it, when the Americans arrested him for treason and put him in a cage in Pisa, but long before, in 1919, when he met Major C. H. Douglas and heard about the doctrine of Social Credit.

Back then, however, Pound was occupied full-time with literature, working on the *Cantos* and selflessly promoting writers he admired, so his eruptions of craziness – ranting on about economic reform and usury to bemused literary audiences – were dismissed as just another eccentricity, rather like his devotion to Ernest Fenellosa's ideograms or troubadour poetry. After he exiled himself to Rapallo in 1924, his attention shifted. He had always been a fervent campaigner and gradually fascism – he met Mussolini in 1933 – replaced literature as his favourite cause. Unlike Lord Haw-Haw, the Englishman who broadcast for the Nazis and was tried and shot for treason when the war ended, Pound the politician seemed so much at odds with Pound the poet that he was considered unfit to stand trial on grounds of insanity. In other words, madness had landed him in St Elizabeth's instead of in front of a firing-squad, but his madness was intermittent and sometimes it looked no different from the folly and pigheadedness that most writers suffer from. He himself seemed bemused by it all, like a bigamist henpecked by both his wives. I felt sorry for him. Even so, I was glad to get away from the hospital and gladder still that, in the rush of admiration and pity I had felt for him during that first visit, I hadn't mentioned that I was Jewish.

As soon as my obligatory six months at Harvard were up, I lit out for New Mexico, the country of Lawrence's heart. The book I was writing included – naturally – a chapter on Lawrence, although his poetry was so distant from the Modernist style that it wasn't much read back then and I think the essay I wrote may have been the first to take it seriously. I justified the trip to the Rockefeller Foundation by saying I needed to talk to his widow. But the truth was, I was still under the spell of Susi's potent, contagious literary imaginings. Since she had cast me in the role of Lawrence, then Lawrence I would be – as far as that was possible for a London Jew with high-minded critical intentions and a fat grant from an American research foundation. I would see his widow, live in a place he had loved, and try to play the part. It was literary infatuation expanded into the realm of dementia. It was also a demented misjudgement of my own abilities and temperament.

Frieda was away in Mexico when I arrived in Taos, and by the time she returned I was already lost to the place itself. I had managed to rent a cabin that once belonged to Dorothy Brett, Lawrence's most devoted disciple, high up on the flank of the Sangre de Cristo mountains, north of Taos and a mile from the then deserted Lawrence ranch. It was a little log cabin on two floors, with big windows all around and an ancient cast-iron wood-burning stove for cooking and heating. There was no running water. I filled the kettle from a stream a few steps from the back porch; the loo was a wooden outhouse, 30 yards off in the trees.

The Lobo Mountain went up behind the place, slowly at first, then suddenly steeper, covered with pine woods and swarming with wildlife – deer, porcupines, jackrabbits, the occasional bobcat and rattler. Beavers had built an elaborate dam upstream; I used to dunk myself in it on hot afternoons. There were also said to be bears in the woods, though I never saw one. But the other animals came regularly in the evenings, rustling around the cabin, sometimes faintly outlined in the starlight. They were my only company. A couple of hundred yards downhill was another, larger log cabin belonging to Lawrence's friends, Bill and Rachel Hawk, who raised alfalfa and a few head of cattle. They were friendly enough, but elderly, shy and not forthcoming. Four miles away, down in the valley at the foot of the mountain, was another elderly couple who ran a tiny general store and post office. Apart from them, the mountain was empty that year.

I had never been in a place so isolated, so peaceful, so beautiful. The woods dropped away below the cabin, and beyond them was a blue sagebrush plain, rimmed by violet mountains and sliced down the middle by the gorge of the Rio Grande. Far off, three or four little volcanic cones, also blue, rose from this desert plain, as though from the surface of the moon. Behind the cabin the Sangre de Cristo mountains swept south to Santa Fe and north into Colorado. Occasionally I would slog up to the top of the Lobo and look down towards Taos, 20 miles away. The air was so clear it seemed almost possible, with binoculars, to pick out people moving about the streets.

In that limpid, Dantesque light and silence I had never felt happier or more ready to work. I got up when the sun woke me, rising from behind the Lobo in the pure pale sky, washed myself in the chilly stream, then wrote for five or six hours. After lunch I drove down to collect the mail, then wandered about the mountain or went off in my ancient car – a 1939 Dodge that I had bought in Cambridge, Massachusetts, for $30 – to explore the canyons and ridges up and down the range. Once a week I drove into Taos to shop, and occasionally I spent the afternoon with Paul Keith, a big bear of a man with a passion for hunting, who had made his money as a wildcatter in the Oklahoma oilfields, and had then settled in Taos and taken up sculpture. Despite his bulk, he had a genius for delicate work and was famous for the tiny figures he carved for commemorative medals.

Every so often I drove the 100 miles into Santa Fe for a boozy evening with the poet Winfield Townley Scott and his wife, Eleanor, whose adobe house on East Alameda was a meeting place for visiting writers. It was a big, handsome place, though too chaotic to be grand: Navajo rugs on the walls, creaking leather chairs, books piled everywhere and, over everything, the smell of wood smoke. It seemed like paradise of a kind and Win and Ellie behaved as though it were. They were affectionate with each other, indulgent with their wild, tow-haired children, and welcoming to everyone who stopped by. But, like paradise, it didn't last. Win was an alcoholic, a genial man who suffered intermittently from bouts of deep depression. He drank, he said, to keep the depression at bay. Eventually the booze got to him and he became unable to write. He committed suicide in 1968, convinced he was a failure. Ellie died senselessly two or three years later, a passenger in a car crash.

But my social trips down the mountain were infrequent. Mostly I kept to myself, and as the summer went on – blazing days, clear cold nights – I think I went a little dotty from sheer isolation. Some evenings I would catch myself in intricate conversations with my own shadow. Then I would get into the car, bump off down the dirt road and drive into Taos to see Paul Keith and his cheerful wife, Rowena. But often my nerve would fail before I arrived and I'd finish up in one of the shabby little bars on the outskirts of town where impoverished Spanish-American farm-hands drank and 'Anglos' were not welcome. I'd tuck myself into the darkest corner, sip a beer and listen to the voices. It was reassuring to know that the world still contained other people, even if they were speaking a language I hardly knew in an accent I couldn't penetrate. Then I'd drive back up the mountain to the moonlight and the silence: only the creaking of the car as it cooled and the faint breathing of the little stream. The rickety gate squeaked when I opened it, the sound of my footsteps was outrageous, the back of my neck bristled with the sense of being watched by whichever creatures had retired into the *piñon* when my car's headlights climbed the hill.

I was used to the peopled loneliness of boarding school and university, but the loneliness I experienced up in that cabin in New Mexico was different – literal, physical, and augmented by the vast indifference of the desert landscape. Underneath, I suppose, it scared me, though I would never have admitted it.

One morning over breakfast I started to read a little paperback translation of Bédier's *Romance of Tristan and Iseult* which I had bought back at Harvard when I was pining for Susi. Instead of settling down to work, I took the book outside and read it straight through, lying on my back under the blazing sun. Then I turned over on to my stomach and read it through a second time. It was our story all over again – the lovelorn young wife with her besotted lover and elderly, not altogether complaisant husband – but transformed into poetry and nobility and doom:

> 'And what is it that you know, Iseult?'
> She laid her arm upon Tristan's shoulder, the light of her eyes
> was drowned and her lips trembled.
> 'The love of you,' she said. Whereat he put his lips to hers . . .

> . . . The lovers held each other; life and desire trembled through their
> youth, and Tristan said, 'Well then, come Death.'
> And as evening fell, upon the bark that heeled and ran to King
> Mark's land, they gave themselves up utterly to love.

As evening fell for me, I reeled back into my lonely cabin, starving hungry, red as a freshly boiled lobster, but utterly content. So that was what it was all about; that was what I had been waiting for. All night I didn't sleep because of the sunburn. I twisted about, trying to find a position that was not entirely agonizing, and fantasizing about Susi and the future and about Frieda, who was due back in Taos a day or two later. The dottiness incubated by my isolation had reached a fine and florid climax. 'Well then, come Death.' I was ready for any stupidity. No rashness was beyond me.

As it turned out, Frieda's return was an anticlimax. Not only because nothing could have survived my expectations, let alone lived up to them, but because she celebrated her homecoming by gorging on rum babas and dark beer at Taos's one German restaurant, then promptly collapsed with a severe attack of diabetes. So it was a couple of weeks before I finally met her. By then, Barbara, the youngest of her three children, had arrived from England to visit her.

I fell for them both in a good-humoured, filial way and did my best not to bore them with the dogged, scholarly questions Frieda had come to dread. Not that I had many questions; I had come to drink at the fountain, not to analyse the water. I was also relieved that the heroine of the most famous literary love affair of the century was now simply a vivacious old lady with a throaty laugh, a thick German accent and a scandalous past she was proud of.

She died a couple of months later. I was back in London by then, so I telephoned Barby, who had also returned to England, to say I was sorry. 'Come to lunch on Sunday,' she said. 'My little daughter will be here.'

The little daughter turned out to be 19 years old and she had Frieda's green eyes. My Lawrence mania grew overnight even more florid. I saw her as the reincarnation of her notorious grandmother. We married seven weeks later, on her twentieth birthday.

In a well-regulated society there would have been a law against marrying so suddenly and so young. If I myself had been well-regulated instead of 27-going-on-12 and unhinged by literature, I wouldn't have needed a law to remind me of the old truth, 'Marry in haste, repent at leisure.' But this was 1956, when everybody married young, especially us literary types who had read Leavis and were keen to demonstrate our maturity. One unqualified good came from the marriage – a son, Adam, who held us together for three or four years. Apart from him, it was miserable for both of us. But at least it cured me of my passion for Lawrence. I never forgave him for getting me into it.

10

BEYOND THE GENTILITY
PRINCIPLE

———————➤◄———————

T he unhappy marriage brought other benefits, although they weren't obvious to me until later. First, it helped make up my mind about the choice I had been putting off since I met Pritchett and Blackmur in Princeton: to abandon my university career and try to make a living as a writer. My reasons at the time were probably as demented as the rest of my behaviour – if the young woman I was marrying was to be my Frieda, then I wanted to be her Lawrence, not her Professor Ernest Weekley. But the dream of living as a free agent, like Lawrence, supported only by my writing and my wits, was real enough and it had real consequences: from then on my life was permanently insecure but continually interesting, and that, I suppose, must have been how I had wanted it all along.

The second benefit of our mutual unhappiness was more complicated and took longer to emerge: it weaned me from the literary world – or rather, from the belief that writing and writers were what mattered most in this world. It may have been that I secretly wanted the marriage to be unhappy, like the one my parents had, in order to prove that marriage was not for me. Whatever my hidden motives, I felt that books – especially Lawrence's – had got me into this mess but they hadn't prepared me for what to do now I was in it and they certainly weren't helping me get out of it again. I had bought the whole smug Leavisite package – love plus marriage equals maturity – and finished up more childish than before. I felt swindled. If books hadn't taught me that there was a world elsewhere, as difficult and demanding as the world I had read about but more varied, more demanding and a great deal less forgiving, then everything my education had led me to believe was skewed. Paradoxically, this revelation sharpened my love of language because language was the best instrument I had to cope with the obdurate non-literary world, and my need to communicate was stronger than ever. (I had never been able to get through to my mother; now I couldn't get through to my wife.) Unfortunately language wasn't enough, not nearly enough.

Unhappiness put the literary life in perspective just as my role in it was getting under way. In the autumn of 1956, a month or two before I married, I had begun what turned out to be a 10-year stint as poetry critic and editor for the *Observer*. One of the earliest reviews I had to write was of the collected poems of Edith Sitwell. She was not a writer I admired but, in those days, you couldn't say so. She was reckoned to be a great poet, untouchable, the sacred cow of English literature. Even the fastidious T. S. Eliot was polite about her work and it was rumoured that the Sitwells and their influential friends made life hard for those who failed to show proper respect. I, however, was young and keen to show off. I also thought, I'm nobody, so what can they do to me? I wrote a long piece explaining why her poems seemed inflated rather than profound, and suggesting that, at her best, she was not quite as talented as Christina Rossetti. The essay was a pleasure to write, but I assumed the *Observer* would spike it. I was reckoning without Terry Kilmartin, the literary editor. He looked like an army officer – handsome, upright and slightly reined in – the perfect English gentleman. In fact, he was Irish and iconoclastic, very much his own man and a shrewd judge of literature and prose style (his translation of Proust is a masterpiece). He also disliked Dame Edith's pretentiousness even more than I did. He ran my piece as the lead review.

On the same day the *Sunday Times* – there were only two posh Sunday papers back then – published a review by Cyril Connolly saying that Edith Sitwell was the greatest English poet of the century. A few days later I met Philip Toynbee, the *Observer*'s chief reviewer. 'I read your piece, then I read Cyril's, and you know what?' he said. 'I heard the great iron door of the Establishment clang shut and knew which side I was on.'

Terry Kilmartin was the best editor I ever worked for until, years later, I began writing regularly for the *New Yorker* and was edited by the laconic and unfoolable Pat Crow and the incomparable William Shawn. Terry and Mr Shawn had one trait in common: once they decided they trusted your judgement, they gave you a free hand. In 1959, for example, Terry sent me Robert Lowell's *Life Studies*, along with half a dozen other slim volumes, for the usual round-up review. I thought Lowell's book was new and important but so different from his previous work that I was sure it would be misunderstood. Up until then Lowell was considered T. S. Eliot's most gifted disciple. His poems were highly wrought and difficult, at once artfully detached and self-conscious, stuffed with the literary allusions and Catholic symbolism that New Critics loved because they sustained every subtle interpretation that could be spun from them.

In *Life Studies* Lowell jettisoned his convoluted high style; the poems were casual, conversational, immediate. More importantly, they dealt with a subject that Eliot had declared off-limits – the poet's private life as a man who suffered periodic manic-depressive breakdowns. I reckoned (correctly) that my fellow-critics would dismiss the book as slipshod and interpret Lowell's colloquial directness not as a new start but as a sign that the strain had been too much for him and the bouts of madness had destroyed his talent. So instead of rounding up the usual suspects in 800 words, I wrote a much longer article on Lowell's book alone. Terry printed it uncut. All he said was, 'Nice piece.'

In the same year he decided the *Observer* should publish poetry and I should choose it for him. This was not something either of the Sunday papers did back then, except occasionally when they needed to fill a column. Terry thought poetry mattered and he wanted it to be a regular feature. We began in March 1959 with a poem by R. S. Thomas, and ended – at least, as far as I was concerned – in February 1977, with four poems by Jean Rhys, the first she published. Some Sundays we printed only one poem and occasionally none at all, but often a quarter or half of one of the literary pages was filled with poems, sometimes by a single poet, sometimes by several – the known, the less known and the unknown jumbled together. Established poets like Graves and Auden and MacNeice all appeared in the *Observer*, as did Larkin, Amis and Enright, but the poets we published frequently were the ones I most admired, especially Ted Hughes and Thom Gunn and Americans whose reputations were not yet fully established in England – Lowell, Berryman, Roethke, Eberhart.

We were also the first journal in Britain to feature groups of poems in translation by Zbigniew Herbert and Miroslav Holub, each with a brief introduction by me. Most important of all, perhaps, the *Observer* was publishing Sylvia Plath's great late poems at a time when few other British magazines would take them, and we treated her death as a tragedy for literature, not as an item of gossip. The Sunday after she died we published 'A Poet's Epitaph': four of her best last poems – 'Edge', 'The Fearful', 'Kindness', 'Contusion' – along with a photograph of her and a paragraph – by me – about her death which I hoped would show – how could I have been so innocent? – that what she had written mattered a great deal more than how she had died:

> Last Monday Sylvia Plath, the American poetess and wife of Ted Hughes, died suddenly in London. She was 30. She published her first and highly accomplished book of poems, 'The Colossus', in 1960. But it was only recently that the peculiar intensity of her genius found its perfect expression. For the last few months she had been writing continually, almost as though possessed. In these last poems, she was systematically probing that narrow, violent area between the viable and the impossible, between experience which can be transmuted into poetry and that which is overwhelming. It represents a totally new breakthrough in modern verse, and establishes her, I think, as the most gifted woman poet of our time. The following poems were all written within a few days of her death. She leaves two small children. The loss to literature is inestimable.

Words like 'genius', 'intensity' and 'breakthrough' are guaranteed to make the London literary establishment cringe, so naturally the claims I made for her work were dismissed as wild exaggeration. Even so, I like to think that the way those last poems first reached a large audience helped establish Sylvia's reputation. Because the *Observer* was a national newspaper and its arts pages were taken seriously – Ken Tynan was the theatre critic – it was, for a time, probably more influential than any poetry journal in the country.

My own relationship with the Establishment – or rather, with the Movement poets who were soon to become the Establishment – was tricky, although I didn't know how tricky it was until I spent a weekend at Kingsley Amis's house in Swansea. During a long, drunken Saturday evening, Kingsley disappeared into the garden with each of the women in the party. While they were gone the rest of us sat around trying to make conversation and pretending not to be embarrassed. Half an hour later our host and whichever lucky lady had gone with him sauntered back in, smoothing their clothes and hair but not quite able to conceal the wild furtive triumph in their eyes.

In one of Thornton Wilder's plays a man with a terrible hangover leans out of a skyscraper window and cries to the tiny figures on the sidewalk far below, 'I apologize! I apologize to everybody!' Kingsley's way of apologizing, over breakfast the next morning, was to launch into a long rigmarole about his fear of death. He was turning it on, of course, indulging himself for our benefit, although what he was saying sounded genuine enough. But he was also missing the point: being an interesting writer with interesting neurotic preoccupations doesn't mean never having to say you're sorry.

What got to me most about the whole performance was that everyone was miserable – the women who went outside with Kingsley as much as those of us who were left behind, even Kingsley himself – but nobody said a word. Whatever our reasons – embarrassment, shyness, humiliation, misplaced good manners – we went on behaving as though nothing unusual were happening. And that, I thought, is what the Movement poets do when they write: they pretend that all's well with the world provided they keep their backs turned on what they really feel. Because my own life at the time was undeniably wretched, that was one pretence I wasn't willing to accept.

My private misery confirmed something I had already learned in America: that the 1950s, the decade in which I came of age, were nothing like as conformist and complacent as, in retrospect, they now seem. 'We are a nation of twenty million bath tubs,' Mary McCarthy wrote, 'with a humanist in every tub.' But behind the moral earnestness an ominous sense of unease was working away, though it was easier to detect it in America than in England. When Auden called the decade the Age of Anxiety he wasn't only referring to the subliminal anxiety of waiting for the end, when their Dr Strangelove – or ours – would push the button on the planet. He also meant anxiety in the Freudian sense – a free-floating neurotic conviction that something dreadful but indefinable had gone wrong.

Senator McCarthy was one of the symptoms of this malaise. He may have been a dangerous, alcoholic buffoon but, before he was discredited, he won more battles than he lost. Until McCarthy got to work, intellectuals on both sides of the Atlantic had thought of themselves as a social force, 'unacknowledged legislators' who lacked political power yet had a profound influence on the moral tone of the nation. The Junior Senator from Wisconsin undermined all that. Like Stalin and the Stalinists on the other side of the Iron Curtain, he succeeded in casting doubt on the reliability of the intelligentsia as a class. As a result all of us in the intellectual world, no matter what our politics or lack of them, were full of foreboding. Yet because we were a wartime generation, brought up not to complain, we didn't know how to express our unease, apart from drinking more than was good for us.

We had also been brought up to believe that writing was a serious business and great literature mattered. 'Thou shalt believe in Milton, Dryden, Pope,' Byron wrote. Also in Shakespeare, Chaucer, Donne, George Herbert, Wordsworth, Coleridge and Keats, in George Eliot, Henry James, Conrad and the great highbrow Modernists like Eliot, Joyce and Stevens. By those lights, *Waiting for Godot* was the literary event of the decade and we looked down at anyone who didn't aim that high. To the English, Ginsberg, Kerouac and the rest of the Beats seemed like a fifties equivalent of the Sitwell gang – their antics had more to do with self-promotion than literature – and the Movement poets were equally unappealing to the Americans. Although the British poets disdained melodrama and showmanship, there was nothing particularly inspiring about the alternative they offered: a tetchy vision of post-war provincial England populated, like a Lowry painting, by stick figures united, above all, by boredom. They were bored by shortages that were no longer justified, bored by the cheap, plastic surfaces of things nobody wanted and everybody bought, bored even by the cosy lives they had fashioned for themselves – books and LPs on the shelves, the gas fire on full, warm bottled beer in the cupboard, and all mod cons. (Philip Larkin, being far more talented than the rest, brought to the mixture genuine depression and anger; but he was careful to keep them at an ironic distance.)

Around 1960 Penguin commissioned me to compile an anthology of contemporary British verse. Nineteen sixty was, I suppose, the worst year of my life. My marriage was on the rocks, I was chronically depressed, and I celebrated Christmas by attempting to take my own life. (I wrote about that episode later in *The Savage God*.) Apart from my personal problems, I had by then spent a long time in the States – almost four of the previous seven years – and was no longer convinced by many of the poets I needed to include if I were to stick to the original plan for the anthology. So I did the job Penguin had paid me to do – the anthology was called *The New Poetry* – but began the selection with poems by two Americans, Robert Lowell and John Berryman, who were writing the poetry that interested me most – that is, poetry that took account of the confusion and sadness of personal life.

I also wrote a fighting introduction in which I explained just what I thought was holding British poetry back in the fifties. In homage to Freud I called the introduction 'Beyond the Gentility Principle'. Gentility, I explained, was a peculiarly English disease, closely allied to the idea of muddling through: 'gentility is a belief that life is always more or less orderly, people always more or less polite, their emotions and habits more or less decent and more or less controllable; that God, in short, is more or less good.' Gentility may have been behind everything that was best about English life – the good manners and restraint, the temperament as mild as the climate – but it didn't seem an adequate response to a century that had spawned two world wars, totalitarianism, genocide, concentration camps and nuclear warfare.

Gentility was not an idea ever likely to catch on in America, a nation, they say, that has no minor poets. Not true in fact, of course, but true enough in spirit. What they mean is, no genuine American poet would ever settle for being minor. All of them want to be up there in the ring, battling it out with Eliot and Pound, if not with Shakespeare and Milton. In the fifties this meant doing to poetry what the Abstract Expressionists, who dominated the art scene, were doing to painting – breaking the traditional moulds and distilling into their work all the troubles of that bleak period of the Cold War as well as the troubles and incoherence of their private lives.

This sense of almost intolerable strain was the mid-century's equivalent of the remoter, more decorous unease that had pervaded T. S. Eliot's poetry 30 years earlier. Even before *Life Studies*, Lowell was expressing it as an anguish that registered in the texture of his verse, in the upset rhythms and troubling imagery of his earlier poems, and later in the abrupt and shocking nakedness of lines like 'I hear / my ill-spirit sob in each blood cell, / as if my hand were at its throat.' In Berryman's poems the strain is less sonorous, more jagged, more on edge. Both poets seemed to be plagued by nervous systems that were badly jangled and too close to the surface, yet there was nothing slipshod or self-indulgent about the way this exacerbation expressed itself in their writing. They thought of themselves as Eliot's rightful heirs, and Eliot, a poet with a faultless ear and all the discipline and technique in the world, was squarely on the side of the classical virtues. The difference was that Eliot believed in the impersonality of art and kept his private troubles strictly to himself, whereas Lowell and Berryman used their disastrous private lives as raw material for their poetry. Ginsberg & Co. also wrote about their private lives but their model was Walt Whitman and they let it all hang out any old how. In comparison, Lowell and Berryman were disciplined, shrewd, technically skilled and very much aware of their link with the great writers of the past – the writers, Eliot said, 'whom one cannot hope to emulate'.

The two younger poets were less modest than Eliot in their aspirations; they wanted nothing less than to emulate the best of them. I loved the seriousness of their ambition, their determination to do all-out what had to be done, without pretending, like the Brits, that everything would work out fine, provided they kept quiet and averted their eyes. Unhappiness was the element they swam in, although I never really knew whether they were determined to get their unhappiness into their work along with everything else or they just wanted to get everything into their work, unhappiness included. Either way, it seemed the honourable way to write; to have settled for anything less would have been a betrayal of their talents.

I met Berryman briefly during my first year in the States, at a New Year party at Hannah Arendt's apartment on Riverside Drive, when he was still a promising young academic who had published just one slim volume of verse. He wore the same anonymous uniform we all wore – tweed sports jacket, Brooks Brothers button-down shirt and sober tie – but uneasily, as though it were a hair shirt. His mouth was tight, his long face was flushed and his manner was fierce and argumentative, as bristling as his poems. When I met him next, in Dublin, a dozen years later, he was labouring to finish his great cycle of 'Dream Songs' and was already famous, fêted, showered with honours and featured in *Life*.

His face was still fierce and flushed, but most of it was shrouded by a wild beard that hung down his chest like a bib. He looked like St Jerome in the desert, emaciated, unsteady, a man at the end of his tether. He smoked five packs a day, coughed ferociously, shouted when he was excited (often), and was usually drunk by midday. Without drink, however, he could barely function. This was a problem because I was in Dublin to interview him for BBC television and the window of opportunity for the interviews was dangerously narrow. First thing in the morning he was too hung over and wretched and sullen to talk, so we collected him just before opening time from the little terraced house he had rented near the Lansdowne Road rugby stadium and interviewed him in a pub around the corner. That gave us about an hour before the booze got to him. What he had to say was brilliant and witty and sometimes moving, but not for long. The half-hour interview took three days to film.

I suspect Berryman was as appalled as everyone else by his alcoholism and impossible behaviour, so he tried to rationalize it. He once remarked, in a *Paris Review* interview, 'the artist is extremely lucky who is presented with the worst possible ordeal which will not actually kill him. At that point, he's in business.' This is a modern version of the old Romantic Agony: the poet as a sensitive plant, born to suffering and able to express it in a way that brings it close to other people. But because Berryman was a sophisticated man, he buttressed this naive belief with twentieth-century theories: an existentialist aesthetic in which art and life are inextricably bound together, and a crude psychoanalytic theory of art as compensation and self-therapy: 'One sheds one's sicknesses in books – repeats and presents one's emotions to be master of them,' was how Lawrence put it. In other words, Berryman's boozing and bad behaviour and the misery they caused other people were the necessary price of genius. The poetry vindicated the cost.

That, at least, is how he saw it; but there was also something else involved, something altogether less tragic and heroic. Towards the end of his life he wrote a novel about alcoholism, *Recovery*, with a hero who has problems very like Berryman's and a c.v. that is even more grandiose. He is Alan Severance MD, Litt.D., a Professor of Immunology and Molecular Biology who also teaches a Humanities course on the side. Like Berryman, Severance is an alcoholic who is being dried out. Like Berryman, he has been interviewed by *Time* and *Life* and can't get over it. He has this to say: 'He had really thought, off and on for twenty years, that it was his duty to drink, namely to sacrifice himself. He saw the products as worth it.' Because I value Berryman's work highly – some of the 'Dream Songs' seem to me as good as any poems written in this century – it took me a long time to realize that the sentence could also mean something else entirely: not that he sacrificed himself to drink for the sake of the poetry but that poetry was his excuse for drinking. He saw himself as a figure in a myth, a leading member of a generation of doomed or suicidal poets – Randall Jarrell, Delmore Schwartz, Theodore Roethke, Sylvia Plath – and by the end the doom and the booze and the myth seemed to matter more to him than the poetry. They set him free to create mayhem whenever he felt like it.

It was an imaginary freedom, more to do with image than with art, but he used it brutally. In the summer of 1966 Berryman came to London to read at a poetry festival. After his reading, Ian Hamilton and I took him and our wives to Chinatown for a meal. Ian was editor of the *Review*, Britain's liveliest literary magazine, and was about to take over from me as poetry critic of the *Observer*. Ian's young wife, Gisela, was German, shy, highly-strung and uneasy in company at the best of times. That evening she was just back from hospital after a bad nervous breakdown and was more fragile than usual.

Naturally Berryman was drunk, but that only sharpened his killer's instinct for the weakest member of the party. He knew all about nervous breakdowns himself, so professional courtesy kept him off that subject. Instead he started in on the Germans, slyly at first – German lack of humour – then with increasing ferocity – German gluttony, German imperialism – finishing with a diatribe about what the Germans had done to the Jews, as though the tongue-tied young woman sitting opposite him at the table were personally responsible. At that point Ian said, 'That's enough' and walked out of the restaurant with Gisela. After they were gone Berryman huffed and puffed and pretended he was sorry, but he couldn't hide his glee. He had scored a double whammy: he had savaged someone who wouldn't fight back and had also committed a minor form of literary suicide by fatally antagonizing her husband. I assume he blamed it on the booze when he sobered up – that is, if he remembered the incident at all.

His behaviour was unforgivable but also curiously innocent. Berryman cared passionately about his literary standing and thought himself to be in permanent competition with Lowell; they circled each other like contenders for the heavyweight title, each acutely aware of the other's achievements, every new book a punch landed and another point on the referee's card. Even so, Berryman was recklessly unpolitical – too much at the mercy of his suicidal alcoholism, or alcoholic self-destructiveness, to care about the damage it did to his reputation. So he ended up as a helpless witness of the spectacle he made of himself. And because he was a witty man he saw the absurdity of what he was doing, and that somehow redeemed him. Henry, Berryman's stand-in as narrator of 'The Dream Songs', is a one-man disaster zone, a comic creation miscast in a tragedy – the Melancholy Jaques playing Hamlet.

Robert Lowell was periodically crazier than Berryman ever dreamed of being, but he never handled himself so badly, even during his crack-ups. I saw him only once when he was mad enough to be hospitalized. That was in London in the summer of 1970, while he was in Greenways Nursing Home, near Primrose Hill. The manic cycle had begun at All Souls, Oxford, where he had a visiting professorship, and his excitable talk, like the lumbering passes he made at his colleagues' wives, was dismissed as the boorish behaviour one expects, alas, from an American poet who drinks too much. When the manic cycle reached its climax, in London, his friends dumped him in Greenways and disappeared. His wife, Elizabeth Hardwick, was still in New York preparing for a year in England, frantic about him but unable to leave town until she had organized their affairs. His newest infatuation, Lady Caroline Blackwood, whom he eventually married, had gone to ground, unable and unwilling to cope with his craziness. Greenways was a shabby establishment, more like a boarding house than a nursing home; it seemed an odd place to park a distinguished poet. It was not far from where I lived so, since no one else was around, I visited him several times until Hardwick arrived.

Despite his crack-up, we did what we always did when we met: we talked about poetry. Or rather, I listened while he talked relentlessly about *Paradise Lost* and Milton's concept of Satan as a tragic hero. Although Lowell was heavily sedated, he still had an uncanny gift for getting inside the heads of other poets and re-creating their work from the inside. He sat in an armchair by the window, in his pyjamas, chain-smoking, talking about the poem as though he had written it and turning Milton's hell into a place very like the one he himself was now in. But as he talked Satan kept mysteriously transforming himself into Hitler and Hitler, equally mysteriously, became the great misunderstood tragic figure of our age, done down by pride, ambition and shady colleagues, and now rewritten and reclaimed by Lowell. And the Jews? The Final Solution was Himmler's work, Lowell answered; Hitler never knew about it. He made his dottiness sound so reasonable and so plangent, and he himself seemed so shaken with grief by the tragedy of it all, there was no way of arguing with him and no cause to take offence.

By the time I visited him in Greenways, of course, he was full of sedatives and the crisis was over, but there was still something menacing about the excitement in his voice and the way he shifted uneasily around in the tatty armchair, as though he might spring up at any moment and start smashing the furniture. Lowell was a disorganized, myopic man with a large, shaggy head, and most of the time he seemed full of sweetness – a sweetness that was intensified by the weird, singsong Southern accent that overlay his Boston vowels. Yet under the mildness – because he was big and powerful and sometimes so awkward as to seem not quite in control of his limbs – he exuded a dangerous whiff of threat. This threat was implicit even in his name: nobody called him Robert; he was Cal, short for both Caligula and Caliban, a schoolboy nickname, acquired at St Mark's, that hinted at some bullying little Hitler beneath the skin and God knows what enormities which he was still trying to live down.

Luckily I never saw him when the madness was truly on him and the little Hitler came raging to the surface and it took ambulance men and cops to subdue him. On the way down from his manic jags, or when he was simply depressed, Lowell was someone else entirely – gentle, alert and terribly sad, as though in mourning for the blunders he had committed and the grandiose rubbish he'd spouted in his folly. When he was depressed the thuggishness disappeared altogether; he seemed young and vulnerable; he made you want to take care of him. That was how he was when he wrote his poetry – he never wrote when he was high or even on the way up – and also when I first met him in Boston, early in

1956, not long before I took off for New Mexico. He was a dozen years older than me and already famous – nine years earlier, his book *Lord Weary's Castle* had been hailed as a masterpiece and had won him a Pulitzer Prize, a Guggenheim fellowship and an award from the American Academy of Arts and Letters – but the man I met for lunch at the Athens Olympia Restaurant seemed so undefended that I felt I ought to protect him, though from what I didn't know.

The answer, I suppose, was from himself, but I was too young and full of myself to see that. Anyway, at that first meeting and the many times we met afterwards, all Lowell ever wanted to talk about was poetry – its craft, its scope, its history – poetry in its purest self, with none of the usual literary gossip on the side. He seemed slightly apologetic about this single-mindedness, as if it were a peculiarly American characteristic, another manifestation of the native ambition that made his countrymen do everything with both hands. 'The artist's existence becomes his art,' he once told me. 'He finds new life in it and almost sheds his other life.' He made it sound like a noble form of self-sacrifice, but he also knew that it had a price, especially for those close to him. Behind the artistic ambition was a different, grieving note, as though he could never quite forget his talent for making a mess of things. Not long before he died he quoted, seemingly as his own epitaph, George Santayana's bitter comment, 'I have enjoyed writing about my life more than living it.' Unlike Berryman, Lowell did not think the sacrifice was worth it.

Lowell had a weakness for what he himself called 'the monotony of the sublime', a kind of high Miltonic rhetoric that rolled along under its own steam. But at his best his voice is unique – supple, vulnerable, eloquent and terribly upset. He writes like a man rinsed with feeling, someone with one skin too few who can turn every trivial incident into poetry, as Plath did in the last year of her life. That suited me fine. Despite Oundle and the rugger-playing and rock-climbing and fast cars, I preferred poets with one skin too few to those with several too many, even if they had to pay for their vulnerability with private lives that were a misery for them and everyone around them. Better that than the Movement poets' glib conviction that they knew all the answers and were thereby entitled to behave like naughty schoolchildren.

Lowell was constantly falling headlong for unsuitable women, but the oafishness of Berryman in the Chinese restaurant or Kingsley Amis in

Swansea was not his style. He was saved from all that by his Boston upbringing – by plain, old-fashioned good manners. Being a Lowell implied certain responsibilities; it meant being civil, alert to other people's feelings, attentive, unintrusive, generous. I looked forward to seeing him almost as much as to reading him – unlike Berryman, whom I read with pleasure but dreaded meeting.

At least they were equal in their determination to 'make it new'. But Pound's famous edict meant something different in the Age of Anxiety, when psychoanalysis had replaced politics as the focus of intellectual interest and the subtitle of *Dr Strangelove* was 'How I Learned to Stop Worrying and Love the Bomb'. Lowell and Berryman inherited the freedom and discipline of the Modernist tradition and applied them to their turbulent inner lives, thereby creating new freedoms and new disciplines, just as the Abstract Expressionists had done for painting.

Although their subject-matter was sometimes dangerously unstable, their standards were as stringent as Eliot's. They handled their troubles as though they were just another impersonal subject, with the artistic detachment Coleridge described in his *Biographia Literaria* when he wrote about Shakespeare at work: 'himself meanwhile unparticipating in the passions and actuated only by that pleasurable excitement, which had resulted from the energetic fervour of his own spirit in so vividly exhibiting what it had so accurately and profoundly contemplated.' From this came what Coleridge called 'the alienation, and, if I may hazard such an expression, the utter aloofness of the poet's own feelings, from those of which he is at once the painter and the analyst'. Eliot had turned his back on traditional poetic forms, but tradition itself mattered a great deal to him and he thought of himself as a classicist, aloof from the feelings he portrayed. Lowell, Berryman and Plath were the same, despite their subject-matter. What they wrote about was private and volatile, but the way they wrote – their discipline and clarity and attention to detail – was as classical as Eliot's.

Unfortunately that detachment became hard to appreciate in the sixties, when R. D. Laing and his followers were preaching the superior wisdom of schizophrenia and Timothy Leary was plugging mind-expanding drugs. A new know-nothing spirit was abroad which fatally confused the distinction between art and life. As a result the so-called 'confessional' poets, like Ginsberg, worked on the assumption that any old bleeding chunk of life or LSD hallucination qualified as a poem provided it was served up with enough chutzpah.

Art, however, is not so easily come by. It doesn't depend on what you experience but on what you bring to the experience. Great tragic poems are not necessarily inspired by great tragedies; on the contrary, they can be precipitated, like pearls, by the smallest irritants, as long as the poet's secret, internal world is rich enough. In the same way, the more exposed and painful the theme, the more delicate the artistic control needed to handle it. The neurotic and the artist may have a great deal in common, but there is one fundamental difference between them: the neurotic is at the mercy of his neurosis, whereas the artist, however neurotic he may be outside his work, has in his capacity as an artist a highly realistic, practical understanding both of his inner world and of his relationship to the materials of his art. With all due deference to Laing, schizophrenia is not a state of grace and there is no short cut to creative ability, even through the wards of the most progressive mental hospital.

'Confessional' poetry was a mindless, loose-lipped style which Lowell, Berryman and Plath never had much time for. Plath explored her ill-lit inner world more resolutely than the others and ended up taking her own life; 'when the curtain goes down,' Elizabeth Hardwick wrote, 'it is her own dead body there on the stage, sacrificed to her plot.' But the poems she wrote in her suicidal depression are sardonic, angry, unforgiving, tender, yet disciplined and always curiously detached; they are full of life, not death. All three poets were interested, above all, in bringing order to their disorderly inner worlds and their reward was not the devious gratification of letting it all hang out but the objective artistic pleasure of writing well. That style of inward exploration has now gone out of fashion even in America – it was always too extreme for British taste – but I think it altered poetry just as much as the great Romantic revolution a century and a half earlier – which was where it all began.

Ted Hughes was the one poet of my generation with a reputation that had nothing to do with the Movement. I first met him in the spring of 1960, just after the publication of his second book, *Lupercal*. I was then in the middle of my 10 years at the *Observer* and *Lupercal* struck me as the best book by an English poet that I had read since I started. When I wrote a piece to say so, the paper asked me to interview him. He and Sylvia Plath and their baby daughter were living in a tiny flat in Chalcot Square, my first wife and I were living near Swiss Cottage, so we agreed to take our children for a walk on Primrose Hill, the no-man's land that lay between.

Ted was already a powerful presence, even though he was just beginning. He reminded me of Heathcliff – another Yorkshireman – big-boned and brooding, with dark hair flopping forward over his craggy face, watchful eyes and an unexpectedly witty mouth. He was a man who seemed to carry his own climate with him, to create his own atmosphere, and in those days that atmosphere was dark and dangerous. It was a darkness that many women found irresistible: one said, 'He looks like a gunfighter, like Jack Palance in *Shane*'; according to another, even more awestruck, 'He looks like God would look if you got there.' Ted himself seemed not to care about his appearance. His clothes were worn and shapeless and his guiding principle for choosing them was Henry Ford's 'any colour as long as it's black': black corduroy jacket, black trousers, black shoes and socks. Later Sylvia Plath metamorphosed him into 'a man in black with a Meinkampf look / And a love of the rack and the screw', but in those days, when Existentialism was the fashion, black was the uniform of chic young intellectuals. It went with spouting Sartre and Camus and smoking Gauloises.

Hughes had no more in common with the would-be Marxist-Existentialists who hung around London's new coffee shops than he had with the Movement poets. He was more self-assured and self-possessed, solidly rooted in a world in which wild animals figured a great deal more prominently than people.

That, too, was nothing new in the fifties, when F. R. Leavis and his acolytes ruled the roost. According to Leavis, D. H. Lawrence was the greatest artist in the Great Tradition because, among other reasons, he was the last writer whose roots were in an England that had not yet been ruined by the industrial revolution. In dingy, pinched, unheated post-war Britain that wasn't an argument that had much appeal for someone, like myself, who had had the luck to cross the Atlantic and see what the industrial revolution could do to make life easy and comfortable. So we concentrated on Lawrence's feeling for nature and his loving descriptions of it. Even a city boy like me knew – or pretended to know – about birds, beasts and flowers because Lawrence had written about them so seductively.

Ted's background was similar to Lawrence's, provincial and working-class, but as people they had little in common. Lawrence had been a delicate, sickly child who bristled with sensitivity, adored his mother and was full of scorn for his brutish miner father. Later in life he changed his mind about his parents' relative virtues:

> My father was a working man
> and a collier was he,
> at six in the morning they turned him down
> and they turned him up for tea.
>
> My mother was a superior soul
> and a superior soul was she,
> cut out to play a superior role
> in the god-damn bourgeoisie.

Even so, he never quite lost his mother's-darling mannerisms; his voice was shrill, his tantrums shrewish and he was in thrall to his domineering wife. Hughes, in contrast, was tougher and more unyielding and there seem to have been no indulgent figures in his early life. According to an interview he gave to an American fishing magazine not long before he died, the most powerful influence on his childhood was an older brother whose passion was hunting:

From the age of two or three, I lived completely in the world of this fanatic. His hunting was getting up at four o'clock every morning to go up the hillside. Sometimes he'd take me with him. He went off to the war when I was eight or nine. I carried on myself. . . . My whole free time . . . was getting away for shooting and fishing. We killed everything. I've got diaries that I kept when I was eleven and day after day I'm killing wagtails and robins and wrens and grass snakes – everything that moved. It was a total obsession . . . I used to trap mice. I had a trapline for mice throughout a big farm. I used to skin them and cure the skins. I'd keep them under the lid of my desk at school and sell them for a penny, and maybe tuppence for a good one. I had a line of gin traps for stoats, weasels and water rats – for their skins. This went on until I was fourteen or fifteen. I was obsessed by shooting first, and then gradually fishing . . . That went on until I went to university. And I always thought I'll keep it up. I had one or two guns and all my tackle. But while I was at university, I got overtaken by the intellectual life.

Hughes was profoundly influenced by Lawrence's writing, but his take on it, like his absorption in the natural world, was very much his own. It was Lawrence without the nerves and the preaching, but also without the flowers and the tenderness. Lawrence's creatures – the snake, the mountain lion and tortoises, the stallion St Mawr, even the mosquitoes – were like the people in his novels: he was always either inside their skins or in passionate dialogue with them, using them to voice his own preoccupations and letting them argue back vehemently. Ted's creatures – the hawk, the otter, the fox, the pike – were different. They were hunters and the hunted, irredeemably alien, and it was their otherness that interested him most: their wildness, their world of instincts and threat and incipient violence, a world in which even thrushes are killers and flowers are rooted in nightmares. When Hughes set out 'To Paint a Water Lily' the flower he came up with was nothing like the ones Monet painted at Giverny. It was suspended between horror and horror, between an air shimmering with murderous insects and the pond's bed where 'Prehistoric bedragonned times/Crawl that darkness with Latin names.' In the domain of Hughes's unforgiving imagination, beauty exists but always perilously, as an act of will, and the forces ranged against it are terrible. Wild creatures, for him, were like dreams; they were his way through to hidden parts of his mind.

He read English when he went up to Cambridge, then changed to anthropology. He switched because of a dream which he told me soon after we first met. He was labouring late at night, he said, on his weekly essay – I think it was about Dr Johnson – bored by it and getting nowhere. Finally he gave up and went to bed. That night he dreamed a fox came into his college room, went over to his desk, peered at the unfinished essay and shook its head in disgust. Then it placed a paw on the scribbled pages and they burst into flame. The next day Hughes wrote a poem about the dream – 'The Thought-Fox' – and left it on his desk when he went to bed. The same night the dream-fox was back. It read the poem, nodded approvingly and gave the sleeping poet a genial thumbs-up. Hughes took the visitation as a sign: the academic study of literature wasn't for him; it was time to change his life as well as his degree course. Anthropology may not altogether have been what he was after, but at least it concerned itself with more primitive and instinctual societies than our own.

That was how he told me the story in 1960 – wryly, almost as a joke against himself. Later, when he told it to Professor John Carey, an eminently sane and reliable witness, he had translated it into something Jungian and more portentous: the fox was another persona – Hughes with a fox's head. Yet it doesn't matter that the wild animals went with a belief in mysteries, the under-life and black magic, or that he increasingly used what I thought was mumbo-jumbo to get where he wanted to be – astrology, hypnosis, Ouija boards, or the dottier forms of Jungian magical thinking. (Jung, like Hughes, was a country boy fallen among intellectuals.) All that mattered was that the poems he fished out of the depths were shimmering with life.

He kept his beliefs to himself, even back then when we were all young and shooting our mouths off at any old bright idea that had come along that week. I remember him as quiet-spoken, shrewd and modest. He was not a man to give himself airs and never came on as a poet. It was not a line of work that would have cut much ice with his neighbours in Yorkshire or Devon and he had no taste for the literary world. But he was utterly sure of his talent and you could never predict what he would say; his reactions to everything – to people, places, books – were always his own.

Like every prolific poet, Hughes published his share of poems that merely go through the motions, poems that might have been written by another of his dream premonitions, the 'Famous Poet' he savaged in his arrogant youth. But even when his duties as Poet Laureate seemed to have got the better of him, he kept his genius for the muscle and sinew of the language, and he saved some of his finest work for the end. *Birthday Letters* was his version of his troubled marriage to Sylvia Plath, a series of short poems written over the years and published on the thirty-fifth anniversary of her death. Up until then Hughes had doggedly refused to talk about Plath or to respond to the wild accusations of treachery by feminists who hacked his name off her gravestone and turned up at his readings with placards calling him a murderer. I assume he decided to set the record straight from his point of view only when he knew he was dying, rather than leave the manuscripts for biographers and academics to pick over and sensationalize.

The poems don't try to soften Plath's violent rages or blur her crippling fears or make their life together seem other than a crazy high-wire act – one slip and they were in the abyss – but they bring her startlingly back to life, often in a style that sounds curiously like hers: tightly controlled despite their apparently free form, packed with images, fast-talking and full of foreboding. They are the most vulnerable he ever wrote and also the saddest: all that love and talent gone to waste, her death, his grief and corroding guilt. The book serves as a funeral monument to them both.

It is also an answer to the story of their marriage as told by Sylvia in the extraordinary poems she wrote in that last year of her life. Part of Plath's genius lay in her ability to take any trivial domestic incident – a cut thumb, a bruise, an unwanted visitor – and infuse it with significance and dread. Hughes was doing something similar. His poems are full of references to hers – quotes, echoes, brief allusions – and several of them have the same names as her poems and describe the same incidents, as though from the other side of the mirror. Like hers, they are scenes from a marriage. His real subject, though, is Plath herself – how she looked and moved and talked, her pleasures, jealous furies and uncanny dreams, what was good between them and where it went wrong. He took the bare bones on which the biographies have been hung – their life together in Cambridge, Spain, America, Devon – and did what no biographer, however diligent and impartial, could ever do: he described how it felt to be there with her.

Plath was a Fulbright scholar at Cambridge when they first met, in 1956. For him, she was 'beautiful, beautiful America', the land of impossible plenty, and he never quite lost his sense of her foreignness and freedom, as though she had been cast in some more generous mould that made him feel shabby. When they married he was 'a post-war, utility son-in-law' and she was 'transfigured./So slender and new and naked./A nodding spray of wet violet.'

In fact, she was a girl with a load of troubles on her back, as everyone now knows: a suicide attempt that had almost succeeded, a nightmare series of electro-convulsive shock treatments and, behind all that, an adored Prussian father who scared her stiff and died when she was eight. Hughes calls her father 'The Minotaur' and a large number of the *Birthday*

Letters chart Plath's gradual, fatal descent into his lair. It was Hughes who showed her how to get there and he did it in the name of poetry.

Plath was already an accomplished poet when she met Hughes. She had won prizes and published at least as much as he had. Her poems were technically skilful and polished but the life in them was locked away out of sight. When I reviewed her first collection, *The Colossus*, I wrote, 'Her poems rest secure in a mass of experience that is never quite brought out into the daylight ... It is this sense of threat, as though she were continually menaced by something she could see only out of the corners of her eyes, that gives her work its distinction.' In comparison to her, Hughes had already arrived. What matters most about his story of 'The Thought-Fox' is that the dream came when he needed it and he was able to listen to what it was telling him. It was this that set him apart from most young poets of his generation, even from Plath when they first met: he seemed to have easy, immediate access to his sources of inspiration, a permanently open hot line to his unconscious.

The weird mishmash of astrology, black magic, Jung, Celtic myth and pagan superstition that got him to where he wanted to be worked fine for him and even made sense, given his unreconstructed *Cold Comfort Farm* view of the world, but for Sylvia it was a foreign country in every sense. Ted's background was rural and relatively poor; his father was a tobacconist and part-time carpenter who specialized in carving toy ducks. Sylvia's background was academic, conventional, middle-class; her father was a professor of biology at Boston University, an ornithologist, entomologist, ichthyologist and an international authority on bumblebees.

Her sensibility was altogether different from her husband's and, on one level, saner: more urban, more intellectual, more governed by nerves than by instincts – in a word, more American. Belief in dark gods and shamans and the baleful influence of the stars didn't come naturally to her, but she had always been good at things, a fast learner and high achiever, fiercely ambitious; anything her husband could do she could do better. She was also desperate to find any trick that might, in Kafka's words, 'serve as the axe for the frozen sea within' her. So she went along willingly when they played spooky games with the Ouija board and read each other's horoscopes, or when Ted hypnotized her to help with the birth of their first child. By the end, the pseudo black magic which Ted used cannily to get through to the sources of his inspiration had taken her over. When her husband left her for another woman, she did what the dream fox had done to his undergraduate essay: she took his manuscripts, mixed them with a debris of fingernail parings and dandruff from his desk, and burned them in a witch's ritual bonfire. As the flames died down, a single fragment of charred paper drifted on to her foot. On it was the name of the woman he had left her for: Assia. 'Her psychic gifts, at almost any time,' Ted wrote, 'were strong enough to make her frequently wish to be rid of them.'

I wonder. Admittedly the Sylvia I knew, the gifted poet who turned up at my studio to read me her new work, was always on her best and brightest American behaviour. She dressed smartly, wore pancake make-up, coiled her long hair into a severe, schoolmistressy bun, and made a great show of being cheerful and in control – a determined, resourceful young mother whose marriage was over and who was now making a new life for herself. Aside from her poems, she gave no hint of her desolation and anger. I never saw her in her other roles – neither as Lady Lazarus who eats men like air, nor as 'the magician's girl who does not shrink' – until our devastating last meeting on Christmas Eve, 1962. I now know that that desolate figure had been around a long time and that I hadn't seen it because, apart from being naive and insensitive, I was fooled by the sardonic energy and wit of her poetry.

Even so, I don't think her 'psychic gifts' were a power that came naturally to her; they were a symptom of her pathology. Hughes's loony methods for getting through to his creative under-life worked for him because, among other reasons, he was a man of unusual inner strength and assurance. Sylvia may have been saner and more sceptical than he was, but only intellectually; emotionally she was altogether more fragile. She had never got over her father's death, never finished mourning him and, because her mother wouldn't let the children go to the funeral for fear of upsetting them, she had never even buried the monster. For her, he was a scary absence, off somewhere out of sight, biding his time. With nightmares like those to contend with, Hughes's creative strategies would have worked on her like, say, the 'recovered memory' games untrained rogue psychotherapists play on unwary patients – releasing the inner demons then stepping aside with no thought of the consequences. Because he truly believed in her talent he did it, as I said, in the name of poetry. He handed her the key she had been looking for to find her dead father and, always the good student, she went down into the cellarage, key in hand. But the ghouls she released were malign. They helped her write great poems, but they destroyed her marriage, then they destroyed her.

As far as Sylvia was concerned, I was a figure in the background, an attendant lord, yet the fact that I was an established critic who responded to her late poems and published them in the *Observer* made our friendship seem important to her – for the time being, at least, until she got back on track. *The New Poetry* was also on her mind. Her work wasn't in the original edition when it appeared, early in 1962, because she was American and the book was initially intended to be an anthology of British poets who had begun to make a name for themselves in the fifties. Although she had only recently started to write the poems that eventually made her famous, she was disappointed not to have been included, particularly because what I had to say about the gentility principle struck a chord in her; she talked about it often when she dropped by my studio to read me her new work in the last months of her life. The essay showed that we had things in common and that I might understand what she was trying to do. Now that she and Ted had split up, there were not many other people around who would listen to her work sympathetically. She was on her own artistically as well as socially, exploring territory where no other poets had been, and I think she was glad to know there was someone out there making a critical case for the new style of poetry she was writing.

It was a literary companionship, a friendly voice at the other end of the black telephone that was off at the root to the voices she really wanted to get through to. My listening to her poems and encouraging her didn't make her any less lonely, but it was all I was able to offer and better, I suppose, than nothing at all. I thought her poems were extraordinary and was frustrated to think they had been written too late to include in my anthology, not least because, more than anyone else's work, they vindicated what I had written in the introduction. But that was no consolation to her. (When I revised the book three years later I included as many of her poems as her literary executors would allow. Only by then it was too late.)

Sylvia had another reason for visiting me, although I didn't mention it in *The Savage God* because the break-up of the Hughes's marriage was incidental to what I was writing about; as Robert Graves wrote of another tragic couple, 'the hazards of their love-bed/Were none of our damn business'. When Ted left Sylvia in Devon, he spent his first nights in London in the spare room at my studio. He left on the third day, saying, 'Guests are like fish. They stink after three days.' He didn't tell me where he was going and I didn't ask him, but I am sure Sylvia wanted to find out what I knew. Or maybe she wanted just to sniff around the lair where he had been. Anything to alleviate her terrible loneliness. After that it was loneliness that made her return – loneliness and her increasing despair. She needed someone to listen to her poems but, even more, she needed someone to live with and take care of her. And that was something I was not willing to acknowledge. I loved Sylvia in the way I loved other friends – for her gifts and intelligence and liveliness, for her fine brown eyes that seemed always drenched with feeling, for the disinterested passion for poetry which we shared – but I was neither willing nor tough enough to shoulder her despair. It wasn't a role I wanted, especially since Anne had walked into my life a few weeks after Sylvia's first visit to my studio. So I stuck to the poetry and tried not to hear what else she was telling me.

Sylvia was not someone who asked for favours, so she kept her needs to herself while she organized a new life in town. She had found a flat near Primrose Hill, around the corner from the square where she and Ted had first set up house in London. The flat was on the top two floors of a Victorian terraced house in Chalcot Road which had a blue plaque above its front door commemorating the fact that W. B. Yeats had once lived there. Sylvia took this as a sign that her life was about to change for the better and set about decorating it appropriately: white walls, rush matting on the floors, no curtains on the windows, a few books and bits of Victoriana and cloudy blue glass on the shelves, a couple of little white-framed woodcuts by the Hughes's friend Leonard Baskin. (Ted gave me one of them after she died.) Her elation in finding a house blessed by Yeats's ghost seemed not to have survived the fitting-out of it. The place was beautiful but chaste and chilly and forlorn – more like a nun's sanctuary than a new home for a mother and her children.

I didn't hear much from her while she was busy moving in, but she called me on Christmas Eve: would I like to come and see the new flat, eat a meal, hear some poems? As it happened, I had already arranged to have dinner with V. S. Pritchett, who lived a few streets away. I said I'd drop by on my way.

I hardly recognized Sylvia when she opened the door. The bright young American housewife with her determined smile and crisp clothes had vanished along with the pancake make-up, the schoolmistressy bun and fake cheerfulness. Her face was wax-pale and drained; her hair hung loose down to her waist and left a faint, sharp animal scent on the air when she walked ahead of me up the stairs. She looked like a priestess emptied out by the rites of her cult. And perhaps that is what she had become. She had broken through to whatever it was that made her want to write, the poems were coming every day, sometimes as many as three a day, unbidden, unstoppable, and she was off in a closed, private world where no one was going to follow her.

While her children slept upstairs, Sylvia sat with her back to the uncurtained night, sipping wine and reading some of the poems she'd written in the past couple of weeks. The ones she chose were all in the minor key, grief-stricken but pared down, without a flicker of self-pity, and hearing them in that stark, cold sitting-room – made doubly forlorn by the flimsy Christmas decorations – made me listen in a different way. This time there was no way of shutting my ears to her desolation.

One of them in particular made me understand how doomed she felt. It was called 'Death & Co' and was inspired by a visit from Dylan Thomas's ghoulish biographer, John Malcolm Brinnen, and a young friend of his. This is what I wrote about it in *The Savage God*:

When she had written about death before it was as something survived, even surpassed: 'Lady Lazarus' ends with a resurrection and a threat, and even in 'Daddy' she manages finally to turn her back on the grinning, beckoning figure: 'Daddy, daddy, you bastard, I'm through'. Hence, perhaps, the energy of these poems, their weird jollity in the teeth of everything, their recklessness. But now, as though poetry really were a form of black magic, the figure she had invoked so often, only to dismiss triumphantly, had risen before her, dank, final and not to be denied. He appeared to her in both his usual shapes: like her father, elderly, unforgiving and very dead, and also younger, more seductive, a creature of her own generation and choice. This time there was no way out for her; she could only sit still and pretend they hadn't noticed her:

I do not stir.
The frost makes a flower,
The dew makes a star,
The dead bell,
The dead bell.

Somebody's done for.

Perhaps the bell was tolling for 'somebody' other than herself; but she didn't seem to believe so.

I didn't know what to say. The earlier poems had all insisted, in their different ways, that she wanted nobody's help – although I suddenly realized that maybe they had insisted in such a manner as to make you understand that help might be acceptable, if you were willing to make the effort. But now she was beyond the reach of anyone. In the beginning she had called up these horrors partly in the hope of exorcizing them, partly to demonstrate her omnipotence and invulnerability. Now she was shut in with them and knew she was defenceless.

I remember arguing inanely about the phrase 'The nude / Verdigris of the condor'. I said it was exaggerated, morbid. On the contrary, she replied, that was exactly how a condor's legs looked. She was right, of course. I was only trying, in a futile way, to reduce the tension and take her mind momentarily off her private horrors – as though that could be done by argument and literary criticism!

Even so, we kept up the pretence – she read, I listened and nodded and made the right noises – until I looked at my watch and said, 'I've got to go.' She said, 'Don't, please don't' and began to weep – great uncontrollable sobs that made her hiccup and shake her head. I stroked her hair and patted her back as though she were an abandoned child – 'It's going to be OK. We'll meet after Christmas' – but she went on crying and shaking her head. So I went on to my dinner party and never saw her alive again.

I left knowing I had let her down unforgivably. I told myself she was Ted's responsibility and Ted was my friend. But that wasn't the whole story. I wasn't up to her despair and it scared me. My own suicide attempt was two years behind me and I didn't want to go that way again. Anyway, my head was full of Anne.

I have never kidded myself that changing from friend to lover would have made a jot of difference to her in the end. Sylvia and Ted were locked together – nurturing each other's talents at first, then pulling each other down – and his affair with Assia Wevill would probably have blown itself out if Sylvia had been able to give him space enough and time. Or maybe Assia might even have left him for someone less demanding if Sylvia hadn't died. She wanted him, in part, for the same reasons as hosts of other women wanted him: because he was gifted, subtle, handsome, manly. I suspect she also wanted him to add to her collection, because she saw herself as irresistible. Assia was a rapacious woman with a delicate, sultry face that seemed out of proportion with her heavy figure, and she made a pass at every man she met so automatically that it was hard to feel flattered. Initially, however, I think she wanted him because he was Sylvia's husband and Sylvia was a woman to be reckoned with. Assia wrote advertising copy and translated a book of poems from the Hebrew, so she knew enough about writing to recognize and resent Sylvia's talent and she badmouthed her poetry relentlessly after her death. But her only way of outdoing her dead rival was in the manner of her death. When her affair with Ted turned out to be just another affair, Assia gassed the child she and Ted had had together when she gassed herself.

Suicide was the other subject Sylvia and I had in common. We were both members of the club and we talked about it often. That, too, is part of the legacy of guilt she left me. As a lifelong adrenalin junky, I had always believed that genuine art was a risky business and artists experiment with new forms not in order to cut a figure or cause a sensation but because the old forms are no longer adequate for what they want to express. In other words, making it new in the way Sylvia did had almost nothing to do with technical experiment and almost everything to do with exploring her inner world – with going down into the cellars and confronting her demons. The bravery and curious artistic detachment – Coleridge's 'aloofness' – with which she went about her task were astonishing – heartbreaking, too, when you remember how lonely she was. But when it was all over, I no longer believed that any poems, however good, were worth the price she paid. And I've sometimes wondered if all our rash chatter about art and risk and courage, and the way we turned rashness and despair into a literary principle, hadn't egged her on.

Lowell and Berryman were in *The New Poetry* from the start because, I claimed, they seemed 'to be concerned with problems that some of the new generation of poets over here are beginning to face'. This was not strictly true. What I really meant was that they were concerned with problems I thought British poets ought to be facing, but weren't. So I put the two Americans at the beginning in order to set a standard, as an antidote to the complacency of the Movement, as a deliberate provocation. 'You may leave out James Whitcomb Riley because you are afraid of being laughed at,' Randall Jarrell wrote of anthologists, 'but if you leave out Spenser you mean business.' I wanted *The New Poetry* to be like the anthologies I admired, such as Michael Roberts' *Faber Book of Modern Verse*. Anthologies of this kind are selective, not inclusive; they are statements of personal taste, literary criticism in disguise, and if no one is offended by them they have failed.

On that level at least, *The New Poetry* was a great success. It received an unusual amount of attention for a poetry anthology and most of it was hostile. The poets I left out hated it because they had been left out and the Movement poets hated it because of the introduction, despite the fact that the book brought their work to a wide audience. (The book was briefly on the best-seller list and became, for a while, a standard school text.) I had set out to make a statement about what I thought was happening in contemporary poetry and why it mattered. So when the poets I respected liked the book and those I didn't much care for took offence, I knew I had done something right.

The anthology also gave me an excuse to get out. I loved poetry, but my relationship to the poetry world had always been ambiguous. I had been part of the literary scene for half a dozen years, going to parties, meeting other writers, gossiping about who was up, who was down and who was touting whom. At the start it was fun to be in the know and to be listened to by strangers. I was making a kind of name for myself – a fresh young tadpole in the puddle of poetry. Although I never cared much for the socializing, I told myself that it was a necessary part of the world of letters I'd opted for when I left academia. It also seemed to be part of my first marriage and the unhappier my private life became, the more I resented the literary world, as though writers and their ways were the cause of my troubles. I no longer liked what I was doing or myself for doing it, but I could see no way out. My mother had never understood what her clever only son was doing in that shady *demi-monde* and secretly I must have agreed with her. The London reaction to the death of Sylvia Plath – the gossip and malice and ill-disguised glee mixed with the shock – appalled me. It was time to move on.

11

UNDER PRESSURE

*T*he New Poetry was published in the spring of 1962, but I had written the introduction 15 months earlier, when I was teaching for a term at Brandeis University in Massachusetts. As I said earlier, 1960 was the worst year of my life and the last months of the year were the worst part of it, though Brandeis had nothing to do with my unhappiness. My marriage had fallen apart and I was chronically depressed, so desperate that I ended the year, back in London for the Christmas break, by swallowing 45 sleeping pills. I survived the pills, but my marriage didn't, although it staggered on into the summer.

I finally moved out just before my wife and child left for a holiday in Greece. I, too, wanted to get away for a couple of weeks, but living it up in the Mediterranean sun wasn't what I was after. During the previous 12 months I had become obsessed with the concentration camps; they were all I read about while I was working myself up to my overdose. In part, it was a way of putting my paltry troubles in perspective. But only in part. I was also identifying with that terrible world, as though the concentration camp were in my own head and I couldn't escape it. (Later Sylvia Plath also became obsessed with the camps during her last months and we talked about them continually.) Seeing Auschwitz, I thought, might lay the ghost. After all, that's where I would have ended up – there or somewhere like it – if the Germans had crossed the Channel in 1941.

In the fifties and sixties the BBC Third Programme was a semi-official patron for writers and intellectuals and I was doing a lot of work for it. So I called the programme's Controller, the novelist P. H. Newby, and told him I was thinking of going to Poland and was bound to meet some writers. If the BBC would buy me an air ticket and lend me a Uher tape-recorder, I'd tape my conversations with them and write a feature about intellectual life in Poland. It was pure bluff. I knew almost nothing about Poland or its writers or its intellectuals, but neither did anyone else back then, apart from the exiles and the experts. This was at the height of the Cold War, when the countries behind the Iron Curtain were blanks on the cultural map. I'm sure Newby wasn't taken in by my pitch, but he had liked the features I'd written for him on Frieda Lawrence and C. K. Ogden, and the new idea intrigued him. Or maybe he just liked my chutzpah. He agreed.

I had two Polish friends, a young couple whom I'd got to know in London and who had just gone back to Warsaw. Both of them had been brought to England at the beginning of the war when they were children, now they were starting over again in their native country. He was a writer – a poet at that time, though he swiftly moved on to steadier, better-paid work – she a doctor. She was also astonishingly beautiful and, like everyone who met her, I fell hopelessly for her Botticelli face and sweet nature. Hopelessly because there was a moral shine to her beauty; she was a faithful wife and no one was ever going to carry her off. But the pleasure of her company made the hopelessness worthwhile.

On my second evening in Warsaw the young couple invited me to their apartment to meet some writers – a few poets and literary journalists, a philosopher, a woman who taught English literature at the university. Also present was a military-looking man, with a duelling scar on his cheek and a ramrod back, who called himself a translator. He was an inspired gossip but seemed curiously uninterested in literature. When I mentioned that later, my host told me he had been a senior intelligence officer in Rome until the Italian press caught him with a rent boy. For all I could tell, the other guests were also intelligence officers, and not yet disgraced or retired. As I said, I knew nothing in those days.

Zbigniew Herbert arrived late. He was then 35, short and powerful, with a deep chest and a head like a boulder – round and heavy and noble. The head was Roman but the face was like a troll's, snub-nosed and impudent, with blue Slavic eyes, slightly slanted and very clear. He had a resonant bass voice, courtly manners and a fondness for expansive gestures: a great bunch of roses for the Botticelli – he bowed when he gave them to her and kissed her hand – and a bottle of vodka for the lucky husband.

In 1961 Herbert's reputation in Poland was high. He had been writing poems since he was a teenager studying in underground schools and fighting in the underground resistance. When the war ended and the Stalinists took over from the Nazis, he went on writing but published nothing, preferring to scrape a living in a series of Kafkaesque jobs – as a clerk in the Department for Retired Pensioners of the Teachers' Co-operative and in the management office of the peat industry, as a lowly administrator in the Composers' Union and a sub-editor of a business review. His first book of poems, *String of Light,* did not appear until 1956, after Khrushchev denounced Stalin at the Twentieth Congress of the Communist Party. By then Herbert was already 31 and had a dozen years of work waiting to be printed. His second collection, *Hermes, the Dog and the Star,* was published the following year. Two brilliant books in two years established him as one of the leaders of what the Poles, who slap labels on every new artistic movement, however transitory, were then calling Generation '56.

In 1958 the cultural *apparatchiks* gave him US$100 – as a reward, he said, for not upsetting the apple cart by publishing his profoundly un-Communist poems during the Stalinist period. He took his 100 bucks to Paris and managed to spin out his stay for two years, working as a fruit porter in Les Halles, giving private lessons in Latin and Greek, living by his wits. French poetry was not his style – too rolling and grandiose, too absorbed in its own importance – but he loved the museums, the countryside, the history, and he travelled to places where the associations were richest – Chartres, Valois, Lascaux, Van Gogh's Arles, the Midi of the troubadours and the martyred Albigensians – then on down into Italy – Siena, Rome, Naples, Paestum, and wherever he could find paintings by Piero della Francesca, the great master of lucidity. All this on a shoestring, 'expropriating a little food along the way', and writing the essays that were eventually collected in his book *The Barbarian in the Garden.*

When I first met Herbert he had been back in Warsaw only a few months and was already in trouble. Soon after his return an agent of the secret police had turned up on his doorstep pretending to be a fan of his poetry but asking questions only about the exiles in Paris. Herbert threw him down the stone staircase of the apartment block where he lived. From then on the police leaned on him, making sure he knew they were always there and spreading the word that he was bad news, though without ever pulling him in. Even the guests at the party on my second evening in Warsaw treated him warily, although they chattered away eagerly enough about Abstract Expressionism and Samuel Beckett and other officially forbidden subjects.

Herbert and I hit it off from the start and also chattered away together. His English was dreadful, I spoke no Polish, so we talked in fractured French, starting with Eliot, whom we both revered. We had other things in common: the same build, the same arrogance, the same love of poetry and distaste for the vanity of poets. We left together when the party ended. 'Thank God that's over,' he said. 'Now let's get drunk.'

A couple of days later someone – not Herbert, who would have considered it immodest – showed me translations of some of his poems. There was something about them – something to do with their clarity and poise and conviction – that made them seem to me, even in translation, to be as powerful and complete as anything that was being written at that high point in post-war poetry by the poets I liked best – Lowell, Berryman, Plath and Hughes. Like them, Herbert was responding to the collective unease of the period.

Norman Mailer had recently published an influential essay called 'The White Negro', in which he talked about 'the psychic havoc of the concentration camps and the atom bomb upon the unconscious mind of almost everyone alive in these years'. Something had happened during the Second World War and its aftermath, he was implying, that had weakened the common decencies and mutual respect on which civilized society depends. In the West, artists responded to this unease by turning inwards, though not as a form of escapism. When Lowell wrote about his bouts of madness, Berryman about his chronic boozing, Hughes about the violence of the natural world, and Plath about her rage and grief, they were using their private troubles as a mirror for this bewildering nihilism.

But they did so from a position of weakness. Robert Frost once said, 'The trouble with poetry is there's no money in it', which may explain why poets squabble and gossip so compulsively and are so unforgiving when they feud. What else can they do when fame is not just the spur but is the only reward? It may also explain why poetry has become a marginalized art in the western democracies. The best poets are thought of as craftsmen who spend their lives distilling and purifying language in order to express something perfectly. For an audience of speed readers, this is a quaint and arcane skill, like carving netsuke – difficult but not quite to the point. The general public prefers poetry as show business, the professional charmers and freaks and wild men of the poetry-reading circuit, with their user-friendly junk. The idea of the poet as a moral authority died, more or less, with Milton. When Shelley called poets 'the unacknowledged legislators of mankind' he was indulging in romantic wishful thinking.

For sound geographical reasons, they order these things differently in Central Europe, especially in Poland. When a country is squeezed between powerful neighbours, constantly fought over, partitioned, steamrollered flat by history, literature matters not just for its own sake but because it is a way of preserving the national identity – its life, culture and integrity, as well as its language. And when a country is occupied by a foreign power or governed by a single party, literature also becomes a form of crypto-politics. Political debate takes place in novels, poems, films and plays, instead of in parliament, on the hustings or on television. In times of national stress it is impossible for a Polish poet to write a lyric about the birds and the bees without someone reading it as a political metaphor or allusion. The Poles call this 'Aesopian language' and it is a long and honoured tradition.

Herbert used this tradition, duly adapted to his own subtle purposes, and it gave him a moral authority which poets in the West lacked. Lowell, Berryman and Plath thought of themselves as inheritors of Eliot's classical style of Modernism – anti-romantic by temperament, strong on intelligence, technically disciplined, culturally sophisticated. But their sensibilities were dangerously frayed and their poise was risky and precarious; like acrobats on a high wire, they needed all the intelligence, discipline and sophistication they could muster to keep their balance. Herbert also considered Eliot to be the greatest of the modern masters but his own poetry, compared with that of his American contemporaries, was truly classical, and not only because it was haunted by figures from Greek mythology and ancient Rome. It was also classical in spirit – calm, lucid, orderly, restrained. Yet his subject was precisely the totalitarian nightmare which Lowell and the others sensed only obscurely – a double nightmare, first the Nazis, then the Stalinists, which Herbert and his fellow-countrymen had been living through since 1939.

He wrote about all this, but obliquely, wryly, without histrionics. In a poem called 'A Knocker' – one of the first I read that summer – he described his style, drily, as though it were a shortcoming:

> my imagination
> is a piece of board

> my sole instrument
> is a wooden stick
>
> I strike the board
> it answers me
> yes – yes
> no – no.

The 'wooden stick' – a style so clear and simple that he could omit all punctuation without ever obscuring the meaning – was not, in fact, his sole instrument. The other was irony, an irony that questions everything – all facts, fables, assumptions, motives, especially his own motives. Herbert was a moralist whose poetry was concerned, above all, with sanity. Back in the sixties, when the Cold War was at its chilliest and the best creative people in the West had turned inward to cultivate their own distinctly messy gardens, sanity was in short supply and his work looked like a miracle. I published five of his poems, with a short introduction, in the *Observer*, in September 1962. It was the first appearance of his work in England. (Two of Miroslav Holub's poems appeared in the same way in June of the following year.)

By that time Herbert's situation in Poland was tricky, despite his reputation. He had never been a joiner and wasn't tempted by the perks that came with literary fame in the People's Democracies – the cushy jobs and plush apartments. He spurned the Writers' Union and his attitude to the police, who hadn't forgiven him for manhandling their agent, remained imperious. He left the country in 1963, when his father died, and spent the next 17 years shifting around Europe, down and out mostly in West Berlin and Paris. Occasionally he stopped off in London and would appear at my house bearing flowers for Anne and Zubrowka vodka for me, and entertaining the kids with boisterous, slightly scary horseplay. (They seemed to understand him perfectly, despite his impermeable English.)

For writers whose language is not much known beyond the frontiers of their own countries, exile is a complex fate. The language itself becomes a homeland and the exiles are caught up in a closed world of special cafés, clubs and salons, none of them too far from where the government-in-exile sits in perpetual session. Everyone knows everyone else and, as in the closed world of poetry, all of them are bound together by malice, gossip and homesickness. Abroad as in Poland, Herbert remained determinedly his own man, a party of one, permanently in opposition, a believer in what the Romans called *virtus* – intelligence, clarity and moral probity.

His independence had a price. During the 1970s he began to write poems featuring an alter-ego called Mr Cogito. Like Descartes, Mr Cogito exists because he thinks about his existence. He is also 'a great judger', a moralist who bleakly refuses the compromises that make for an easy and successful life. 'The Envoy of Mr Cogito' – which is perhaps Herbert's greatest poem – is a final statement of principles, the poet's epitaph on himself, and it leaves no room for human weakness. No room, either, for poignancy or regret. All that is left to Mr Cogito is outrage, scrupulously controlled but wholly despairing:

> go upright among those who are on their knees
> among those with their backs turned and those toppled in the dust
>
> you were saved not in order to live
> you have little time you must give testimony
>
> be courageous when the mind deceives you be courageous
> in the final account only this is important
>
> and let your helpless Anger be like the sea
> whenever you hear the voice of the insulted and beaten
>
> let your sister Scorn not leave you
> for the informers executioners cowards – they will win
> they will go to your funeral and with relief will throw a lump of earth
> the woodborer will write your smoothed-over biography
>
> and do not forgive truly it is not in your power
> to forgive in the name of those betrayed at dawn . . .

One of the paradoxes of Herbert's early, pre-Mr Cogito poems was that they confronted historical disaster calmly and with a wonderful mixture of playfulness and arrogance, tenderness and wit. But as the strains of his self-imposed exile began to tell on him his poetry gradually became more sombre. Mr Cogito is not amused and he does not forgive, and this made the younger Polish poets uneasy. They read Mr Cogito's scorn as a condemnation of their own triviality, incompetence and slipperiness, and they resented Herbert for it. 'He aspires to the role of the only just man,' one of them told me resentfully. It was a source of great bitterness among the next generation.

Another paradox of Herbert's early poems was that their elegant classicism was sharply at odds with the life he was leading. The poet I met in Warsaw was a wild man, despite his elaborate courtesy, and a serious drinker. Adam Zagajewski, a Polish poet who loves Herbert and his work, called him a 'hooligan poet', like the Russian Yesenin. The German poet and publisher, Michael Kruger, who had been a friend of Herbert since his Berlin days, said he once turned up with a huge three-litre bottle of cheap Italian wine under each arm. When Kruger asked if he could help him with them, Herbert replied, 'When they get too heavy I'll drink them!' 'Six litres of Italian plonk!' Kruger said. 'One bottle would have lasted a large family for a week.'

Herbert survived the drink in the same way as he survived the other tribulations of his indigent, footloose life – by having the physique and will-power of a bulldog. But the drinking was a symptom of more serious trouble. In the seventies and eighties he used to arrive in London looking strong enough to take on the world, yet talking mysteriously about cancer, hospitals and operations. The hospitals were real enough but the illnesses were mostly in his head: terrible bouts of depression punctuated by periods of mania. It was as though the effort to create a poetry that was unwaveringly sane and lucid out of – or in the teeth of – the terrible times he had lived through was too great. For the poetry to stay sane, something had to give elsewhere.

Booze and mania are a fearful combination and they provoked Herbert, in his chosen role of a party of one in permanent opposition to whomever happened to be in power, to new heights of provocation. He had always been reckless – he claimed to have fought a duel over a lady's honour when he was young, despite never previously having met the lady or handled a sword – now he seemed set on alienating everyone. He gave interviews in which he attacked not only the folks at home – the

Communists, the Church, his fellow-writers – but also his translators and publishers in the West. The latter wrote off his behaviour as eccentricity but the Poles were less forgiving. When Herbert returned to Warsaw in 1980, none of his poetry was in print. 'He was a poet in translation,' Kruger said. 'He existed in German, English, French, Italian, Spanish, Greek, but he did not exist any more in his own country. It was a nightmare. I remember he sent me his book *Report from the Besieged City*, published in Polish by Kultura in Paris in 1983, with a letter saying, "Keep this book. It's the only Polish edition of my poems that will survive me." That 60-page volume was his only Polish book in print at that time. Nothing else was available. Not a line. Imagine it. You come home, you know the people, you hate a lot of them, and they say, "Here's the famous Mr Herbert. What can we read of his?" And the answer is nada. At the age of 60 he was confronted with the fact that he was a writer without a language.'

Herbert had always had a taste for trouble. His scorn for the careerists and compromisers had kept him out of Poland in the relatively relaxed years when he might have made a comfortable life for himself, and while he was in exile he refused the alternative cushy career of the professional dissident. But he headed home as soon as Solidarity was established and the situation hotted up, and he stayed there all through the period of General Jaruzelski's martial law, ignored by his fellow-writers and harried by the police, who stationed a car outside his apartment and served him with subpoenas (which he ignored). He stuck it out for five years, but eventually the strain broke him. He returned to Paris but Paris was no easier for him than Warsaw. He had always suffered from hand-to-mouth disease, the occupational hazard of poetry; now he was seriously broke. He couldn't write, he was drinking heavily and he was desperate, as though emptied out by his own scorn and bravery. Finally he was hospitalized with severe depression.

Apart from the hospital staff, only his wife Katarzyna knew what was wrong with him and she wasn't saying. This was partly because she was the type of devoted spouse who scarcely exists any more in the West: well-educated, an excellent linguist, but content to live uncomplaining in her husband's shadow because she knew he was a great poet. She took care of him, she typed his work, she cooked, she protected him from intruders, and when he cracked up she protected him and his pride with silence. As a result rumours began to circulate: Herbert was in Paris, dying of some unspecified malady, penniless, unrecognized and unread in his own country. None of this was strictly true – his *Collected Poems* had been published in Warsaw before he returned to Paris – but it sounded uncannily like a rerun of the death of Cyprian Norwid, the great nineteenth-century Polish poet, and it put the wind up his admirers.

When he was young Herbert's friends loved him for his energy and playfulness and off-the-wall erudition, as well as for his poetry. His moral probity was so transparent that it seemed like innocence; it made you feel responsible for him. Feeling responsible for Herbert, however, was a tricky business, not least because he was full of Polish pride and refused to accept anything that looked like charity, no matter how dire his circumstances. And after his crack-up his circumstances were dire indeed.

So he went back to Warsaw once again, to the apartment he had bought with hard currency earned by a spell of teaching in Los Angeles during his exile. Only the Poland he returned to had changed. When I first went there in the early sixties the citizens of Warsaw looked down on Prague and Budapest; Warsaw, they claimed, was the Iron Curtain's Paris, the place to go for culture and argument. (In Budapest they said that Poland's fragile intellectual freedom was a sham; it was the price the Russians paid the Poles for keeping quiet during the Hungarian uprising in 1956.) But physically the place was more drab and battered than London in 1945. The Nazis had razed the city, boasting that they would turn it into 'a second Carthage', and the rebuilding was slow and shoddy; there were still wastelands of cleared debris and the new buildings were grey Stalinist slabs. There were few cars on the streets, the planes overhead were military, not commercial, there was nothing to buy in the shops, the restaurants were awful, the clothes shabby and life generally was hard. When I went back to Warsaw to see Herbert in the winter of 1994, five years after the collapse of Communism, the drabness had vanished but the liveliness, the intellectual buzz, had vanished with it.

So had the reverence for culture. During the bad times of the war, the Stalinist repression and martial law, Herbert had been a moral leader – a pure man, outside the system and poor by choice – who was writing some of the finest poetry of this century. None of this seemed to matter in the new would-be capitalist Poland where poetry had become what it is further west – another marginalized minority art. When I put it to a younger Polish poet that Herbert's achievements should guarantee him a comfortable old age, I got a dusty Thatcherite answer: 'He's written half a dozen books – poems, radio plays, some essays. Why, in a free market, does he think he's got the right to live well on that?'

Herbert himself had never hankered after the good life: 'A poet needs a library, a comfortable chair, a room to sleep in, hot water for a bath, and perhaps some trees outside the window. Nothing more,' he told me during one of our last evenings together in Warsaw. 'Those are the comforts necessary to organize a working life. Without them, your strength diminishes and you're fighting all the way.' By those modest standards, he had all he needed. His Warsaw apartment was on the first floor of a nondescript block, overlooking a ratty urban square full of trees. There were engravings on the walls, a vast number of books, his and her typewriters, a copying machine and, as a bonus, a small tortoiseshell-and-white cat which seemed to spend most of its time asleep on a chair. By Stalinist standards, it looked like high living, but Herbert still had trouble paying his bills and the world outside didn't let him forget it.

The free market in Poland is not attractive. The centre of Warsaw has been jazzed up, the shops are crammed with expensive luxury goods, the billboards advertise Pepsi and Camels instead of the Party, but the suburbs look as rundown and ill-lit as ever and the whole town still seems closed for business by midnight. In the bar of the recently refurbished Bristol Hotel – the Poles claim it is the most luxurious and expensive hotel east of Berlin and they are probably right – the new entrepreneurs check the stock market prices in the *Financial Times* and do deals, while their brassy wives gossip together and their children play games on notebook computers.

I mentioned what I'd seen to Herbert – casually, as a joke we could share. Instead it triggered a furious denunciation. Everyone in power, he said – the politicians, the businessmen, the police, the whole rotten gang – were old *apparatchiks* in sheep's clothing. He couldn't keep away from the injustice of it, the cynicism and corruption, and it was driving him crazy. Instead of writing poems, he was spending his days churning out what he called '*feuilletons*' – political squibs designed to provoke – and, as ever, he was giving outrageous interviews. Even the Polish intellectuals who admired him were embarrassed by his outbursts and said he was being manipulated by a bunch of anti-Communist fundamentalists who were using his fame to lend themselves respectability; 'Herbert,' they said, 'is their *pièce de résistance.'*

When his tirade ended I asked him why he bothered. He answered, 'Doctors have skills, priests have a uniform, but poets have no proper public identity. When I write my *feuilletons* I have readers.' Then he added, 'And I'm trying to liberate the greatest of human gifts – laughter.' His tone was reasonable, faintly professorial, but his expression was baleful. Then he was off again, his bass voice steadily deepening with rage: 'The most important thing is distrust, and mine is immense. My relationship to my fellow-countrymen is like a bad marriage. After a few years my strength is exhausted and I say, "Enough. Goodbye. I've done everything I could. I'm leaving with a clear conscience." The truth is, they've betrayed me – spiritually, not physically; I'm talking about the sources of poetry. I'm drowning in their stupidity.'

I was on one side of the dinner table, Herbert on the other. He gradually leaned forward while he spoke, closer and closer, until his face was inches from mine. He looked like one of the classical gods he used to poke fun at in his early poems, like Zeus thundering in his wrath. It was a fearsome sight and I barely recognized him.

When Herbert was a young man he exuded energy and seemed indestructible. Now he was 70 and all he exuded was rage and impatience. He said his lungs were bad – although that didn't stop him smoking – and his legs, damn them, weren't working properly. His many illnesses over the years seemed to have combined themselves into one – an asthma so chronic that he could scarcely manage the few steps up from the street to his apartment. Even indoors he moved reluctantly and with difficulty and, although he ate little, slept badly and had given up drink, he had put on a lot of weight. His hair, which he used to keep short and neat, was long and wild and white, and his eyes were sombre. He was a man running on empty, kept going by stubbornness. He had been hospitalized, he said, the week before I arrived, 'But when I heard you were coming I unplugged the tubes and came home. You must treat the body like a horse. If you want it to go in a certain direction, you pull the reins and kick it with your heels. If you don't fight you're dead.' He sounded amused and defiant, but moments later the asthma got him; his face turned blue and he had to stagger out of the room to take oxygen.

Katarzyna seemed as appalled as I was, and also embarrassed. 'Morally, he's extremely demanding,' she said. 'He makes no distinction between behaviour in daily life and in art. He wants everything to be crystal-clear. He bases his life on ideas, and ideas, he thinks, should be crystalline. But life isn't crystal and so he suffers. I think now that he's emptied out by it all. He tells me sometimes, "I can't exist here. I detest Warsaw." But with this illness of his, he can't get away, he can't budge. Sometimes I drive him out of town. There's this little place I know where the air is good. We walk in the forest there when the weather is not too hot. But I have to measure out the number of steps he takes.'

While we were talking, Herbert, in the next room, began coughing violently. Katarzyna winced.

When Herbert was living in exile and the people he denounced as bandits and liars were running his native country, Mr Cogito had been a rallying point for Poles; but after the Berlin Wall came down in 1989 Herbert ceased to be an exile and became just another Pole who preferred to live abroad. So he came back home and found himself preaching morality to an audience that didn't want to know.

Herbert, Czeslaw Milosz and Tadeusz Rózewicz were the only Polish poets left who had lived through the horrors of the Second World War and made great poetry out of them. Unlike the others, Rózewicz was a Communist and he never left Poland. Even so, when he was asked who was reading him now, the poet replied, 'Nobody. I'm famous and my books are published, but the younger generation is reading completely different stuff. I'm a dinosaur in my own country.' Herbert's standing in his native country had always been trickier than Rózewicz's and that made him less philosophical about accepting oblivion. And because he had never believed in giving an inch, he was still in there fighting, denouncing his enemies in public, making his situation worse. But the effort was destroying him and when he started in about the people who had betrayed him and the publishers who robbed him blind, even his friends threw up their hands in despair. 'The old Herbert – youthful, funny, innocent – is still there,' Adam Zagajewski said. 'But every so often he's eclipsed by this furious, unforgiving guy. The rage lasts for only five crazy minutes, then it's gone. But it's terrible to witness and I don't know what to do.'

None of us did. Our best hope was that he would get the Nobel Prize for Literature: 'I'd love to see it,' Kruger said. 'Herbert in Stockholm, the penguin with the Tintin haircut, saying to that funny German lady, the Queen of Sweden, "I'm so obliged." He kissing her hand, she trying to pull it away ... But it's just a dream.' Many other people who knew about poetry, including two Nobel laureates, Joseph Brodsky and Seamus Heaney, had the same dream. It seemed so obvious. Herbert had already received a number of distinguished literary prizes, especially in Germany, where his poetry influenced a whole generation, and the money from them had kept him afloat for a while. But at Herbert's level the Nobel was the prize that mattered most, the one that would have rescued him finally from poverty and confirmed his achievement even with the Poles who shunned him.

But the Nobel committee is famous for moving in mysterious ways – for preferring Galsworthy to Proust and Pearl Buck to James Joyce, for passing over Graham Greene and Auden and Primo Levi. It is also famous for tailoring the award to current events. Milosz was the first Polish writer to receive the Nobel Prize and that was in 1980, soon after the election of the first Polish pope and the rise of Solidarity. By the time Herbert was back in Warsaw, ill and broke and desperate, Poland was no longer in the news. Shortly before he died, however, they gave the Nobel to another Pole, a charming minor poet called Wislawa Szymborska. For Herbert, it must have seemed like a final insult, though by then he was probably beyond caring.

I spent three days with Herbert in the winter of 1994, and every evening, when I went back to my hotel, the same two poems were running in my head. The first was Eliot's grim lines in his *Four Quartets*:

> Let me disclose the gifts reserved for age
> To set a crown upon your lifetime's effort.
> First, the cold friction of expiring sense
> Without enchantment, offering no promise
> But bitter tastelessness of shadow fruit
> As body and soul begin to fall asunder.
> Second, the conscious impotence of rage
> At human folly, and the laceration
> Of laughter at what ceases to amuse ...
> Then fools' approval stings, and honour stains.
> From wrong to wrong the exasperated spirit

Proceeds, unless restored by that refining fire
Where you must move in measure, like a dancer.

That was Eliot's epitaph on a life devoted to poetry, but at least he had international fame, a comfortable living and the Nobel Prize. Herbert in his old age lacked honour and even fools' approval in his own country.

The other poem was Herbert's 'Pebble,' one of the handful I had read on my first visit to Warsaw three decades earlier:

The pebble
is a perfect creature

equal to itself
mindful of its limits

filled exactly
with a pebbly meaning

with a scent which does not remind one of anything
which does not frighten anything away does not arouse desire

its ardour and coldness
are just and full of dignity

I feel a heavy remorse
when I hold it in my hand
and its noble body
is permeated by false warmth

     – Pebbles cannot be tamed
     to the end they will look at us
     with a calm and very clear eye

I remembered reading that poem for the first time under a 40-watt lamp in my hotel room, and thinking, That's what I've been looking for, that's how poetry should be: full of feeling but without 'false warmth', wakeful, ironic, even-handed, intransigent. Herbert was the first contemporary poet I had read who could talk about nobility and, more important, sound noble without also sounding false.

It made me feel shabby. In my introduction to *The New Poetry* I had sounded off about the need for what I pompously called 'a new seriousness . . . the poet's ability and willingness to face the full range of his experience with his full intelligence; not to take the easy exits of either the conventional response or choking incoherence'. All I really meant was that it was better to write like Lowell than like Larkin or George Barker, better to face your troubles as clearly as you can than to pretend they don't exist or to work them up into melodrama. Now I was faced with a poet with a different scale of values.

Herbert and Miroslav Holub, whom I met in Prague a few months later, had both endured what I think is called 'an exemplary Central European education'. They had survived the Nazis by sheer good luck and the Stalinists by keeping their heads down and writing exclusively for their desk drawers. (Holub also had an official career separate from poetry; he was a distinguished clinical pathologist who travelled widely to conferences on both sides of the Iron Curtain and was famous in the international scientific community for his work on subjects like the immunology of nude mice.) Neither of them wrote about the concentration camps or the purges. As far as they were concerned, terror had a limited shelf-life in poetry and, anyway, they had a more insidious disaster to deal with – namely, the philistinism, venality and inertia of the *apparatchiks*, the sentimentality of socialist realism. Holub called this leaden oppression 'codified stupidity', and thought the only answer to it was 'Authenticity, living every-day authenticity, plain human speech'. In the world of agitprop and political self-righteousness, he meant, private values and private life, even when it was unhappy, kept people sane and it was the business of poetry to remind readers of their shared, troubled humanity.

None of that did justice to the subtlety of the poems he and Herbert were writing. I preferred a remark Herbert once made to me: 'Poetry is a very calm force for persuasion.' The two men were different in style and temperament but they had the same ambitions for poetry: a poetry based on clarity, irony and a distaste for whatever was exaggerated or ornate or overstated, a poetry of private life, good behaviour and what the English call 'decency'. Perhaps that was what Eliot had meant when he talked about classicism in the early great days of Modernism – classicism, that is, as a force for sanity, as opposed to the hothouse deformations of late Romanticism. If so, it was Modernism without the experimental hype. That didn't mean that it wasn't often the result of intense experiment, but the experiments had one aim in common: the elimination of hype in the steady pursuit of emotional precision.

I had always disliked the pretensions of poetry and the fancy airs poets assumed as though by right. When I collected some essays together, in 1968, I called the book *Beyond All This Fiddle* in honour of Marianne Moore's wonderful poem 'Poetry', which begins: 'I, too, dislike it: there are things that are important beyond all this fiddle.' It turned out there was a poetic world elsewhere that was truly beyond all this fiddle, but I had to go behind the Iron Curtain to find it.

The feature on Poland went down well with the Third Programme and P. H. Newby asked me to follow it up. So I went to Czechoslovakia, Hungary and Yugoslavia and wrote features on each of them. Then I went back to the USA, soon after President Kennedy's assassination, to look at the same problem – the writer in society – from a different perspective. The series was called *Under Pressure*.

One of the people who had listened faithfully to all the programmes and liked what he heard was Tony Godwin, who was then the editorial boss of Penguin Books. Godwin was an important figure on the scene during the sixties. I'd first met him when he was running a book shop in Charing Cross Road. It was called Better Books and it lived up to its name. It not only stocked highbrow and avant-garde titles which were hard to find elsewhere, it was also a literary hangout. Godwin was punchy and clever and he kept a pot of coffee on the cash desk. All sorts of writers – myself included – used to drop by to schmooze with him. This gave him a reputation among publishers as a man who was in touch. Eventually, Allen Lane, the founder of Penguin Books, Britain's first paperback publisher, brought him into the company as his heir-apparent.

As a publisher Godwin belonged to what, even then, was an endangered species – a book-lover who was more interested in good writing and ideas than in the bottom line. That made him a natural for Penguin, which, in those days, played an important role in British life:

most people went to Penguin for their culture in the same way as they went to Sainsbury's for their food and Marks & Spencer for their clothes. *Under Pressure* was the kind of ideas book Godwin loved and he published it as a Penguin Special. He also brought me in as advisory editor to beef up a newish project called Penguin Modern European Poets. At that point the series had published two famous dead poets, Rilke and Lorca, two fashionable Frenchmen, Apollinaire and Prévert, the Italian Nobel Prize winner Quasimodo, and one Russian, Yevtushenko, who was constantly in the news. Godwin thought the choice too conservative. If there was interesting poetry being written behind the Iron Curtain, then it was Penguin's duty to make it available. The first three poets published under my aegis were Herbert, Holub and Vasco Popa. I helped with the choice for 12 years and a further 22 volumes, until the accountants decided that enough was enough.

Godwin was a spiky, difficult man – you had to make allowances for his temperament, as though he were the author, you the publisher – but he took care of his writers like no other publisher I have known. He knew that writers write better when they are not continually fretting about money. So he haggled with his fellow-directors, more like an agent than a publisher, for advances large enough to buy his authors time and peace and freedom. As a gesture of goodwill to the board he made economies in areas in which they indulged themselves. Business lunches with Godwin were strictly business-like. He specialized in third-rate restaurants where there would be no distractions – particularly not from the food. He paid you the compliment of assuming you would prefer a larger advance to an overpriced, drunken meal.

He also paid you the compliment of assuming that your priorities were the same as his. He may have been generous to his authors but he was frugal and exacting with himself, and this frugality went with his monk-like dedication to his job. He was up at five each morning, put in four hours work, walked miles to the office, then kept up the pressure all day and usually on into the night. Despite the chronic asthma which plagued him all his life and eventually killed him, he was inexhaustible, sprightly, buzzing with energy.

The focus of this buzz and concentration was the books he edited. To me, he was the Platonic ideal of a reader. He had the instincts of the good critic for the tone and underlying purpose of a book, and also for the hesitations and padding and false notes. When I handed him the manuscript of *The Savage God* I had been working on the thing for four years and had put it through at least seven rewrites. I simply couldn't see what more I could do to it. He kept me waiting three days, then telephoned, asking me to come around that evening. He was waiting with black coffee and six foolscap sheets of notes in his tiny handwriting – notes on everything from details of punctuation to the reorganization of a whole chapter. Beside him on the table was a second foolscap pad on which he had made, for his own use, a page-by-page synopsis of the book so that he could be certain of following the argument clearly; I think there were another 12 pages of that. He made me feel that no one had ever before really read anything I had written. It was a sobering, even moving experience.

So, too, was his objectivity, his critical disinterestedness. The literary world has never been short of editors who fancy themselves as closet authors; instead of coming out and exposing themselves dangerously in print they prefer to impose their own notions of style on the authors whose work they have to deal with. Godwin had no taste for that kind of bullying. When he made a suggestion which you thought was mistaken, he would listen to your arguments and then, if he was convinced, he'd let the matter go. His ego wasn't involved.

He got on better with writers than with his fellow-publishers. He fought with Allen Lane, moved from Penguin to Weidenfeld, fought with Weidenfeld, then went to New York, where he started up his own list at Harcourt Brace Jovanovich. By then he had divorced for a second time and was living alone in a little walk-up apartment above a sports shop on Lexington Avenue, a couple of blocks north of Bloomingdale's. He'd always been a shrewd art collector; he'd bought paintings by the Australians Fred Williams and Colin Lanceley, when they were still virtually unknown in London. He also made a point of having one portable treasure which he could pop into a briefcase and take with him if the going got rough. In London, it had been a Benin bronze which he sold before he left; in New York, it was a Renaissance statuette he had picked up for a few dollars in California. Slowly the scruffy apartment began to fill with his stylish bits and pieces. The traffic hooted and fumed below, the view was of iron fire-escapes, rooftop water tanks and the new skyscrapers on Third Avenue, yet the place seemed curiously English.

So did Godwin. And because of that, he seemed very lonely. He said he missed his London cronies, which was, for him, an unusual admission of weakness. When he started working in New York his colleagues had been intrigued by this middle-aged English cuckoo in their nest. But his pugnaciousness and unorthodox ideas gradually scared them off and, like their British counterparts, they were offended by his voracity for work. Although it wasn't necessary, he had arranged his contract with Harcourt Brace Jovanovich in such a way that there could be no let-up in the pressures on him. He seemed to work even longer hours than he had in London, and eventually the strain began to tell. The New York climate was bad for his asthma – the winters were too cold, the summers too hot – and the attacks became progressively more savage. But he went on with his insane routine, as though not to have done so would have been a loss of face as well as a dereliction of duty.

In October 1975 I got a letter from Godwin saying he had found a beautiful little cabin far out on Long Island 'in an acre of woodland on a saltwater creek and marsh'. It would do as a hideaway when Manhattan got too much for him. Then he added:

> The asthma is still guerrilla warfare ... When I feel really bad I comfort myself with the remark an NY doctor made when I was having a really bad bout, wondering if I was for the high jump. Managed to get to the phone, dial and croak into it. 'Look,' he says, 'are your lips blue yet? If not you'll be OK till I get there.'

> Dear Al, are your lips blue yet?

Five months later he had another devastating asthma attack and this time he wasn't able to reach the phone in time. It was three days before he was found.

12

AUDEN

———————➤◄———————

W. H. Auden also changed my life, though not in the way Tony Godwin did. I only met Auden a few times, but the meetings stuck in my mind and taught me things I needed to know about the ways of the literary world. What I learned was not particularly cheering, but it was valuable, so I owe him a personal debt.

I first met him in Princeton, at the end of January 1958. I was in my late twenties, but young for my age and not a nice figure – edgy, confused, ambitious, unhappy. Auden, with his Wallace Beery face and twanging Oxford-American accent, was confident and famous and doing his best to appear interested, though he was obviously bored rotten by the chattering adulation which erupted wherever he went in literary academia. (Later he stopped pretending. The last time he appeared at London's International Poetry Festival, in 1973, he treated the audience to a poem which ended: 'I'm so bored with the whole fucking lot of you I could scream.' Needless to say, the audience chose to believe his throwaway charm and battered face, even on stage, rather than the words. The applause was overwhelming.)

We were both at Princeton to give the Gauss Seminars and we met at the usual post-seminar party in Richard Blackmur's house. Auden had just given the first of his six seminars and was unwinding over one of Blackmur's gigantic mahogany whiskies. The feeling in the room was strained. Although everyone was delighted by the great man's presence, they were put out by the talk he had given. Instead of a meticulously prepared lecture, Auden had simply chatted – allusively and wittily, of course, but in a rambling way and not always coherently – from a few notes scribbled on the back of an envelope. The Gauss seminarians were a distinguished bunch – people like Edmund Wilson, Hannah Arendt, V. S. Pritchett – and all of them had come with carefully written papers which they eventually turned into books. Auden hadn't bothered. The audience was offended, a bit contemptuous, and vaguely embarrassed on his behalf. Everyone at the party was polite and deferential, but the room vibrated with free-floating malice.

I myself was secretly pleased, and also relieved that Auden seemed, at least on this first occasion, to have blown it. After all, I was to give the six seminars which followed his and was terrified by such eminent competition. On another level I was full of admiration. For me, the Gauss Seminars represented the biggest of all possible deals; I was the first person under 30 to give them and had been writing and rewriting my lectures for months. Now here was Auden with his half-dozen words on a torn envelope, obviously not giving a damn. Listening to him, I realized that there was a self-confident adult world elsewhere that I had never even dreamed of. I was a couple of years short of my thirtieth birthday, with a wife and a new-born son, yet he made me feel like a child.

We got on rather well in a partyish, chatty way. He mentioned that he had read articles of mine – 18 months earlier, I had begun my stint at the *Observer* – and, of course, this was flattering. More importantly, we had England and Oxford in common. And Auden remained implacably English, despite all his years in America, despite the weird, flattened vowels which kept jolting his accent unexpectedly, like so many potholes. He had the shabby, shop-soiled look of the English intellectual who, no matter how smartly he tries to dress, invariably finishes up looking like an unmade bed and doesn't mind a bit. He also had that quick, sideways-on way of talking, all allusive jokes and sudden jumps in the argument, which flourishes on the belief that anything, no matter how serious, can be settled by a witty aphorism. And his aphorisms were very witty indeed. He made me homesick for Oxford, although it was two years since I had packed in a career there in order to write freelance. It was nice to be back, provided it was just for an evening and in another country.

To Auden, I was simply another face in a swarm of faces. My own reactions were more complicated: I knew, and he didn't, that my first book, *The Shaping Spirit*, was about to appear, and in it was a long essay highly critical of his work. I suppose it had to be that way, since every young writer trying to sort out his own values from the mass of received opinion does so, in part, by giving the finger to the established great of the preceding generation. In those days, as I have mentioned, Dr Leavis and his followers dignified this primitive Oedipal gesture with a term from

Henry James. They called it 'placing' – a smug, judicial word implying that once you had put an author firmly in his rightful place you were thereby mysteriously superior to him. It was a particularly British affliction, like catarrh. Reading the essay I'd written on Auden now, it seems to me overbearingly cocksure and pleased with itself, pleased with its own cleverness and determination to lay down the law. In other words, more than a little offensive and also ungrateful since, in my time, I had been besotted by Auden's poems. As a student, I had known dozens of them by heart and, like every versifier who came of age in the fifties, I had written my share of Auden pastiche. Someone once said that when you have had a youthful love affair with a writer it is hard to be friends afterwards. Apparently I felt that the only way to break free of my infatuation was by kicking the loved one, metaphorically and literary-critically, in the groin.

Now there the great man was – charming, witty, subtle, sympathetic. I felt ashamed. But, of course, I didn't want to admit that even to myself, so I made a resolution: from now on I would avoid poets – or rather, avoid poets about whose work I had mixed feelings. It was hard enough to react freshly to the words on the page without complicating them with personal details – the faces, voices, the grating or ingratiating mannerisms, sometimes even the plain niceness and goodwill. I imagined I was preserving my independence; more likely, I was being cowardly. Even so, it was a decision I have never regretted. Thanks to Auden, I have been spared a great deal of literary gossip and cheap booze.

Although I now dislike the bumptious tone of that essay, I still agree with its basic premise: a change occurred in Auden's work – a change mostly for the worse – and it coincided with the outbreak of war in Europe, in 1939, when he left England for America. As he got older and his life became apparently easier, his poetry relaxed and lost its sharpness. Perhaps this was inevitable in a poet as precocious as Auden, since precocity is the most ambiguous gift in the world, particularly in verse. It depends on a creative arrogance which rarely survives the erosions and compromises of age. Yet Auden's gifts at the start were so absolute and unexpected, and his technical mastery so great, that it was unlikely he could ever relapse into the inertia which overtook many of his contemporaries. What happened, instead, is that he retained his skill and lost his cutting edge.

When *The Orators* was reissued, in 1966, Auden wrote, 'My name on the title-page seems a pseudonym for someone else, someone talented but near the border of sanity who might well, in a year or two, become a Nazi.' Maybe, but it was precisely this borderline quality which made his poems tick – what I called in a review of the book

> an unnamed, probably unnameable, but utterly pervasive sense of guilt and fear of retribution, which made him cast around unceasingly for solutions. So he went to politics, psychoanalysis and sociology, and refracted them all through a tense, thickened language, the poet's mind leaping like a salmon with energy and despair.

Auden seemed to put these anxieties behind him when he moved to New York, and the longer he stayed there the more he came to dislike his younger self. That, I suppose, is why he so savagely mutilated his early poems when he reissued the *Collected Shorter Poems* in 1966, omitting many of the most famous – 'Sir, No Man's Enemy', 'Spain, 1937', '1st September 1939' – and reducing his fierce poem on Oxford to four toothless stanzas. His refusal to lapse into the most tempting of easy solutions, self-plagiarism, was admirable; so, too, was the self-knowledge. But the effects on the poetry were unfortunate.

There were still moments when he wrote like an angel. *The Sea and the Mirror* is as rich and moving as anything he ever produced; though even there the tone has altered: renunciatory, calm, adjusted, all passion spent. The years in Manhattan transformed a poet who, in his youth, had been a combination of Ariel and Caliban – at once stunning and dangerous – into a mature, autumnal Prospero.

In his later years that persona took over completely. The verse became increasingly more comfortable, determinedly more mellow. New York set him free to adopt a role he would probably neither have dreamed of nor been allowed in Britain: that of the fuddy-duddy English gent, a little eccentric perhaps – he wore carpet slippers in public and lived openly with another man – but basically sound, basically clubbable, basically Christian. Who else among the modern poets – who else even among the Victorians – accepted all the Church of England's 39 Articles? Who else was such a genius with crossword puzzles, clerihews and limericks? It was as though his time in New York were ultimately a preparation for that Honorary Fellowship at Christ Church, Oxford, where he spent his last years.

That is, God knows, an unjust way of expressing the obvious fact that Auden changed as he grew older, changed as he had to since he was far too gifted and self-aware to relish being stuck with a parody, however successful, of himself when young. So in his maturity he came to accept what he was and what he could do – to accept it and enjoy it. He became the supreme technician, a cosmopolitan, highly social figure with an extraordinarily wide range of cultural interests. The emotional current of his poetry, previously so turbulent and powerful, did not, however, deepen as it became broader and calmer. Instead it seemed to run more and more shallow as it became, like his themes, obstinately social.

I think he saw himself as a kind of latter-day Roman: a dedicated craftsman and past master of worldly wisdom, writing long, chatty, decorously knowing epistles, mostly to his friends, while the Visigoths hammered at the gates: a deliberate choice, deliberately and skilfully pursued. Yet somehow I have never quite believed that, for Auden, ripeness was all. Had it been so, the late verse would have been less thin; it would have been convinced as well as casual. In other words, it would have got its effects not through all those brilliant, beady-eyed aphorisms of maturity and adjustment – which are what, if anything, you remember of it – but through the more insidious, underground disturbances which occur when a poet of Auden's stature is writing about something that really concerns him. It is only rarely that that note is sounded in any of his last books. Instead the real, unspoken content of his late verse is, simply, boredom – a crippling, unceasing, demoralizing and ultimately destructive boredom: 'I'm so bored with the whole fucking lot of you I could scream.'

And maybe bored with himself, too. He knew he had more talent than all his contemporaries rolled into one; he knew that he was so famous and revered that he could do whatever he wanted without hesitation or question, and with flamboyant technical aplomb. But he also knew that there was not much he wanted to do and, more depressing still, that the Muse who had once so shaken him, and whose unforgiving embraces he no longer relished, had now gone elsewhere, leaving him in ambiguous peace. No wonder he found, when he paid his much-applauded annual visits to the London Poetry Festival, that the other poets got on his nerves, and even the audience's adulation seemed, after remarkably little time, to be more a persecution than a pleasure.

I met Auden at the first of those festivals, and once or twice later, but only briefly and with other people. The last time I spoke to him alone and at length was in New York, in 1964, when I went to his apartment to interview him for the American section of my *Under Pressure* programmes.

He was living in St Mark's Place, which, in those days, had not yet become like one of Gustave Doré's illustrations of the Inferno. It was merely rundown, going to seed. But the smell of disaster was already in the air: too much litter, too many derelicts, a feeling that somehow the whole area, like the city itself, was slowly cracking open, 'revealing what was much better hid – Unpleasant'. Eventually the drug addicts, muggings and dilapidation were too much for Auden and he left for the ordered spaces of Oxford's most elegant college, where they have perfected a higher style of decay.

Back in 1964 he was still well ensconced, shuffling around in his slippers, dropping cigarette ash and talking, while the tape-recorder was running, wittily, originally, and to the point. The apartment was dark and unswept. I remember dusty piles of books and papers, overflowing ashtrays, a sink full of dirty glasses waiting to be washed. Like the neighbourhood, it was shabby and on the seedy side.

When the recording was finished we chatted for a while, mostly about how hard it was to scrape by as a freelance writer without falling back on a university job. Terrible, he agreed, but he was all right now, thank God. He didn't have those worries any more. I remember wondering enviously how it must be not to have to fret about next week's money, not to have to hustle around between literary editors, producers of radio talk shows and the smart operators in television. I wondered what it would be like to write what you wanted to write without having to churn out an article a week to pay the rent. At the same time I was thinking, I don't know whether or not he is still a great poet, but he has a great face. It was like the limestone he loved so much: seamed, rifted, pocked, unbelievably complex, with a long upper lip and shrewd, hooded eyes surrounded by a wild network of wrinkles, like shattered rock. A face like a city, lived in and swarming with life.

Then he said, 'Still, writing for the *Observer*, you have great power.'

He's got to be joking, I thought. But his eyes, watching me, were serious, neither amused nor friendly. I was dismayed.

Thanks to my encounters with Auden in Princeton, I had carefully steered clear of poets' pubs and readings and jamborees, so it had never crossed my mind that serious poetry inhabited a world in which the idea of power – literary political power, as Auden obviously meant – had any meaning. I knew about the power of art critics and had watched Clement Greenberg throw his weight around brutally at a conference on criticism in Sydney. After each session I would be surrounded by ladies in floral dresses with poems concealed about their persons, while Greenberg was whisked away in a chauffeur-driven Rolls-Royce to advise millionaires about their art investments. According to Australian painters I knew, it was years before the art market recovered from his visit. But that was the point: paintings are valuable commodities and there's no money in poetry. The only literary person I had ever heard talk about power was George MacBeth, who edited poetry for the Third Programme. But MacBeth was a sardonic Scot as well as a gifted poet, and he grinned like a death's head when he said 'power', expecting you to see the joke. And that, I felt, summed it up: the social politics of poetry were a substitute for the art itself, a frivolity that kept you busy in place of writing. Of the thirties generation, I might have expected someone like Geoffrey Grigson to be interested in power, never W. H. Auden.

I believed this not just because the poetry world is small and obscure, but because poetry itself is the most private of all the arts. The real work is done and the real satisfactions are obtained long before the poem reaches print. Naturally every poet wants his work to be read sympathetically and with pleasure; though that is just an added bonus. The ultimate pleasure is in getting the poem right, making it as true and strong as you are able, and then, perhaps, having it pass muster with the two or three people whose judgement you respect. After that, publication is usually automatic, a matter of where and when. Sooner or later anything of any worth will be published, since the magazines are jammed with so much that has none. Auden obviously knew that far better than I did and, anyway, he had been beyond such problems for more than 30 years.

Thinking later about what he had said, I realized that by 'power' he meant power to influence taste, so maybe there was truth in his remark. The *Observer* was an influential paper and for eight years I had chosen the verse it published and had been its regular poetry critic, so at least there had been a certain personal consistency of taste – or prejudice. Moreover, the period when I was writing for the paper had begun drab but had become intensely interesting: Lowell and Berryman first publishing in England, Hughes and Gunn writing their best stuff, Plath appearing like some marvellous comet then burning out. As I've already explained, I was deeply committed to this style of poetry and I had done my best to plead its cause. Even so, I knew that my readership was tiny: the poets reviewed and their relatives, their friends and their enemies (i.e. other poets) were the only guaranteed audience, apart from a few teachers of English who still made a pretence of keeping up, and even fewer 'poetry-lovers' – whoever they were.

It had never crossed my mind that Auden bothered to read the things I wrote, except occasionally and out of curiosity, still less that he might take them seriously. He was beyond such problems, a major international figure whose reputation and devoted readership were unlikely to be affected by what anyone said about him in a Sunday paper. I expected young or minor poets sometimes to resent what I wrote and take it personally. But Auden was Auden. Now it seemed I had been wrong all along. I felt like the lady in 'Prufrock': 'That is not what I meant at all. / That is not it, at all.'

I suppose I should have known better. But I didn't, and that still puzzles me. Perhaps I was being irrational, or disingenuous, or perhaps I was still disproportionately young for my age, although I no longer felt so. More likely I was nurturing a contempt for the whole critical enterprise, a contempt which I did my best to hide even from myself, since it did me no good to admit it. To explain this, I must go back a little.

I decided to give up my university career – such as it was – in 1956, the year of the Suez affair and *Look Back in Anger*, when I was in my middle twenties. Unlike most of the choices I have made, this one was deliberate and clear-cut, not sidled up to on the sly or in a dream. My second year-long visit to the States was over and I was back in Oxford, hanging around indecisively, and about to launch into my first marriage. One of the colleges was looking for a tutor in English and it was suggested, in the conventionally roundabout way, that it might be a good thing if I were to apply. 'You understand,' I was told, 'that nothing is certain in this world, old boy. But . . .' One thing I understood clearly was that the job meant security for life because, in those days, a fellowship at an Oxford college brought instant tenure. Since I had at that time about 30 shillings in the bank, security was a tempting proposition. But I also understood, however obscurely, that if I had security I would probably never write another word, since teaching and writing are both full-time occupations, and to my mind mutually exclusive – maybe equal but certainly separate. I also believed, equally obscurely, that I was a writer, not an academic. I had just finished my first book of criticism, I was writing poetry, publishing articles here and there on both sides of the Atlantic, and making my first abortive start on a novel. At least it was a beginning, and anyway, I realized, that was what I wanted and had always wanted. So I said no. Or rather, I didn't apply.

I had a moment of pure elation, then a long period of panic when I realized that I had no money and no prospects. They say that two can live as cheaply as one. I found that, with luck, two can live as cheaply as three, but it took some doing. So I began frantically to review everywhere: the British weeklies, American quarterlies, the BBC and occasional, better-paid pieces for glossy magazines. Within a few months I was so busy writing for a living that I had no time to write for myself.

During those 10 long years I wrote criticism regularly, seriously, and sometimes even passionately; but secretly I believed that criticism was somehow not a wholly valid occupation. It was more like a holding operation while I waited for the unlikely moment – it became more and more unlikely as the years went by – when my luck would change and my number would come up. I thought of what I was doing as a long apprenticeship in the discipline of prose – good for me, like callisthenics, but somehow to one side of my real concerns. And because I wrote so much about contemporary poetry – always the shabbiest and most malicious fringe of the literary world – I felt doubly ashamed. 'One cannot in some degree help but judge a man by the company he keeps . . .' Now here was the great W. H. Auden implying that that was precisely what he had been doing all along.

There was no good reason why he should have done otherwise. He might possibly have glanced at *The New Poetry*, but apart from that book and a lot of articles my collected works at that time consisted of a second dour book of criticism – *The School of Donne* – and a couple of slim volumes of verse. Auden was unlikely to have set eyes on any of them. So far as he was concerned, I wasn't a genuine writer and never had been. I was just another one of them: one of the critics, editors and commentators, the peddlers of opinion and influence, one of the literary world's necessary evils. I had assumed, for no good reason, that he and people I respected would never be stupid enough to be taken in by appearances which even I found unconvincing. Now I realized that I had assumed wrongly.

'Power,' he said sourly, and I wanted to reply, 'No, thank you. Thanks very much, but no.' Instead I just blushed and grinned like an idiot and hung my head.

We had nothing more to say to each other. As I walked off down the dingy street, I thought, 'Well, that's it. I must change my life.' And I did. Not immediately, of course, since it took time to arrange alternative ways of keeping the wolf from the door. But within a couple of years my career as a regular reviewer of poetry was over. It was a great relief. Ten years is too long to do anything. I had gone stale and lost interest; more importantly, I was no longer convinced. If there were ever to be a collective noun for a gathering of bards – on the model of 'a pride of lions' or 'a gaggle of geese' – it should be, I decided, 'a bellyful of poets'. I had had mine. But it took Auden, the idol of my adolescence and a very subtle man, to show me how tired and uneasy I was with the scene. I am grateful to him for that.

Auden had called my bluff. Writers write books, not bits and pieces, not books about other people's books. If I was really a writer with something to say and my own way of saying it, then it was time I got on with it. Tony Godwin thought so too. He had left Penguin not long after he published *Under Pressure* in 1965, and had moved to Weidenfeld. In 1967 the *Times Literary Supplement* ran a long essay of mine – it was called 'Beyond All This Fiddle' – about the situation in contemporary arts. It was a literary sermon on the text of John Berryman's 'Dream Songs' – 'We are using our skins as wallpaper and we cannot win' – and it must have touched some nerve in Godwin because he called me at seven in the morning to tell me how much he liked it. I had been playing poker the night before and was still half asleep, so I didn't take much in. Then he said, 'It's time you wrote a real book. You dream up a subject and I'll get you a decent advance. Think about it for a couple of days, then come and see me.' That woke me up. But when I sat down to consider his idea all I could think of was Sylvia Plath's terrible end five years earlier and my own brutal attempt to do myself in a couple of years before that. When I told Godwin I wanted to write a book about suicide his face fell, but he kept his word and got me a good advance – £5000, which in those days was enough to live on comfortably for two years.

Unfortunately *The Savage God* took me four years to write and I was desperately strapped for money by the end. It took me so long because I have always written slowly and rewritten obsessionally. But there was another reason: I didn't want to finish up with just another dry discussion of suicide, or suicide and literature. If I wanted to write a real book, I mustn't lose sight of my real motives for writing it.

In February of 1962 I had gone back to Poland with the Australian painter Sidney Nolan. The *Observer* had asked me to write about Auschwitz and Nolan wanted to illustrate the piece. Auschwitz is a difficult experience to handle, even as a tourist. You grab hold of whatever you can to keep your mental balance. Nolan seemed curiously upset less by the obvious horrors – the crematoria, the mountains of shorn hair, discarded spectacles, suitcases and artificial limbs – than by the orderliness of the camp's layout. The interiors of the barracks were dreadful – the tiers of bunks in which the prisoners slept, six men to a bunk, like battery hens waiting to be slaughtered – but the neat grids in which the buildings were arranged troubled him even more. 'It looks like a bloody Mondrian,' he said. This was one way of putting an idea we had often talked about: that the arts didn't just reflect society, they were a kind of early warning system that obliquely predicted what would happen. (This, remember, was during the Cold War, when global annihilation and nuclear winter were on everyone's mind.) But I also knew that my own suicidal behaviour had given me a personal stake in the idea of a murderous century reflected in murderous art, and that it wasn't enough to write a critical study of suicide to prove it. What was needed was something more – well, existential: something that would make the subject come as alive and urgent for the reader as it was for me and had been for Sylvia Plath.

So I planned the book as a modern *Anatomy of Melancholy*, a personal meditation on suicide in all its manifestations: a history of suicide as a social taboo and of the false beliefs generated by that taboo; a geography of the closed world of chronic depression and the many psychological theories for it; finally, suicide as a black thread running through literature from Dante, through Donne and the Renaissance to the Age of Reason and the Romantics, then emerging as a major theme in the twentieth century.

I knew there was a danger that, however sharply I tried to write it, all this dour research might end up sounding abstract and theoretical. To prevent this happening, I began and ended the book with two detailed personal histories – an account of Sylvia Plath's suicide (the first, in fact, to appear in print) and of my own failed attempt. Suicide is an intensely private act and, to do justice to it, *The Savage God* had to be equally personal.

Apart from Tony Godwin, no one at Weidenfeld liked the project. A highbrow book on a downbeat topic wasn't their idea of a sure-fire hit, so they prepared for disaster by printing 1500 copies – just about enough to sell to the public libraries. What they got instead was a miracle. Despite their indifference and the initial print-run, the book sold well enough in Britain and is still in print nearly 30 years later. But in Europe and America people are less shy about acknowledging their depression and, like a 100–1 outsider winning the Grand National, *The Savage God* became a best-seller.

Nan Talese, my editor at Random House, had called me in London to say that the *New York Times* was running a review on the front page of its book supplement but I had no idea of what that meant until I arrived at JFK on the Sunday the article appeared. There were not many people on the flight and the immigration officers were taking their time. Mine was swarthy and suspicious. He examined my passport closely, stared at the photo in it, stared at me, and took what seemed an age searching through his files. Then he stared at me again. Here goes, I thought. It's the Spanish name. They're going to take me to a locked room, tell me to drop my trousers, then check to see if there are drugs hidden in my rectum. Instead he said, 'Are you the guy who's written a book about suicide?' I nodded. 'I just read about it in the *Times*,' he went on. 'It looks real interesting. Welcome to America, Mr Alvarez.'

As a best-seller, *The Savage God* was never a big deal, but publishers are optimistic people, like punters at the racecourse, and that wasn't how they saw it. So far as they were concerned, any unlikely horse that could make it past the winning-post and on to the *New York Times* best-seller list was worth backing again. During the next decade I wrote two novels, a book about divorce and, as a gesture to my past life, a short critical study of Samuel Beckett. But *The Savage God* was my first real book, written in my own voice on my own terms, and it changed my life. Finally, in my forties, I had became what I had always wanted to be: someone who wrote books rather than someone who wrote about them.

PART TWO

13

THE PLEASURE PRINCIPLE

I

So where did it all go right? The change began around the time of my fateful meeting with Auden in New York. My ex-wife had remarried by then and moved to Rome, taking our small son with her. Adam and I had always been close and the separation was hard for both of us, so I went to Rome as often as I could afford the fare. Mercifully that wasn't often, because my visits drained the life out of us.

The routine was always the same. It began with small talk with the ex- and her new husband at the door of their apartment, each of us bright and cheerful and brittle as glass. Then Adam and I would wander off into the city, stopping at toy shops and the joints that sold his favourite ice-cream. We usually finished up eating hot dogs on the Spanish Steps or dabbling our sweaty feet in the fountains of the Borghese gardens, while sleek Romans paraded past on their glossy horses. This was the time of *La Dolce Vita*, when Rome was reckoned the smart place to be, but its charm always eluded me. My reaction to the Eternal City was much the same as Arthur Hugh Clough's:

> Rome disappoints me much; I hardly as yet understand, but
> Rubbishy seems the word that most exactly would suit it.

I didn't even manage to get the hang of the city's geography because I was too miserable to take anything in. We were both too miserable, although we pretended it was all great fun, and I never knew which of us was the more exhausted by the end of the day. I'd have him home before seven, as instructed, then I'd wander off again to the noisiest dive I could find, hoping to get drunk or laid or both. I think Adam dreaded the visits as much as I did, but we hated the separation even more. Since he wasn't coming back to London, there was nothing else to be done.

One Friday afternoon I was locking the door to my studio in London, already late for the evening flight to Rome, when I realized I had nothing to read. I rushed back inside, grabbed the nearest book off the nearest shelf and stuck it in my briefcase without looking at the title. Any old book would do to read myself to sleep. It turned out to be *Bleak House*. I started reading on the plane and went on reading on the bus into town; I read it over an unusually sober dinner and I read it in bed at the hotel. The novel was all I could think of next day and the following morning, while Adam and I were trudging around the city. I couldn't wait to get back to it.

At some point during one of those long, chaste evenings with *Bleak House*, it occurred to me that the book was giving me something I no longer necessarily associated with reading: it was giving me pleasure. I was totally caught up in Dickens's story and his people; I wanted to know what would happen to them, I wanted to know how it would all work out. I was reading without a pencil in my hand, without consciously being on the lookout for technical tricks or layers of meaning or ultimate intentions. Critical habits die hard, so I suppose I was too watchful to swallow everything whole, but I was far too absorbed in the alternative world Dickens had created for my pleasure to be irritated by his mannerisms. So this is what Coleridge meant by 'a willing suspension of disbelief'. I hadn't dreamed it could be anything so simple. I knew about music and the pleasure of being taken over by it, but had forgotten that reading, too, is a solitary delight: turning the pages, at one with the book, while a stranger's voice in my head – a voice like no one else's, with its own accent and speed and hesitations and emphases – told me a story. Then I thought, Here I am, a paid-up, card-carrying literary critic and I've forgotten that people read books for pleasure; more importantly, I've forgotten that authors write books in order to give pleasure. I must have known that when I first decided that writing was what I wanted to do with my life, and if years of churning out criticism have made me forget it, then I must give up criticism and get back to where I started.

It seems obvious enough now, but at the time I felt like Saul on the road to Damascus. Above all, I was astonished that it had taken me so long to find out about the pleasure principle because, in those days, most of the people I hung out with in London were painters, and painters are better at pleasure than writers. I had discovered that truth back in the autumn of 1956, soon after my second trip to the States. I was stopping off in Glenilla Road on my way back to Oxford, but after three months in Brett's log cabin in the mountains north of Taos I was no longer sure if Oxford was where I wanted to be. By then, as I have said, my first book was almost finished, I was writing poetry and earning a dodgy income as a book reviewer. I knew I wanted to write, not teach, but reviewing is a hard way to make an uneasy living and I had no money. I was still working up my nerve to take the plunge when I met a painter called Denis Mathews and mentioned that I was looking for somewhere to live for a month. He said he was about to go out of town and offered to rent me his studio for £3 a week.

The studio was in Merton Rise, a side-street between Swiss Cottage and Primrose Hill, not far from where my parents lived. It had once been a stable but all that was left of that was now a garage with a cobblestone floor and a vine, heavy with grapes, growing under its glass roof. The studio itself lay behind a big oak door in the far corner. It was a romantic place and very beautiful. The old hitching-post stood in the centre of the living-room, an enamel stove throbbed away in one corner, a couple of rugs and spidery Windsor chairs floated on the red linoleum. A small kitchen was tucked below the steep staircase and there were two bedrooms and a bathroom on the floor above. Outside the windows was a walled garden that had run to seed and half a dozen ancient apple trees hung with fruit. Denis's pictures were on the walls, mostly paintings he had done during a recent visit to China, full of colour, swarming with life and busyness. Over everything was the rousing smell of oil paint and turps.

It was the smell that got to me – the smell of art, of making things, of the bohemian life, of everything that wasn't to be found in Oxford's musty libraries. That heady smell, the beauty of the place, the liveliness and subtlety of the pictures – all of them seemed to be expressions of Denis himself and of the kind of life he led. He was easy and good-humoured and utterly free of the pompous moral earnestness that passed for seriousness in English departments in the fifties. Meeting him made me realize that it might be possible to live an interesting life on my own terms, provided I kept my nerve and didn't worry about security. This was not something he and I ever discussed, then or later, and I'm not sure if I myself even thought about it deliberately. But he and the place and the atmosphere must have been working away on me subliminally because, within a couple of months, I had made up my mind: I abandoned my university career and set out to earn my living as a freelance writer.

Four years later, when my marriage broke up and I had nowhere to go, Denis was the first person I called. By some miracle, my timing was right: he was about to move to Wales and the studio was free. I moved back in and stayed until the place was sold to a property developer, who tore it down, flattened the secret garden and built three bijou, Georgian-style terraced houses in their place. For the two or three years before that catastrophe I lived a bachelor life in one of the most beautiful and hidden little houses in London, dirt cheap, and with the faint smell of oil paint always in the background.

I know where my love of music and books began and I know where they have ended – writing is what I do and music is what keeps me sane – but where my love of the visual arts comes from is a mystery to me. It has nothing to do with thwarted talent; I was hopeless at art at school and can scarcely draw a map, let alone a face or a figure. Grandpa Levy's splendid flat was hung with paintings – mostly soft-core Victoriana, variations on the theme of the Egyptian harem – but I suspect he collected them less because he liked art than because that was what you did if you were rich. There were also a few pictures on the walls at Glenilla Road, including a couple painted by my mother when she was at the Slade, but they seemed to be there only to fill the empty spaces and no one ever looked at them. Yet painting has always been the art I associate with freedom. Perhaps this is because I read *The Horse's Mouth* and *The Moon and Sixpence* and spent hours poring over my collection of two-and-sixpenny Penguin Modern Painters when I was shut away in Oundle during my impressionable teens.

Or perhaps it began much earlier. I can remember passing the elegant little houses at the edge of Hampstead Heath when Nanny took me for my daily walk, looking into the windows at the pictures on the walls and the books on the shelves, and thinking, That's how life should be. I was far too young to know about books or art or anything much, but maybe the chaos of life with Bertie and Katie instilled in me some vague yearning for order – maybe even for beauty – and I sensed that somehow that was what books and pictures added up to.

Whatever the reason, I have been buying pictures whenever I could afford them since I was at school. I bought the first, for 30 shillings, from Scottie Wilson. That was in 1948, the first year of what became an annual art market on the broad stretch of pavement up at the top of Hampstead, near the Whitestone Pond. Most of the works on show were chocolate-box landscapes and Scottie must have been more than usually broke to have set out his wares in that crowd. He was also the only artist showing who didn't look the part. The chocolate-box merchants were doggedly bohemian; beards and corduroys for the men, long, flowered skirts and beads for the women, and all of them wore sandals. Scottie was small and gnarled and working-class; he had a thick Glasgow accent, a boozer's bulbous nose and flaming complexion, his spectacles were held together with insulating tape and he was wearing a flat cap, a muffler and a filthy blue-serge suit. He looked like a street trader – which was what he had been before the urge to paint possessed him – the kind of man who used to peddle junk from a barrow in the Caledonian Road market.

I'd never heard of Scottie Wilson, of course, and his pictures were like nothing I'd seen before. The one I fell for was like a mediaeval map of the universe: an elaborately bordered circle, resting on the backs of two startled birds and presided over by two deities, one stern, one benign. The terrestrial globe at the centre of the picture and the smaller globes within it swarmed with creatures, mostly fish, and were dominated by a fierce humanoid head with gaping jaws, which seemed to be gobbling them up. The picture was drawn in coloured inks – Woolworths inks, unfortunately, which have faded over the years – obsessionally cross-hatched and precise. Looking at it was like being handed the key to a stranger's private world.

I wanted to buy it, although 30 shillings was about all I had in the world. But this was a Sunday and Sunday trading was illegal in those days, so we had to sneak around the corner and do the deal on the sly. Scottie waited until the 30 bob was in his pocket before he handed over the picture. 'Sorry about all them fucking fish,' he said. 'I've been living on kippers for a fortnight.'

I was home from Oundle, overdosed on the sporting spirit, full of gentleman's relish, and now I'd met a real-life Gulley Jimson. I was overwhelmed. The key he had handed me was not just to his private world; it was to the life I wanted to lead.

Around the same time the Tate put on a great exhibition of wartime paintings by Picasso and Matisse. It fatally enraged the readers of the *Daily Telegraph* – i.e. every member of my family – so naturally I loved it.

In Paris, on my way back from Grenoble, I bought a Picasso etching – a satyr's sly, grinning face conjured up in a dozen or so faultless lines. It was authentic, but because it was unsigned it, too, cost 30 shillings.

Thirty shillings is a derisory sum – today £1.50 wouldn't buy a pint of beer or half a gallon of petrol – but it was half what I earned each week teaching French at Maidwell Hall and more than enough for etchings: I picked up a couple of exquisite little Callots at a junk shop off St Martin's Lane for a shilling each (or was it sixpence?). But even in those days paintings came dearer, too dear for me, and there is one that still haunts me. It was in the Leicester Gallery, a still life of some lemons on a table. It was small – not much more than about 12 inches by four – but it glowed with so much life that it seemed to fill the whole wall: *nature vivante*, not *nature morte*. I wanted it more than I have ever wanted anything. It was painted by Vuillard – naturally I had never heard of him – and the price was 25 guineas, way out of my range. I thought of asking my parents for a loan, but my father was having another financial crisis and fighting about it bitterly with my mother every evening. I didn't want to add to the mayhem. So I went back to the gallery the next day and the next, and stood in front of the painting like a jilted lover face to face with the woman he has lost.

The following year, my beloved aunt Lou gave me 21 guineas for my twenty-first birthday. I went straight down to the Leicester Gallery but the Vuillard, of course, was long gone. So I walked over to Colnaghi in Bond Street and bought a Dürer woodcut and two of Callot's *Grandes Misères de la Guerre*. Twenty-one guineas went a long way in 1950.

I hung those pictures wherever I settled. At Oxford, during the gloomy year when I was pretending to start my doctorate, they were a steadying influence, a constant reminder of another style of life. Every day, late in the afternoon when I got back from my stint at the Bodleian, feeling soiled and unaired and stupid from the lumber-house of unreadable books in my head, I used to look at them and wonder what it would be like to be free.

II

The farce of the doctorate ended, but not in freedom. It ended with the sudden marriage which seemed to put the lid on everything, and I didn't begin to find out about freedom until 1958, when I went back to New Mexico. I had spent the year at Princeton, giving the Gauss Seminars and teaching creative writing; now my wife and baby son and I were staying on the Lawrence ranch, a mile across the mountain from Dorothy Brett's old cabin, where I had lived a couple of years earlier. Frieda had left the Lawrence ranch to the University of New Mexico and they had inaugurated a Lawrence fellowship for a writer to use the place. Or rather they provided the house and the Rockefeller Foundation gave me the money to live there.

The ranch was still the same as it had been when Frieda was living there with Angelino Ravagli. The university had installed a caretaker, a laconic cowboy called Al Pierce, who packed a pistol to blast rattlesnakes when they came to visit: he never missed. He lived in the main house, a grand alpine-style chalet Ravagli had built for Frieda after Lawrence's death. The Lawrence Fellow got the log cabin Lawrence and Frieda had occupied 30 years before. It was a ramshackle little place, infested with pack rats, but very romantic. Lawrence's old rocking-chair stood on the rickety porch, below a nest of bats which hissed malignly when you went in and out. One of the outer walls had been plastered over with adobe to protect it from the weather; on it was the fierce figure of a buffalo, like something from the Lascaux caves, painted by a Pueblo Indian the Lawrences had befriended. The view was as heart-stopping as the view from Brett's cabin – down over the blue sagebrush desert rimmed by purple mountains – and the only sound was the wind in the great ponderosa pine that overshadowed the house.

Every day I drove down the mountain to collect mail from the store cum post office in San Cristobal. The road was a dirt track and nobody used it except Al Pierce and me (the Hawks were away that year). I fancied myself as a driver and had done some rallying in a friend's car at Oxford, so I used to roar downhill, power-sliding every corner, pretending my weary old Studebaker was a rally car and I was unmarried and fancy-free. One afternoon I careered around a corner and just managed to avoid a shiny Chevy station wagon which was plugging cautiously uphill. I got out of my car and went back. I was wearing jeans and sneakers; it was too hot for a shirt.

There were three people in the Chevy, a middle-aged couple and a teenage girl. All of them were white-faced with shock and dressed to kill. The man was wearing a dark suit, a white shirt and a tie, the women wore fancy summer dresses.

'Sorry about that,' I said. 'Can I help?'

The man said, 'We're looking for Señor Alvarez.' He made it sound so Spanish that, for a moment, I didn't recognize the name.

'That's me.'

The man took off his jacket and tie. 'My name's Sidney Nolan,' he said. 'I'm a painter.'

He had got my name from someone at the Rockefeller Foundation, who gave him a copy of *The Shaping Spirit*, the book I had written on my first Rockefeller fellowship, and told him to look me up when he got to New Mexico. Nolan had dutifully ploughed his way through the book and concluded, from its pompous, cocksure tone, that I was some white-haired Spanish sage who, for no good reason he could think of, knew about modern British and American poetry.

He was delighted not to have to be on his best behaviour and I was delighted to have someone to talk to. It was the beginning of a great friendship.

His wife Cynthia did her best to discourage it, just as she discouraged his other friendships. She was a Cerebus at the gate, opening every letter, fielding all the phone calls. Not that there were many. Their number was strictly ex-directory and she changed it whenever she thought Nolan had spread it around too far. I had it in my diary but one evening, years later, when I was married again and our son Luke was a baby, I forgot to leave it with the au pair when Anne and I went to dinner with the Nolans in Putney. Directly we got there, Anne asked Cynthia if she could call home with the number in case of emergency. But there was no number on the telephone and Cynthia took a lot of persuading before she would give it to her. Finally she scribbled it on a scrap of paper and said, 'Tear it up straight away and make sure you forget it.'

After dinner Nolan took me up to his studio to show me his new pictures. He was an artist who was possessed by certain images – Ned Kelly, Mrs Fraser and the convict, desert flowers – and he painted them over and over, hundreds of variations on the same theme, until he had exhausted whatever they had to give him. Leda and the swan was his current obsession and the paintings, mostly in gouache, were discreetly erotic and very beautiful.

I pointed at one of them and asked, 'How do you get that thick texture?'

'Dead easy,' he said. 'You do it like this.' He took a sheet of paper to his workbench and stared at it, seeming to disappear into his own head, like a sprinter before a race. Then he was off, washing on the gouache fast and without hesitation: a burnt and hilly landscape, a stormy sky, a chilly lake and Leda reclining beside it, half submerged in the water, while the swan swooped down on her, its neck urgently extended, its wings blurred in haste. A couple of smears with a finger and their faint reflections were on the water, then a few quick strokes of waxy yellow crayon to indicate divinity in action. The whole miracle, from start to finish, took about 10 minutes.

'Jesus,' I said.

'If you like it, keep it. Plenty more where that came from.'

While this was going on Cynthia was lecturing Anne on the unreliability of men, beginning as we went out of the dining-room, 'That's typical. Sidney always wants to be off with the boys.'

Maybe she was right and Nolan himself knew it. He liked company and he liked drink, he was clever and funny and a pleasure to be with. In order to get on with his work without interruption, he needed someone at the gate to keep off his many friends. He didn't take kindly to a prison-camp regime, but Cynthia's unflinching disapproval probably intimidated him almost as much as it intimidated everyone else. He and I used to meet often for lunch, but he always phoned at the last moment, on the sly, from a public call-box.

Their marriage ended dreadfully. They were shopping at Fortnum & Mason; he said he wanted to go to an art gallery; she said she was tired and would go home. When he got back late in the afternoon she was dead. She had swallowed a bottle of sleeping pills and washed them down with gin. There had been no warning at all – they had not been quarrelling and she did not seem depressed – and Nolan never seemed to understand why she had done it. He was right to be bewildered. From what I knew of her, Cynthia wasn't the type to commit suicide; if she was ever depressed, she kept it icily to herself; she had a flair for scaring people off and seemed to enjoy the power it gave her too much to let it go. She certainly scared me and that is how I interpreted her suicide: as a distillation of the bad will she brought to everyone and everything, an act of supreme malice which she turned finally against herself.

For Nolan, the story ended better than he could ever have imagined. Mary Boyd, the beautiful, sweet-natured sister of the painter Arthur Boyd, looked after him during the awful weeks after Cynthia's death. They fell in love, married and lived happily ever after. So happily, in fact, that they could never find any good reason to be apart. They moved to Herefordshire, up near the Welsh border, rarely came to London, and that was the end of my lunches with Nolan and our long afternoons trawling art galleries and talking about painting and poetry. Whenever I saw them – usually at concerts – he and Mary were hand in hand and absurdly content. If Cynthia had guessed how well it would all turn out, she would have risen in outrage from her grave.

In 1959 Bryan Robertson mounted a great show of new Australian painting at the Whitechapel Gallery. Its huge success brought a number of the artists to London: Charles Blackman, Arthur Boyd, Lawrence Daws, John Perceval and, a little later, Colin Lanceley. These were the people I hung out with while I was living in the studio in Merton Rise. We used to meet on Sunday evenings at a pub at the north end of Archway Road, in Highgate. (Arthur Boyd was painting red dogs at the time and he always arrived with a blush of ruddy pigment on his cheeks which made him look, for him, unnaturally healthy.) The pub was big and ugly and noisy, which was probably why the Australians liked it: it reminded them of the pubs down under and showed how little they were taken in by pretty Olde England. It also had a piano for singsongs and a small stage. Towards closing time Barry Humphries used get up on the stage and try out what later became his Edna Everage routines. This was at the beginning of the sixties, when men didn't yet wear long hair (Barry's was down to his shoulders) and the only female impersonator in town was the famously camp Danny La Rue. We used to cheer Barry on raucously, but the regulars – mostly elderly and working-class – were not always amused.

Australia after the war was an isolated, narrow-minded place and it gave its avant garde a hard time. The painters came to London to get away from all that as well as to see European art at first hand and make their reputations with a wider audience. But the London they came to was bleak and class-bound, badly fed and badly heated, and what they brought to the scene was disproportionate to what they gained. They were friendly and energetic, feisty and utterly unimpressed by British snobbery. The model for them all seemed to be Nolan's Ned Kelly, the outlaw in his home-made armour, a home-grown anti-establishment rebel, casually brutal, casually generous and famously laconic (on the gallows, with the noose around his neck, his last words were, 'Such is life').

Being lively and irreverent was only part of their charm. They also, from my point of view, seemed to live more interesting lives than writers. Most of the writers I knew sat at their desks on their own and wrote; and when they weren't writing they went to publishers' parties where they met other writers and talked about money. Sometimes they were forced out of their burrows for research, but not often and not if they could help it, especially in the early sixties, when hatred of 'abroad' was a matter of principle for the likes of Amis and Larkin, an inverted snobbery, a source of pride. Camus once said that it is possible to live a life of wild adventure without ever leaving your desk, but the adventures are all in the head and a very little reality is enough to set a writer off. The wilder their imaginings, in fact, the more boring the lives they lead. *Portnoy's Complaint* and *Sabbath's Theatre* are two of the wildest novels of our time, but Philip Roth himself is a man of meticulous habits and lives the austere, regulated life of a monk. Writing well is too slow and difficult a process to leave much time for an interesting life.

Perhaps the painter in his studio is no better off, but that is not how it appears. To the desk-bound writer, spinning his work out of his head like a spider spinning its web out of its innards, the visual world itself is freedom – colours and shapes and textures instead of abstract ideas and disembodied voices. And when a painter can't paint he always has other things he can do – canvases to stretch, paints to mix, brushes to clean – handyman's jobs that make him feel virtuous even when real creative work won't come.

The ultimate handyman's studio, and the one I liked best, belonged to Colin Lanceley. Colin was an original, part Surrealist, part craftsman, a meticulous draughtsman of strange creatures that looked like anatomical drawings of cerebral processes – thoughts with limbs and digestive systems, wit and attitude. His paintings were also halfway to being sculptures; the surfaces of his canvases rippled and curved and the images seemed to solidify and step down off the wall into the room. It was an eerie effect and he achieved it by a kind of three-dimensional collage. For the artist the special charm of this form lies in the way found objects bring an element of chance into the formal frame of a painting. But Lanceley is intellectual in his tastes and even his found objects had intellectual weight. He had come across most of the ones he used initially when he was scavenging for junk in an abandoned engineering works in Sydney and found, in the basement, a great treasure-trove of outlandish, carefully machined objects. As far as he was concerned they were just intriguing shapes; in fact, they were wooden patterns that had once been used for sand-casting parts of marine engines. An engineer would have recognized them as cams, pinions, flywheels, flanges and cogs, but once they were incorporated into a picture they became forms in their own right, full of their own meaning, purposeful and strange.

The corners of Lanceley's London studio were piled with these mysterious, dusty chunks of carved wood, his workbench was cluttered with tools, and yet more tools were nailed haphazardly to the wall above it. The place looked more like a carpenter's shop or a garage than an artist's studio. At the centre of this chaos there was always a calm, cleared space: a painting on an easel or an immaculate sheet of heavy paper spread on a draughtsman's table, tins of paint and jars full of clean brushes and fine pens in carefully ordered rows. Because I like fixing things and have always been fascinated by machines, whenever I went into Colin's studio I used to think, This is how work should be: practical as well as delicate, an orderly chaos in which you imagine something, then make it with your own hands. It seemed a far more agreeable way to live than what Pound called 'this damn'd profession of writing, where one needs one's brains all the time' and has very little to show for it at the end.

The Lanceleys were a golden Australian couple, blonde and bronzed and fit, who looked as if they had stepped on to the plane to London straight from Bondi Beach. Colin had been a champion swimmer, Kay was beautiful and clever, a good businesswoman and an inspired cook. She used to get up before dawn to buy the best meat at Smithfield Market and the freshest vegetables at Covent Garden, and the dinners she produced were right out of Elizabeth David's *French Country Cooking* – rich, bountiful feasts served up on a scrubbed wooden table. Lanceley was a little too young to be included in the Whitechapel show and he and Kay didn't arrive in London until 1965, the year before Anne and I married. They stayed for 15 years, until Colin grew weary of grudging gallery owners and badly paid teaching jobs and went back to Australia, where he was already famous.

While they were in London the Lanceleys were our close friends; we lived in and out of each other's houses, I saw all his paintings, he read whatever I wrote and sometimes used it wittily as a theme for his pictures. Like us, they were always broke, but that didn't stop them being the most stylish couple we knew. Colin wore white suits and white shoes and when he sold a picture they'd lash out on whatever obscure object of desire was currently obsessing them – anything from an Eames chair to an outrageously expensive pair of sandals: 'Each bloody strap cost a week's housekeeping,' Kay said when she showed them off. 'But aren't they lovely?' When they left London for good, in 1980, it was as though a part of our lives had been snuffed out – the best part, when we were all young but not too young, full of feeling and appetite and ambition, and determined, this time, to make our marriages work.

The poems I was writing in the backwash of my first marriage were about unhappiness. It seemed to be the only subject I had. But it was a subject I shared with the painter Charles Blackman and, during the first half of the sixties, we spent a lot of time in each other's company. I had seen three of his paintings at the Whitechapel show, and one of them in particular had stuck in my mind: a series of brooding, melancholy faces – girls' faces, most of them – each separate and arranged on a great black canvas, like photographs in an album. A few months later I met Blackman at his one-man show at the Matthiesen Gallery. He looked like a jockey, short and slight and pugnacious, with a round face, big ears, a small chin and inquisitive eyes. He reminded me of something Keats wrote in a letter: 'The Creature has a purpose and his eyes are bright with it.' We started arguing almost immediately, but purely for the pleasure of it, because argument was something we both enjoyed.

It wasn't the only thing we had in common. I also recognized in his paintings something I was after in poetry – an emotional starkness, images that worked on you with the immediacy of dreams. Blackman, at that time, was painting the same two female images over and over again: one was of a grieving woman, accusing and apparently sightless; the other was of a young girl, playing or lost or dancing or brooding over flowers.

The eyes of both the women and the children were turned inwards, their hands were eloquent and the flowers they played with were delicate and formal, but the focus was always on the faces: grim or rapt or shocked or dreaming, faces behind faces, and faces behind them, a cloud of witnesses to the act of painting. The formal means varied continually: at times the figures were striped like convicts, so that their shapes solidified through bars of colour or were violently brought up short against them; or they emerged from an intense background glow, as though looming out of fog; or they were painted flat and hard, like pop images; or the whole painting was subdivided into separate frames, like a comic strip. But it was always the same images and variations on the same few situations. The paintings were as loaded and obsessed as recurrent dreams.

His paintings were like dreams yet they weren't dream-like, which is another way of saying 'vague' or 'self-indulgent' or 'self-hypnotized'. Nor were they Surrealist; Blackman was never interested in the wit of the unconscious or the bizarre topology of dream landscapes. Instead his pictures seemed to cut through to the emotional raw material which is transformed and made tolerable – in however loony a way – by what Freud called the 'dream-work'. Blackman seemed to be trying to create images for grief and guilt, for loss and persecution and tenderness in their most naked forms – soaked in feeling, dredged up alive and kicking from the unconscious. His images were the figurative equivalents of what the Abstract Expressionists called 'gestures'.

They were also sightless and that is what, mostly, saved them from sentimentality. When Blackman met his first wife, Barbara, he was vaguely artistic and bohemian but he had produced almost nothing. Barbara encouraged him to paint and then, just as he was hitting his stride, she lost her sight. That didn't prevent her raising three children, running a house and coping with her temperamental husband, but its effect on him was complicated. On one level the unease her blindness aroused in him may explain something of the guilt and masochism that underlie the paintings. But I think Blackman also used it in a subtler way – less as a subject than as the beginning of a style. He created visual images that somehow conveyed an uncannily heightened awareness of the other senses – touch, silence, isolation – visual images of a non-visual world. Some psychoanalysts talk of art as an act of reparation; but Blackman was doing something more complicated: he wasn't only making up for his wife's blindness, he was in some way inhabiting it; he was painting how it must feel to be blind.

Blackman had been brought up in a house full of women – a mother, three sisters, no father – and that had made him preternaturally alert as to how they feel. It had also given him a feminine vulnerability and I suspect that being married to someone who couldn't see his paintings must have been at least as hard for him as it was for Barbara. That, too, was something he and I had in common. Maybe he liked the poems I was writing at that dismal period of my life because my subject was the grief that comes when you can't get through to the person you think you love. Whatever the reason, the poems were doing something he understood. I used to pass them on to him as I wrote them and he muttered about doing a book together, but I thought nothing of it. Another pipedream. Then one day in 1963 he arrived at my house with a sheaf of my poems and seven gouaches – not illustrations but stern, glowing variations on the same themes. The book, *Apparition*, was published in Australia in 1971.

Fifteen years later we did another book together, but this time it didn't work out so well. Blackman had painted a series of pictures inspired by the Daintree rainforest and had lined up a publisher to reproduce them in a book. He wanted me to go with him to the Daintree and write the text. By then he and Barbara were divorced. They had fought all the time while they were in London, but more out of mutual exasperation than rancour and, beneath the squabbling, they seemed wholly dependent on each other. Back in Australia, with the kids gone, the marriage unravelled. When I arrived in Sydney, in 1986, Blackman was drinking heavily and surrounded by impossible women, some of them no older than his daughter and all of them seemingly interested more in his celebrity than in him or his work. I couldn't imagine what he saw in them.

Or maybe he didn't see them at all and that was his secret. He loved women, but indiscriminately – because they were female, not for who they were. It didn't matter to him that he and his young women had nothing to talk about or that one or two of them were truly scary. All he could see was their femininity and that was enough to get him going as a painter. He had a genius for seductive images and he himself was seduced by them. Being able to impose beautiful patterns on the world, to reduce it fluently and feelingly to composition and perspective, meant that he didn't have to look closely at the jagged bits that didn't fit into his scheme. Perhaps the women he painted were unseeing not because his wife was blind but because he himself wasn't interested in looking into their eyes. Back in the early sixties, when my own life was mess and confusion, I felt he and I were trying to do similar things. Two decades later, I'd done my time with blind romanticism and it no longer appealed to me.

So we went to the Daintree together, to a little hourglass-shaped clearing between the rainforest and the Pacific, and while we were there I tried to talk to him about the mess he was in. I knew it was a mistake but it seemed the decent thing to do for an old friend in trouble. Maybe it was time to make life easier for himself, I said. He was gifted, charming, famous, and women fell for him all the time. He was also pushing 60. Why not go for someone who is kind as well as beautiful, I asked, someone who cares about you, someone who is on your side? If a basket-case like me could do it, why couldn't he? I might as well have been speaking Magyar. He looked at me with round eyes and said, 'Love's not like that.' Then he added, irritably, 'And anyway, if I'm not miserable I can't paint.' There was no answer to that, so I shut up. Since then, whenever I hear of some new disaster he has wished upon himself, I remember Gore Vidal's epigram: 'The rocks in his head fit the holes in hers.' I admire his steadfastness.

Twenty-three years earlier – in the summer of 1963 – Macmillan's Conservative government had tottered and almost fallen when John Profumo, the Secretary of State for War, lied to the House about his affair with Christine Keeler, a call-girl who was also sleeping with a military attaché at the Soviet embassy. The week the scandal broke I had lunch with Nolan and dinner with Blackman and both of them gave me their gleeful comments, in pictures. Nolan made Keeler into an anti-establishment rebel: he took what was then a famous nude photo-portrait of her, gave her Ned Kelly's iron helmet, put a rifle in her arms and sketched in behind her a bleak Australian outback. At the top of the picture he wrote, 'The real Christine Keeler'. Blackman's picture was altogether non-political, although he painted it on the front of the left-wing *New Statesman*. It was of three figures – Adam and Eve and the serpent. Eve was dead centre, lush and yielding, pressing herself against a great green phallic serpent. Adam was at her other side, a featureless shadow, solid black, tentatively reaching out to her. Nolan the iconoclast, Blackman the romantic. I've kept the pictures on the mantelpiece of my study ever since.

I had learned from my father that romanticism is a crippling affliction. I had also learned from my mother that generosity can be a great redeemer. And Charlie Blackman was recklessly generous. That, too, is an area in which painters have an edge on writers. The best an author can do for his friends by way of a present is to dedicate a book to them. More usually, all they get is a signed copy: an ambiguous blessing, part gift, part imposition – the receiver is expected to read the thing and say something nice about it. Artists, in contrast, create beautiful objects, things that make people's eyes light up and their blood race. Blackman seemed to love that response and, over the years, he gave me literally dozens of pictures – casually, as a token of affection, out of pure bigness of heart. He called me, for example, one Christmas Eve when he was living in London: 'Just checking that you're in,' he said. 'I'm sending you the biggest fucking Christmas card you ever saw.' It arrived an hour later, a huge charcoal drawing of a dancing girl – six foot by five foot – the kind of picture that stops you in your tracks when you see it in a museum. When I tried to thank him, all he said was, 'It's Christmas, isn't it?' Giving was his greatest pleasure and he couldn't believe that everyone else didn't behave in the same way – especially women and, with his artist's eye, even more especially beautiful women. He seemed to believe that beauty and generosity were one and the same thing, as they should be in a properly ordered world. So maybe he painted to put the world right.

Nolan, Lanceley and Blackman loved literature and ideas in the same amateur way as I loved paintings – passionately but without finally knowing too much about them. And not knowing enough allowed us a certain freedom; it meant we were comfortable with each other and didn't compete; we admired each other's mysterious expertise and couldn't intrude on the professional privacy. (Later, I had a similar, equal-handed friendship with the pianists Alfred Brendel and Imogen Cooper.)

Maybe the Australians also liked me because I didn't fit their idea of the emotionally costive Englishman. In their different ways all three artists thought of themselves as Ned Kellys, subversive by profession as well as by nature and permanently in opposition, no matter what honours were showered on them later in their lives. I like to think that they thought of me as an outsider like themselves, at odds with the ruling pieties despite Oundle and Oxford, a Jew with a Spanish name disguised as a true Brit.

14

ON THE ROCKS

O ne afternoon in the early sixties Blackman asked me over to his London studio to sit for a portrait, one of a series in charcoal he was working on at that time. He was unusually business-like and brusque. There was no small talk and every time I caught his eye he seemed to be sizing me up like a coffin-maker. For a while he laboured away carefully on two solemn profiles on a single sheet of paper. When he was done he asked me what I thought of them. They were Alvarez the critic, bearded and pensive, and I didn't much like them. 'Very flattering,' I said. Blackman sniffed. 'Too bloody true. That's the kind of thing your mother would love.' (He was right. Naturally he gave me the picture, and when I passed it on to Katie she hung it in the dining-room and showed it proudly to everyone. It made her think I might be serious, after all.)

He dropped the first picture on the floor, took another, larger sheet of paper and began to sketch irritably. This time there was no attempt to flatter me. He drew me slouched sideways on a chair, glaring at someone out of the corners of my eyes. My mouth is squeezed tight on a cigarette. My right elbow rests on the back of the chair, and my forearm dangles across my chest, the hand loose, the fingers sensitive. My left arm rests on my thigh and the fist is clenched. My shoulders are slightly hunched and I look dangerous – a borderline paranoid – not so much hunched as coiled and ready to spring at the slightest offence.

And that was truly how I was back then when I was between marriages and my adrenalin addiction was running high. I drove too fast, I played poker for more money than I could afford and spent most weekends off in the Welsh hills, climbing rocks with my pals. All this cut me off even more from the London literary scene. As far as the poets were concerned I was a wild man, not to be tangled with, but I see now that I was reverting to type. I had been wild as a child – these days the word would be 'disturbed' – until the Blitz provided something outside myself for the wildness to batten on to. Oundle added rugger and boxing to my repertoire and gave me my first heady taste of rock-climbing, but I didn't climb again until the end of my first year at Oxford, just after my twentieth birthday, when I spent a week in Wales with the Oxford University Mountaineering Club.

As I mentioned earlier, I wasn't a natural athlete. I didn't have an eye for a ball like my cricketing father, and I had been a scrawny, delicate child. But once I was at boarding school I worked harder on turning myself into an athlete than I ever worked on exams. I still wasn't a natural but the compulsory daily exercise built me up and made me strong and, on the rugger field and in the ring, my wildness gave me an edge. I didn't scare easily. Or rather, I was unreasonably frightened of all sorts of things other people take in their stride – especially spiders with their dangling bellies and eight scuttering legs – and my experience on the operating table when I was a baby left me nervous of doctors and hospitals and butchers' shops. But I was never scared of being hurt. I'd fling myself at a lumbering forward twice my weight or batter away at a boxing opponent with a reach six inches greater than mine without any thought of the consequences. It had nothing to do with bravery. It was simply that physical danger turned me on; it increased the adrenalin high.

Climbing was different. I had discovered I had a flair for it on my first schoolboy visit to Wales and when I took it up again at Oxford it seemed to suit me even better, as though I had unknowingly grown into it. It is, after all, a sport in which strength and nerve go a long way – not least because they can get you out of trouble when things go wrong – and wildness is taken for granted. I had the right build and the right temperament, although, compared with the hard men on the climbing scene in the fifties and sixties, I was a minor player. In terms of really hard routes and piss-ups, I wasn't in their league. They accepted me because I was a good man to have second on the rope – strong and unbothered – and also because most of them were part-time fugitives from the straight world – businessmen, engineers, plumbers, doctors, teachers – and I worked in what they considered an odd, exotic trade.

Not that they ever mentioned this, and that in itself was one of the pleasures. I have always believed that Mallory's famous reason for wanting to climb Everest – 'Because it's there' – was only half the story. The other half was 'Because you're here' – where 'you' included the town, the job, the wife, the kids, the dog, and, above all, the kind of person who would ask such a question in the first place. In the same way I loved climbing for all the things it wasn't: not Glenilla Road, not my first marriage, not poets or poetry or literary criticism. Climbing has its own specialized language and hierarchies, subtle gradations that mean nothing to outsiders, and a whole range of people, like a secret society, with whom I had otherwise nothing much to talk about. A few of them became close friends – there is nothing like shared risk and extreme discomfort for cementing a friendship – but with the majority I had just this one activity in common. And I enjoyed their company because climbing is a maverick sport and the people who do it consistently are usually interesting and rather private. Some lead very successful lives, because the drive that will get you up a mountain will also stand you in good stead in a career; but many are natural anarchists who have chosen to grub along outside the system in order to make their own timetables and not to answer to any boss. What most of them have in common – the employed and the unemployable – is a taste for black humour and a wicked eye for pretension. The climbing world has its phoneys but, unlike the world of letters, they are not given an easy time.

Climbing is also, like poker, a truly democratic activity. At the poker table nobody cares about the colour of your skin or who you are or how you earn a living – they wouldn't even notice if you were a little green man from outer space – provided you sit down with enough money and ante up on time. Climbing is equally classless. I climbed until I was well into my sixties and in my latter years, when big routes were beyond me, I went most weekends to a little sandstone outcrop called Harrison's Rocks, near Tunbridge Wells, where the crowd I climbed with included a security guard, an odd-job man, a municipal gardener, a schoolboy and a tycoon who had made a fortune in the software industry. The tycoon and I, being older and less athletic than the others, were benignly tolerated. What any of us did when we weren't climbing was never mentioned.

Climbing is also one of the least cluttered of sports; it depends on the climber, not the equipment. When I began, back in 1950, all you needed was a rope, a pair of boots, a government-surplus anorak, some carabiners and a few nylon slings. Since then safety equipment has improved and the modern hard men are festooned with gear when they hit the rocks: artificial chockstones – called 'nuts' and 'friends' – bags of chalk to improve their grip, sticht plates, nut-keys, descendeurs. They also dress up in coloured Lycra tights and snappy singlets that show off their muscles. Yet no amount of flashy gear will get you up a climb or add to the pleasure you feel when mood and fitness and rock all come together and everything goes right. No doubt every athlete feels the same on his best days, but in climbing that style of contentment is attainable long after you pass your physical prime.

Whatever standard you climb at, the rewards are much the same. You get to wild, lonely places and the people you go with are mostly funny and irreverent and impervious to pretension. Climbing is also a physical activity of a special, rather intellectual kind. Each pitch is a series of specific local problems: which holds to use, and in which combinations, in order to climb it safely and with the least expenditure of energy. Every move has to be worked out by physical strategy, in terms of effort, balance and consequences. It is like playing chess with your body: you have to think, and think clearly, because if you get it wrong there is a risk of being hurt.

It was that aspect of climbing that I always found peculiarly satisfying – perhaps because I am a professional writer and writing is a sedentary middle-class occupation, like psychoanalysis but more lonely. (The analyst at least gets to see patients.) For five or six days each week I sit at my desk and try to get sentences right. If I make a mistake I can rewrite it the following day or the next, or catch it in proof. And if I fail to do so, who cares? Or even notices? On a climb, my concentration is no less, but I am thinking with my body instead of with my addled head, and if I make a mistake the consequences are immediate, obvious, embarrassing and possibly painful. For a brief period and on a small scale, I have to be directly responsible for my actions, without evasions, without excuses. In the beautiful, silent, useless world of the mountains, I can sometimes achieve a certain brief clarity, even seriousness of a wayward kind. It seems to me worth a little risk.

That, at least, is how I used to justify the time I wasted when I should have been gainfully employed. But it was all a sham. The truth was, I was addicted to the adrenalin rush and I also had something to prove that couldn't be done through books. When I was a sickly child I despised my fragility and the fuss it provoked in other people. But the lesson I'd learned at my Nanny's knee that day on Primrose Hill was that I had a choice: I didn't have to lie back and be cosseted; I could walk if I wanted to; all it took was a little effort and a little risk and I could be out there playing games with the healthy kids. So I turned myself into a pint-sized tough and made quite a convincing job of it. But secretly I wasn't convinced and my housebound, cerebral profession was a constant reminder of the invalid I'd left behind.

Moving up steep rock, at ease with my body and in control of it, was one way of confirming that all was well with the world. I loved the curious on-off physical rhythm of climbing – blinding effort on the pitches, then long periods of goofing off on the belays while I paid out the rope, puffed my pipe and stared at the view. For years I climbed regularly with Ian McNaught-Davis, the man who was making a fortune in software. We struggled up some hard climbs, giggling like schoolchildren and egging each other on. It seemed the best possible way of spending my time and the best possible company to spend it in.

But there was always something else niggling away, something to do with hardship and what my friend Mo Anthoine called 'feeding the rat'. Mo was a great mountaineer who had climbed all over the globe and confounded the statistics by surviving 15 Himalayan expeditions – the death rate in Himalayan climbing is one in seven, higher than Grand Prix driving – before brain cancer ambushed him at the age of 50. But even Mo, who was wild and anarchic and independent in ways that left me standing, and apparently had nothing to prove, knew that there was a gap between what you seem to be and what you really are. This is how he put it to me in a book I wrote about him called *Feeding the Rat*:

There is always a question mark about how you would perform. You have an idea of yourself and it can be quite a shock when you don't come up to your own expectations. If you just tootle along you can think you're a pretty slick bloke until things go wrong and you find you're nothing like what you imagined yourself to be. But if you deliberately put yourself in difficult situations, then you get a pretty good idea of how you are going. That's why I like feeding the rat. It's a sort of annual check-up on myself. The rat is you, really. It's the other you, and it's being fed by the you that you think you are. And they are often very different people. But when they come close to each other, that's smashing, that is. Then the rat's had a good meal and you come away feeling terrific.

As it happens, I was with Mo when my own rat had its first big meal, and maybe the creature got fed only because I was with him. I have written about the incident before – at length in *Feeding the Rat* – but I want to tell the story again briefly because the way it turned out mattered a good deal to me.

Mo and I first met at the Lavaredo hut, in the Italian Dolomites, in August 1964. We romped up a fairly hard climb together, rested for a day, then went round on to the north face of the Cima Grande to try our luck on the far more intimidating Comici route. But taking a day's rest with Mo meant drinking quantities of beer, so we overslept and both of us were hungover when we started two hours late. We were also too young and cocksure to take the climb seriously. We packed no bivouac gear, no extra clothes, no food, and got caught in a snowstorm when we were too far up the route to be able to retreat. We had reckoned to be up the climb in five or six hours, but the storm slowed us down and we were still 500 feet below the summit when night fell. When it became too dark to see the holds we were forced to bivouac. Then the snow stopped, the sky cleared, the temperature plummeted, and there was nothing to do but sit it out on a tiny ledge – each of us had one buttock on, one buttock off, and 1100 feet of air below our boots – and hope we would make it through to the morning.

Silence is one of the attractions of the mountains – a total silence you find only above the timber-line, where nothing moves but the wind. But not on this occasion. The lower 600 feet of the route had been up a steadily overhanging wall; the last 1000 feet followed a crack that was partly overhanging and never less than vertical. Because the rock on the summit had been warmer than that of the north face we were on, the snow had melted above and turned the crack into a waterfall. Our bivouac ledge was halfway up this crack and, although it was protected by an overhang, we were soaked to the skin by the time we stopped. We took off our shirts, wrung them out, put them back on and settled down for a long night, while the clouds lifted, the stars came out and the air froze. Body temperature drops when you sleep, so we swapped limericks and sang songs and tried to stay awake. Even so, we kept nodding off, lulled by the sound of falling water.

At some dead point of the night I woke, feeling something was wrong. I nudged Mo and said, 'What's up?' To my surprise I realized I was whispering.

We huddled together, listening. But there was nothing to hear.

Then Mo said, 'The waterfall's frozen.' He, too, was whispering.

It occurred to me that this was how freezing to death would be – numb and soundless. First the waterfall, then us. But I didn't say so, and that surprised me, too. Usually I'm a talkative person, but I knew that talking about what was on my mind would do no good. It would also, in some obscure way, have been an invasion of privacy. Since Mo was behaving as though everything was perfectly normal, for me to have suggested that we were in trouble would have been – well, impolite. It would also have been a waste of precious time. If my account had finally come due, I might as well make the best of the hours I had left. So we sang songs and blew on our hands and pummelled each other to keep the circulation going, until the sky slowly lightened and we could start climbing again.

The last 500 feet up the vertical crack to the summit were disproportionately hard. There were plaques of verglas where there should have been holds and both of us were frostbitten – Mo in the feet, me in the fingers. By the time we had got to the top and scrambled down the easy south side of the mountain and were back at the hut, I had reached the far, frayed end of my tether.

But perhaps that was what I had been after all along. Like most young people, I had been worried about how I would behave under pressure. I wanted to know how much I could take, at what point I would or would not crack. I had arms like a lumberjack, heavy shoulders and a bull neck, but none of that meant a thing to my rat. In its beady gaze, I was still a nervous little Hampstead intellectual with a wonky ankle and a Nanny to catch me if I fell. Mo was nobody's Nanny. His mother had died when he was four, his stepmother was a Dickensian tyrant and, to get away from her, he had been out of the house, camping in the wild, at an age when I was still a coddled brat in the nursery. His rat was different from mine and demanded a sterner diet. But at least I hadn't let him down. Or myself. After that night on the bare mountain I no longer felt I had continually to justify myself, apologize and explain. I had learned that I was a survivor and didn't fall apart in a crisis.

Maybe I should have known that already. I had survived surgery as a baby and a lead boot packed with radium, I had survived my unreliable parents and their emotional tempests, then, four years before the incident in the Dolomites, I had survived 45 sleeping pills. But those were private nightmares, loaded with despair, whereas what Mo and I were doing had started out as fun. There was no emotional build-up to it at all – no fights, no misery, no sign of Auden's 'Hump-backed surgeons/And the Scissor Man'. The Via Comici was famously demanding, but that was why we were on it: because we were fit and strong and competent and we wanted to push the envelope. I expected to be exhausted when it was over, though Mo probably reckoned to be no more than pleasantly tired. What neither of us expected was a freak storm which almost changed a long day out into the big chill.

'Life is impoverished, it loses in interest, when the highest stake in the game, life itself, may not be risked.' When Freud wrote that he was talking about the Great War and the insidious glamour of danger. For years it was one of my favourite quotations, my excuse for craziness, trotted out whenever I was challenged about my addiction to risk. But my night out with Mo had nothing to do with the adrenalin rush. It was about character – about patience and good behaviour – and, like an initiation rite, the mere fact of surviving it in decent style changed my life.

I went on climbing regularly until 1993, 43 years after I started. Climbing wasn't just something I did to pass the time; it was part of who I was. So it seems just that it should have been climbing that finally laid me low. In the spring of 1960 the Soviet Union sent six mountaineers to Britain and I was enlisted to climb with them in Wales. The Russians were vigorous, funny men, brimming with Slavic soul, though slightly bewildered to be on the other side of the Iron Curtain where nobody cared what they did or said. Even their interpreter, the cadre who was there to keep them in line and make sure they didn't defect, seemed intent on enjoying himself while he could. All of them were powerful climbers – they had probably been chosen to put us decadent bourgeois Brits in our place – but they weren't used to slippery Welsh rock. When one of them fell off and broke his leg they lapsed into Dostoievskian gloom, as though the Soviet Union itself had lost face.

I cheered them up the next day by falling off, too, and breaking my right leg. It was not a deliberate gesture towards Anglo-Soviet friendship, but they took it that way. The whole group was waiting at the foot of the cliff while I was lowered down and their lead climber had me on his shoulders before I touched the ground. He then took off like a goat down the steep scree slope, whooping, laughing, and shouting up at me, 'Not to worry. Iz all OK.'

I was carted off to hospital to have my leg set, then spent the next few days in the hut with the injured Russian, our plastered legs propped companionably in front of the fire, gorging ourselves on Mother's Pride toast heaped with the Beluga caviar the Russians had brought with them in industrial-size tins.

The hospital I was taken to was Bangor General, which, in those days, was primitive, ill-equipped and staffed by doctors who resented having to cope with injured climbers. They set my leg badly and it had to be reset back in London. (When Mac drove me to the London hospital, the doctor examined my leg and asked him if he'd set it.) But none of the doctors in either hospital seemed to notice that the ligaments in my ankle were torn and the foot was loose. As a result they set the leg into the ankle at the wrong angle and the cartilage in the joint eventually wore away until bone was grinding on bone and walking itself was painful.

Mercifully the cartilage took a long time to disintegrate. I was 30 when the accident happened and was back on the rocks within a couple of months. To celebrate my fiftieth birthday, I did a hard route on the Procinto, a 500-foot overhanging sugar-cube in the Apuan Alps. I climbed it with Mo and an Italian friend, Damasco Pinelli, who, with generous Italian exaggeration, swore he knew no one of my age who could have got up the thing. Six years later I climbed the Old Man of Hoy – again with Mo – then repeated the Procinto route with Damasco on my sixtieth birthday. This time I found it easier and came away thinking, I can go on doing this for ever. I was wrong. Within three years there was no cartilage left in my ankle joint and I couldn't even walk to the foot of the cliff.

I could still hobble from the car to Harrison's Rocks, but climbing one-legged was graceless and painful, and eventually I gave up. Not long after, I dreamed I was climbing again, moving easily up a steep open chimney. It is rare to smell things in a dream – the olfactory neurons are usually quiescent – but in this dream all my senses seemed to be working. I could smell the faint, smoky scent of rock and another scent, harder to define – the pervasive, gunpowdery smell of climbing rope. I was moving effortlessly and my body was suffused with a physical sweetness. Then I woke to my throbbing ankle and old man's aches and pains; but there was nothing to be done and no point in complaining. As Bette Davis said, 'Getting old ain't for sissies.'

That was when I was most grateful for the lesson I had learned years before, on the Cima Grande, about patience, good behaviour and that Edwardian virtue fortitude. It had already stood me in good stead in different risk situations – bad runs of luck in my professional life, bad runs of cards at the poker table. But it helped me most when I had to give up climbing and accept that my status as an upstanding member of the human race had only been temporary. I entered this world limping on my left leg. I will exit limping on the right.

15

THE BIGGEST GAME IN TOWN

A fter that, all that was left to feed the rat was swimming – in the chilly amber ponds on Hampstead Heath, where I have swum since I was 11 years old – and poker, a traditional refuge for ex-athletes who have lost their physical skills but not their desire to stay in the action and compete.

It is one of the ironies of my life that although I helped change the way poetry was read in Britain during the fifties and sixties by speaking up for American poets like Lowell, Berryman and Plath, and introducing the poets of Eastern Europe to British readers, the one place where I am truly famous is Las Vegas, Nevada. And that is only for three weeks a year, while the World Series of Poker is in progress. Another irony is that I should ever have thought of playing poker. I had no interest in cards when I was young and the Sunday bridge games at Glenilla Road – Grandpa Alvarez and the black widow versus my parents – created so much bad blood that I vowed never to learn the game. Added to that, I'm not a gambler. After my disasters with the Wykehamist horse-fancier at Maidwell Hall, I no longer believed in luck and rarely placed even a small bet on anything.

But poker isn't about gambling. In *My Little Chickadee* someone asks W. C. Fields if poker is a game of chance. He answers, 'Not the way I play it.' He was speaking as a card-sharp but he was also speaking true. Serious poker is no more about gambling than climbing is about taking risks. You fall into it from time to time, but not if you can help it. The point of the game is to develop enough skill to minimize the element of chance. Chess is a game of pure skill, like poker with all the cards exposed – the better player will always win – but in poker the cards are shuffled and dealt haphazardly, so the sucker can sometimes beat the expert, though only in the short run. Yet that's not how the uninitiated – or the suckers – see it. Poker looks like gambling – and at a low level is gambling – because it has to be played for money. Poker chips are more than just a way of keeping score; they combine with the cards to form the very language of the game. What you do with your chips – when and how you bet or check or raise – is a form of communication. You ask subtle questions with them and receive subtle answers. The questions and answers may be misleading – a big bet might be a sign of weakness, an attempt to drive the other players out of the pot because you do not have the hand you purport to have – but the combination of cards and money and position at the table creates a complex pattern of information (or illusion) that controls the flow of the game. In poker, betting and what is called 'money management' are as much an art as reading the cards and reckoning the odds.

But I didn't know that in my late twenties when I started playing. Like all beginners, I thought poker was like baccarat, a game of pure chance where you gambled money on the turn of a card. Perhaps that was why it appealed to me – for the risk and the machismo that goes with risk-taking. To gamble more than I could afford blindly, like a dare, seemed a dashing thing to do. It proved what was not otherwise apparent: that I was one of the boys, that I didn't care. It was also a misapprehension that cost me a good deal, both in money and self-esteem. I lost regularly and was fortunate that the people I played with in those days were as innocent and self-deluding as I was.

Then one summer evening a young American appeared in our game. He was a pale, sweating youth, grossly overweight, with a face like that of the oaf on the cover of *Mad* magazine – the same carrotty crew cut and freckles, the same small, close-set eyes. In comparison with our fast-talking, rather literary group, he seemed graceless and dull – a hick with no small talk and even less charm, who didn't get our jokes and couldn't pick up our allusions. But he cleaned us out effortlessly two weeks in a row, until the man who had brought him was told to withdraw the invitation.

He handled the cards like a professional, crisply and deftly, and all of us suspected he was cheating. We were flattering ourselves. Not even W. C. Fields would have bothered to fix the deck for a group of mugs like us. Anyone could have taken our money simply by playing the game as it should be played, by the book, while we gambled wildly, unable to believe that hands that had started well wouldn't necessarily finish that way, or that we didn't have some secret, special claim on the chips we had recklessly contributed to the pot.

The money I lost to the fat American turned out to be a good investment. He shamed me by taking it so easily, calling every pathetic bluff, then turning over his hole cards and scooping in the pot casually, scarcely bothering to wait to see what I had – not even interested, as though my pretences were below the level of his attention. But humiliation is a great teacher and two long nights of it taught me that I knew nothing about the game. If I was going to play poker I would have to study it. So I got hold of the classic introduction, Herbert O. Yardley's *The Education of a Poker Player*, and read it through twice – first, incredulous that anyone could play so conservatively, then ashamed of my own naivety. I went back to the game and tried to apply what I'd learned. For two years after that I played by the book – that is, by Yardley, whom I solemnly reread cover to cover each afternoon before the game. And for two years, with a couple of minor hiccups, I didn't lose.

It was a good period. For the first time in my life I had money to spare in my pocket – one night I was so successful that I went out the next day and bought myself an E-type Jaguar – and I was earning it in a way I enjoyed. In fact, I enjoyed it so much that, for a few zany moments, I imagined I might be able to make a modest living without having to churn out a review every week. It was all nonsense, of course. I was nailed to literature for life, but because I found the sheer labour of writing so hard I was always casting around for other things I could do, and do well, that would give me pleasure.

Poker, in those days, wasn't one of them. It is a deep game and you never stop learning. Thirty-five years later, I'm still learning, although now, when I play in casinos instead of private games, I've learned enough to know that I will never be as good as the professionals I sit down with. But I didn't know that back then and I was spared further humiliation only by an invitation to lecture for a term at an American university. When I got back to London my regular Friday game had broken up and there were no more easy pickings. I joined another, more sophisticated group that met on Tuesday nights and began learning all over again.

Poker gave me company, something every writer who avoids the party circuit needs. The Friday game was made up of guys I played cards with; I enjoyed their company, but poker was all I had in common with them, although I knew them in oddly intimate ways. If one of them tugged his ear when he called a bet it meant he had nothing and was hoping to fill his hand; another always cleared his throat before he bluffed; a third said, 'Raise' when he had you beat, and 'Raise the pot' when he was bluffing. I got to know their nervous tics as well – maybe better – than their wives did, yet I rarely saw them away from the table. The Tuesday game was different. I played in it for over 20 years, arranged my week around it, and at least three of the players became close friends.

Terry Steinhouse was my introduction into what I romantically considered to be the real world – the cynical, hard-headed realm that lay all around literature but impinged on it only in American thrillers. He looks like a line-backer gone to seed – a massive, lowering man with a square head, a powerful belly and a strong line in black humour. He had run a floating craps game in Montreal when he was a teenager and that had given him a taste for low-lifers which blossomed after he moved to London and made money in real estate. Age and illness have now forced him out of the action, but at that time he played poker not just on Tuesdays, like the rest of us, but most nights of the week – seven-card stud at the Victoria Casino and the Sportsman, then strip-deck poker at the illegal private clubs in Soho that opened when the casinos closed, stank of stale frying oil and were popular with gangsters and thieves, people who worked nights and preferred to play with cash, not chips – wads of soiled notes piled high around the tables, plenty more in their pockets, all of it untaxed and no one to ask where it came from.

Terry organized his life around poker. He was in his office every day, wheeling and dealing, from nine in the morning until four in the afternoon, when he went home and slept until 10. Then he showered, shaved and drove off to the casinos, arriving bright-eyed and implacably good-humoured when the amateurs were running out of steam. He was that rare creature, a Jew with a serious drink problem, though he never showed it. He was also absurdly generous to people he liked. He used to say, 'When I do business deals and play poker, I want to be a tiger. With friends it's different.' I gave him a starring role in one of my novels, *Hunt*, but the book has been out of print for years.

John Moorehead has generosity in common with Terry, but not much else. Terry looks like a heavy in a *film noir*, wisecracking and hard-headed, resolutely North American. John, as it happens, is Australian – his father was the gifted writer Alan Moorehead – but he has lived most of his life in Europe and is as English as Eton and Oxford can make you – modest, hesitant, with beautiful, you-first manners and a barking laugh that make him seem alarmingly self-deprecating until he sits down at the poker table. Then his English mannerisms intensify almost to the point of eccentricity – he stirs his chips around like soup, fiddles irritably with his cards, sips his whisky, taps his foot, shifts about in his chair – but the innocence vanishes. And you begin to wonder if maybe all that English diffidence is itself a bluff, part of some arcane game he plays with his life, because John is a true games player and rules exist for him only to be broken or twisted or turned on their heads. Most solid poker players wait for good cards then try to make the maximum from them. John knows how to do that but prefers not to. Solid play bores him. The challenge, as he sees it, is to take bad cards and turn them into winners by outmanoeuvring his opponents, raising when he should call, flat-calling when he should raise, and bewildering everyone with illogic. He doesn't play his cards, he plays the other players', and that is a skill which only true mind-game players ever master. He and I have played together, on and off, for nearly 30 years and I still can't read him.

Mind-game playing is an art I've never properly mastered. It's all done with mirrors, by thinking back to front or laterally but never straight: '"Contrariwise," continued Tweedledee, "if it was so, it might be; and if it were so, it would be; but as it isn't, it ain't. That's logic."' But it's only logic on Lewis Carroll's chessboard world through the looking-glass. Poker, as it is played in casinos by the likes of Terry Steinhouse, is a ruthless game which, according to Walter Matthau, 'exemplifies the worst aspects of capitalism that have made our country so great'. It embodies, that is, all the elements of that Social Darwinism – the doctrine of the survival of the socially and economically fittest – which is the reality behind the American dream. That is what I like about it and why I owe it something that has nothing to do with playing games. Quite simply, poker taught me qualities I lacked – patience and cool-headedness – that steadied me when I most needed them.

When I first began to play the game I had the profound ignorance that often goes with excessive education. I had been through the most high-minded academic mill, read a vast number of books and written a couple of my own, but in my personal life I was naive to a degree that still makes me blush. I had a marriage I couldn't handle, a childish desire to be loved by the whole world and an equally childish conviction that everything would turn out right in the end. I lived my life as I played poker, recklessly and optimistically, with my cards open on the table and nothing in reserve. I also assumed that everybody else was doing the same.

I was wrong, of course, and it was about the time I began to realize this that I first read Yardley's book. Read: 'You should study your own weaknesses as well as those of your opponents. Keep a poker face. Keep silent. Don't gripe when you lose a hand or gloat over a winning one.' Read, above all:

> A card player should learn that once the money is in the pot it isn't his any longer. His judgement should not be influenced by this. He should instead say to himself, Do the odds favour my playing regardless of the money I have already contributed?

What was true of money in a card game was equally true of the feelings I had invested in my disastrous personal affairs: 'Do the odds favour my playing regardless of what I have already contributed?' I knew the answer. The only puzzle was why I should have discovered it not in Shakespeare or Donne or Eliot or Lawrence or any of my other literary heroes, but in a how-to book about cards written by an American cryptographer. It was more than absurd; it was humiliating, an insult to all the effort I had made.

The Education of a Poker Player was the beginning of my own education in the ways of the world beyond literature and Las Vegas was my graduate school. 'Las Vegas is like a parasite that feeds on money,' a local poker professional once told me. 'It sits here in the middle of the desert and produces absolutely nothing, yet it supports half a million people.' That was in 1981. Since then the parasite has more than doubled in size and grown subtler in its methods of extracting money from visitors, but its spirit remains the same. Behind the illusion – the fantasy worlds of the casinos, the cascading lights, the remorseless cheerfulness – lies the profoundest disillusion. It is the most cynical place on earth. But its cynicism is also its saving grace – a form of vitality so shameless that it is endearing. Years ago, for example, when George Burns was performing at Caesar's Palace, I called to book a table. A rasping voice at the other end said, 'Whaddya want? The 10 o'clock show or the midnight show?' 'Which do you recommend?' 'The guy's 88 years old. Take the 10 o'clock show.' Even the *maître de* was working out the odds. In Vegas everybody has an angle, from the casino bosses to the saddest cocktail waitress. They weigh you up in gold and call it the golden rule: he who has the gold makes the rules.

Las Vegas is a peculiarly American creation: a resort surrounded by a cordon sanitaire of desert and designed simply to take money from holiday-makers by cashing in on their dreams and never giving a sucker an even break. I didn't know that when I first went there, in 1980, with my wife and kids. I thought I'd died and gone to poker heaven; there were games everywhere and of all sizes 24 hours a day. I'd never played in a casino before. I thought it would be like the Tuesday game, where everybody ran outrageous bluffs, showed off and had fun. Instead it was as dour and unrelenting as labouring in a salt mine. I played for three days and lost steadily. But I loved the energy of the place, its brutal swagger, and I came away feeling justice had been done.

The following year I went back and stayed for three weeks. I wanted to know if I had the discipline and hard-headedness to play poker in the same way as I'd sat through the cold night on the Comici route with Mo. Poker as played in Vegas by the professionals has nothing to do with the adrenalin rush. On the contrary, it is about patience and self-control, and for an impatient, volatile person like myself to play in that way took balls of a kind. I'd read the books and talked about what was needed. Now I wanted to put my money where my mouth was.

I had gone back to Vegas to write a long piece for the *New Yorker* about the World Series of Poker, a competition which is held each May at Binion's Horseshoe Casino to decide who will be world champion for the year. William Shawn, the editor of the *New Yorker*, was not interested in poker – unlike his predecessor Harold Ross – but he liked the idea of an English poet writing about professional card players. And culture clash was what he got. The World Series is now poker's equivalent of Wimbledon and poker players flood in from all over the globe to play in it, but it had started, in 1970, as a casual get-together of Benny Binion's high-rolling Texan cronies and when I first went there 11 years later they were still in the majority: cowboys in alligator boots, wildcatters wearing Stetsons and Dior ties, gnarled good old boys with eyes like ferrets, who farmed in West Texas. I felt like I had walked into a Sam Peckinpah movie.

Almost none of them had even heard of the *New Yorker* and they reacted to my English accent warily, as if it were some shrewd play I was trying to put on them. But not the highest rollers of all – men like Jack Straus, Doyle Brunson and Eric Drache, who regularly played for hundreds of thousands of dollars and could handle any company. They read me as easily as they read their opponents at the poker table, saw that I was genuinely interested, and decided they liked me because I was a good listener and I made them laugh. So they let me sit in on their giant games where the kind of money that would have made me rich for life changed hands as casually as small change. For me, it was a revelation as well as an education.

It was also pleasurable in a way I had never dreamed research could be. I came home with a vast amount of material to work on, but length and deadlines were never a problem when you wrote for Mr Shawn. He believed that each piece has a natural length of its own and takes as long as it takes to write. Mine took me 15 months and finished up as *The Biggest Game in Town*, the only book I have ever enjoyed writing. It appeared in two long instalments in the *New Yorker* in March 1983, and was published the following year as a hardback. I think it was the first of its kind – a poker book about the characters who play, rather than about the strategy of the game. It didn't sell particularly well – poker players prefer not to waste good stake money on books – but by some gambling sleight of hand almost every serious player seems to have read it. That is why I am famous for three weeks a year, when the World Series is in progress at Binion's Horseshoe in Glitter Gulch, Las Vegas. Like the cup I won for diving at my prep school, it is a touch of glory I am unreasonably proud of – maybe because it is the only thing I have done that the high-rolling Levys might have respected.

Since that initiation I have been back at Binion's for the World Series every May. Or almost every May; the years when I couldn't rustle up enough money to go were always a harsh reminder of the sorry state I was in. In 1994, courtesy of Tina Brown's *New Yorker*, I even competed in the World Championship itself – the $10,000 buy-in No-Limit Hold 'Em event. I didn't do well – it's hard to take notes and concentrate on the game at the same time – but I suspect I am the only published poet to have done so. The Levys would have liked that, too.

Usually I go with Tony Holden, another regular from the Tuesday game. Tony is the kid brother I never had. Both of us are besotted by America and both of us have North American second wives. (Tony's blonde Bostonian wife, the novelist Cindy Blake, plays a tough game of poker.) We also have Oundle, Oxford and poetry in common, which is how we first met. Tony is someone who has always worn several hats – journalist and biographer, librettist and translator of Greek poetry. Although he was only 21 when we first met, back in 1968, he was already wearing two – president of the Oxford University Poetry Society and editor of the student paper *Isis* – and he gave me the benefit of both. First, he invited me to read my poems, then, later that year, when my name was put forward for the Oxford Professorship of Poetry, he organized the undergraduate vote on my behalf. Unfortunately undergraduates have no vote in the election – only MAs are eligible – and my candidacy got nowhere. But we had fun working out strategies to beat the opposition – Enid Starkie's candidates always won; that year she was backing Roy Fuller – and the 18 years' difference in our ages seemed not to matter. If I was looking for a kid brother, maybe Tony was looking for a raffish uncle, but because we shared the same background and the same interests and laughed at the same kind of jokes neither of us noticed the age gap. We have been friends ever since, especially after I inducted Tony into the Tuesday game.

At the start I think we were both astonished to find anyone who could have gone through Oundle and still be interested in poetry. Even now, we sometimes remember our literary connection and talk about the things writers usually talk about – books and other writers' advances. But mostly we talk about poker and what poker players call 'bad beats' – the hands we should have won but didn't, because the cards were freakish or, more often, because some other player made a stupid call. Bad-beat stories are long-winded and ill-tempered and they never have a happy ending. Their punch line is always roughly the same: 'I mean, what was the schmuck doing in the hand with a lousy pair of deuces?' Bad beats haunt you like bad dreams and seem far more significant than the hands you win. Because they go against the rules that govern the game – the law of averages and immutable odds – they put your beliefs in doubt.

For a couple of weeks most years Tony and I go to Vegas, where we swap bad-beat stories and behave as we both must have behaved when we were home on holiday from Oundle – without a care in the world. For hours each day we try to take each other's money – and everyone else's – at the poker table. But away from the table nothing seems to matter and everything seems funny. Our mutual friend Eric Drache, for example, who organized the World Series and ran the poker room at the Mirage, suddenly vanished from town owing, they said, $4 million. (That was the rumour. When I finally met up with him, I asked him about the debt. He shrugged modestly and said, 'They're exaggerating. It's seven million.') A couple of years ago Tony called me in my room between games to say he had tracked Eric down and solved the mystery of his disappearance. 'I'm going to astonish you, delight you and appal you with just two words,' he said. 'Erica Drache.'

'Jesus, he's had a sex-change.'

'No, he's had a daughter.'

That was the start of a fortnight of silly jokes about literary London, featuring, among others, Francesca Kermode, Martina Amis and Salmonella Rushdie. One morning we were giggling over them at breakfast in the Sombrero Room. Jack Binion, the president of the Horseshoe and one of Drache's closest friends, was at the next table. He asked what we were laughing about, then sat for a while, solemnly weighing up our answer. Finally he pronounced judgement: 'It's his only out.'

When Tony and I are in Vegas the flip side of the joking is poetry. We talk about it more often there than we ever do in London, perhaps because it's the only town either of us knows where art means Liberace and if you mention books they assume you're a bookmaker. I've always had a knack for remembering verse. When I was young I could read a poem two or three times and know it by heart. It was a mnemonic trick that has vanished with age, along with all the other tricks – the fingertip push-ups and one-arm pull-ups. But the poems I once knew are hard-wired in my memory and in Vegas they come pouring out, especially in the small hours, after a hard day in the salt mines, figuring the odds and keeping a poker face. I recite Donne and Lovelace and Berryman, Tony sings excerpts from his translation of *Don Giovanni,* and occasionally we do stretches of *King Lear* in chorus. It is a reminder of a world elsewhere and it adds to the pleasure of hacking it with a close friend in the most tough-minded town on earth.

16

A PACT WITH MR SHAWN

Once I began to write regularly for the *New Yorker* my strange, lonely profession became something I could never have imagined; it became pleasurable. The magazine had published a short story of mine in 1971, but that was a one-off and nothing I submitted for the next decade seemed to appeal to the choosy Mr Shawn. That, of course, was part of the *New Yorker*'s strength, and the reason why most writers of my generation wanted to publish there. It was impossible to predict what the editor would like. He was a chronically shy man and celebrity didn't interest him at all. He was famous for turning down famous writers. Although many of the writers he first published – Cheever, Salinger, Updike – went on to become very famous indeed, they were merely part of the *New Yorker*'s attraction and there were others, equally talented – staff writers like Jane Kramer, William Maxwell, John McPhee and Mark Singer – who, although they published excellent books, made their reputations almost entirely in the magazine and on whom the magazine's reputation for immaculate writing depended.

I never became a staff writer for the *New Yorker*, but after *The Biggest Game in Town* Mr Shawn let me write on more or less any subject I chose. He was a nervous man who suffered from claustrophobia and scarcely left New York, but I think he had a taste for adventure – for other people's adventures – and he encouraged me to feed my rat. After poker in Las Vegas I went out to the oil installations in the North Sea to write about Britain's offshore oil, climbed the Old Man of Hoy in terrible weather as part of a profile of Mo Anthoine, then wrote a profile of another friend, Torquil Norman, which gave me an excuse to fly in his ancient De Havillands, the kind of aeroplanes I'd worshipped as a kid.

The only project Mr Shawn wouldn't hear of was the one I lusted after most: I wanted him to help me hitch a ride on a space shuttle. I knew that because I was a 50-something Brit the *New Yorker* was my only hope with

NASA, so I did everything I could to persuade him, though I was careful to make my pitch in writerly terms and keep my hungry rat out of it. I told him that the exploration of space was going to remain a mystery unless the agency found room on a spacecraft for someone who knew how to write. Until that happened no one would know how it really feels to be blasted off beyond the pull of gravity, or to live weightless and in slow motion while the capsule circles at an insane speed in that huge darkness. We wouldn't even properly know what the planet looks like from out there in space. The astronauts, I said, are too busy with their scientific chores to bother with anything else. And even if they knew how it was done, writing is not their brief. As they report it, I said, life in space sounds like a spell in a Best Western motel in Topeka, Kansas. And so on.

I pitched it to him as a perfect *New Yorker* project, the kind of piece the magazine owed its readers now there was someone willing to write it. Mr Shawn looked away, fiddled with the papers on his desk and said no, he didn't want any of his writers taking that kind of risk. It's not risky, I said airily; NASA has built so many fail-safes into the system that riding in a spacecraft is safer than crossing Fifth Avenue at rush hour. But he just shook his head. A couple of months later *Challenger* exploded right after blast-off and that was the end of the argument.

Even before the disaster, when I was still seething with impatience at his implacable timidity, I realized that I was involved in something quite new to me: I was writing for an editor who cared about my well-being. In fact, I had already learned that, though in a different way. When I was 50 pages into my piece on offshore oil I ran out of money. So I sent the finished pages off to Mr Shawn with a letter saying I'd got this far and didn't want to stop now in order to write short pieces to pay my bills. If he liked what he read, would he consider advancing me some of the fee, on the understanding that, if the finished piece wasn't good enough for him, I'd repay the money when it was published as a book? I'd never written a begging letter before and I found it hard.

Courier services were rare in 1985 and beyond my means, so I airmailed the package from the local post office on a Monday. At three o'clock on the following Friday afternoon – 10 a.m. New York time – my telephone rang and I heard Mr Shawn's unmistakable, creaky voice: 'The pages are very strong. Would $15,000 help?' From where I stood, $15,000 was a fortune. 'It would solve everything,' I said. I was so relieved and so grateful that I could scarcely get the words out, but he cut me short when I tried to thank him. The cheque arrived three days later.

That kind of generosity and solicitude was like nothing I had ever come across in 30 years of writing for a living – not even from Tony Godwin. But what mattered even more was knowing that what I wrote was thought well of by the most fastidious editor in the world. In a way the *New Yorker* took good care of its writers because it cared, above everything else, for the written word. Pat Crow, who edited my pieces before they went to Mr Shawn for final approval, had a passion for fly fishing and kept his fly-tying tackle – a vice, tweezers, bunches of feathers, spools of coloured threads – on a side-table in his crowded office. I assumed he tied flies to calm his nerves after dealing with writers, though I never caught him at it. He was burly and bearded like a sea captain, but he read prose with the attention most people read poetry – alert to the inner rhythms and the placing of every word. I do the same – it was poetry, after all, that first turned me on to literature – but I've always been secretly ashamed that I never learned to read diagonally, to scan a page for the facts without listening to the writer's voice, which is the only way to cope with pulp fiction or newspapers. However hard I try, I still read aloud silently in my head and sometimes my lips move, like an old Jew praying in synagogue. This is a disadvantage for someone who spends a great part of his professional life with a book in his hand.

But that was how everyone seemed to read at the *New Yorker*, though I never saw Pat Crow's lips move and he turned the pages faster than I ever managed. He listened intently to the rhythm of each sentence and the flow of the paragraphs, to the tone of voice, and the echo and reverberation of every word. And whenever he found something he thought was amiss, he'd pause and say, hesitantly, 'Now, about this . . .' Every change, down to the last comma, was discussed and nothing was ever cut without long, almost tender deliberation. (Philip Hamburger famously spent a whole day wrangling with Mr Shawn about whether or not 'stone cold' should be hyphenated.) I have always thought of myself as a meticulous rewriter, but the *New Yorker* made me feel like an amateur.

Every writer has two audiences: one he never knows, the other he invents. The first reads his work once it is written; the second is the inner audience which is present while he is writing – four or five listeners in his head whose judgement he trusts and whose good opinion he cares about.

Those inner listeners are powerful presences, but they are not reliable. One or two of them may be figures from the past, literary heroes and mentors who stay silent because they are long dead, and even the living don't always bother to pick up the telephone or drop you a line when they approve of what you've done. Writing is always a lonely trade, but writing in the dark, never knowing if there's anyone out there who hears what you're saying, makes it the loneliest trade of all. 'I don't want criticism,' Joseph Conrad told his wife when he handed her the manuscript of a new novel. 'I just want praise.' Praise was never part of the *New Yorker*'s house style – Crow was notoriously laconic and the others seemed embarrassed when they told you they liked something you had written – but you knew they understood what you were trying to do and they expressed their approval by a mute geniality, as though to say, Welcome to the club.

The effect was curiously heartening, though not in a narcissistic way. Although it was good to be listened to closely and taken seriously, the focus was on the writing, not on the writer. When Mr Shawn and his brief successor, Bob Gottlieb, were in charge at the *New Yorker*, there was a pact between the editors and the writers and the readers to produce and support a magazine which didn't concern itself with the stuff that filled other weeklies and glossies – news, celebrity, gossip, fashion. It was a pact about literary style, not stylishness, and we were all in it together. Any subject, no matter how quirky or arcane or seemingly trivial, could be made interesting provided the writing was cool and lucid and a pleasure to read. The common goal was journalism that read like literature, but modestly and without drawing unnecessary attention to itself. It was a unique publication and to have been part of it for a few years was a unique experience.

17

OTHER FRIENDS

After I married Anne I more or less dropped out of the literary world. The people I saw most of were climbers and poker players, friends like Mac and Tony Holden, and a funny, generous South African couple, Bunny and Berenice Krikler. Berenice, like Anne, was a psychologist turned psychotherapist, a woman with a vocation, intuitive and sure of herself. Bunny was equally self-confident, but only intellectually. He was formidably intelligent and well-read, a man with real taste whose good opinion was important to everyone who knew him, though he himself did virtually nothing with his talents. He had dropped out without even bothering to drop in. No doubt he had any number of private reasons which I knew nothing about to explain his bloody-minded refusal to compete, but one of them was an excess of fastidiousness and I admired him for that. While his brother became a judge and the clever South African friends who looked up to him published books and became professors – one received the Nobel Prize – Bunny taught at a secondary school, then joined the staff of the Wiener Library. It was honourable work – the Wiener is Britain's leading research source for the history of anti-Semitism and the Nazi period – and he took it seriously enough, but it wasn't exactly challenging to a man of his ability. He wrote none of the books he planned and his failure to use his many gifts haunted him.

He made up for it, however, in the end. He had always put himself down in a witty, gloomy way, but when he learned he had terminal cancer the self-deprecation fell away. He seemed somehow strengthened, even invigorated by the prospect of death. It was as if the bad news had finally forced him into a decision: having betrayed his intelligence during his life, he would at least use it to die well.

The first time I saw him after his cancer was diagnosed he said, in an off-hand way, that there were some lines of Andrew Marvell that he couldn't get out of his head.

'Which lines?'

'You know. The ones about King Charles's execution: "He nothing common did, or mean,/Upon the memorable scene:/But with his keener eye/The axe's edge did try."'

Bunny had always set the intellectual standards for his friends, now he was setting moral standards both for them and for himself. And he kept to them scrupulously – without complaints, without self-pity. He went on reading, judging, joking; he remained interested in things – glad, especially, to have lived to see the collapse of Communism – and was less concerned about what was happening to him than about the grief it was causing his friends. At his daughter's wedding his skin was waxy-yellow and he looked hollowed out by the disease, but his speech was funny, tender, stylish, the best wedding speech any of us had ever heard – the masterpiece he'd never written. He was saying goodbye – but subtly, without mentioning the subject, an example for the rest of us to live up to. I think he was also saying, 'See what I might have done if I'd tried.'

Through Berenice Krikler I got to know Stirling Moss in 1962, soon after the terrible accident at Goodwood which put him out of Grand Prix racing. Berenice was working at the hospital he had been sent to and she gave him psychological tests to check for brain damage. (There was none. The doctors also expected him to be crippled for life but he was walking normally after six weeks.) She introduced us because I had a passion for fast cars and she knew that he was a hero of mine; Stirling and I have been friends ever since. Occasionally he took me with him when he tested cars. I had done some rallying when I was at Oxford – in someone else's car – and fancied myself as a driver, but being driven by Stirling, like climbing with Mo or Joe Brown or playing poker with Eric Drache, made me realize that there are ranges of skill I never knew about – ranges beyond ranges, and I was still in the foothills.

When the motoring journalist Denis Jenkinson went as his map-reader in the Mille Miglia race around Italy, he wrote that Moss drove for 10 hours on that fine edge on which the rest of us drive for 90 seconds before we crash. That was how it was, on a smaller scale, when he tested a car. He'd go through the routine checks, muttering into a tape-recorder, then he'd say, 'Let's see what she can do.' And we were off, always on the limit, always in control. On corners where I, driving flat out, would have left a margin of six inches, he left less than one – but smoothly, without hasty corrections, without panic, a single effortless progression. He seemed to sense the balance of the machine in the same way as he sensed the balance of his own body. When we stopped after a long, fast run, the interior of even the most expensive cars smelled pleasantly of hot oil and sometimes the brake-discs glowed red. Stirling would nod and say, 'Nice piece of machinery.' It was a professional judgement and also a professional courtesy, the matador saluting a brave bull.

Driving of this order is a high art, as thrilling and controlled as any poem or painting – thrilling because it is so controlled. Stirling is brisk and practical, he likes gadgets and fixing things and is not at all interested in the arts. But behind the wheel of a car he is as sensitive as any artist I have ever met.

The last time I taught was at Buffalo in 1966, the year Anne and I were married. Since then my only link with the academic world has been Frank Kermode. When we first met early in the fifties, while he was at Reading and I was a student at Oxford, English departments were divided into two warring camps: scholars who knew everything about texts and their authors and critics who made judgements and weren't bothered by boring details and facts. Frank was the exception; he had read all the books and formed his own shrewd opinions of them; he had also read all the books about the books, as well as the learned articles and footnotes, and he went on to produce authoritative editions of major writers like Shakespeare and T. S. Eliot. Despite his learning, his grand professorships and knighthood, the roll-call of honorary degrees from famous universities, he has never acquired the king-of-the-castle arrogance that often goes with academic eminence. This may be because he is a modest, private man who has an interesting life outside academia, a life where learning doesn't count for so much. There is a more fundamental reason still: he is too involved in literature to put on airs. Because he is a fine critic and understands what he reads from the inside, he knows that feelings are always mixed and motives ambiguous and he applies this knowledge to his own life. He himself may not have written novels or poems – although he wanted to when he was young, he has said – but he is full of authorly self-doubt; his intellectual world is peopled, like Eliot's, by 'men whom one cannot hope to emulate' and he judges his own achievements accordingly.

Talking to Frank about poetry – especially seventeenth-century poetry – sometimes reminds me of what I have missed by opting for the lighthouse keeper's isolation of the professional writer: the pleasure of swapping quotes, conversing in shorthand without having to explain the references, the pleasure of the mutual obsession. But when Frank talks about academic power struggles and what has happened to teaching now that theory, politics, race and gender have replaced the study of literature as a living art – words on the page, sounds in the head, images in the mind's eye, imaginary presences with lives of their own – I know I was right to get out.

The same goes for the poetry world which I know, these days, only through Ian Hamilton. Ian and I first met in 1960, when he was 'president, chief executive and general mastermind of the Oxford University Poetry Society'. That is how he described himself in his wicked *New Yorker* profile of Stephen Spender, and I suppose it's a miracle that we ever saw each other again, given what he goes on to say about the lessons he learned as boss of the OUPS:

The week before Spender's visit, we had dinner with W. H. Auden . . . The week after, we would be getting Robert Graves. Why these grand figures put themselves to this inconvenience – no fee, no audience to speak of, and a dinner that few of them ever seemed to touch – remains a mystery to me. But it was rare for a poet, however famous, to turn down our invitation. One or two of them, unbelievably, came back for more.

In retrospect, I can see that this was my introduction to the limitless vanity of poets: they'll put up with anything provided that they get to read their works.

Maybe I got through Ian's net because there was no way I qualified as 'grand'. I wasn't famous, I had no backlist – at that point, my collected works ran to two books of criticism, a couple of pamphlets of poetry and a lot of reviews – and, anyway, I was far too young – 30 years old to his 22. Eight years may have seemed a lot when we first met, but it rapidly became nothing at all, particularly after Ian founded the *Review*, in 1962, and began to publish things of mine in it. The relationship of editor to contributor is a great equalizer, no matter how small a fee is involved.

As it happens, we became close friends and have met every month or two ever since. I have just two or three good friends who actually write for a living, and Ian is the only one who keeps in touch with who's in and who's out in contemporary verse. He dislikes the vanity and follies of poets as much as I do, but he is stuck with them professionally. Once a literary editor, I mean, always a literary editor. Although Ian, unfortunately, is no longer in charge of a magazine, he still seems to feel that it is his duty to know what's happening in Grub Street. Or maybe everyone in Grub Street wants to know Ian because his standards are so high. Certainly, the fact that we have continued to meet makes me feel obscurely pleased, as if I had passed a difficult test.

The truth is, Ian is a hard man to please and his beady eye for whatever is phoney or sentimental makes him almost impossible to fool. This combination of shuddering distaste for overstatement and a sure instinct for clear, emotionally precise language gives his reticent poetry its strength; he has made an art out of looking away without disguising the price you pay for doing so. The same qualities also make him a formidable literary critic, although they mean that, on his scale of values, nobody escapes whipping. Mention the name of any prominent operator in the lit. biz and Ian's sardonic mouth tightens, his eyes glint and somebody's done for, his or her vanity fatally skewered with a joke. I have never for a moment kidded myself that Ian doesn't see right through me, too. I simply assume that he is willing to overlook my failings because he likes me.

To be fair, he is even harder on himself than he is on other people. Once we were talking about his mother, who was old and ill and miserable. 'If my life were like hers, I'd rather be dead,' Ian said. 'Come to think of it, if my life were like mine, I'd rather be dead.' He was only partly joking. For as long as I've known him he has been engulfed in disasters, most of them financial. He has also steadily refused to extricate himself from them, as though he believed that making an effort on his own behalf were morally distasteful, a gesture that might somehow be construed as self-promotion rather than self-help.

Moral scruples aside, Ian takes a perverse pride in being broke. He has written eloquently on 'The Trouble With Money' – it is the title essay of one of his collections of essays – but his particular trouble with money is not that he is above it but that it has always been above him. At the start there may have been what he called 'a near-priestly kind of romance in the idea that a high-purposed literary career would be profitless, at least in terms of cash', but that didn't last long. He has the usual expensive habits – he smokes, he drinks, he likes to eat out – and he swiftly acquired the usual expensive responsibilities – a family, a mortgage, alimony. He worked hard to support them all, but his heart wasn't in it. It was in poetry, the least profitable of all the arts, and no matter how solemnly he pretended otherwise he couldn't take money seriously. I used to chivvy him about keeping records and getting himself a good accountant but the look he gave me – amused, disdainful – made me feel cheap, so I gave up trying.

Money, however, is like the godhead – it never manifests itself to those who don't truly believe in it – so the disasters kept on coming and kept on getting worse. There may be one or two people who know as much as Ian about contemporary poetry, but I can't believe that any living writer is more expert on how to cope with creditors, bailiffs, Inland Revenue auditors, the Official Receiver and the bankruptcy court. It must be a nightmare for him but, from the outside, the whole show has come to seem so much out of control that it is laughable. Or almost laughable. As Adlai Stevenson said when Eisenhower beat him to the US presidency, 'I'm too old to weep and it hurts too much to laugh.'

As each new calamity rolls in, Ian reports on it deadpan, with a high critical impartiality, like a theatre critic at a dreadful farce at which he is a helpless spectator like you, not a participant. He can't beat it, so he might as well make fun of it, and he is an effortlessly funny man. For me, in fact, one of the great pleasures of his company is that he makes me laugh more or less all the time. And not just about literature: for example, when I told him my daughter was working for the man who invented virtual reality, he replied, without missing a beat, 'How can she tell?' Mostly, however, the jokes are at his own expense. Another example: a meal with Ian goes on for hours. It is like a science-fiction experience in which time implodes, waiters age before your eyes and generations of diners come and go, while Ian toys disdainfully with the food on his plate and ends up eating almost nothing. I'm the opposite: I wolf my meal and often end up eating his, too. Once, when I had long finished and he was being more dilatory than usual, I asked him if he minded if I smoked while he was eating. He looked at me in amazement. 'Mind?' he said. '*I* smoke while I'm eating.'

Ian's nose for literary talent is as spectacular as his lack of financial success. As editor of the *Review* and the *New Review*, he was the first to publish all sorts of writers who went on to become rich and famous: Julian Barnes, Ian McEwan, Clive James, Jim Crace. While they moved up in the world, he stayed broke, went bankrupt and watched his magazines fold. But none of them would seriously claim to have more literary taste and intelligence than Ian.

Justice isn't a concept that carries much weight in the literary world. Freud was wrong when he said that writers are kept going at their dreadful trade by the prospect of 'fame, riches and the love of beautiful women'. Of course, the winners accept the rewards as their natural right and the losers glower from the sidelines, but that's not the point. All that matters is the work itself:

> Western wind, when will thou blow,
> The small rain down can rain?
> Christ, if my love were in my arms
> And I in my bed again!

The anonymous poet who wrote that at the beginning of the sixteenth century wasn't thinking about fame and riches. He may have had a beautiful woman in mind but she was only one part of the story: absence, freezing weather, loneliness and longing; he was bringing all his uneasy yearning together as perfectly as he could in four bare lines.

Poetry is the sparest, most concentrated and exposed form of verbal communication, and writing it is like trying to break into a bank: the giant lock on the vault won't budge until every tumbler has clicked open; the poem isn't finished until every word is precise, weighted, necessary and in its right place, and the true poet knows it. 'Perfection, of a kind, was what he was after.' What Auden wrote as an epitaph on a tyrant also applies to poetry. It is a tyrannical craft and it demands sacrifices. In his devotion to the art Ian has suffered all the indignities of Grub Street, churning out ill-paid reviews, dodging creditors, standing glumly aside while the bailiffs walk off with his worldly goods. It's a messy life but because he has stuck by – or is stuck with – his idea of perfection, it is also curiously selfless.

*

When Henry James called novels 'loose and baggy monsters' he was talking about the shapelessness and infinite malleability of the form, although prose, too, is loose and baggy compared to poetry. You can go on tinkering with it forever, no matter how many times you've rewritten it. Once, when Philip Roth was living in London, I went to the little apartment where he worked to collect him for lunch. While he was putting on his coat, I glanced at a page of manuscript lying beside his typewriter. Philip has one of the strongest voices of any novelist alive, effortless and apparently unhesitating, yet the page was black with tiny corrections.

'Who's going to notice the difference?' I asked.

'You are,' he answered. 'I am.'

Meticulousness is just one of the obsessions Philip and I share. When we first met 40 years ago we were both angry young men with bad marriages, troublesome parents and a yearning for shiksas and literature. We had both been good students, full of high seriousness, and even now when we talk about books it's usually about the masterworks we were taught to admire back in the fifties when we were at college – Kafka, Gogol, James. Since then I have written three novels, yet whenever I am with Philip I realize I lack the novelist's temperament. A real novelist is an invigilator, constantly on the watch, listening, making mental notes, using whatever happens to happen and weaving it into stories. Maybe that was what James meant by 'loose and baggy monsters': the novel can accommodate everything.

Philip manages to feed his monster while living like a hermit. He writes, he reads, he swims, he works out and occasionally he watches baseball on television, but everything he needs is in his head and he ventures abroad hardly at all. David Cornwell (aka John Le Carré) is as prolific as Philip but always on the move, checking out locations and collecting characters for his plots. He has a Dickensian eye for people's quirks and an unstoppable Dickensian energy. In the 20 years I've known him he has never paused for breath, off on the next novel as soon as the ink is dry on the last. I once said to him, 'If I earned in my whole life as much as you earn on one book, I'd never write another word.' Although he laughed politely, it was a joke he didn't share. Money is beside the point for David. He uses it to travel in comfort and have fun, to wine and dine his friends in a manner to which they are not accustomed, but mostly to look after his children – 'to see them right' is the expression used by the father he made famous. But his real pleasure lies in turning high intrigue into high art. Unlike most writers I know, he genuinely enjoys writing.

He is a brilliant mimic and has a wicked eye for weakness. When he tells you, say, about a dinner at the Russian embassy what he gives you is less an anecdote than a drama in three acts: the accents, the body language, the clothes and the sweat, the brand of vodka and caviar, the make of the security guards' guns and where exactly they were packing them. Best of all, there is always a plot. One of his greatest advantages as a novelist is that the world he knows best has nothing to do with literature, for he honed many of his most unique skills while working for MI6. It is the world of spies and diplomats and civil servants in which every motive is veiled and betrayal is the only game in town. There is always some level beyond the level the players are on, some point being made they don't quite understand, some item of information to be gleaned which they didn't know they possessed or why anyone should want it. His genius is to have combined a peerless gift for storytelling with the art of the interrogator.

Jean Rhys is the one writer I have ever met whose life was more of a mess than Ian Hamilton's, although, unlike Ian, who detests excess and handles people sardonically but gently, Rhys was a nightmare for anyone who came close to her. Her novels are spare, concentrated, without a flicker of self-pity and her seemingly casual prose is pure and austere, but she herself was a chronic alcoholic and when she drank she became a monster – vengeful, sullen, manipulative, violent, abusive. Mercifully, on the few occasions when I saw her she was always on her best behaviour.

The first time we met was in 1974. Her books were belatedly being reissued in the States and the *New York Times* asked me to write about them. Because I was a fan and she was still almost unknown in America, I wanted to do her justice and the piece I wrote was almost twice the length they asked for. I assumed they would cut it to shreds. (As it happens, they didn't cut a word and I like to think that, thanks to the *New York Times*'s influence, it helped establish her reputation over there.) So I sent her a copy of the original version, thinking it might give her pleasure, and thereafter we exchanged letters.

She was living in Devon, not far from Exeter, where I had a good friend, Cliff Fishwick, a talented painter who was also a mountaineer. One weekend when I was going climbing with Cliff, I arranged to pay Rhys a visit. She was holed up in a draughty, jerry-built bungalow which she had bought sight unseen – she had a flair for wrong choices – in a bleak village called Cheriton Fitzpaine. She asked me to come at two o'clock and I was warned by Diana Athill, Rhys's friend and editor, that whatever I did I mustn't arrive early: 'Jean's very careful with her appearance. She doesn't like being surprised.'

Rhys was 84 by then but, apart from her ragged smile, she only looked her age when she laughed. Then she collapsed suddenly forward and her head tumbled almost into her lap, as though a string had snapped in her spine. Otherwise she behaved like a demure young girl with a gentleman caller. She had dressed and made up with enormous care. She had marvellous eyes, blue as blue velvet, and she wore a blue brooch at her throat to bring out their colour as well as a large blue cameo ring on the middle finger of her left hand, which she held carefully at her cheek. Her black skirt was long and elegant, slit to the knee at the front to reveal a frilly white petticoat.

We sat facing each other in her L-shaped sitting-room and for a while there seemed to be nothing to talk about. She was shy and tongue-tied, and that made me shy. She kept crossing and re-crossing her legs under the frilly petticoat until I registered that this bashful old lady had the calves of a young girl, long and immaculate. So I stared at them admiringly as I was supposed to do, and suddenly she relaxed. She began to talk about her incompetence with machines – she wasn't sure which knob switched on her television and using a typewriter was beyond her – then about the unfriendliness of the villagers and the snags of her poky bungalow. Her voice was soft, hard to catch. 'Before I bought it,' she said, 'I was thinking of going to a little hotel in Belgravia, but now it's been turned into flats.' Her eyes widened in panic. 'What would have become of me if I'd moved?' she whispered.

We talked hardly at all about books. I mentioned that I was just finishing my first novel. 'Forty-four's a bit late to start,' I said, trying to make a joke of it. She muttered something polite and I replied, 'You'd written most of yours by then.' Her face collapsed and for a moment I thought she would weep. She didn't care to be reminded of her age.

When I tried to get her to talk about her own books she changed the subject. The only one she mentioned – in passing – was *Wide Sargasso Sea*.

She said a man used to come and see her once a week while she was writing it. (She made it sound as if he had been an admirer but I think she was talking about Max Hamer, her third husband.) 'He didn't like my books. He thought they were ephemeral. That helped somehow. Without him, I suppose I wouldn't have written it.'

A few months later I met her again when she came to London. She was staying at the Portobello Hotel, which was as close in style to her beloved Left Bank as London hotels get. By then her books were selling in America as well as in Britain and, after a lifetime of poverty, she finally had money to spare. She had rented a suite with big bay windows, a desk to write at and a fridge full of champagne in a mahogany cabinet. She was dressed in a shimmering silver caftan and carried a silver-topped cane. She looked beautiful and knew it.

She was in London to recover from one of her periodic disasters. A tax inspector had visited her in Cheriton Fitzpaine and bullied her about money she owed. When she told him she knew nothing about it, her accountant was in charge of that stuff, he started to relent. 'I was only obeying orders,' he said. She replied, 'That's what the Nazis used to say.' A couple of days later a letter arrived from HM Inspector of Taxes saying her house would be seized in lieu of payment. It frightened her so much she lost her balance and fell. She didn't break any bones but she bruised her ribs and was badly shaken. Friends drove her to London to recuperate.

She had already written to me about my piece in the *New York Times* – a polite thank-you note, dutiful and formal. When she thanked me again I said someone should have written it 40 years earlier. She replied, 'Perhaps it would have been nice to have had money and fame then. It would have saved a lot of trouble.'

'You'd have found trouble,' I answered. 'You have a genius for it.'

She giggled, hung her head and whispered, 'I suppose you're right.'

I saw her again a few times when she came up to London. This woman who seemed to have been doomed from birth and moved relentlessly downwards from one disaster to the next lived to be 89 and died honoured by the Establishment she despised. (In one of her stories she wrote, 'I got the feeling that I was surrounded by a pack of timid tigers waiting to spring the moment anybody is in trouble or hasn't any money. But tigers are better-looking, aren't they?') It should have been a happy ending but in fact nothing changed. The boozing, manipulation and violent rages went on as before and she continued to behave shamelessly to the people who tried to care for her. Jill, the good-natured young woman who looked after her in Devon, momentarily thwarted her and was frightened out of her wits when her sweet, 87-year-old charge leapt out of her wheelchair and became a taunting, threatening witch, straight out of the girl's worst nightmares. Near the end she almost destroyed Diana Melly, who, because she loved Rhys's books and was enchanted by the old lady when she was sober, invited her to stay with her in London the whole of one winter. Whenever I visited Rhys in the Mellys' house near Parliament Hill, Diana would meet me at the door, ashen-faced, with her coat on, ask me how long I was going to stay, mutter 'I'd like to murder the bitch', then scurry out. Upstairs, Rhys rested in state, all sweetness and light, charming, flirtatious and dressed to the nines. Diana's genial husband, the writer and jazz singer George Melly, nicknamed her 'Johnny Rotten'. Jean Rhys was an extraordinary writer, scrupulous and self-denying, who laboured obsessively at her prose until it followed, with uncanny precision, the sidelong, casual, flickering movement of her sensibility. But thank God I never got to know her well.

Samuel Beckett was the one writer I would like to have known but I met him just once, in April 1976, at a party for his seventieth birthday. A couple of years earlier I'd published a short introduction to his work in Frank Kermode's series of Fontana Modern Masters. The choice of subject was Frank's, not mine. I had wanted to write about Jean-Luc Godard but Frank wasn't sure if he wanted to include books on the cinema, so he persuaded me to tackle Beckett. At that time Beckett was a one-man academic industry, the subject of hundreds of books and articles, none of which I had read. When I mentioned this to Frank he was not discouraged; he seemed to think that it would be an advantage to come at the work with an innocent eye. Maybe he would have thought differently if he'd known just how innocent my eye was: I'd seen *Waiting for Godot* and *Endgame* but none of the other plays and had read not one of Beckett's difficult novels. However, one of the bonuses of the mendicant critic's life is that you get paid to further your education. I settled down and read the collected works and decided to skip the commentaries.

I was entranced not only because Beckett's one unchanging subject was depression and I'd just spent four years writing a book about suicide. It was his deadpan black humour that got to me, the technical fecundity which enabled him to play endless variations on a single theme, the stern distance he kept between himself and his narrators, the purity of his language – everything pared down to the essentials, not a comma out of place. He was a master stylist who despised style – 'a bow-tie about a throat cancer' he once called it – and had nothing good to say of the vocation he was condemned to – the sorry, 'balls-aching' labour of putting words on paper.

The birthday party was at the flat of John Calder, Beckett's publisher and friend, and not many people had been invited because Beckett hated crowds. He was also notoriously disdainful of critics, so I was surprised to have been asked.

There were only a couple of other guests there when I arrived and I was introduced to Beckett straight away. He looked at me warily and said, 'Now we can't talk about my work.' He spoke so softly I had to strain to hear him. When I replied, 'Of course not', he exhaled gratefully.

There was a long, awkward pause. Then he said, 'I was very interested in *The Savage God*.'

I said, 'If we can't talk about your work we can't talk about mine.'

After that the conversation went easily. We moved over to a corner, next to the table with food and bottles on it, and talked for almost an hour. I no longer remember what the conversation was about – sport probably, certainly nothing cultural – but I remember clearly what he looked like. This great celebrator of derelicts, whose work is populated by hoboes and crazies and the prematurely senile, by cripples with 'spavined gait', by people stuffed in urns and dustbins, up to their necks in sand or crawling in the mud throughout eternity, by the bodiless, limbless and unnameable, was himself a man of extraordinary presence and dignity – tall, erect, alert, ascetic, like a noble saint in a Spanish painting. In *Malone Dies* the abused child Sapo is allowed one moment of release:

But he loved the flight of the hawk and could distinguish it from all others. He would stand rapt, gazing at the long pernings, the quivering poise, the wings lifted for the plummet drop, the wild reascent, fascinated by such extremes of need, of pride, of patience and solitude.

With his hawk's profile and steady, uncanny gaze, Beckett had a similar beauty – not wild but stern and remote and self-contained.

We drank whisky while we talked; or rather he drank and I sipped; there was no way I could keep up with him. Meanwhile the room had filled and the guests were heaping their plates from the table beside us. Calder had laid on a great spread for the occasion and I have always been fonder of food than drink. I eyed the board lustfully until I could bear it no longer.

'Fancy something to eat?' I asked.

Beckett glanced disdainfully at the feast, then looked away.

'I'm not much of a trencherman myself,' he answered mildly.

A trencherman! It was as if I'd offered St Jerome a hamburger. I blushed with shame.

Later in the evening one of Beckett's cronies told me, strictly off the record, that the great man had liked the book I'd written about him. Then he added anxiously, as if he'd broken some Mafia code of silence, 'Maybe I shouldn't have told you.'

When I went to say goodbye to Beckett he smiled sweetly, shrugged and said in a resigned voice, 'A pity we couldn't talk about your book.'

He may have been referring to *The Savage God*, but somehow I was convinced that the book in question was the one I had written about him. I will never know.

18

DANCING ON A CLOUD

———————➤ ◆ ————————

I never managed to hitch a ride with NASA and I missed my chance to learn to fly at post-war Oxford by catching the climbing bug instead of joining the RAF-sponsored flying club. But, in the end, I did get to fly in the kind of aircraft which I had yearned for and studied and made models of when I was a schoolboy – delicate, nimble machines one generation on from the Sopwith Camels my uncle Teddy had flown in the Great War.

I flew in them, though only as a passenger, with Torquil Norman, who comes from a family of fliers and has been messing around in planes since he was a kid. His father, who held one of the first pilot's licences issued in Britain and died heroically in the Second World War, flew him to Switzerland in his three-seater Leopard Moth when Torquil was just one year old. His brother Desmond, who is equally obsessed with flying (and eventually designed and produced the highly successful Britten-Norman Islander), taught him the rudiments while Torquil was still a schoolboy at Eton. Torquil got his pilot's licence at 18, the minimum legal age, flew Seafires and Sea Furies with the Fleet Air Arm during his National Service and, while he was at Cambridge, spent most weekends flying Meteor jet fighters with 601 Squadron, the RAF's wild bunch (since disbanded), who jazzed up their drab uniforms with scarlet jacket linings and scarlet socks and were renowned for their rowdy parties and outrageous behaviour. He has been flying ever since whenever he could get time away from his work as founder and chairman of the board of Bluebird Toys, which was, until he retired, Britain's most successful toy manufacturer.

The planes Torquil flies are more like the planes I used to make out of balsa-wood and rice paper in my childhood than the cramped, impersonal metal tubes flown by commercial airlines. Torquil has a unique collection of ancient De Havillands, all of them 50 or 60 years old, and their only metal parts are the engines and the bearers that hold the engines in place.

Everything else is a miracle of old-fashioned craftsmanship: wings, fuselages and tailplanes made of wood and covered with Irish linen, cabins kitted out like Rolls-Royces with Connolly leather, polished wood and cloth head-linings. But the machines are sturdy and reliable and, skydiving apart, flying in them is as close as you can get to a bird's three-dimensional freedom and a bird's-eye view of the earth.

In a commercial jet you know you are airborne only if you are lucky enough to be sitting by a window. Even then, all you can see from 35,000 feet is a flat carpet of clouds far below or, in clear weather, a small-scale map of the country. Torquil's planes can only climb to a few thousand feet and flying at that altitude is like being on an invisible seam between the earth and the sky. All the details below are intensely sharp: the harvest neatly stooked in the fields, a man walking his dog, a child waving from his back garden, the bright-blue swimming pool of a country house and, off in the distance, the office blocks of a town. Maybe this is what builders of luxury cars mean by 'grand touring': effortless progress across a road map, without dust or sweat or hassle, in a hand-built machine so beautifully crafted that it is itself a source of pleasure.

It is also a source of adventure, as flying itself used to be before it became just another form of boring mass transportation. Twice I have flown with Torquil from Tuscany to England in a single day – first in his Leopard Moth, then in his twin-engined Dragonfly. Neither plane could climb high enough to go over the Alps, so we went through them, threading the mountain passes, level with the seamed faces and well below the summit ridges. It was as though we had the whole range to ourselves – a private, inward experience, despite the steady roar of the engine. Moving across those bowls of rock in the little Leopard Moth, a couple of thousand feet above the valley floors, I was aware of the fragility of the aged machine and also of its sturdiness, the sureness with which it balanced on the air, the steady beat of its engine, the ingenuity and adventurousness of flight.

In the luxurious Dragonfly the flight from Arezzo to Rendcomb, in Gloucestershire, was stately and uneventful, but it was different in the Leopard Moth. We thought the leg through the Alps would be the hard part of the trip; in fact, it was merely the appetizer. The sky darkened steadily as we flew north over France. By the time we passed Amiens we had dropped from 3000 to 1000 feet, just below the clouds, and the rain was lashing down. Torquil sat up front with a map on his lap and one hand on the joy stick. He peered out at the shrouded landscape below, then back at the map, moving from side to side, tick-tock, like a metronome, and muttering to Air Traffic Control at Lydd Airport in Kent. The weather there was dreadful, he said: heavy rain and wind gusting to 30 knots. 'But we'll give it a try. If we can't make it, we'll go back to Le Touquet.'

By the time we crossed the French coast and moved out into the Channel, our altitude had dropped to 800 feet, the visibility was worse and the little plane seemed not to be making much headway against the wind. Because of the sheeting rain, there was nothing to be seen ahead through the windscreen. Torquil's metronome beat rose as he peered from side to side. From where I sat, behind him, the view was like Beckett's *Endgame*, 'Light black. From pole to pole': grey air, grey sea and great white horses rolling back towards France. So I watched the altimeter: 800 feet, 550, 400, 300, on down until the white horses seemed almost close enough to touch. Just off to our left, a huge container ship loomed out of the murk, the top of its superstructure level with our undercarriage.

After half an hour of blind man's buff there was still no sign of the English coast. Torquil shouted, 'I don't know exactly where we are' and put the plane into a wide, banking right-hand curve, until we seemed to be going in the same direction as the white horses. It's back to Le Touquet, I thought, and felt irrationally disappointed, as though the whole point of the journey had been missed: two old buffers with a secret agenda, Italy to England in one day, in a plane not much younger than we were. I knew that wasn't really the point, of course. The point was the pleasure in flying this immaculate old machine. But the bad weather had raised the ante, turning a pleasant trip into an adventure, and it seemed unfair to be beaten now, so close to home.

Five minutes later we were over land: a wide beach, tussocky dunes, pylons. England or France? I wondered. Then suddenly, Bingo! There, through the veils of rain, was the great bulk of Dungeness power station.

We landed gingerly and crabwise in the howling wind. As we taxied to a halt, the Lydd flight controller said, 'Welcome to terra firma.' 'Pleased to be here,' Torquil replied. The Leopard Moth was trembling like a whippet in the gale.

For the Customs officer, we were comic relief on a quiet day. He laughed when he saw us and went on laughing while he checked our bags. 'Had some fun, did you?'

'Piece of cake,' said Torquil, on his dignity.

'Where've you come from today?'

'Italy.'

The Customs officer's smile faded. 'Bugger me,' he said.

Later, on the train to London, Torquil said, 'Actually, I was a little doubtful when they said the wind was gusting to 30 knots.'

'Why?'

'Our stall speed is 42 knots.' He paused, then added reassuringly, 'Not that that was the real problem, of course.'

'Oh?'

'The real problem was the army firing-range at Dungeness. It was active. They had the red flags out. But the control tower told them to stop.' Another pause. 'All part of the fun,' he said.

The rat had a great meal that day, but it was as nothing compared to my first flight in Torquil's Tiger Moth. It's a trim little biplane with two open cockpits, one behind the other, a deep blue fuselage, white wings and tailplane, and struts of polished wood – every detail bright and clean and perfect. It was light enough for the two of us to manoeuvre it easily out of its hangar – we lifted it by its tail strut and pushed – and the engine started sweetly at the first swing of its propeller. We strapped ourselves in, Torquil behind, I in front. The seat harness was a four-point contraption made of three-inch khaki webbing. At the start it felt uncomfortable to be held so rigidly in place; later, when we were upside down, I was glad of it. We taxied out on to the runway, Torquil revved the engine to a pleasant roar, the plane moved forward, the tail lifted, and in less than 100 yards we were airborne. The instruments on the dashboard were minimal: an air-speed indicator, a rev counter, an altimeter, a turn-and-bank indicator, an oil-pressure gauge and a compass – ageing black dials with yellowish needles and figures. The joystick in my hands and the rudder-control pedals were linked to those in the rear cockpit, so I could follow what Torquil was doing to control the plane. My head was out in the air, the wind was in my face, the sun shone peacefully.

In an open cockpit in an English summer, you don't have to stop to smell the flowers; they come to you. At 300 feet on a warm day, great clouds of perfume envelop you as you go: mayflower from the hedges that bound each little field, wafts of pine scent from the intermittent patches of plantation. Torquil pulled back gently on the joystick. At 3000 feet we flew suddenly into cloud. One moment the clouds were above us, looking as solid as rock; the next we were moving through them at 90 miles an hour – great, softly streaming masses, as beautiful as the hair of one of Blackman's girls. Then, just as suddenly, we were out of them again in the sunlight.

The intercom was an old-fashioned air tube plugged into the headphones of my borrowed leather flying helmet. Torquil's voice came in above the noise of the engine: 'Feel like some aerobatics? Nothing fancy.'

I nodded vigorously.

'Loop,' said the cheerful voice in my ear.

Torquil dipped the nose, then pulled back hard on the joystick. My mouth dropped open with the g force, and my stomach dropped with it. The sun, which had been obscured by the upper wing, came into view. Then the pressure on my stomach eased and we were moving downward fast. There was a blur of blue and green and yellow, which cleared slowly. I looked up and saw the fields, with their bales of hay in tidy rows, right in front of my face. I'm upside down, I thought. That's strange. I don't feel upside down. Then, still slowly, the sky was back where it should be and the horizon was steady.

'OK?'

'Terrific.'

'Right ho, then. Let's try a spin.'

Again the plane dipped and climbed, my mouth dropped open, my stomach lurched. At the top of the curve – this time I was ready for it and could see the earth clearly above my head where the sky should have been – the engine stopped and the plane seemed to hang motionless. There was a violent movement of the rudder pedals, and suddenly we were falling in silence like a sycamore leaf, round and round, the landscape and sky spinning fast, until the plane steadied, the engine burst into life again and the world reassembled itself.

There was a third manoeuvre, a barrel roll, during which, I learned later, the aeroplane spirals like a corkscrew. I couldn't make that out at the time, because my stomach was rolling faster than the barrel and my mouth had dropped open so wide I thought it would unhinge itself. All I saw was a spinning vortex of sky and ground.

'Sorry about that,' Torquil said over the intercom. 'Bit untidy.'

The loop, the spin and the barrel roll are formal procedures – three of a large repertoire of aerobatic manoeuvres – with set rules and criteria for performance. You get it right or you do it shoddily or, worse still, you foul up. But essentially they are all variations on a single theme: play. And what distinguishes this particular style of play from earthbound equivalents is that it is in three dimensions. When Torquil put the Tiger Moth into a steeply banked turn it felt as if the plane had poised one wing-tip on an invisible pinnacle then pirouetted around it. It was dancing in three dimensions, playing in space, and the effect it produced was one of total freedom.

It was freedom from gravity in every sense: from the earth's heavy pull and from the responsibilities of everyday life. Torquil calls it dancing on a cloud. As for me, my heart was pounding and the blood was coursing sweetly through my veins. I recognized my old friend and bad habit, the adrenalin rush, but this was purer than anything I had ever experienced on a rock face or a diving board or at the poker table. It wasn't just adrenalin, it was happiness. It was as if I'd got my childhood back in the way childhood is supposed to be – without the tantrums and confusion. I was a 60-something grandfather, with a gammy ankle and a walking stick, absurdly dressed up like the Red Baron in a leather flying helmet and goggles. But I was also back where I started on the high board at the Finchley Road swimming pool. Free as a bird.

19

AUDIENCE OF ONE

———➤ ◆ ———

I've been lucky in other ways, if luck means having some of the things you want come true, like a happy marriage after an unhappy one, or the chance to replay childish pleasures in grown-up terms. As it happens, I never much associated pleasure with childhood. As far as I was concerned, happiness began when I went off to boarding school and started to lead my own life. The only truly happy memories I salvaged from Glenilla Road are of the long evenings I spent with my father listening to his records, and later I revived them in a perfect and very privileged way.

Thanks to those evenings, music became as much a part of my life as literature and listening on my own became a habit. Although I know I am missing whatever it is that makes a live performance special – the artists' presence, the sense of occasion, the interplay between the players and the audience – I still prefer sitting alone in front of the hi-fi to sharing a concert hall with strangers, distracted by the man with a cough, the woman who rustles her programme, the kid who can't sit still. Sometimes distracted, too, by the showmanship and vanity of the performer. 'There are two kinds of musician,' Isaiah Berlin once told me. 'The virtuosi love playing. That's what virtuosity is: you use the music for some kind of self-exhibitionism. When Shura Cherkassky was asked why he played so fast, he answered, "Because I can." The musicians I admire – Schnabel, Toscanini, the Busch Quartet – have a vision of the music they play, not of the playing of it.' Berlin was talking about our mutual friend, the pianist Alfred Brendel, part of whose genius lies in his selfless respect for the works he plays. As a musician he is a thinker with a wonderful grasp of the structure of each piece, of the way it develops intellectually as well as emotionally, and this makes his playing strangely inward, as though he were following the composer's own train of thought as it develops note by note, bar by bar. Listening to Brendel is like sharing in the act of creation, an austere experience, in which showmanship and self-importance play no part. His purpose is to make the audience marvel at the composition, not at him.

Perhaps this is partly because Brendel has many interests outside the closed world of music. He is well-read in two languages – German and English – and in a highly intellectual, Central European way: philosophy and criticism and art history, along with fiction and poetry. He contributes subtle, learned articles to the *New York Review of Books* and has published two collections of essays about music. He also writes witty and profoundly subversive poems, most of them poking fun at his own grandeur as a musician. When he was starting out, in fact, music was just one of the many things he did. 'I was a genius in those days,' he once said, 'like everyone else of 17. I composed, I painted, I wrote poetry.' When he was 17 a local gallery was showing his watercolours and gouaches at the time he gave his first public recital in Graz, his home town. The recital itself was an aggressively high-minded occasion. It was called 'The Fugue in Piano Literature' and included works by Bach, Brahms and Liszt, as well as a sonata with a double fugue by Brendel himself; the encores were all fugues. The teenager was making a point about art and intellectual rigour and since then he has never looked back. These days he no longer paints, but he has a passion for Dada and kitsch and an idiosyncratic collection of art – tribal, ancient and modern. An admirer once said, 'Everything about him is Jewish, except him.'

Brendel and I have been friends for almost 20 years and, because we are also neighbours, he sometimes invites me around, before recitals, to listen while he runs through the programme. It probably helps that I love music but cannot read a score, though, even if I could, comment is not what he is after. Brendel disdains gush and he assuredly doesn't need my praise. What I assume he wants is a sounding-board, a sympathetic and attentive presence in the room, not for vanity or reassurance, but simply to complete the artistic circle.

Literature and paintings are two-way communications – the poem needs a reader, the painting needs someone to look at it. But music, like theatre, is a three-way exchange – from the score to the interpreter to the listener – and the art of performance depends on the relationship between the musician and the audience. 'In the concert hall,' Brendel wrote in one of his essays, 'each motionless listener is part of the performance. The concentration of the player charges the electric tension in the auditorium and returns to him magnified.' He also once said to me, 'I like the fact that "listen" is an anagram of "silent". Silence is not something that's there before the music begins and after it stops. It is the essence of the music itself, the vital ingredient that makes it possible for the music to exist at all. It's wonderful when the audience is part of this productive silence.'

Brendel has two pianos in his studio and when he first began asking me around to listen, in 1981, he would place my chair off to one side where I could see him play. It was like watching a conduit under too much pressure: the music seemed to flow through him, from head to fingers to piano, and he was twisted and racked by the pressure of it. His neck distended, muscles twitched in his cheek, he pursed his mouth, bit his under-lip, smiled suddenly at some particular sweetness. Occasionally he made little grunting noises or sang along with the music *sotto voce*. In the small room, the sound was intense, reverberating, daunting. Sometimes, halfway through, the beautiful Reni Brendel would bring in tea and biscuits, and she and I would gossip for a few minutes while Brendel stood fretting pianissimo, not wanting his concentration disturbed. Immediately she left, he was back at the piano, head tilted to the ceiling, eyes closed, neck and cheeks tensed. Then he was playing again.

But those marvellous, disciplined cascades of sound don't come easily. Isaiah Berlin said that a public recital by Brendel was 'a dedicated sacrifice on an altar, an exalted experience'. Those private sessions with him made it clear to me how much a performance cost him. After one of them, when he was soaked with sweat and looked more than usually drained, I asked, inanely, how he remembered it all. He answered, 'Memory is not a problem. What matters is the musculature.' His body, for him, is an instrument that he must care for and respect like his piano – except that he has at least three pianos and only one body. One summer Brendel spent a month in Provence without playing a note – the first time in decades, he said, that he had kept away from the piano for so long – and when he got back to London and began playing again he complained that his little finger was bruised. I was still climbing in those days and my hands were permanently battered and scarred. When I failed to register an appropriate degree of dismay, he added reproachfully, 'The little finger has to withstand a lot.' He cocked the finger as if to play a note and a great ridge of muscle rose up along the side of his palm. His musculature, I realized, is as specialized as an athlete's.

A few years ago Brendel moved his studio to a different-shaped room and, since then, he has sat me immediately in front of the instruments. From there I can't properly see him and the effect is strange. Because of his extraordinary gift for projecting himself into the heads of the composers he interprets and playing as though he himself were thinking out the music for the first time, sitting right in front of the piano while this is happening makes you part of the process. The sound, in the small room, is huge. It is like being inside the music, hearing it breathe, exploring its structure as it unfolds around you. Occasionally I get a glimpse of his moving head or hear him mutter fretfully, but in a way he no more exists for me than I do for him. Only the music exists and both of us, in our different ways, are witnesses to it. I suppose this is what Eliot meant by 'music heard so deeply/That it is not heard at all, but you are the music/While the music lasts'.

A few times in my life I have written a poem that really works – at least, for me – so I understand a little about the disinterested pleasure of making something as perfect as you can. But to be present at the creation of great art is a different order of experience. Maybe this is what my father and I were hankering for, in our amateur way, when we sat together for hours in front of his ancient gramophone. Certainly, the old man is always hovering around when I am Brendel's audience of one. Of all the good things that I have had and he missed – a loving wife and children, travel, adventure, satisfying work, a chancy life lived on my own terms as my own boss – this is the one that would have given him most pleasure.

20

WRITING WHITE

———◆·———

I

Ten days after I walked out of my marriage and moved back into the studio in Merton Rise, Denis Mathews invited me to dinner at his other London home, a flat up the hill in Hampstead Village, less beautiful than the studio but easier in winter because it was centrally heated and more comfortable. The other guest was a young Australian friend of his called Jill Neville. As far as Denis was concerned, bringing Jill and me together was a simple piece of social engineering: we were both writers and had both just escaped from bad marriages. (Jill's first husband was Hetta Empson's lover, Peter Duval Smith, who had conveniently set up house with Jill in a flat directly across the road from the Empsons.) But Denis's scheme worked better than he could ever have imagined.

Jill was a dazzling presence – auburn hair, hazel eyes, mobile mouth – although that evening she was doing her best to disguise her looks. She was dressed in a dowdy black frock, as though for a funeral, and seemed not to have bothered with make-up. But she couldn't disguise the dazzle. She was funny, talkative, self-deprecating and so full of life that, even when she was sitting at the dinner table, she seemed somehow on the move, not quite anchored to her chair, ready to take off under her own steam. She was also friendly, a characteristic that made her seem positively eccentric in chilly, post-war Britain. Her friendliness, however, didn't extend to the timorous, class-bound English, who didn't know how to let go and enjoy themselves. The word she used to describe them was 'dank'.

Jill and I hit it off from the start and were together for two years. It was a real love affair, a mutual tenderness that lasted long after we had split up and were happily married to other people, but there was too much in our way to make it stick. Maybe we were too alike – too literary, too touchy, too needy, too ready to put ourselves down. Or maybe we were both still too obsessed by the lousy marriages we had escaped from. Our new-found freedom was so precious and precarious that we didn't dare make claims on each other. We also needed to prove that we were attractive to other people. Whatever our reasons or excuses, we slept around, not in order to make each other jealous – we both took great care to keep our stupidities to ourselves – but simply to prove to ourselves that it could be done. After all, this was swinging London and everyone else was doing it. I suppose I had more to prove about my attractiveness than Jill, who was always besieged by admirers, and she was more anxious about her freedom, but in practice each was as bad as the other. It was a stupid game, although we pretended it was light-hearted and cool, and it did for us in the end. After two years we had played ourselves out and drifted apart.

I met Anne a couple of months later, on 11 November 1962. Remembrance Day, appropriately enough, although I don't remember the appropriate things, like wearing a poppy in my buttonhole or listening, as everybody then did, to the service from the Cenotaph on the radio – the one minute of solemn silence while Big Ben struck the hour, then the muffled guns and the buglers sounding the last post. What I remember is her smile – 'a smile like daybreak' I called it in a poem, 35 years later. I'd known Mary McCarthy in New York and Mary was famous for her dazzling smile, but she used it as if it were a sophisticated instrument, something electronic and miniaturized that she could switch on and off as she needed it. Someone once said of her, 'Mary can do anything with that smile of hers – even smile with it.' Anne's smile was the real thing. It was about pleasure. It made you welcome.

She was staying temporarily in Fellows Road, just around the corner from my studio in Merton Rise, camping out in a flat that belonged to a friend of mine called Jimmy Vaughan. Jimmy was a hustler, half Scot, half Nigerian, charming and utterly unreliable. He worked on the fringes of the movie business, in the grey area between art films and pornography, and played poker on Friday nights with me and an assortment of other literary types – people like Lukas Heller, who wrote highly paid movie scripts for Robert Aldrich, and Leon Griffiths, and who in those days was writing anything for anyone who would pay him but later cashed in on the years he had wasted in low-life drinking clubs with the television series *Minder*. Jimmy, Lukas and Leon were all old lefties who had quit the Party in 1956, after the Hungarian uprising. But they were still political enough to be embarrassed by doing well in the capitalist system they claimed to despise, so they made a point of throwing their dirty money away at the poker table. My way, often enough, so I didn't complain. Not that I was any better at the game than they were – none of us really knew how to play poker back then – but after the fat American humiliated us I had read a couple of books and they gave me an edge. Jimmy was the wildest of us all, a gambler not a poker player. He'd call on anything – a pair of deuces, ace high – and sometimes he got lucky, though not often enough. This made him a popular figure in the game.

Jimmy had been out of London that autumn, hustling some obscure deal in China, and had rented his flat to a South African divorcée called Marna. Being a schoolteacher and short of money, Marna was sharing the place with her friend Anne Adams. Marna was small and combative and troublesome, a woman who made a point of always knowing better than everyone else. She reminded me of some of the friends my sister Sally had surrounded her-self with before she married – bullies who kept her noisily in her place – and I didn't much like her. But she liked me enough to invite me to lunch that Remembrance Sunday when Jimmy was briefly back in town, and I went because I had seen her with Anne at a distance across the street.

Anne looked like all the girls in the fifties college movies I had ever hankered after: blue eyes, heart-shaped face, long dancer's legs and that sun-up smile. I had registered all that a week or two earlier from the glimpse I'd had of her out walking with Marna, both of them too busy talking to notice me. But on the Sunday we met she had a dreadful cold and her looks were on hold: her perfect shiksa nose was red from too much blowing, her hair was a mess and – I had arrived early – she was bundled up in a hideous, shaggy, sky-blue dressing gown. She hurried off to change, but meeting her when she was looking her worst created an odd, domestic familiarity between us, as though we had known each other for years. And, in a way, we had – or at least, I had – though it seemed strange to find her in Hampstead after all my weary searching in the States.

It turned out that she was Canadian, not American, and had come to England on a research fellowship to work as a clinical psychologist at a mental hospital in Essex. But the hospital was a brutal institution that performed lobotomies as casually as it doled out aspirin. The place appalled her and the Rorschach tests and Thematic Apperception Tests no longer seemed to answer the questions that really interested her, which were mostly about her weak and handsome father and his alcoholism. Shortly before we met she had ditched the research and had begun to train as a child psychotherapist.

I remember her smile, she remembers me making her laugh when I had to climb on to the kitchen table to change a light bulb and made jokes about being stunted. Another short cut to intimacy. 'Among animals, one has a sense of humour,' Marianne Moore wrote. 'Humour saves a few steps, it saves years.'

After lunch the four of us went for a walk on Primrose Hill. When I said, 'Race you to the top', Jimmy and Marna rolled their eyes and deliberately walked more slowly, but Anne took off on her long legs like a racehorse. She ran as though she meant business and enjoyed it. I kept behind because I wanted to watch her move.

As I was leaving, I said, 'Why don't we have dinner?'

She hesitated. 'I don't think I can do that,' she said. 'I'm seeing someone else.' Then she gave me the smile and added, 'But I'm glad you asked.'

I phoned her a week later and got the same hesitation, then the same answer. So I let it ride. I, too, was seeing someone else – or rather, I was gloomily playing the field now Jill and I had split up – and there was something about the straight-on way Anne looked at me from under her broad forehead that told me she had no intention of being part of a team.

Even so, I was surprised how pleased I was to see Marna's truculent face in the grocer's shop in England's Lane. She launched instantly into her latest grievance: Jimmy wanted his flat back over Christmas, so she and Anne had to find a place to stay. 'At Christmas, for God's sake, when nobody goes away.' 'Funny you should mention it,' I said. I was going climbing for a few days, leaving on Christmas Day, back on the thirtieth. I told her they could use my studio. I was hoping Anne would come with her to collect the keys and check the place out, but Marna had other ideas and arrived on her own.

The terrible freeze-up that helped kill Sylvia Plath began just after Christmas. I spent the first few days of it in a climbing hut on the north coast of Cornwall, west of St Ives, with Peter Biven, his wife Polly and their baby. The Cornish sea cliffs were always my favourite place to climb – the place where everything felt right and looked right. The pinkish granite of the Bosigran Face is steep and faultless, the sea boils along its base, there are small, salty flowers in the soft turf at the top, and the view west, beyond the crest of Bosigran Ridge, is of headland succeeding headland, with the white thumb of Pendeen lighthouse sticking out against the Atlantic horizon. There are harder climbs in North Wales, and more of them, but the weather there, as I remember it, was usually bad and the atmosphere sterner; climbers seemed to get hurt more often and their friends made a point of dwelling on the gruesome details. Cornwall, in comparison, always seemed like a holiday resort – warm rock, blue sea and sunshine.

I also climbed better when I was there. Maybe that was because, more often than not, I climbed with Peter Biven, who, for a decade or more, beginning in 1955, was the genius of the place, the pioneer who had opened up the Bosigran cliffs with a series of bold, imaginative routes up what had previously been thought to be impregnable rock. He was a big man and very strong, though he climbed so precisely and effortlessly that he seemed to shed weight as he moved. As climbers we were in different leagues, yet we climbed together as often as we could – he, I suspect, because he liked talking about books and music, I because I loved doing hard routes with someone who found them easy. And because he liked what I wrote, he somehow assumed that I climbed as well as he did. This wasn't true, of course, but since he took it for granted I always climbed better with him than anyone else. So well, in fact, that I can't remember ever having had a bad day on the rocks in his company.

Those few days between Christmas and New Year were as good as any we ever had. We spent most of the time making a second ascent of a route called the Diamond Tiara which Peter had put up six years before and no one had yet repeated. It was a high-level traverse of the whole cliff, 900 feet of difficult rock, starting high up at the landward end of the Bosigran Face, finishing at sea level on the farthest tip of the Seaward Cliff. It took us three days to complete the route and every day a blizzard was blowing.

It was the great blizzard that eventually brought the whole country to a standstill, freezing trains on their tracks, lorries on the roads, water in the pipes, overloading the power stations, numbing the mind and stilling the heart. It was like the worst period of the war – the months after Dunkirk when invasion and defeat seemed inevitable – but without the heroics or the excuses. The harshest winter, they said, for 150 years.

By some trick of the wind, the blizzard scarcely touched us on the Diamond Tiara. It howled across the top of the cliff and froze our fingers, but no snow settled on the face. Only one pitch was unclimbable – a friction traverse that was covered with verglas. We avoided it by climbing 20 feet or so to the top, walking a few yards, then climbing back down. That was what we also did at the end of each day, since it was too cold to climb for more than three or four hours at a stretch.

Peter was always modest and laconic, but even he seemed impressed to have finished the route in such terrible weather. 'One for the record books,' he said.

There was snow on the road back to Exeter, where the Bivens lived, but my Mini-Cooper had front-wheel drive, so it coped well enough. The only trouble we had was on Bodmin Moor, where the wind had scoured away the snow and left black ice. On the long climb to the top Peter sat on the bonnet to help the wheels grip, while Polly placidly fed her baby in the back.

It snowed all night – deep, serious snow that brought the whole country to a halt – and it was still snowing when I set out the next morning. I could have stayed on with the Bivens, but I had told Marna that I'd be home by late afternoon and somehow I'd convinced myself that she and Anne – or rather, Anne on her own – would be waiting for me in the studio if I kept my word. I told myself that it didn't matter if I got stuck on the way; I had a sleeping bag and some leftover food in the back of the car and could sit it out until someone dug me out. Anyway, after three days on the Diamond Tiara in a blizzard, I wasn't going to let snowy roads stop me.

There were no motorways in those days and very few snowploughs. The old A30 was twisty and narrow and lined with cars, but most of them were stationary and I managed to creep through. By the time I reached the start of the long climb on to Salisbury Plain, there was no traffic at all, the snow was still falling and it was already dark. At Mere, a rope with a sign on it was stretched across the road. The sign was plastered with snow, so I got out to read it. 'No Through Road,' it said. I stamped around in the snow for a while, wondering what to do. The village was already shut up for the night. Then the snow slackened for a moment and I saw up ahead the winking red light of what could only be a snowplough crawling uphill. I drove under the rope, tucked in behind the plough and followed it to the top. From there on I reckoned it was downhill all the way.

A car was coming slowly towards me when I overtook the plough, the first I'd seen in hours from that direction. It was a Citroën, another front-wheel-drive car, like my Mini. We both stopped and rolled down our windows.

'How's the road west?' the driver asked.

'Just about passable. What's it like towards London?'

'Likewise.'

At that point I knew I was going to make it.

Anne was on her own when I walked into the studio that evening around nine. I wasn't even surprised. It seemed the most natural thing in the world to find her sitting by the stove reading a book. I half expected her to be wearing her hideous blue dressing-gown.

Like me, she had had an eventful few days. I'm not sure if I figured much in her calculations, but she'd had the studio to herself – Marna had decided to stay with her mother, who lived close by – and maybe something in the magical atmosphere of the place got to her. Whatever the reason, she had decided to break up with her boyfriend. Marna was not so easily disposed of. I don't think she liked me any more than I liked her, but she'd seen me first and that made her feel proprietorial. She had arrived in the afternoon, saying she'd help Anne tidy up, and then settled down to wait her out while the blizzard raged outside. Anne had arranged to go back to a room she'd rented before she moved in with Marna. It was up at the top of Hampstead, overlooking the Heath, too far to walk in the storm. When I hadn't arrived by seven, Marna started nagging her to call a taxi. But there were no taxis to be had in the foul weather and by 7.30 Marna's mother, who could out-nag anyone, was phoning every five minutes to tell her that dinner was getting cold. At eight o'clock, when still no taxi had arrived, Marna gave up. Anne closed the door on her, pulled a chair up to the stove and settled down with a book. The taxi never came.

She moved in with me a couple of weeks later. A month after that she moved out again. And that is how it went for three years or more: coming together, splitting up, coming together again, kept apart, despite ourselves, by an unappeasable itch for trouble. Each time we got back together, the first thing I saw was her smile and I'd wonder what I'd been doing all these weeks or months or whatever it was. Being together felt natural and inevitable. We made each other laugh, we found each other interesting and attractive. In other words, we were happy. But for a long time happiness didn't seem to be what we were after.

We were equally to blame. Both of us were children of unhappy parents and both of us were convinced that marriage existed mainly to make people miserable. We held that truth to be self-evident but reacted to it differently: Anne was so scared of choosing wrong that she might never have married at all, despite the flocks of would-be suitors who surrounded her, whereas I had married in the same way as I had dived off the high board when I was a kid, before I knew how to dive properly or even swim – headlong and foolishly, as if to prove that marriage was not for me. Now I was free again, all I could think of was the good times I'd missed out on when I was young: my misspent adolescence playing games at a monastic boarding school and my owlish twenties swotting in university libraries and feigning maturity. Now I was 30-something and divorced and it was my turn to misbehave. I chased women, drove too fast, played high-stakes poker and spent more time than I could decently afford off in the hills, climbing rocks with the boys. I wrote just enough to pay my bills but my heart wasn't in it. My real life was elsewhere, catching up on the fun that had passed me by. I was not a suitable candidate for matrimony, especially to a marriage-shy young woman who had recently gone into psychoanalysis.

It went on like this for nearly three years – on and off, on and off, like the lights in a fun fair – yet in some ways we were never really apart. We marched out of each other's lives, swearing never to come back, we took up with new lovers and stayed away from each other for months on end. But even when we were living separate lives each of us always seemed to know when something important was happening to the other.

During one of our off periods, for example, I took up with a glamorous, tough-minded American actress called Linda Gates. We met in San Francisco, then flew to New Mexico, rented a car and spent a week that seemed more like a movie than real life: the beautiful blonde, the white convertible, the country of my heart. Back home I could think of nothing else and imagined Linda and I could recreate the idyll in dreary London, so I persuaded her to fly over. Naturally it didn't work out as planned, but at least we were trying. Then Anne called me out of nowhere, after months of silence. She was in hospital, she said; she had had her wisdom teeth out; would I bring her something to read? It never occurred to either of us that the town was full of people – including her current boyfriend – who would willingly bring her books. I drove straight to the hospital. Anne was propped up in bed with her hideous blue dressing-gown around her shoulders. Her face was drained and bruised and dreadfully swollen. I said, 'You look like a chipmunk.' She said, 'Don't. It hurts to laugh.' And we were back where we had left off. Linda flew back to San Francisco a few days later. She was too independent to make a fuss, and anyway she hated London. I think she was glad to get out so cleanly.

My sixth sense for what was happening in Anne's life was as finely tuned as hers was to mine. During another of our long freezes, she finally met a man who seemed to be everything she was looking for: cultured, bookish, handsome and alert to what she was feeling. One evening he took her to a performance of Monteverdi's *Vespers* and when he drove her home after dinner she let him stay. Usually I am addicted to sleep, but that night I didn't sleep at all. I knew nothing about this new man of hers and had girlfriends of my own to worry about, but all I could think of was Anne. I got up around seven and walked over to the flat she had recently moved into. I stole a rose from a garden along the way and presented it to her when she answered the door. I asked if I could come in. She shook her head: 'I'm not alone.' I went back down the steps. When I got to the bottom she was still standing at the open door. 'I'll meet you at the Cosmo,' she said. 'Give me half an hour.' Then she went upstairs and bundled the other man out of her life.

She had acquired her new home as a gesture of independence, in order to live on her own terms and not to have to rent some temporary bolt-hole whenever she moved out on me. But even the flat she chose showed we weren't safe from each other. She called me when she found it and described it in detail. 'I don't know what it is about the place, but it some-how feels right,' she said. 'It's even got a stove like the one in the studio.'

I said, 'It's number 148 Fellows Road and the telephone number is Primrose 0054.'

'How on earth do you know that?'

'I lived there with the first lucky Mrs Alvarez.'

The signs were all there but we couldn't read them. Despite what I'd learned from my near-fatal addiction to Lawrence, I still believed that great love had to be as Denis de Rougemont described it – 'fatal, frowned upon, doomed by life itself'. Since Anne and I felt natural and easy together, it couldn't be right. I think Anne's delusions were different. Maybe she couldn't allow herself to be happy while her classy, devoted mother was wretched, or maybe her parents' mutual unhappiness had convinced her that marriage was necessarily a way of institutionalizing misery and she wanted no part of it. Whatever her reasons, walking out on me was a way of placating her inner demons, and in the end she walked out for good.

Some time after that seemingly final break, I had a dream about her. By then we hadn't seen each other for months. She had made her choice and settled down with someone she planned to stay with and I was preoccupied with another young woman – very attractive but very elusive – who was giving me a hard time. And because she was giving me a hard time and I, being slow to grow up, still believed that great love was always a misfortune, I imagined I was in love with her. In my dream, however, Anne and I were dancing, something we always did well together. Both of us were smiling. I made a joke, she laughed, then, still dancing, I pushed her out to arm's length and looked at her. I saw that her hair was white and realized that mine, too, was white. We're old, I thought in my dream, and we're together. And I was perfectly happy.

I woke flooded with happiness and I couldn't understand why. I knew I found her enormously attractive and I knew I liked being with her, not just for the moments of high romance but for the casual pleasure of her company – chatting while we did the dishes in the evening, shopping at the supermarket, sitting together in silence, reading or watching TV. But somehow I imagined that wasn't enough. It was too easy, too natural, not sufficiently doomed. The dream was telling me what I refused to know: that I wanted to spend the rest of my life with her.

A few days later I met Anne on the street and told her the dream. If I'd said, 'I love you. You love me. Let's stop all this nonsense and get married,' she wouldn't have believed me. But the dream was too raw and guileless to be a sham. Soon after, we were back together again.

Even then, it didn't last. The itch for trouble was still too strong for both of us and we wearily split up once more. And that seemed to be that, despite my dream. We were finally rescued from our bloody-mindedness, though not by a dream or a revelation or a sudden change of heart or anything great lovers like Tristan and Iseult would have recognized as a sign. We were saved by a joke about a dumb blonde in a supermarket. The joke went the rounds fast and is now a classic, part of every amateur comedian's repertoire. But this was 1965, I hadn't heard it before and I thought it was brilliant. I was driving past Anne's house the day after I heard it and saw her in the front garden gloomily stuffing a bag of rubbish into the dustbin. I slammed on the brakes, jumped out of the car, told her the joke and drove away. I noticed that she looked pale and drawn and dejected, but at least the joke made her laugh. What I did not know was that she was chronically depressed and this was the first time she had laughed in months. And that did it. Laughter, said Thomas Hobbes, is 'sudden glory'. We were married six months later.

A few years ago I wrote a poem called 'Anne Dancing':

You sashay in, twenty years-old again,
Sweatshirt and jeans, eyes closed, a cat-like smile,
Self-satisfied, self-absorbed, hips swaying,
Weaving your intricate steps across
The intricate carpet. The merest glance

At me does it. You're a North American
College girl out on a date, a '50s-style
Dazzler – great legs, cute ass, sweet smile. That's Satchmo playing
Your youth back loud and clear. You toss
Your greying, lovely head. You say, 'Come on, let's dance.'

Only after I had written it did I remember the dream I had had a quarter of a century before.

The dumb-blonde story that brought Anne and me back together was a great joke, but the best and least likely joke of all was that we made the marriage work. Although both of us were old enough to know our own minds when we married – she was 30 and I was 36 – the smart money said that we wouldn't last three years and the odds against our staying together for the rest of our lives, as my dream had predicted, were astronomical.

The wedding was at her parents' apartment in Toronto and, as though to prove the smart money right, we staged the worst fight we ever had at the airport right after the ceremony, while we were waiting for the plane to take us down to New York. We squabbled later, as any two people are bound to squabble when they spend their lives together, but never as savagely as that first time. I don't know what we were fighting about, but I know why: both of us were aghast at what we had done. We were so convinced that marriage was a fatal institution that we believed that merely by going through the wedding ceremony – standing up before witnesses and saying, 'I do' – we would poison our relationship. It didn't happen and I remember waking up the next morning in the Fifth Avenue Hotel, astonished that everything was fine, just as it always had been when we were together. The truth is, the fight was over and more or less forgotten before the plane took off. Neither of us has ever had any talent for bearing grudges and, despite our dread of wedlock, we were determined to make a go of it – if only because her parents and mine had failed so dismally. It helped that we had had so many divorces before we married; we were simply too exhausted to go through all that fuss and fury again.

We were also too exhausted to be caught up in the fuss and fury that later turned the sixties into what Richard Rovere famously called 'a slum of a decade'. Nineteen sixty-six seems now like a good year to have married. It meant we had had the best of the decade to fool around in – the early years when, for perhaps the first time since the 1920s, it was possible to be young in England and feel free. We had a little money in our pockets, our own music (Bob Dylan especially), our own fashions (Anne looked great in mini-skirts, I looked foolish in bell-bottomed trousers), and the contraceptive pill to free us from the threat of unwanted pregnancy. More crucially, the Establishment had lost its magic; after the Profumo affair, it was hard to believe that our 'betters' were any better or more entitled than we were. It was an easy-going time, egalitarian and innocent, but because Anne and I had come of age in the fifties rather than the sixties, the freedoms we had won were all strictly personal. She got hers from psychoanalysis, I got mine from literature, and both of us distrusted political ideologies because we were wartime children and had seen them in action. So when the decade began to go wild we weren't swept along with it. We grew our hair long, but not too long, and we were too old to tune in, turn on, drop out. Eastern mysticism, love-ins and Ginsberg's tinkling Buddhist bells had never been my style and, as someone who had been brought up on hard liquor, drugs seemed to have less to do with expanding the mind than with constricting irony and muddying conversation.

By the time the violence started – student riots in Paris, Soviet tanks in Prague and protests everywhere against the war in Vietnam – I was pushing 40 and had been left behind. Anyway, I had other things on my mind. I became a father again – first of a son, Luke, then of a daughter, Kate – and they brought me back into the kind of world I wanted to live in. In my loveless first marriage Adam had been the focus of all the affection which, in better circumstances, would have been shared with his mother. It brought him and me very close and made leaving him the hardest part of the divorce. But that is not a burden a child should have to bear and I don't think he was free of it until he himself was happily married and had children of his own. Luke and Kate had an easier time – or rather, since no childhood is easy, they were less weighed down by their parents' emotional needs and had more room to manoeuvre. But from my point of view they weren't instead of a marriage, they were an extension of it – two people becoming three, becoming four, becoming a family, inextricably intertwined.

Having a real family made it easier for me to disengage myself from the literary world. The year I married Anne – 1966 – was also the year I stopped reviewing poetry for the *Observer*. I went on reviewing books sporadically in order to pay my bills, but I was no longer writing for a regular audience. And because I had no university job, there were no students to test my ideas on or spread the word for me. *The Savage God* was a success, especially in America, and for a while it gave me some financial security.

Then, in 1982, I began to write regularly for William Shawn's *New Yorker*. But the subjects I wrote about – professional poker players in Las Vegas, North Sea oil, mountaineering – didn't fit my sober image as a literary critic and dissipated whatever audience I had. Of all the books I've produced, *The Biggest Game in Town* is the one that gave me most pleasure to write. But it wasn't reviewed in the *Times Literary Supplement* and when I asked one of the editors why, he answered, 'We don't know how to classify you.' He sounded offended, as though I had done something wrong. I took it as a compliment.

I I

I sometimes claim I married Anne because she is a child psychotherapist, so she knows how to cope with my age group. That isn't altogether a joke. I sidled up to matrimony with the same anxieties as some people sidle up to psychoanalysis – scared that the compromises I would have to make would dull me down, spoil my edge, emasculate me. And maybe it did, but that is not how it felt. We certainly reshaped each other's lives, knocked off some of the rough edges and wore others down, but carefully, even playfully, because the differences between us mattered; they were part of the mutual attraction. Since neither of us was interested in gaining the upper hand, we never came at each other brutally, like a couple of bulldozers flattening whatever was in the way. We were more like the sniffer dogs they bring in after earthquakes, working in the dark, looking for signs of life, smelling out what the other was good for.

Anne had always been blessed with a clear mind and the intellectual honesty to follow her ideas through to their end once she was convinced she had them right, although she disguised her tough intelligence under that friendly North American manner which always baffles and secretly enrages the English. The friendliness didn't change but gradually she became braver and more independent, less bothered by transgressing against the orthodoxies of her profession, while I, who had always been spiky and iconoclastic, became less driven, less pugnacious and more aware of what I was feeling.

Especially about my mother. I have written earlier about Katie Alvarez and her confusions, about the spell her bullying father cast on her, and how exhausting it was to be her child. She yearned to be loved, in her troubled way, but because she was terrified of physical contact normal motherliness was beyond her. During my sickly childhood it never occurred to me to turn to my mother for comfort; I went to Nanny. Yet to strangers, who owed her nothing and made no claims on her, Katie was wantonly good-hearted. Witness the platoon of tramps she kept on her payroll, the household pets she spoiled, the lonely widows and jittery stray cats she fed and watered.

This was the woman Anne fell for: Katie the Bountiful who cooked great meals and stuffed her grandchildren with chocolates, the Woman in Red, with her wonky make-up, who appeared in the maternity ward bearing gifts, who made shrewd jokes and, in her scatty way, had everybody's number. Anne even fell for her cavalier misuse of the English language. My mother took stabs at words and when she couldn't get the one she wanted she invented it. I've mentioned some of them earlier: 'schakaboodle' for hullabaloo, 'schnippy' for small-minded. If I asked her what on earth she meant, she'd lie airily, 'A Yiddish word, darling. Mr Dreen uses it all the time.' Since I knew no more Yiddish than she did, I couldn't argue, but it got on my nerves. For Anne, the old lady's verbal make-believe was a sign of life, part of her buzz and bustle, and she loved her for it. Once I began to see my impossible mother through Anne's eyes, I slowly began to understand that, although she was pigheaded and frustrating, there truly was no malice in her. Better to take what she had to offer than to resent her for what she couldn't do.

But it wasn't easy and I don't want to sentimentalize what happened. I didn't suddenly start seeing my mother through a rosy mist any more than she saw me that way. Her pottiness went on driving *me* potty. So did her obdurate refusal to look after herself – to put a plaster on her finger when she cut it or to lock the doors and windows at night when she went to bed in her big empty house. And she was driven equally crazy by my obdurate refusal to get a properly paying job. (By then I couldn't even pretend I had a university career.) My father was proud of having a son who was a writer; he read some of my articles and slogged dutifully through my books. But my mother didn't read anything and after the old man died, in 1966, she lost track. Occasionally she saw me on television or heard me on the radio and thought maybe I might make a decent living after all. But not often. When people came to visit she sometimes showed them the books I wrote; she handled the things with baffled pride, but never read a page of any of them. I was a disappointment to her, more even than my sisters because I was the one she had pinned her hopes on. Privately I agreed with her about the vanity of writing, but that didn't make her disappointment any less frustrating. The frustration was mutual, of course, and exasperating, but gradually, as we learned to tolerate each other's follies, the exasperation became good-humoured.

The death of her father and then of her husband set Katie free. Once she was on her own, relieved of the burden of being the daughter who couldn't do anything right married to a husband who wasn't interested in money, she flourished. She pottered around the house, walked her dog, cooked great meals when she felt like it and squabbled half-heartedly with the cleaning lady. Her Indian summer was good while it lasted but her friend Doris, whom my father called Black Bess, put paid to it by falling in love with her osteopath.

Doris had aged badly. The only exercise she took was when she walked her tubular Sealyham to the shops or down to my mother's house, and even that seemed too much for her. She moved as though her joints were rusted and complained constantly of her aches and pains. But her husband was long dead and, apart from the dog, there was no one to comfort her physically. The osteopath was young and bearded and commanding, and his clever hands knew how to ease every tension in her neglected back. She went to him twice a week and her eyes glowed when she told my mother about the wonders the young man performed.

Katie didn't believe in cures. She distrusted doctors and medicines, refused to fuss about herself and believed there was only one sure remedy for any sickness: 'Wrap up warm and get a good night's sleep.' She also believed she would stay healthy provided she kept away from hospitals and walked her evil-tempered dog every day. She covered insane distances, always pretending it was for a sane purpose. If she wanted a quarter of a pound of smoked salmon, she trotted three miles to Panzer's in St John's Wood, instead of buying it at the local delicatessen up the road. 'There's no comparison in the quality,' she'd say. She was right, but that wasn't the point. The point was a long walk through familiar streets, the people she met and schmoozed with along the way, the pleasant exhaustion when she got back home, and the sense of another day innocently passed. She used to say, 'I want to die with my boots on.'

But as she got older she became more and more arthritic. Her joints ached, her neck creaked when she turned her head, her fingers became stiff and swollen and gouty. When she complained to Doris about her condition – for companionship's sake, because Doris was always complaining – Black Bess began nagging her to see the osteopath. 'He'll cure you,' she said. 'He can work wonders.' Then she'd titter falsely and add, 'And you can't believe how good it feels.' She kept on in this way – part friendly concern, part girlish conspiracy – until my mother, who was terrified of giving offence and incapable of saying no, finally allowed Doris to make an appointment for her. I know nothing about the osteopath – neither of the old ladies would tell me his name – except that he was young and, presumably, inexperienced. Instead of giving her a soft-tissue massage and sending her off for an X-ray of her neck, he went straight in for the kill – a quick, brutal manipulation. My mother screamed in pain, the osteopath jumped back in dismay. I still don't know how she managed to get herself and her dog back home, but she never walked properly again.

For a while she managed to keep secret the damage done to her spine. All I could see was that she was moving unsteadily and had started to use a walking-stick – a stylish Malacca number of her father's, with a horn handle and a gold band. She also complained more than usual about her various discomforts. But if I asked her what was wrong she'd say, 'Old age, darling. It happens to everyone', and when I suggested consulting a doctor she refused indignantly: 'What do they know?'

She kept up the pretence until Christmas Day. Doris came to lunch, stayed for tea, stayed for supper, and then just stayed on doing what she always did, moaning about her miserable existence. She went home at 11.30, leaving the dirty dishes to my mother. On her way to bed, around midnight, Katie decided to fill the ancient kitchen boiler which heated water for the house. She picked up the empty scuttle and started down to the cellar where the coal was kept. Halfway down the steep steps, her legs gave way and she fell to the bottom. God knows how she managed to drag herself to the top and then up two more flights to her bedroom, though I know very well why she didn't phone me – for the same reason that she hadn't phoned when my father died in the night: she 'didn't want to be a trouble'. Maybe she even thought a good night's sleep would do the trick. She called the next morning when she knew something was seriously wrong.

By the time Anne and I got to Glenilla Road, Katie had somehow managed to put on a dress and daub her face erratically with make-up, but that didn't disguise the fact that she was in shock. I knew I would get nowhere if I mentioned this, so I called the doctor – 'You're making a fuss about nothing,' my mother said tearfully – then I played the one game she and I had in common: mutual exasperation.

The only traces of my Sephardic inheritance remaining in my life were three elaborate dishes with deceptively simple names: white-stewed chicken, white-stewed fish and brown stew. (The names were also misleading; the chicken and fish were cooked with saffron and were vivid yellow.) Katie had been taught how to prepare them by Minnie the cook and, to keep me happy, she had grudgingly passed two of the recipes on to Anne: white-stewed chicken because she didn't reckon it highly, white-stewed fish because it took a day or more to prepare and she assumed Anne would never have the time. The recipe for brown stew, however, she kept to herself, knowing I would always come home to her when she cooked it.

My mother was hunched in her chair at the dining-room table. She looked defeated. I took a sheet of her most expensive letter paper from the sideboard drawer – heavy bond paper, embossed with her address, supplied by Harrods and used sparingly. Then I sat down opposite her and took out my pen in a business-like way. 'Have it your way,' I said briskly. 'If you're determined to do yourself in, no one can stop you. It's your call. But you're not taking the recipe for brown stew with you to the grave.'

For a moment I thought I'd overdone it; she was, after all, in shock. Then her eyes brightened, her back straightened and she giggled like a naughty child. 'What did I do to merit a son like you?' she said.

She was still giggling when the lady doctor arrived. She even seemed glad to see her. But by then it was too late; I had the recipe in my pocket.

From then on nothing went right for her. There was a spell in St Mary's Hospital, in Paddington, which reduced her to despair. The nurses bullied her, the food was uneatable, the patients in the beds either side picked fights and shouted her down. Each time I went to see her she seemed more diminished. She kept saying, 'You've got to get me out of here.' So I did – against the hospital's advice.

Back home there were no more strenuous, soothing walks with her dog; she dragged herself precariously around with a Zimmer frame. Her doctor also procured a wheelchair for her but it sat in the hall for months before she agreed to use it. I used to push her to Primrose Hill, just like Nanny had pushed me in my pram. It was Katie's favourite park and she loved the view from the top, clear across London to the Surrey hills. But the journey to and from Primrose Hill terrified her – not because of the traffic but because she was afraid of meeting people she knew along the way. In her own house, enthroned at the head of the dining-room table, dispensing food and drink and sympathy, she was the one who called the shots. Out in public, slumped in her wheelchair, she felt foolish and somehow shamed, as though she were a child again – in her second childhood – someone whom everyone could patronize and condescend to. 'A penny for the Guy,' she used to say when we helped her into the wheelchair. 'All I need is the bonfire.'

Arthritis crippled my mother and cataracts made her almost blind, but in a way they protected her from the casual damage she had done to herself when she was up and about on her own. Not being able to cook any more meant she couldn't scald herself with boiling water or slice her fingers with kitchen knives or trip headlong over the dog when she was carrying a tray. And because she never otherwise got ill – no common colds or flu for Katie, and she had a system like the ostrich which 'digesteth harde yron' – she even seemed, oddly, to thrive on her incapacity. Once it was clear that she wasn't going to get her wish to die with her boots on, her natural cynicism flourished, especially at the expense of her companions.

There were two of them in the last years. Violet, who did the cleaning, had spent most of her life working for my mother and her family. She was a parlour-maid at my grandparents' flat at Harley House, then housekeeper for Uncle Teddy before he married, and when I was a child she used to come to Glenilla Road every Friday to clean the silver. She was a bossy little woman with a sharp tongue, who piled her tightly permed curls high on her head to make herself look tall and painted her face as though for battle. She loved a fight, especially with Mrs Hughes, who moved into Glenilla Road as housekeeper when my mother became too crippled to look after herself.

Mrs Hughes was a doctor's wife, a lady who had come down in the world, and she was a good deal older than Katie, although she never admitted it. She was bent over like a question mark and moved around the house in carefully calculated bursts, from one piece of furniture to the next, pausing to rest and catch her breath at each stop. She prattled unceasingly in a vague way, presumably for the sheer pleasure of hearing her own genteel Irish voice, since she never paused for an answer. My mother needed her, so she rolled her eyes to heaven and held her peace, but Violet, who felt usurped, lit into her brutally. Sometimes, when it got really bad, I would be called in to referee the fight. It didn't end until Violet, who had always liked 'a Guinness or two or maybe a drop of gin at night', took seriously to the bottle – to Katie's bottles mostly – and began insulting everyone. Even then, my mother put up with her 'for old times' sake', sitting immovable in her chair, like Rockall in an Atlantic storm, while the two rivals raged around her. But when Violet drunkenly turned on Katie's beloved sister Lulu she had to go.

Lulu used to come for tea at Glenilla Road every Monday and I always made a point of dropping in. The two old ladies consoled each other about their ailments, but only as a matter of courtesy. Mostly they talked about their childhood, about the good old days in the grand house in Tavistock Square, when Queen Victoria was still on the throne, life was orderly and affluent, scandalous uncles kept mistresses 'over the water' (not in Paris but across the Thames, in south London) and – a nod towards the kitchen, where Violet was banging around and cursing – when 'servants were servants'. When they talked this way – about their sweet-tempered mother or a nanny who was kind to them or my mother's favourite teacher, Miss Messervie – they seemed to shed years. Once, when Aunt Lou was talking about the foolish things she had done on her honeymoon in Penzance, she exclaimed, 'God, wasn't I young!' And at that moment, she really was 20 again and full of hope.

In fact, she was well into her eighties, still elegant and energetic, but increasingly bewildered and forgetful. (Alzheimer's was not a word much used 20 years ago.) One evening, for example, she came to dinner at our house and stole the show, charming everyone with her talk about her favourite subjects – books and wine and France. The next morning a letter dropped through the box when I was in the hall. I opened the door and saw Aunt Lou scurrying down the front steps. She looked tired and flustered and I knew she had walked from West End Lane to the top of Hampstead because, like my mother, she thought taxis were a sin. But when I asked her in for a coffee she just shook her head vehemently and said, 'It's bad enough as it is without keeping you from your work. I'm quite appalled at myself. I woke up this morning and realized I hadn't written you a thank-you note for that lovely dinner.' Then she was off down the road before I could say another word. When I told my mother what had happened, she shook her head and said, 'Darling Lulu, how dreadful.' Then she gave me her 'old-fashioned look', sly and sideways-on, and asked, 'Do you think the poor dear isn't with it any more?' Katie, who had always been treated by her parents as the family idiot, was with it to the end. It was her body that let her down.

Things began to go badly wrong with her early in 1980, when Doris died suddenly. Katie got the news over the telephone and the grief hit her like a physical blow. She wobbled out into the hall on her walking-frame to call Mrs Hughes, who was upstairs taking her afternoon nap, but her legs began to buckle and she started to fall. She managed to steady herself long enough for Mrs Hughes to stagger down and help her back to her chair, but for weeks after she seemed stricken, as though the shock had given her a kind of stroke. Then gradually her beady eye for the absurd began to reassert itself. 'Doris was always saying, "I wish I could wake up dead,"' she told me. 'I'd say, "You've got everything to live for – all the money you want and not a care in the world. Enjoy yourself. Take a cruise or something." But she never did and now she's got her wish. Poor old girl, always so miserable.'

Even so, the fight had gone out of her. At Easter, Anne and I and the kids went to Cornwall for a holiday, although we made sure we were back in time for my mother's birthday. In the 10 days we were away she seemed to have shrunk. Her clothes hung around her like a sack, her voice was muted, her prodigious appetite gone; she ate nothing and complained of feeling sick. Usually she stayed up until midnight. That evening she went to bed at 8.30, saying she was exhausted. The next morning, for the first time since her stay in hospital, she did not get up. The doctor diagnosed cancer of the liver and gave her three weeks.

We didn't tell her, but she knew anyway. All she said was, 'I don't want to die in hospital.'

'Of course not.'

I called an agency and hired a series of night nurses, so that Mrs Hughes could get some sleep, and suddenly my mother perked up. She began to eat again and seemed to regain a little strength, although there were terrible hollows in her neck, below the Adam's apple and at her collarbones. Her skin itched and she kept scratching vaguely at herself. Her legs, she said, 'felt like sticks of wood, but heavy'. Mrs Hughes, however, perked up even more. She went around the house humming tunelessly and chattering to no one in particular, delighted by the idea of outlasting her younger employer. Katie watched her balefully. 'As I get iller, she gets more cheerful,' she hissed at me.

The doctor was a competent and sympathetic woman but she was wrong in her prognosis: Katie took three months to die, not three weeks.

My father's death had been like a conjuror's trick, sudden and unexpected, with no visible strings or trapdoors, no rustling curtains, no farewells. My mother's was a slow dissolve – each day a little dimmer, a little worse, but with no end in sight. Yet somehow the prospect of death seemed to cheer her up, as though she had never much cared for the cards she had been dealt and was glad to quit the game. Her favourite saying had always been 'You can't win', and now she was being proved right.

Not that she ever talked about dying, except obliquely. Her bed had been moved downstairs into the drawing-room, with its satinwood furniture and treasured knick-knacks. The linings of the heavy curtains were in tatters and damp had left a large black stain on the Chinese silk carpet on which my sisters and I were not allowed to tread when we were children. My mother saw none of this. Her sight was now so bad that all she could see was shadows and the paleness of the French windows, beyond which the garden was running to seed. 'At least I won't have to pay that do-nothing gardener this year' was one of the few references she made to the death she knew was coming.

She also made jokes about it. My sister Anne had died the previous year. The week before her tombstone-setting Katie said, 'If I time it right, dear, you can have two funerals for the price of one.' And when the doctor, whom she had scarcely seen before her illness, began to visit her daily, dispensing cheer, my mother was not fooled. 'Every time that young woman breezes in she seems more astonished,' she said. 'She can't believe I'm still here.'

'What did she say about you?'

Katie raised her sightless eyes to the ceiling. 'What do you think she said?: "You're on your last legs."' She shrugged. 'You can't win, dear.' Her words were slurred, her mouth was down-turned, her skin was yellow and her breastbone showed through, but at least she was going out with her sense of absurdity intact.

Most of the agency nurses were from New Zealand – brisk, efficient young women, habituated to death. They washed her emaciated body, cheerfully cleaned up her wastes and injected her with Brompton Cocktail, which subdued the pain and brought hallucinations: a giant hand opening and closing before her eyes ('Such silly things!' she said), disembodied voices – mine and my sisters' and malicious strangers' – gossiping together about unpaid bills and the collapse of Levy & Franks.

Even when she became used to the drugs and the hallucinations passed, she fretted about the expense of the nurses. 'How are we going to pay for all this?' she would ask. And when I replied, 'It's only money. Don't even think about it', she'd shake her head and say, 'You're just like your father.' But fondly, without recrimination, as though finally she could see there was no point in worrying any more.

I visited her every day and at some point during the three months she took to die we seemed to forgive each other and draw close. Before her final illness Katie's refusal to take care of herself had given me bad dreams. I used to dream that I was driving past her house on some urgent errand and saw the light on in the hall and the front door open – not wide open, just carelessly ajar. I knew I ought to stop because the old lady was in there on her own, anyone could walk in and it was up to me to take care of her. But I was already critically late for whatever it was I had to do and I didn't have the time to go in and check the place out. So I drove on by, full of dread, but also outraged by her fecklessness. Those devouring dreams seemed to sum up my tangled feelings for her – guilt, frustration, impatience, thwarted love. I used to wake up from them in a panic, then telephone her as early as I decently could, trying to sound casual.

Once death got its foot in the door at Glenilla Road, the dreams stopped and my mother and I became almost peaceful together. We even began to depend on each other. She depended on me to keep the show on the road, pay the bills on time and swap jokes with her. I depended on her being there and battling on, and on her total refusal to sentimentalize what was happening.

As the weeks dragged by, the skull beneath her white hair turned yellow, her thigh bones showed through, her blind eyes reflected the light. She hated her helplessness, her incontinence, her debility, and gradually she stopped making jokes, even about Mrs Hughes. For a while she kept saying, 'Isn't it sad?' whenever she mentioned her daughters or her sister – Anne dead, Sally in a wheelchair, Lulu becoming senile. She meant her own condition, of course, although she never complained about the pain she was in. And when she said, 'It won't be long now', she was no longer making fun of herself and I no longer answered, 'Nonsense.' We both wanted it to be over.

She had never believed in happy endings and refused to kid herself now. One sunny afternoon I was sitting at her bedside while she slept.

Suddenly she opened her unseeing eyes and said, 'All that stuff about the afterlife. It's just fairy stories, isn't it?'

The cancer was everywhere by then and the doctor had told me she had only a few days to go. I knew I should say something encouraging, but when I saw the bleak expression on her face I shrugged and answered, 'I think so.'

'Thank God,' she said.

I always left when the night nurse arrived. That evening, as I reached the door of her room, Katie said, 'You've been a good son.' Her voice was slurred, so maybe I misheard her. But if I didn't it was the first loving compliment she had ever paid me. And also the last. That night she went into a coma.

I had never thought of my mother as a stylish woman in the way Aunt Lou or Barbara Kerr were stylish. She was generous and shrewd and funny, but too confused, too much at the mercy of feelings she didn't even want to understand, to be stylish. Yet up until then, she had been stylish in her dying – refusing to make a fuss, determined to keep the tone light. The coma put paid to all that. It lasted three days and was dreadful.

When I arrived the next morning – it was a brilliant summer day and the streets, as I drove down the hill, were full of pretty girls in summer frocks – her eyes were turned up and gummy, her lips were loose, there were deep lines around her mouth, starting at the middle of her nose and running down to the chin, her breathing was rasping and unsteady. For long moments she seemed to stop breathing altogether, then she would sigh deeply, pant, sigh again, mouth slack, tongue lolling. Occasionally she hiccuped and retched, bringing up a little mucus, and the nurse would wipe her lips, feel her pulse, smooth the pillow. Once, towards the end, she had a kind of fit: her body stiffened, she braced her arm and clenched her fist as though enraged. The nurse and I looked at each other and held our breath, like Katie was holding hers. But her heart would not give up and the remorseless sighing began again. I had no idea it could be so hard to die.

All her life, whenever there was any misfortune in the family, my mother used to announce, 'I feel we've been cursed.' She said it each time my father hit another financial rock and when my sister Anne died and when Sally was knocked off her bike and nearly killed during the war. I assume she also said it when her only son was born with a growth on his ankle. It was Katie at her least lovable – melodramatic and self-pitying. She didn't know what was coming.

Aunt Lou arrived during the first afternoon of the coma. She sat beside the bed, leaning over her sister, stroking her hair and singing nursery rhymes: 'Rock-a-bye baby on the treetop' and 'Ride a cock horse to Banbury Cross,' repeating the last line – 'She shall have music wherever she goes' – with an emphasis on the 'she'. At the end of each song she stroked her sister's forehead and murmured, 'There, there, there, there.' Like my dying mother, she was oblivious to me and the nurse. She was back at Tavistock Square, in the night nursery at the top of the house, comforting her frightened younger sister as she must have done when both of them were small.

Katie died during the third night of her coma. The duty nurse called around two to tell me the news, but told me not to come because nothing could be done at that hour. When the cancer had first got hold of my mother, her body began to waste away but her face had smoothed out, as my sister Anne's had done. The bone structure became clearer and I could see her as she must have been when she was young, before I was born: dark eyes, long mouth, a beauty in her time. The coma and the terrible sighing changed her face into a tribal mask, but when I went down to Glenilla Road the next morning the mask had gone. She was cold and stiff and very small, but her face had regained its calm, although the mouth was down-turned. Disappointed to the end.

'You've been a good son.' Did she really say that or did I imagine it, like my elder sister, when she was dotty, imagined our father cursing her on his deathbed? I don't think I'm out of touch in that way, though I can't be certain. Anyway, it isn't true; I wasn't a good son until my wife showed me what there was to be good to. Even if my mother did say what I think she said, she couldn't have believed it. The good son she wanted would never have had my perpetual money worries. Also, declarations of love were not her style. Tears came easily to her, recrimination and disappointment were her daily diet, but love was too complicated and unreliable. It wasn't something she could ever count on or risk talking about out loud. She couldn't get her tongue around the word and the only way she could express it was by indulgence. (Her last words to her adoring, stricken grandson Michael were, 'On your way out, pour yourself a nice gin and tonic, dear. Make sure it's a double.') So why did she tell me I'd been a good son? Because she knew she was dying and decided finally, now it was too late, to say something she knew I wanted to hear? Or is it my own sense of having disappointed her that stops me believing she meant it? Or maybe, in the end, she realized that things had worked out OK after all and it was possible to live a good life without the Levy millions. I would prefer that to have been as true for her as it is for me. But I can't be sure.

'Happiness writes white. It does not show up on the page.' When I first came across those words of Montherlant I typed them out in 20-point letters and pinned them beside my desk. A tribute, I thought, to my wife and children and the good times we have had. But that wasn't the whole truth. I was also using the quotation for my own ends, as an excuse for not having written as much as I should. I love language and the things you can do with it and the intricate business of getting it right, but sitting at a desk, churning out a set number of pages day after day, is not a discipline that comes easily to an adrenalin addict with itchy feet.

About 10 years after my father died I had a dream about him. We were together at Glenilla Road. He was sitting where he always sat – in front of his beloved gramophone – I was standing by the door. I said, 'Come on, Pa. It's a beautiful day. Let's go for a walk on the heath. It'll do you good.' He nodded and smiled, which made me happy. So I turned and walked into the hall, expecting him to follow. But when I opened the front door – it really was a shining day – I realized he couldn't come with me because he was dead. I woke up crying.

I was grieving for his death, but I was also grieving for what he had done with his life. The truth is, my father had never been for a walk on Hampstead Heath – with me or anyone else or even on his own. He'd spent his life in a business he didn't care for and had never been anywhere. I didn't want that to happen to me.

> The intellect of man is forced to chose
> Perfection of the life or of the work.

For Yeats, the choice may well have been a great torment; but without the burden of his genius and fluency, it seemed easy enough to me. However much I loved literature I had always believed that there truly are 'things that are important beyond all this fiddle'. They filled me with curiosity and I wanted to try my hand at as many of them as I could. That's one of the things writers do, of course: they look and listen and make something unique out of it. But I didn't just want to be a spectator watching from the sidelines; I wanted to be a player.

I sometimes feel I've led my life back to front, atoning for my sins before I committed them. My first 30 years, when almost nothing went right, were purgatory. They seemed to go on for ever and I couldn't get out. The last 40 have passed in no time at all. A blur of years, all written white.

INDEX

Abstract Expressionism 189,
  196, 214, 260
Adams, Henry 146
Albee, Edward 153
Aldrich, Robert 313–14
All Souls College 193
Alvarez, Aaron 6
Alvarez, Adam 148, 182, 247
Alvarez, Al
  America 144–68
  antecedents 3–23
  Auden's influence
    232–43
  childhood 53–70
  Eastern bloc 212–31
  flying 302–7
  friendships 288–301
  grandparents 24–38
  love-life 169–82
  marriage 183–211
  music 308–11
  New Yorker 284–7
  painting 247–63
  parents 39–52
  poker 274–83
  pre-university jobs
    90–108
  rock-climbing 264–73
  school 71–89
Alvarez, Alfred 8–9, 12–16,
  18
Alvarez, Anne (sister) 3, 42,
  49, 50, 64, 333
Alvarez, Anne (wife) 46–8,
  55, 206, 209, 217, 254–5
  early meetings 313–15,
    317–25
  friendships 288, 290
Alvarez, Barnet 8
Alvarez, Bertie 3–5, 9–17, 35,
  39–52, 54–5, 57
  arguments 62
  bar mitzvah 83

death 333, 337
family business 92,
  93–4
holidays 58
paintings 250
school 76
sport 87–8
university 133, 138
war 64, 65, 67–9
Alvarez, Harry 6
Alvarez, Isaac 49
Alvarez, Kate (daughter) 55,
  324
Alvarez, Katie 3, 5, 17,
  19–20, 22
  arguments 62
  armed forces 90–1
  art 264
  bar mitzvah 83
  business 93–4
  death 326–37
  family life 28–35, 39–52,
    54, 56–8, 62
  paintings 250
  school 76–7
  university 132–3, 135
  war 64–5, 67–9
Alvarez, Luke 47, 254, 324
Alvarez, Madge 10
Alvarez, Nancy 10
Alvarez, Renée 10
Alvarez, Sally 3, 5, 42, 48–53,
  59
  family life 64, 334
Alvarez, Sophie 10
Alvarez, Vicky 10
American Officers' Club 39
Amis, Kingsley 86, 115–16,
  122–3, 170
  reputation 185–7, 195,
    257
Anastasia, Albert 159
Anouilh, Jean 103

Anthoine, Mo 268–72, 284,
  289
Arendt, Hannah 7, 190, 232
Aristotle 114, 152
Arnold, Matthew 126, 129,
  131
Ashkenazis 7, 20
Ashworth, Phil 85
Astaire, Fred 88
Athill, Diana 297
atom bomb 125, 151, 196,
  215
Auden, W. H. 23, 78–9, 81,
  127–8
  friendships 291
  influence 174, 232–43
  poetry 294
  reputation 185, 187,
    225, 247, 271
Auschwitz 212, 242
Austen, Jane 126
Australia 140, 256, 259, 261
Austria 4

Baader–Meinhof gang 124
Bach, Johann Sebastian 82
Baez, Joan 176
Bailey, Pearl 165
Ball, George 164
Balliol College 110
bar mitzvah 83, 105
Barker, George 78, 117,
  227
Barnes, Julian 294
Bartlett, Lynn 144–5
Bartók, Béla 10
Baskin, Leonard 206
Bateson, F. W. 112–13, 115,
  132, 135, 141
Bath Club 73
Battle of Britain 70, 71
Baudelaire, Charles 41, 86,
  100

339